Praise for *Peddlers of Hate*

"In the Ku Klux Klan's ascent to power between 1921 and 1924 the Klan could command audiences of thousands to attend its rallies, lectures, parades, and cross burnings in every nook, cranny, city, town, and village throughout the state of Oregon. Steve Law's powerful new book, *Peddlers of Hate,* documents these events in intimate detail, naming names, dates, locations for all to see. It is a scary story."
—DARRELL MILLNER, Black Studies professor emeritus, Portland State University

"In this thickly researched work, Steve Law brings together the complex strands of the second KKK's presence in Oregon. Instead of night-riders and murderous vigilantes, readers are introduced to a political and social movement that combines white Protestant nationalism, immigration restrictionism, and support for Prohibition with the defense of public education, gestures of community service, and the rituals of a fraternal lodge."
—DAVID A. HOROWITZ, editor of *Inside the Klavern: The Secret History of a Ku Klux Klan of the 1920s*

"*Peddlers of Hate* provides today's justice advocates with a meaningful insight into the fissures of American democracy that will continue to be exploited until the cores of bigotry, xenophobia, and white supremacy are met with the same understanding of history as the operators of oppression. Law's warnings are to be heeded lest the heirs to the Klan ride to power once again." —TAYLOR STEWART, executive director of the Oregon Remembrance Project

Peddlers of Hate

How the Ku Klux Klan Seized Power in 1920s Oregon

STEVE LAW

Oregon State University Press Corvallis

Library of Congress Cataloging-in-Publication Data

Names: Law, Steve (Newspaper reporter) author
Title: Peddlers of hate : how the Ku Klux Klan seized power in 1920s Oregon / Steve Law.
Description: Corvallis : Oregon State University Press, 2026. | Includes bibliographical references and index.
Identifiers: LCCN 2026003058 | ISBN 9781962645706 trade paperback | ISBN 9781962645713 ebook
Subjects: LCSH: Ku Klux Klan (1915-)—History—20th century | Oregon—History—20th century | African Americans—Crimes against—Oregon—History—20th century
Classification: LCC HS2330.K63 L347 2026
LC record available at https://lccn.loc.gov/2026003058

∞This paper meets the requirements of ANSI/NISO Z39.48-1992 (Permanence of Paper).

This edition first published in 2026 by Oregon State University Press
Printed in the United States of America

Oregon State University
OSU Press

Oregon State University Press
121 The Valley Library
Corvallis OR 97331-4501
541-737-3166 • fax 541-737-3170
www.osupress.oregonstate.edu

Oregon State University Press in Corvallis, Oregon, is located within the traditional homelands of the Marys River or Ampinefu Band of Kalapuya. Following the Willamette Valley Treaty of 1855, Kalapuya people were forcibly removed to reservations in Western Oregon. Today, living descendants of these people are a part of the Confederated Tribes of Grand Ronde Community of Oregon (grandronde.org) and the Confederated Tribes of Siletz Indians (ctsi.nsn.us).

I dedicate this book to my adorable mother,
Stella (Yosha) Law,
who taught me right from wrong;
and to my lovable father
Albert Law,
who inspired me to fight for what's right.

Contents

Oregon KKK in the 1920s

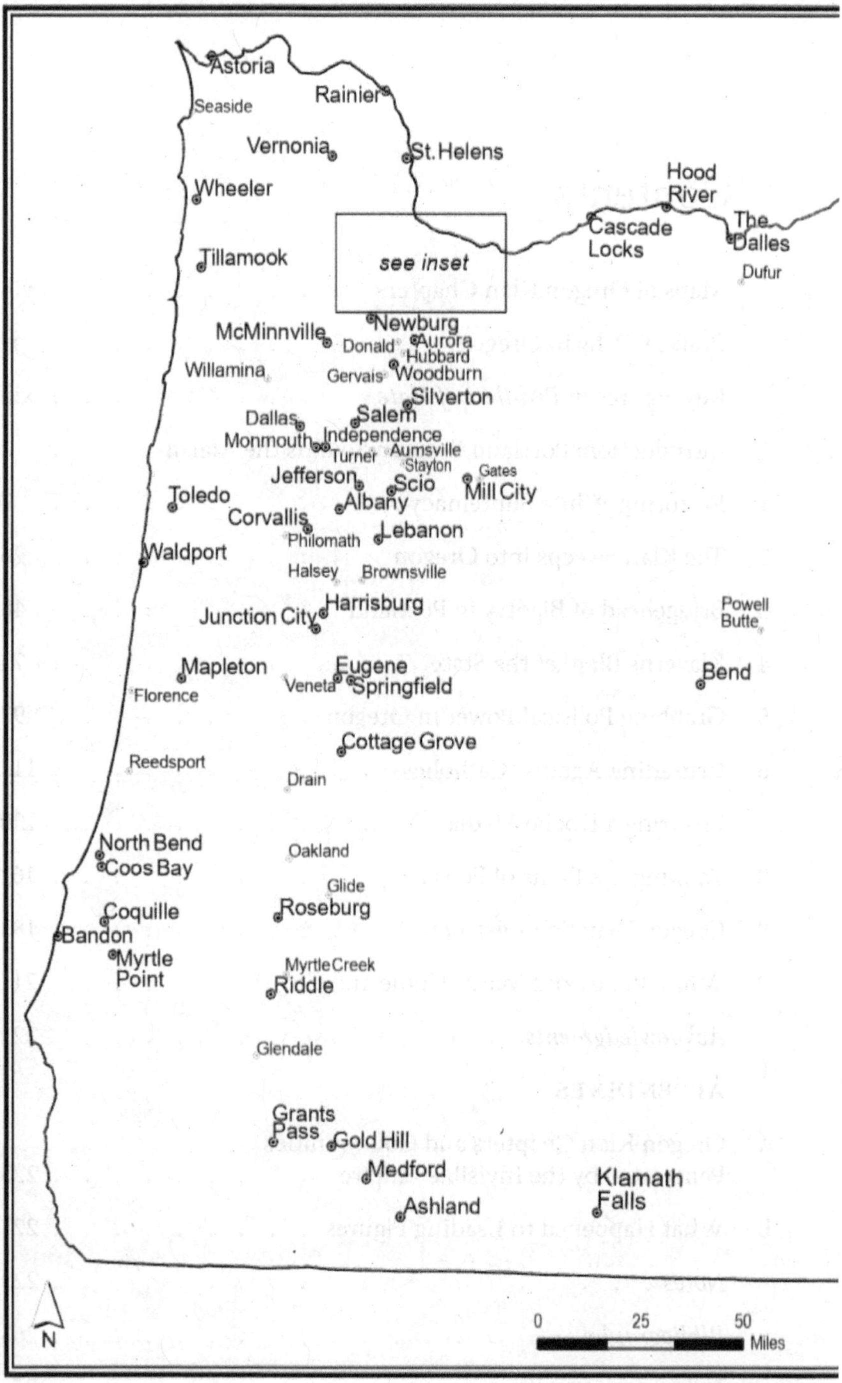

There were documented Klan chapters in at least 66 Oregon cities and towns, plus Klan lectures, rallies, or other activities in 28 additional communities. Map courtesy of Sara N. Lohse

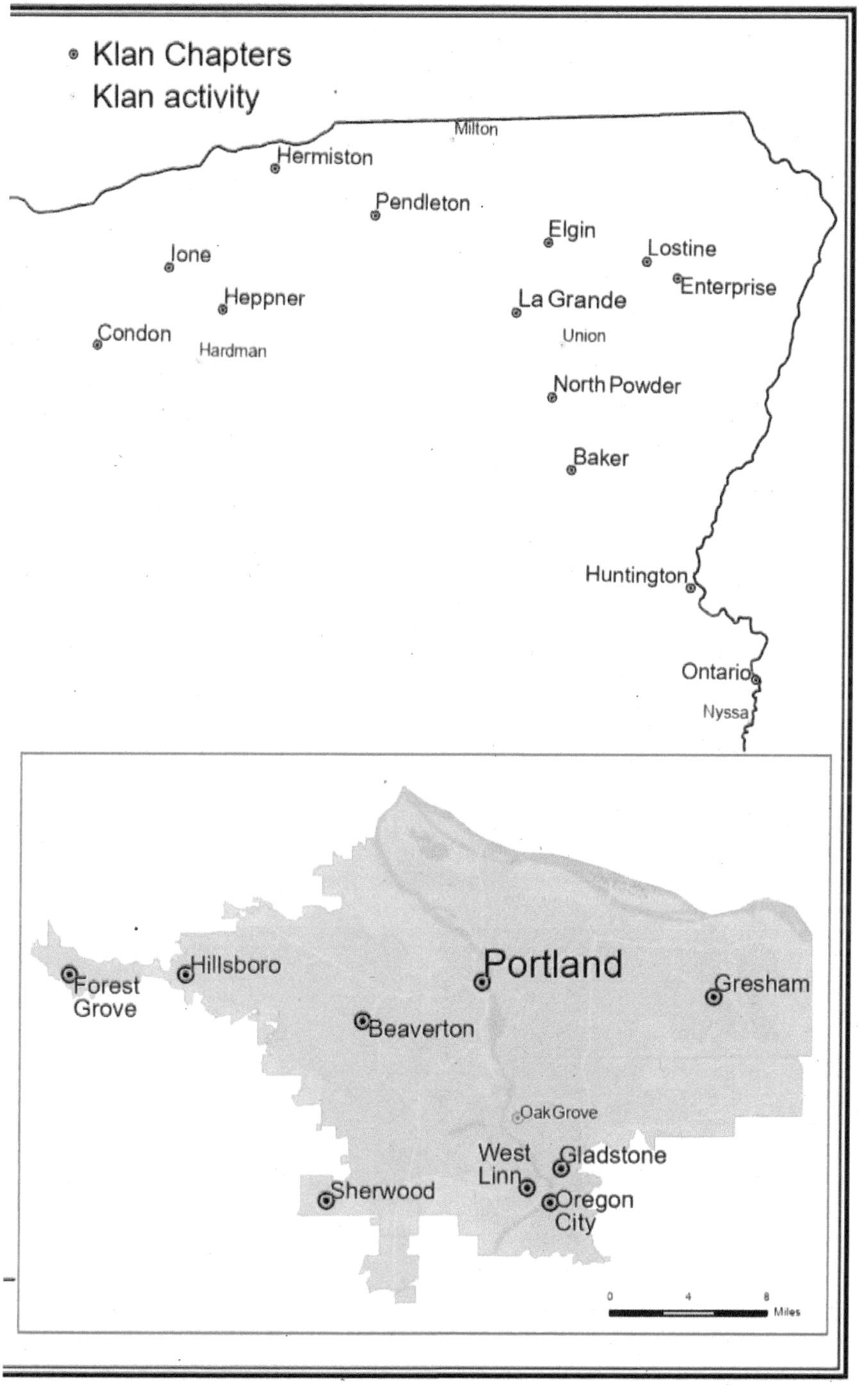
Klan Chapters
Klan activity
Milton
Hermiston
Pendleton
Elgin
Lostine
Ione
Enterprise
Heppner
La Grande
Condon
Hardman
Union
North Powder
Baker
Huntington
Ontario
Nyssa
Portland
Hillsboro
Forest Grove
Gresham
Beaverton
Oak Grove
West Linn
Gladstone
Sherwood
Oregon City
0
4
8
Miles

Preface
Why in Oregon?

We Oregonians tend to be awfully proud of our state. We treasure its natural beauty, its friendly people, and pioneering policies such as direct democracy and universal vote by mail. But Oregonians are increasingly reckoning with the darker side of our history. Many are shocked to learn the Ku Klux Klan dominated the state after the KKK was reconstituted more than a century ago. As a former history teacher and then newspaper reporter who covered Oregon for thirty-three years, I wanted to explore how such a magnificent place became a seedbed for hate, and what lessons we might draw to combat bigotry in the future.

Starting in 1921, the revived Knights of the Ku Klux Klan found fertile soil in Oregon for their message of religious prejudice, racism, and anti-immigrant nativism. *Peddlers of Hate* chronicles how a fleet of salesmen working on commission sold that philosophy of intolerance to build one of the nation's largest Ku Klux Klan enclaves. Over the course of just three years, the Klan established more than sixty Oregon chapters, from Portland to Medford and Astoria to La Grande. Fiery crosses lit up the sky from Skinner Butte in Eugene, Mt. Tabor in Portland, and Reservoir Hill in Roseburg. Klansmen disguised in white robes, masks, and hoods paraded through city streets in Salem, Ashland, and Grants Pass. Zealous Klan preachers mesmerized audiences in Vernonia, Philomath, Myrtle Creek, and Brownsville.

The second version of the Klan enlisted up to four million or more men and women across the United States, becoming the largest anti-Catholic, anti-immigrant, anti-Black, or anti-Semitic group the nation had ever experienced. At the Klan's 1923 peak of influence in the Beaver State, Portland was home to the nation's sixth-largest urban chapter and Oregon boasted more Klansmen per capita than all but one other state.

Peddlers of Hate documents how the Klan exploited that popularity to topple an incumbent governor and congressman, enact a ballot initiative to shut down Catholic schools, and seize control of the state House of Representatives, local city councils, and school boards. It explains how the Klan intimidated political opponents and the news media into complacency or silence. It highlights some of the brave Oregonians who challenged the Klan and explains how Klan leaders' thirst for power and profit led to the hate group's demise. *Peddlers of Hate* relies heavily on century-old newspaper accounts and sparse original documents that survived Klan purges. It synthesizes the work of historians and others who chronicled the Oregon Klan, providing the first comprehensive statewide account in book form.

Key Figures in *Peddlers of Hate*

George L. Baker: Portland mayor from 1917 to 1933 who cozied up to Klan but later parted ways.

Lemuel (Bragg) Callaway: first Klan recruiter (kleagle) to organize Portland chapter, in summer 1921.

Beatrice Hulon Morrow Cannady: manager and editor of the *Advocate* and Oregon's foremost Black civil rights leader.

Edward Young Clarke: marketing and public relations whiz who partnered with Elizabeth Tyler to take charge of Klan recruitment and business operations in 1920.

Lemuel A. (Lem) Dever: editor of *Western American*, the Oregon Klan newspaper; later wrote a devastating tell-all.

W. C. Elford: secretary of Oregon Federation of Patriotic Societies, or FOPS, a secretive anti-Catholic group that allied with the Klan but later parted ways.

Hiram Wesley Evans: Texas Klan leader who ousted William Simmons to become imperial wizard of the national KKK in fall 1922.

Frederick L. Gifford, exalted cyclops of Portland klavern (chapter) who rose to grand dragon of Oregon Klan and regional Klan leadership.

Charles Hall, Republican state senator from Marshfield (now Coos Bay) who supported the proposed ban on private schools, then ran for governor in 1922 with Klan and FOPS backing.

Maybelle Jette: mother counselor of Portland's Ladies of the Invisible Empire, or LOTIE, a Klan women's group.

Reverend James R. Johnson: militantly anti-Catholic pastor and the second exalted cyclops of Portland klavern.

P. S. (Philip Schuyler) Malcom, sovereign grand inspector general of Oregon's Scottish Rite Masons who spearheaded the initiative to ban Oregon private schools, in tandem with Klan.

Father Edwin V. O'Hara: Priest in Portland and later Eugene who oversaw Catholic schools and clashed with the Klan.

Ben W. Olcott: Republican governor of Oregon from 1919 to 1923 who issued proclamation raising alarm about the Klan, then lost re-election bid to Walter Pierce.

Walter M. Pierce: Democrat who earned Klan support by endorsing ballot measure to ban private schools, capturing governorship in 1922.

Luther I. Powell: first recruiter (kleagle) to organize Klan in Oregon in early months of 1921, later king kleagle for state and then region.

Reverend Reuben H. Sawyer: first Klan lecturer in Oregon, created Ladies of the Invisible Empire.

William Joseph Simmons: revived the Ku Klux Klan in 1915 in Atlanta, naming himself imperial wizard.

D. C. (David Clarke) Stephenson: leader of Indiana Klan and Midwest empire who jousted for control of KKK; his 1925 conviction for murder sped the Klan's demise.

Mary Elizabeth Tyler: marketing and public relations whiz who partnered with Edward Clarke to take charge of Klan recruitment, propaganda, and other operations in 1920.

Introduction
Portland Woman Sounds the Alarm

Race relations in Portland were relatively peaceful in 1915, in no small part due to the tireless efforts of Black newspaper manager Beatrice Morrow Cannady. But Cannady saw trouble ahead. The National Association for the Advancement of Colored People had sounded an alarm about a new, deeply racist feature film, *The Birth of a Nation,* which glorified the Ku Klux Klan, a Reconstruction-era terrorist group that rolled back Black gains after the Civil War. Fearing the film would provoke attacks against Blacks, the NAACP sought to block its screening in New York City and Boston, and invited far-flung chapters of the civil rights group to join the campaign.

Cannady, secretary of Portland's one-year-old NAACP chapter and manager of the *Advocate,* a weekly newspaper covering the city's small Black community, teamed with colleagues to pen an urgent plea to Portland Mayor H. Russell Albee. *Birth of a Nation* is a "very vicious play designed to create prejudice and race hatred against the colored people," civil rights leaders wrote in a June 21, 1915, letter.[1] They asked the city's new seven-member Board of Motion Picture Censors to bar *Birth of a Nation* screenings in Portland, and submitted a petition signed by 300 people. Cannady, in a separate letter to the editor of Portland's largest newspapers, called the film a "diabolical scheme" that glorified the cruelty of the Ku Klux Klan and denigrated efforts to advance Black social, economic, and civil rights after the Civil War. "Portland cannot promote progress when 2,500 of its citizens are held up to public shame and ridicule."[2]

The NAACP's protests were for naught. *Birth of a Nation* opened in Portland's Heilig Theatre on August 29, 1915, with patriotic flags draped over seats and balconies and a twelve-piece orchestra

Journalist and civil rights leader Beatrice Morrow Cannady lobbied in vain to prevent Portland screenings of *The Birth of a Nation*, a racist film glorifying the original Ku Klux Klan, a terrorist group formed after the Civil War. (Oregon Historical Society)

performing live during the silent film. The audience "went wild with enthusiasm," wrote a reviewer from the state's leading newspaper, the *Oregonian*. The crowd was especially moved when hooded Klansmen rode up on horses to save the day from what were depicted as greedy Northern intruders and corrupt Union soldiers, many of them Black. "They applauded, they cheered, they stood up in the intensity of their emotions as they saw the great army of the mounted Ku Klux Klan sweeping down the road, fording streams, dashing to the rescue of either Northerners or Southerners in peril."[3]

David Wark Griffith's three-hour silent movie was Hollywood's first blockbuster and a landmark filmmaking achievement. Reviewers raved about D. W. Griffith's artistic and technical innovations, glossing over his historical distortions and slanted portrayals of Blacks, Reconstruction, and the KKK.

Launched by President Abraham Lincoln, Reconstruction was designed to reintegrate and rebuild Southern states that seceded from the union during the Civil War. A new Freedmen's Bureau, staffed by Northerners, helped secure voting rights, education, and economic advances for newly freed Blacks, under the protection of Union troops that had just won the war. The Ku Klux Klan arose to counter Black gains and the erosion of white supremacy. Masked Klansmen in the cover of darkness staged raids, lynchings, and other intimidation tactics to terrorize Blacks and their white defenders.

Griffith's film was based on Thomas Dixon Jr.'s 1905 novel, *The Clansman*, which promoted the fictitious view of Klansmen as valiant saviors of a South besieged by Union soldiers, "uppity" Blacks, and corrupt Northerners derided as carpetbaggers. Dixon, grandson of a slave owner and son of a Klansman, dedicated the novel to his Scotch-Irish uncle, a former grand titan of the Klan.[4] The author concocted a false image of the Klan using burning crosses as its calling card.[5] (Cross burnings were an ancient Scottish tradition used to call clans together and weren't deployed by the post-Civil War terrorist group.)[6]

Griffith, son of a Kentucky Confederate colonel,[7] adopted the erroneous image of cross burnings for his film, as well as a false depiction of 1860s Klansmen all wearing the same white masks, hoods, and robes.[8] His film portrays most Black male characters as lazy, corrupt, and lusting after white women. They are characterized as uppity for demanding equal rights, and sinister for demanding the right to marry white women. One Black father, after his toddlers fall out of his horse-drawn carriage, picks them up like sacks of potatoes and whacks them for having the gall to fall out. After newly enfranchised Blacks elect some of their peers to office, an uncouth Black lawmaker is depicted taking off his shoes and resting his dirty bare foot on a desk in the middle of a legislative session.[9]

Griffith also depicts some "good" Blacks who are still subservient to whites. In one scene, enslaved people cheer wildly as their Southern masters go off to fight for the Confederacy in the Civil War. During post-war Reconstruction, Black house servants in the South are portrayed as openly hostile to other Blacks seeking equal rights. One sinister-looking Black veteran pursues a white woman he fancies, but she jumps off a cliff to escape his clutches. "And none grieved more than these," a block of text states, cutting to the Black servants.

In Griffith's distorted history, Klansmen are the ones violently attacked by Blacks and Union soldiers, and they take up arms only in self-defense. Donning white robes and hoods, they ride up on horseback to save the day, restoring plantation owners to their rightful places and ridding the South of Northern interlopers. Griffith said he "felt driven to tell the story, the truth about the South, touched by its external romance which I had learned to know so well."[10]

The NAACP's premonition bore out when William Joseph Simmons launched a new version of the Klan on Thanksgiving, 1915, timed with the upcoming Atlanta debut of *Birth of a Nation*. Portland's Sunset Theatre booked the film for a second run the week before Easter in 1918. Cannady and others met with new Portland Mayor George L. Baker, who pressed the cinema owner to remove some of the footage she found most objectionable.[11] When those edits didn't satisfy her, Baker said his hands were tied because the film had been approved by the city's Board of Motion Picture Censors. Baker did ask his city attorney to draft an emergency ordinance so the City Council could overrule the censorship board, but one city commissioner blocked the ordinance, which required unanimous consent. Witnessing the vote in City Council chambers, Cannady broke down and wept, saying she'd gone for a week with little sleep and irregular meals, and the strain was too great after her mission failed.[12]

The Birth of a Nation, Hollywood's first blockbuster film, prepared public opinion for the 1915 revival of the Ku Klux Klan in a new form. (Library of Congress, left; Wikimedia Commons, right).

After the second Klan had penetrated Oregon and formed numerous chapters, Portland's Blue Mouse theatre scheduled a third run of *Birth of a Nation* in March 1922. Cannady asked the national NAACP for help, noting the Klan had enlisted five thousand members in Portland. "This film has caused serious race clashes in many places by stirring up race prejudice," NAACP leader James Weldon Johnson telegrammed Oregon Governor Ben W. Olcott.[13] But the effort proved futile. In an ominous sign of the times, the theatre's newspaper ad included a small 100 in the corner, denoting its support for the Klan mantra of "100 percent Americanism."[14]

In 1923, when the Klan reached the peak of its influence in Oregon, the film returned to Portland a fourth time. Cannady was then at odds with timid NAACP leaders, and she lamented in her newspaper that "not a word of protest was heard from the local branch." By then, the Portland Klan outnumbered the city's Black population by more than five to one.

Seven founders and leaders of the original Ku Klux Klan: D. L. Wilson, Major J. R. Crowe, Captain John C. Lester, General Albert Pike, General W. J. Hardee, Calvin Jones, and Ryland Randolph. (Alabama Department of Archives and History)

1
Restoring White Supremacy

> *In 1873, the Ku Klux Klan, outside the South, was a synonym for the most sinister and dangerous force in American life. Who then would have dared to prophecy that within less than a half-century this secret, oath-bound order would be revived and spread to every section of the country?*
>
> —John Moffat Mecklin, historian[1]

1865 to 1870s: Founding of the Ku Klux Klan

The original Ku Klux Klan, like the second Klan that arose fifty years later, took root on the heels of social upheaval and sweeping economic and cultural changes. The two versions of the Klan were vastly different in approach and composition, but in each case Klansmen portrayed themselves as champions of a besieged majority facing uncertainty, anxiety, and the threatened loss of their dominant position in the social order.

April 9, 1865: Confederate General Robert E. Lee surrenders to Union General Ulysses S. Grant, ending Civil War.

April 14, 1865: John Wilkes Booth assassinates President Abraham Lincoln. Vice President Andrew Johnson, a former slave owner from Tennessee, sworn in next day as president.

December 1865: Six former Confederate soldiers from Pulaski, Tennessee, form club later named the Ku Klux Klan.

November 1866: Radical Republicans win control of Congress, enabling them to enact Reconstruction policies that advance newly enfranchised Blacks and weaken Southern Democrats.

April 1867: Ku Klux Klan delegates meet in Nashville, elect former slave trader and Confederate general Nathan Bedford Forrest as grand wizard.

1867–1868: Radical Republicans help establish GOP-led state governments in former Confederate states, spurring Klan's expansion.

November 3, 1868: Grant elected president, restoring Republican control of executive branch; Grant vows to destroy KKK.

January 1869: Grand Wizard Forrest, pressured by federal prosecutions of Klansmen and increasing violence by newer recruits, orders KKK disbanded and its records and garb destroyed. Many members fail to comply.

1871–1872: Remaining Klan chapters disband after wave of federal arrests and convictions.

March 2, 1877: A secret Congressional deal dubbed the Compromise of 1877 hands GOP the presidency after disputed 1876 election; Democrats gain withdrawal of federal troops from South and end to Reconstruction.

Pulaski Pranksters

The most potent terrorist group in US history didn't start out that way. John C. Lester and five buddies, all Confederate soldiers idled after the Civil War's end, gathered in Pulaski, Tennessee, in December 1865 to form a secret club. The young men called it a den and dubbed their officers "grand cyclops" and other silly names. Each member would create his own club outfit: a white face mask, a tall cardboard hat, and a gown or robe of any color to cover his body, according to a 1884 book co-authored by Lester.[2]

The six pranksters adapted a ritual used by colleges to initiate new members. Club members led blindfolded recruits past obstructions placed in their path, ultimately descending into a cellar. "Then the grand cyclops commanded: 'Place him before the royal altar and adorn his head with the regal crown.' The royal altar was a large looking glass. The regal crown was a huge hat bedecked with two enormous donkey ears." Once the blindfold was removed, "the den rang with shouts and peals of laughter" as the recruit saw his ridiculous head gear in the mirror.[3] The founders included two former Confederate officers, two lawyers, and a newspaper editor. All were of Scotch-Irish background, and most were Presbyterians.[4] They continued planning their club until May 1866, when they agreed to formally launch the organization after convening in the law office of one of their fathers. After tossing around potential club names based on the Greek word *kuklos*, which meant circle, ring, or band, they came up with the name Ku Klux Klan. "The origin of the order had no political significance," wrote Major James Richard Crowe, one of the six founders. "It was at first purely social and for our amusement."[5]

The club's formal founding came one year after Lee surrendered at Appomattox Courthouse. The South was devastated by the war, and its economy was in shambles. Emancipated Blacks, no longer the legal property of white masters, were eager to exercise their new rights, with support from Union soldiers in the South and the Freedmen's Bureau created by Congress. Once-enslaved men could now reunite with dispersed relatives, seek paid work, vote, buy land, form businesses, attend church, and learn to read and write at newly established schools.

Many white Southerners were nervous about the impending loss of white supremacy, as regions with major Black populations managed to

Ten smartly dressed members of an original Klan den pose with a skull and bones, circa 1870. (Library of Congress)

elect former slaves to state legislatures and Congress. Plantation owners struggled to maintain operations without slave labor and were dismayed by threats to their political dominance. Poorer whites looked on with trepidation as formerly enslaved people sought to rise out of the lowest caste and compete with them for jobs. Many whites complained about Northerners who'd arrived to set up schools and other services for newly freed Blacks, accusing them of corruption. Northerners were ridiculed as "carpetbaggers"; Southern whites who cooperated with them were derided as "scalawags." The Ku Klux Klan den evolved from mischievous pranksters donning masks to scare Blacks into a militant group with a penchant for violence. The Freedman's Bureau in Pulaski began receiving reports of floggings and shootings of Blacks.[6]

Vigilantes and Terrorists

As word spread about the mysterious Pulaski order, new dens sprang up across Tennessee, then in eight other states from Virginia to Mississippi. The Klan emerged as one of several groups purporting to represent aggrieved whites in unsettling times, along with the Knights of the White Camelia, the White Brotherhood, the White League, the Pale Faces, and the Constitutional Union Guards. Discharged Confederate officers and politicians joined the KKK, enabling it to absorb and dominate other white supremacist groups.[7]

Klansmen avoided majority-Black rural areas, operating mostly in white-majority areas in the mountain and Piedmont regions, the plateaus between the Appalachian Mountains and coastal plains.[8] The Klan became known for dispatching masked and hooded marauders on nighttime raids to intimidate Blacks and their white allies. Members became more violent and defiant. Masked Klansmen set fire to Black school classrooms and attacked white schoolteachers who dared instruct former slaves how to read and write. Klansmen attacked Blacks deemed too uppity, such as those who dared to acquire land or start businesses, and attacked whites helping them assert voting rights. Brazen Klansmen strung up whites and Blacks from trees, instigating a wave of lynchings that enthralled supporters. Sympathetic Southerners hailed the Klan as a protector of white rights at a time when Union soldiers were siding with emancipated Blacks they were sent to protect. Others saw the Klansmen as killers in bed sheets, organized to reimpose white supremacy.

Newspaper editor Ryland Randolph, a Klansman in Tuscaloosa, Alabama, offered a frank portrayal of the order: "It originated with returned soldiers for the purpose of punishing those Negroes who had become notoriously and offensively insolent to white people, and in some cases to chastise those white-skinned men who, at that particular time, showed a disposition to affiliate socially with Negroes."[9]

In the wake of Lincoln's assassination, the South had one of its own in the White House. President Johnson, a Tennessee Democrat, favored lenient treatment of his defeated Southern brethren. But in November 1866 elections, progressive lawmakers known as Radical Republicans gained commanding majorities in the US Senate and House of Representatives, enabling them to override a series of Johnson vetoes. Congress proceeded to install Republican administrations in most of the Southern states, further inflaming the white backlash and spurring more Klan violence and expansion.[10]

The Klan's far-flung chapters operated independently and grew increasingly out of control. Pulaski members, hoping to bring more structure to the secret order, summoned delegates from each den to a conference in Nashville in April 1867. Delegates named former Confederate General Nathan Bedford Forrest as the Klan's new grand wizard. Forrest was a scrappy and brilliant general whose reputation was tarnished by the wartime murder of more than two hundred unarmed Union troops, many of them former Black slaves, who had surrendered to his command after the Battle of Fort Pillow.[11]

Nathan Bedford Forrest, a controversial former Confederate general, took command of loosely affiliated Ku Klux Klan dens in 1867 when he was named grand wizard. (Library of Congress)

Forrest set out to impose military-style control of the Klan, though that proved elusive. Klan violence continued unabated, especially in advance of elections, when Klansmen sought to intimidate Blacks and their Republican allies to keep them from voting. Spencer Griffin, a fifty-four-year-old Black man, was whipped with 150 lashes and told that Blacks "had to do what they were told." John Dunlap, a white teacher in a Black school, was stripped, whipped, and ordered to leave Tennessee. Mrs. Lewis Powell, a Black woman, was shot to death for being active in the Union League, a group that originated in the North to advance Black rights.[12] Being elected to public office provided no immunity. Black state legislators James Martin and B. F. Randolph of South Carolina and Benjamin Inge and Richard Burke of Alabama were murdered.[13]

In August 1868, Forrest told a newspaper reporter that the Klan had grown to 40,000 members in Tennessee and 550,000 throughout the South.[14] By November, Civil War hero Grant was elected president, restoring Republican control of the executive branch. Grant vowed to quash Klan violence. As arrests and prosecution of Klansmen loomed, Forrest ordered the Klan disbanded just two months after Grant's election. Forrest also ordered Klansmen to burn their records and uniforms, but many ignored his orders, especially in North and South Carolina.[15]

Klan violence persisted, prompting Grant to seek passage of the Ku Klux Klan Act of 1871, which empowered him to impose martial law where needed to curb the terrorist group.[16] When Grant invoked the law in October 1871 for nine South Carolina counties where Klan violence was rampant, fifty local chapter leaders fled the state. In short order, an estimated eight hundred Klansmen were arrested, jailed, or vanished.[17]

By 1872, the Klan faded away, but it had succeeded in turning back the clock on Black advancement. With many Blacks intimidated from voting, Democrats won back control of Southern state governments. After a disputed 1876 presidential election, Republicans in Congress agreed to yank Northern troops from the South and end Reconstruction. In exchange, Democrats agreed to anoint Republican Rutherford B. Hayes as president. The white South "won the racial battle," observed Darrell Millner, emeritus Black studies professor at Portland State University.[18]

Second Coming of the Klan

1905: Thomas Dixon Jr. novel, *The Clansman: A Historical Romance of the Ku Klux Klan*, glorifies KKK as heroic savior of the South during Reconstruction.

July 28, 1914: Hostilities break out in Europe, igniting World War I.

January 1–2, 1915: *The Birth of a Nation*, D. W. Griffith film based on Dixon's novel and screenplay, previews in Riverside, Los Angeles, and San Francisco.

February 18–19, 1915: President Woodrow Wilson screens *Birth of a Nation* for his cabinet at White House. National Press Club shows it to members of Congress, the Supreme Court, and diplomatic corps.

August 16–17, 1915: Jewish businessman Leo Frank kidnapped by anti-Semitic mob and lynched in front of three thousand gawkers.

August 29, 1915: *Birth of a Nation* premieres in Portland.

September 2, 1915: Georgia politician Tom Watson calls for revival of Ku Klux Klan.

Thanksgiving, 1915: William Joseph Simmons leads ceremony atop Georgia's Stone Mountain to herald a reconstituted Ku Klux Klan.

1916: New book, *The Passing of the Great Race*, claims "Nordic race" is superior to others but is becoming outnumbered.

February 1917: Congress enacts Immigration Act, overriding Wilson's veto, and creates literacy test to limit US immigration.

April 1917: United States enters World War I. Wilson and others warn of "hyphenated Americans" whose loyalty might be questionable, stressing need for "100 percent Americanism."

June 1917: Espionage Act makes it a crime to interfere with war effort or support US enemies.

October 1917: Bolsheviks prevail in Russian revolution. Russia withdraws from World War I.

March 1918: Flu pandemic begins, eventually killing 675,000 Americans.

May 1918: Sedition Act makes it a crime to cast the war effort, the flag, or military in negative light.

January 1919: Automaker Henry Ford acquires *Dearborn Independent* newspaper to spread anti-Semitic propaganda.

February 1919: General strike shuts down Seattle waterfront.

Summer 1919: Wave of violent attacks on Blacks in Chicago; Washington, DC; and several other cities.

November 1919: US Attorney General A. Mitchell Palmer launches Red Scare. Thousands of foreign-born socialists, communists, and anarchists are arrested and several hundred are deported.

November 11, 1919: Six people die in Centralia, Washington, after violent clash between American Legion veterans and members of Industrial Workers of the World (Wobblies).

1920: Henry Ford distributes 500,000 copies of bogus document, "Protocols of the Elders of Zion," which supposedly reveals Jewish drive for global domination.

June 7, 1920: William Simmons hires public relations whizzes Edward Young Clarke and Elizabeth Tyler to handle Klan recruitment, leading to surge in membership.

August 18, 1920: Nineteenth Amendment passes, granting national women's suffrage.

1921: Emergency Quota Act restricts emigration from Southern and Eastern Europe by capping annual newcomers at 3 percent of each nation's immigrant population as of 1910.

May 31–June 1, 1921: White mob destroys thirty-five blocks of prosperous Black Wall Street district of Tulsa, Oklahoma; up to three hundred people die and eight hundred are hospitalized.

Stone Mountain Ceremony

Americans flocked to see *Birth of a Nation* after its theatrical release in early 1915, gleaning distorted images of heroic Klansmen saving the South from imagined abuses after the Civil War. That summer, a Jewish businessman from Atlanta named Leo Frank was yanked from his prison cell by an anti-Semitic mob. Instigators were incensed that Frank received life imprisonment instead of the death penalty after he was wrongly convicted of raping and murdering a thirteen-year-old girl under his supervision. The mob strung up Frank from an oak tree and lynched him in front of three thousand gawkers.[19] Two weeks later, Georgia politician and journalist Tom Watson wrote that it was high time to revive the Ku Klux Klan to "restore home rule."[20]

William Joseph Simmons, who'd watched *Birth of a Nation* several times, seized the opportunity. Simmons, who sold insurance to

William Joseph Simmons, an insurance salesman for fraternal lodge members, recreated the Ku Klux Klan as a privately owned corporation in 1915, timed with the Atlanta premiere of *Birth of a Nation*. He's shown here during a break in Congressional hearings on the Klan in October 1921. (Library of Congress)

fraternal lodge members in Atlanta, purchased an ad in an Atlanta newspaper promoting a new "high class order for men of intelligence and character," which was placed alongside ads for the December 6 Atlanta premiere of D. W. Griffith's masterpiece.[21] Three weeks before the premiere, Simmons had submitted a petition signed by thirty-four white Protestant men seeking to charter a new fraternal lodge called the Invisible Empire of the Knights of the Ku Klux Klan. Three of the men were surviving members of the original KKK.

On Thanksgiving, twelve days before the film's premiere, Simmons assembled his recruits at Atlanta's Piedmont Hotel. The charismatic redhead then led fifteen of them on a nighttime drive aboard a sightseeing bus to Stone Mountain, a sheer granite dome twenty miles to the northeast. Illuminating their way with flashlights, the men trudged up a rocky trail to the windy summit. They erected a simple rock platform to support a crude wooden cross drenched in kerosene, accompanied by a US flag and a Bible opened to Romans 12, and lit the cross. In front of a fiery cross visible for miles, Simmons led the men in a solemn ceremony pledging themselves to his new fraternal order.[22]

Later recruits would commit to a formal declaration written by Simmons, which began: "We solemnly declare to all mankind that the Knights of the Ku Klux Klan, incorporated in the original Ku Klux Klan organized in the year 1866, and active during the Reconstruction period of American history, and by and under its corporate name is revived, remodeled, and expanded into a Ritualistic, Fraternal, Patriotic society of national scope."[23] On July 1, 1916, Fulton County, Georgia, officially granted the Klan its charter as a private corporation owned by Simmons. He granted himself the title of imperial wizard.

Impractical Dreamer

The founder of the second Klan liked to be called Colonel Simmons, but it was an honorary title bestowed by the Woodmen of the World fraternal lodge, not earned from his undistinguished service in the Spanish-American War.[24] Born in 1880 in Harpersville, Alabama, Simmons was the son of a country physician who'd been a Confederate officer in the Civil War and a member of the original Ku Klux Klan. "I was always fascinated by Klan stories," Simmons would say later. "My old Negro mammy, Aunt Viney, and her husband, used to tell us children about how the old Reconstruction Klansmen used to frighten the darkies."[25] Simmons apparently wanted to follow in his father's footsteps, claiming that he completed pre-med studies at Johns Hopkins University. However, the university had no records of that.[26]

Simmons was charismatic, honing his public speaking skills as a traveling minister for the Methodist Episcopal Church. But he was an impractical dreamer, possessing great ambitions that he often failed to fulfill. He left the ministry after a dozen years, when the Alabama church failed to grant his wish to lead a decent-sized congregation of his own.[27] Simmons also tried his hand as a garter salesman and a Southern history instructor at Atlanta's Lanier University.[28]

Simmons found his niche with fraternal orders. He joined fifteen of them, including the Masons and Knights Templar, and moved to Atlanta to handle promotional duties for the Woodmen of the World, then sold insurance to fraternal lodge members.[29] Simmons finally found success when he conceived of resuscitating the legendary Ku Klux Klan, though it took several years and vital assistance from more-competent organizers. In Simmons's later telling, creating a new version of the Klan was the culmination of a fourteen-year-old dream. Roaming through rural Alabama one summer evening in 1901 as an itinerant minister, Simmons claimed to have had a mystical vision—a row of white-robed figures on horseback racing across the sky. In the background was a map of the United States.[30] In 1911 Simmons was injured in an auto accident and confined to bed for three months. It was then, he claimed later, that he conceived of rituals for a new fraternal group inspired by the original Ku Klux Klan.[31] He called the rituals Klankraft. Much like the six founders of the original Klan, Simmons had no idea how his scheme would morph.

"Certainly in the earliest years of the Invisible Empire," concluded Klan historian Kenneth Jackson, "Simmons intended that the secret order be no more than a genuine fraternal lodge, with largely ritualistic activities and a selective membership policy."[32] Simmons's initial newspaper ad boasted that he was forming "The World's Greatest Secret, Social, Patriotic, Fraternal, Beneficiary Order."[33] Early on, he shopped around his proposed Klan constitution and bylaws to Atlanta city clerk Walter Taylor, referring to it as a locker club. Locker clubs were devised to evade Prohibition-era rules against liquor, enabling fraternal lodges like the local Elks to be essentially boozing dens.[34] "It is entirely possible that Simmons was thinking of the lucrative fraternal insurance field when he organized the Klan," Jackson wrote. "Of the ninety-two persons who joined the secret order in the first few months, forty-two signed up for a total of $53,000 worth of Klan life insurance."[35]

Spinning His Wheels

Simmons was a spellbinding orator but lacked basic administrative and organizing skills, never bothering to compile a full roster of his initial recruits to the Atlanta Klan chapter.[36] To help launch the new version of the Klan, Simmons turned to Jonathan Frost, whom he met through the Woodmen of the World. Frost also edited a local magazine that covered new junk-science theories about racial distinctions. "It seems likely that much of the Klan's racial philosophy came from Frost, and it is almost certain that he supplied the organizational acumen to get the movement under way," wrote Simmons biographer Charles O. Jackson.[37] By 1916, though, Simmons parted ways with his co-founder after a bitter court battle. Simmons accused Frost of embezzling $5,000 in cash from the Klan.[38]

Simmons devoted much of his energy to creating Klan rituals, which dictated how meetings would be run and how members could be initiated into the order. He concocted odd names for officers, along with acronyms for Klansmen to use as secret greetings. He freely borrowed some of the original Klan's titles, traditions, and costumes, gaining legal rights to appropriate those when he secured his charter in 1915.[39] He also adapted rituals from the Masons, whose lodges often were the most important institutions in small American towns. Simmons enfolded his ideas into a fifty-four-page booklet called the *Kloran,* which he decreed would serve as a secret Klan Bible. The *Kloran* spells out Simmons's names for officers (mostly starting with the letter k), provides a diagram of where officers and others should sit during meetings, lists text and rituals for opening and closing meetings, and specifies songs to sing during such ceremonies ("Greenland's Icy Mountains," sung to the tune of "Home, Sweet, Home") and procedures for inducting new members.[40] Simmons was so proud of his creation that on January 16, 1917, he obtained a copyright for the *Kloran.*

Much like its namesake, the new Klan evolved from a fraternal-style lodge whose members took a secret oath of loyalty into a vigilante group marked by intimidation and violence. White-sheeted Klansmen prevented a work stoppage and abducted a labor leader in the Mobile, Alabama, shipyards in 1918. In a similar action, a strike leader disappeared as a walkout loomed in the Birmingham mills.[41] But the second Klan grew modestly and was little known even in its hometown of Atlanta.

In 1919, an enterprising Atlanta newspaper photographer named Matty heard rumors the Klan had been revived in Georgia, and he asked Simmons to pose for a photo. Simmons, who had a penchant for secrecy, turned him down, recalled an *Atlanta Journal* reporter. But the photographer decided to get creative and set up his own photo. Matty fashioned sheets to create twenty outfits modeled after those seen in *Birth of a Nation,* and hired twenty Black men to pose under the sheets for twenty-five cents each.[42] The paid models then marched down Atlanta's Peachtree and Whitehall Streets in a Confederate veterans reunion parade, carrying two burning crosses rigged by Matty.[43] The staged photo was picked up by newspapers, giving much of the country its first glimpse of the new Klan, thanks to an enterprising photographer engineering fake news.

In those first five years, Simmons signed up fewer than four thousand Klan members. Besides Atlanta, the only active chapters were in Mobile, Birmingham, and Montgomery, Alabama.[44] It's unclear whether the Klan would have survived if Simmons hadn't handed the reins over to two public relations professionals in 1920.

Revamped Hate Group

The duo that propelled the second Klan into a robust hate group met at a wholesome community festival in Georgia. Elizabeth Tyler had taught new moms living in tenements how to improve hygiene practices for their infants. She sponsored a Better Babies Parade at an Atlanta harvest festival, where she met Edward Young Clarke, a promoter who organized the festival.[45] The pair decided to parlay their talents in marketing and public relations by creating the Southern Publicity Association. Their two-person company snared contracts handling fundraising, publicity, and promotional work for the Anti-Saloon League, along with Salvation Army, Red Cross, and Near East relief efforts. Clarke and Tyler deployed cutting-edge public relations techniques, favoring monster events and eye-catching spectacles. Once, they dropped Anti-Saloon League pamphlets from an airplane.[46]

Both Clarke and Tyler became acquainted with the fledgling Atlanta Klan chapter. Clarke, a slim, curly-haired man with horn-rimmed glasses, was rumored to have joined the Klan in late 1919.[47] Tyler's son-in-law, a member of the Atlanta chapter, reportedly introduced her to the group. A large woman with blue eyes and auburn hair, Tyler had been divorced multiple times. She was well known for her entrepreneurial skill and became financially independent. Tyler also was vice chairman of the Georgia Committee of the Republican Party,[48] and a member of the women's auxiliary of the Junior Order of the United American Mechanics, an anti-Catholic fraternal lodge.[49] In June 1919, the *Searchlight* newspaper was launched, cosponsored by the anti-Catholic group and the Klan and owned by Tyler.[50]

In 1920, Simmons grew frustrated by the Klan's tepid growth and measly earnings from his private enterprise. "There were times during those five early years when I walked the streets with my shoes worn through, because I had no money," Simmons said later.[51] "By 1920, the Invisible Empire was on the verge of organizational if not financial collapse," wrote his biographer.[52]

Simmons turned to Clarke and Tyler for help, inking a June 1920 contract granting them responsibility for Klan member recruitment and publicity. The contract awarded Clarke and Tyler 80 percent of the revenues they could collect from the Klan, with Simmons pocketing the remaining 20 percent. In practice, Simmons outsourced much of

Public relations and marketing whizzes Edward Young Clarke and Elizabeth Tyler took over recruiting and business operations for Simmons's sagging company, propelling the Klan into a nationwide hate group. (Alabama Department of Archives and History)

the administration, finances, and organizing to them. "Mr. Simmons hangs around the office when Mr. Clarke has need of him, possesses the biggest-sounding title and draws a weekly check as a stockholder of the ideas," observed a Georgia newsman.[53] Clarke was named the Klan's imperial kleagle and head of a new Propagation Department to conduct recruiting. His real estate company handled Klan property transactions, and he set up the Gates Manufacturing Co. in Atlanta to make Klan hoods, masks, and other paraphernalia. Klansmen would be commanded to buy such regalia from the Atlanta headquarters at a significant price mark-up. Tyler's newspaper, the *Searchlight*, became the official Klan propaganda organ, and published Klan membership forms and other literature sold to chapters. Tyler also oversaw training of recruiters by sending them weekly newsletters filled with sales tips.

Clarke and Tyler's master stroke was hiring recruiters, known as kleagles, who were paid solely by commission. "They set up this pyramid scheme," said David Horowitz, a retired Portland State University professor and historian who has written extensively on the 1920s Klan in Oregon.[54] Of each ten-dollar initiation fee paid by a new member, Clarke and Tyler awarded four dollars to the kleagle (a lucrative commission worth more than sixty dollars in mid-2020s currency). One dollar went to the king kleagle, or chief recruiter for the state; fifty cents went to the grand goblin, the district sales manager. That left two dollars to pay Simmons his share, and a nifty two-and-a-half dollars in profits for Clarke and Tyler, not counting their earnings from ongoing member dues and sales of outfits, literature, and real estate commissions.

Initially, Tyler said they had modest goals of recruiting in the South and appealing to men seeking a fraternal lodge that preached white supremacy. But the veteran PR pros soon realized they had their hands on something with greater potential. "The minute we said, 'Ku Klux,' editors from all over the United States began literally pressing us for publicity," Tyler observed.[55]

In 1896, the US Supreme Court legalized racial segregation in its infamous Plessy v. Ferguson ruling. By the 1920s, a wave of Jim Crow laws had re-established rigid racial segregation in the South, leaving Blacks in near-servile status again with negligible political clout. In 1880, half the Black men in the former Confederate states voted; by 1920, less than 1 percent did.[56] But when 200,000 Black soldiers returned home after fighting for their country in the Great War, they were more assertive about demanding better treatment. Many gave up on the Jim Crow South, joining a massive wave of Black migration to the North and West that began in the 1910s. As a result, racial tensions and violent attacks against Blacks were on the rise, culminating in a wave of so-called "race riots" in Chicago, Washington, DC, and several other Southern and Northern cities in the summer of 1919.[57]

In addition to the KKK's historical hostility to Blacks, Clarke and Tyler determined the Klan needed new adversaries to expand its nationwide appeal. "Now Catholics, Jews, nonwhites, Bolsheviks, and immigrants became targets, a shift that greatly increased the Klan's recruitment potential in Northern states," wrote historian Kathleen Blee.[58] The two Klan leaders-for-hire also incorporated moral outrages that appealed to the nation's growing numbers of socially conservative Protestant ministers and their congregants: tirades against bootleggers, nightclubs, dope, adulterers, and urban corruption. Those moral transgressions were conveniently blamed on Catholics, Jews, and Blacks.

Clarke and Tyler's new Propagation Department contracted with more than 1,100 kleagles, training them in modern sales techniques and dispatching them to Oregon and elsewhere across the country to recruit members. Tyler, in her weekly newsletters, instructed kleagles how to find and exploit local hot-button issues when entering unfamiliar terrain. The Klan also contracted with professional lecturers, typically conservative Protestant ministers. Clergymen's paid speeches, promoted by kleagles, garnered publicity and spread the Klan's message.

By the summer of 1921, the Klan was a thriving corporation. Clarke and Tyler, aided by hundreds of kleagles hungry to make sales, had created a new, dynamic Klan with a broader hate-filled message, while Simmons was raking in the money. In little more than a year since inking their contract with Simmons, Clarke and Tyler had expanded the Klan from perhaps 4,000 members to 85,000, collecting more than $750,000 in revenues.[59] "There can be no little doubt that the purely commercial motive had much to do with the successful promotion of the Klan," wrote historian John Moffatt Mecklin in the first major book about the second Klan in 1924.[60] "Money was pouring in," Simmons said later. "I owned the Ku Klux Klan like I own my hat or car."[61]

Ripe Conditions

Clarke and Tyler are widely credited—or blamed—for the dramatic growth of the Klan after five years of obscurity. But the United States also was in a far different place in 1920 and rife with social upheaval. One week after the United States entered the Great War in April 1917, President Woodrow Wilson established the world's first wartime propaganda agency, the US Committee on Public Information.[62] Germans, now clearly the enemy, were derided in Portland newspapers as "Huns," while sauerkraut was renamed "liberty cabbage" and hamburgers "liberty steak." German nationals were barred from coming within one hundred yards of Portland's ten waterfront shipyards, which were churning out cargo vessels for the war effort.[63] Wilson, trying to unify the country, bashed "hyphenated Americans" who still identified with their country of origin and might be prone to divided loyalties, such as German-Americans or Irish-Americans. Government appeals to buy war bonds to finance the war effort called for "100 percent Americanism."[64]

The Great War whipped up Americans' emotions and had a chilling effect on foreigners and new immigrants, especially those who retained their native language, had darker skin, and seemed very different from the white Protestant majority. During the war, Congress enacted a literacy test designed to stem the flow of immigrants; an Espionage Act making it a crime to interfere with the war effort or show support for American enemies; and the Sedition Act, making it a crime to use "disloyal" language that cast the war effort in a negative light.

After the war ended in 1918 and soldiers came home, there was a rise in labor union militancy. One-fifth of all US workers went out on strike during 1919.[65] The reduction in wartime demand spurred two recessions within five years, stoking fears that immigrants were taking jobs from native-born Americans. After Bolsheviks prevailed in the October 1917 Russian Revolution, there were new fears about the spread of communism. That, along with a series of bombings carried out by anarchists, led to the nation's first Red Scare in 1919 and 1920. Wilson's Attorney General A. Mitchell Palmer, assisted by his young underling J. Edgar Hoover, conducted a series of violent raids against alleged anarchists, socialists, labor militants, and communists. More than six thousand were arrested, and more than five hundred who were foreign citizens were deported, including anti-war radical Emma Goldman.

Though accounts of the second Klan are curiously silent about it, the influenza pandemic of 1918–1919 devastated families and communities, adding to social anxieties. Dubbed the Spanish Flu, though scientists say it more likely originated in Kansas, the virus infected more than one in four Americans, killing 675,000 of them. The flu was particularly brutal for children and young adults, the major factor in the plummeting of US life expectancy by twelve years.[66] Worldwide, the flu led to three times as many deaths as the Great War.

When Republican Warren Harding ran for president in 1920, his winning slogan was a call for a "return to normalcy." Life in America was changing at a dizzying pace. For the first time that year, more than half of Americans lived in urban areas, continuing the shift from farming to industrial and office jobs. Greater access to cars, airplanes, radios, telephones, and motion pictures revolutionized transportation, communication, and entertainment, bringing people out of their homes more.

A new burst of prosperity, dubbed the Roaring Twenties, sparked broad cultural changes. Couples could now go out on dates away from their parents, "necking" or "petting" in Model T cars, dancing the

Charleston, and listening to jazz at night clubs and speakeasies. The advent of Prohibition in 1920 made alcohol a forbidden pleasure, and drinking actually increased rather than decreased as intended.[67] Young women seeking more independence became "flappers," donning high heels, makeup, and revealing clothing. More of them left the confines of home to join the workforce.

Backlash

Many Americans feared that their traditional way of life was vanishing. Among majority Protestants, a new term appeared in 1920, "fundamentalist," to describe the increasing numbers of conservative ministers preaching a stricter, literal interpretation of the Bible.[68] Fundamentalist and evangelical preachers were particularly alarmed by widespread violations of Prohibition, which had proven virtually impossible for police to enforce. The complexion of cities also was changing due to Black migration and recent waves of Catholic and Jewish immigrants from Southern and Eastern Europe.

The second Klan exploited Americans' anxieties about the rapid pace of change. Its leaders championed old-fashioned values, capitalizing on mainstream prejudices to build a robust political movement that scapegoated minorities and blamed them for America's woes. While leaders of the second Klan expressed a nostalgic fondness for the original KKK, the 1920s version was quite different. It was a private company, structured to earn profits for the owner, officers, and recruiters. The second Klan never abandoned the racism or commitment to white supremacy that was so foundational to the original KKK. But its leaders ultimately saved most of their venom for immigrants, especially the surge of Catholics and Jews who had arrived in recent decades. "Nationwide, it was more of an anti-immigrant movement and also a purity crusade," said Horowitz, the historian of the Oregon Klan. "It's a white Protestant supremacy organization."[69]

Klansmen didn't view the second Klan as a hate group. Rather, Klan positions on race, religion, and ethnicity largely reflected mainstream views of the era. Madison Grant, a respected New York conservationist, argued in his popular 1916 book, *The Passing of the Great Race*, that the "Nordic race"—Northern European Protestants—was inherently superior to all others. Grant warned that Nordics were being outbred by inferior white ethnic groups in America. "Nordics deteriorate when mixed with other races," concurred President Calvin Coolidge.[70]

The Klan highlighted its support for "100 percent Americanism" and treated the US flag and the Bible as sacred symbols. It melded its moral platform with aggressive attacks on Catholics by focusing on Prohibition. Many Catholic immigrants from Ireland, Germany, and Italy retained their cultures' affinities for whiskey, beer, and wine. Catholics also viewed the alcohol ban as an attack on their use of wine in rituals. "The 18th Amendment had been a Protestant triumph over Catholic voters, most of whom opposed it," wrote Father Wilfred P. Schoenberg, a historian focused on Catholicism in the Northwest who taught at Gonzaga University in Spokane.[71] The Klan depicted alcohol consumption as a vice committed by Catholics, and frequently bashed Jews and Blacks as bootleggers who carried out underground sales and production.

Those stances gave the Klan a righteous appeal among Protestants and aided recruitment. But the Klan's moral stances didn't seem to apply to its top leaders. Simmons was a heavy drinker, known for frequenting prostitutes and having a fondness for horse racing and pornography.[72] Clarke, who was married, became romantically involved with Tyler. They were arrested by police in a 1919 romantic "tryst" that came to light two years later.[73]

Mecklin traced the Klan's anti-Catholic obsession to the large numbers of Scotch-Irish immigrants who settled in the South in the eighteenth century.[74] England's King James I lured their Presbyterian ancestors to the northern part of Ireland in 1610 as a Protestant counter to Irish Catholics chafing under English colonial rule. King James awarded Protestant newcomers some of the best land,[75] creating bad blood between Catholics and Protestants that lasted for centuries and carried over to the American shores. Descendants of those Scotch-Irish immigrants formed the core of Orange Lodges who became some of the most militant Klansmen.

2
The Klan Sweeps into Oregon

> *Oregon, as much if not more than that of any other state in the union, headed into the stream of war spirit and was swept through the years 1917 and 1918 under the stupor of patriotism and intense nationalism. When the weapon of intense nationalism so indispensable to the prosecution of the war suddenly left without a war to spend itself upon, it turned introspective and vented itself on the 'enemies' of America at home.*
>
> —C. Easton Rothwell[1]

> *"The Klan is a war-time product. It was born of psychopathic hysteria and religious delusion."*
>
> —Lem Dever, former Oregon Klan propagandist[2]

1921: First Kleagles Arrive in Beaver State

The second Klan went national in late 1920 and 1921, when Edward Clarke and Elizabeth Tyler trained and dispatched recruiters to all sections of the country. The first three assigned to Oregon arrived by the spring of 1921. They swiftly enrolled enough Klansmen to form chapters in Medford, Portland, Eugene, and elsewhere, earning lucrative sales commissions.

Winter or spring: Kleagle Luther Powell arrives in Medford, enlists Ku Klux Klan's first Oregon members.

June: Bragg Callaway arrives in Portland to sign up members, while C. N. Jones recruits in Eugene.

July: Powell replaces Callaway as main Klan organizer in Portland.

August 1: Portland Klan stages press conference with local public officials to promote Klan's entry into Oregon.

Klansmen raise a giant cross for a Klan ritual in August 1925. Burning crosses, popularized by *Birth of a Nation,* became the second Klan's calling card. (Library of Congress)

August 20: Portland NAACP petitions Governor Ben Olcott to promote law and order by restraining Klan.

September 6: *New York World* begins twenty-one-part series exposing violence and other unsavory behavior by the second Klan.

September 22: Governor Olcott tells *New York World* the Klan has failed to make headway in Oregon.

October: Klan holds first Portland chapter meeting.

October 11: US House Rules Committee launches investigative hearings on Klan.

December 22: Portland Mayor George Baker creates one hundred-person police vigilante squad, many of them Klansmen.

December 22: Klan holds first public event in Portland, attracting six thousand people to Municipal Auditorium lecture by Reverend Reuben Sawyer.

On a Mission from Atlanta

Oregon was ripe territory for the Klan. The state was overwhelmingly white and Protestant, with a long history of hostility toward Blacks and

Catholics.[3] During the Great War, the state stood out for its patriotism. Oregon had the highest military enlistment rate among all the states;[4] Portlanders topped all their big-city peers buying up Liberty Bonds to finance the war effort;[5] and Oregonians eagerly supported the Red Cross and other war-related causes. Oregon was swept up in a "stupor of patriotism and intense nationalism" as intense as any other state, concluded C. Easton Rothwell, who wrote the first detailed account of the Oregon Klan for his 1924 Reed College thesis.[6] Wartime fervor stirred up Oregonians' suspicions of foreigners and made the state more receptive to the Klan's appeal to "100 percent Americanism."

In the winter or spring of 1921, Major Luther I. Powell stepped off a northbound train from California to Medford, dispatched from Ku Klux Klan headquarters to expand the second Klan into Oregon.[7] Powell, who turned forty-three that May, sold advertising back in Shreveport, Louisiana, then switched to selling memberships in the reconstituted Ku Klux Klan, first in Louisiana, then in California.[8] Now the Missouri native was opening new terrain, starting in a Southern Oregon city of 5,700 people that was a center of the orchard industry.

Powell was a master pitchman and experienced kleagle—part recruiter, part salesman—earning hefty commissions by signing up new members to the secretive white supremacist group. He was big, jovial, and magnetic, and he made friends easily. Later he reportedly organized an entire Klan chapter of one hundred sailors aboard the USS *Tennessee* battleship while it was anchored in Puget Sound.[9] Powell's political and religious views meshed with the Klan's. He was a Spanish-American War veteran and member of the Scottish Rite Masonic lodge and an Orange lodge, two fraternal groups that provided fertile recruiting ground for the Klan.[10]

Powell followed the standard Klan organizing formula by combing rosters of Medford's Masonic and other fraternal lodges for potential recruits. Kleagles were trained to ferret out and exploit hot-button issues when entering new communities, and Oregonians in 1921 were more concerned with religion, education, and politics than with racial issues.[11] Kleagles focused on "scabs they could pick," said Ashland historian Jeff LaLande, who chronicled the Klan in Southern Oregon.[12]

In Medford, the scab was the ongoing battle over Prohibition enforcement. Oregon had allowed local communities to ban alcohol

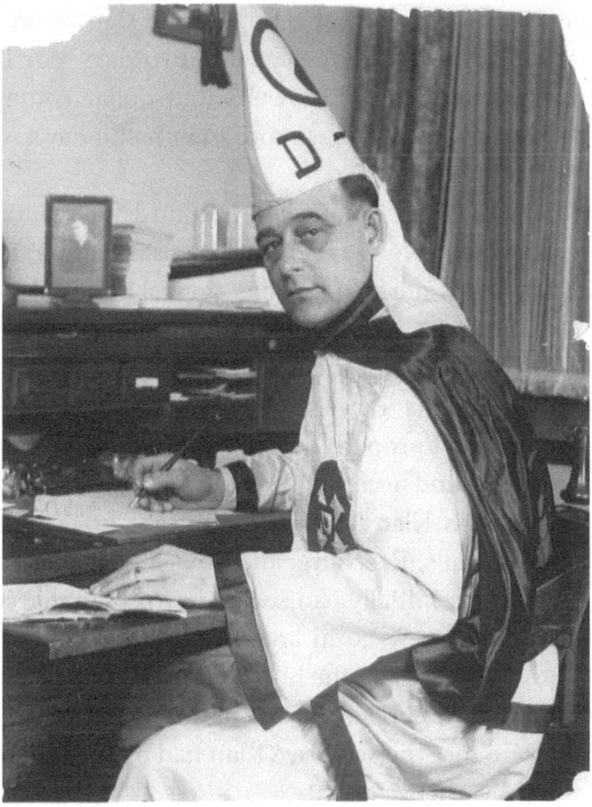

Veteran salesman Luther Powell organized Oregon's first Klan chapter in Medford, then moved on to Portland and other cities. Powell, shown here in Seattle in 1923, later organized the Klan in Washington. (MOHAI, *Seattle Post-Intelligencer* Collection, 2000.107.108.16.02)

since 1905, and voters approved a statewide ban on booze in 1914 that took effect in 1916, three years before passage of the national Prohibition amendment. Enforcing the ban on alcohol sales and manufacturing proved elusive. Powell arrived in town shortly after an itinerant evangelist, Reverend E. J. Bulgin, preached there about the evils of alcohol and lax law enforcement. Bulgin later joined the staff of the *Searchlight*, the KKK newspaper in Atlanta.[13] Powell piggybacked on Bulgin's moral crusade, promising that the Klan would take action against bootleggers and others skirting Prohibition laws.

The first three recruits signed up on the afternoon Powell arrived in town, according to an account by one of those men.[14] They in turn helped Powell enlist twenty-six more men to attend a meeting that night in the Masonic Hall. The agenda was reportedly so secret that none of the other men knew the exact purpose of the gathering. All of them were Protestants and most were Masons. After hearing Powell's pitch, twenty-five of them agreed to sign up as Klan members.[15] The ten-dollar initiation fee equaled two days' pay for the average skilled workman in Oregon. Powell's four-dollar commission for signing up just one Klansman was more than half a day's wage for a union longshoreman in Portland.[16]

The kleagle remained in Medford for several days, conducting at least three evening meetings. In a short time, Powell recruited about eighty-five Klansmen, earning several hundred dollars in commissions. Those recruits formed the nucleus of Oregon's first chapter of the Invisible Empire of the Knights of the Ku Klux Klan.[17] Klansmen later complained that Powell was too eager to make a buck and move on, and that he didn't properly screen Medford recruits or court the city's more influential and accomplished citizens. The Medford chapter, known as a klavern in Klan lingo, failed to take hold once Powell departed for Klamath Falls, Roseburg, and other new pastures to sign up recruits.[18] The klavern initially had such a low profile that *Medford Mail Tribune* editor Robert W. Ruhl boasted in July 1921 that his community was more peaceful than the big metropolis of Portland, where the Klan had just surfaced publicly for the first time in Oregon. Ruhl apparently was unaware that the secretive Klan had organized its first Oregon chapter months earlier in his city.[19]

Klan Expands into Portland

As Powell organized klaverns in Southern Oregon, C. N. Jones was dispatched from Louisiana to sign up members in the lower Willamette Valley, and Bragg Callaway made his way from Texas to recruit in Portland. Callaway arrived at Portland's Union Station on June 12, 1921, after a long train journey from his home in Houston.[20] The thirty-one-year-old tried to impress Portland recruits with a business card listing himself as vice-president of Barringer Norton Co. Inc., Houston Tailors and Shirt Makers.[21] He was no longer selling shirts; now he was selling memberships in the Ku Klux Klan on commission.

Callaway brought along membership applications and KKK pamphlets, including a handout explaining the Klan's philosophy of putting "America First."[22] He was searching out white male Protestants born in the United States who shared the Klan's views. Catholics were considered beholden to the pope in Rome and thus not loyal Americans. Jews,

Blacks, and people of Chinese or Japanese ancestry also were excluded. The membership application asked applicants to note whether they believed in white supremacy and to list the secret fraternal orders they belonged to and the church they attended.

Racial composition of Oregon in 1920

Whites	769,146	98.2%
Native Americans	4,590	0.6%
Japanese	4,151	0.5%
Chinese	3,090	0.4%
Blacks	2,144	0.3%
US-born whites	666,995	85.1%
Foreign-born whites	102,151	13.0%

Source: US Census

Portland may have seemed an unlikely target for a white-supremacist group. Only 1,556 Blacks lived in the city in 1920, less than 1 percent of the population.[23] The tiny Black community had suffered from racist treatment since before Oregon became a state.[24] There were signs of a new assertiveness as Black soldiers returning from Europe chafed at Jim Crow-style segregation they encountered at Portland movie theaters, swimming pools, and other public facilities. And Beatrice Cannady and other Black activists had formed that NAACP chapter in 1914, the year the war started. Yet when the Klan expanded into Portland, Blacks well-understood its terrorist history and had good reason to fear being victimized again, observed Darrell Millner, an emeritus Black history professor at Portland State University.[25]

Portland once had a substantial population of Chinese immigrants, but a series of racist attacks and federal restrictions had caused their numbers to plummet two-thirds during the 1910s, leaving only 1,846 Chinese-born residents when the Klan arrived.[26] However, many Americans didn't think of Jews or olive-skinned Italians and Greeks as whites, and those groups had grown substantially in recent years. Portlanders couldn't help noticing new enclaves of Yiddish-speaking Jews from Russia and Eastern Europe; Catholics from Italy; and Greeks, whose Orthodox Christian faith was alien to Protestants.

Oregon's changing immigrant mix

Nationality	Change from 1900 to 1920
Greeks	up 1,929%
Italians	up 326%
Russians	up 254%
Finns	up 184%
Norwegians	up 149%
Austrians	up 146%
Swedes	up 131%
Canadians	up 84%
On the flip side:	
Germans	up 3%
Irish	flat
Chinese	down 77%

Source: US Census

Jews now accounted for an estimated 3 percent of Portlanders, or eight thousand people, the bulk of them living in an immigrant enclave in South Portland.[27] There was an international spike in anti-Semitism in the early part of the century, though Jews had a relatively higher level of acceptance in Oregon than in other states.[28] They had long thrived as merchants in Portland and many smaller Oregon towns, propelling many of them into civic leadership. In the nineteenth century, Jews were elected mayors of Albany, Astoria, Burns, Eugene, Heppner, North Powder, and Pendleton.[29] Three Jewish men had served as Portland mayor.[30]

Homelands of Portland Immigrants, 1920

Canada	6,437	Ireland	1,969
Great Britain	6,104	China	1,846
Germany	5,384	Japan	1,715
Russia	5,161	Austria	1,599
Sweden	5,060	Finland	1,394
Norway	2,915	Denmark	1,365
Italy	2,847	Switzerland	1,283

Source: US Census

One in five Portlanders were immigrants when the Klan arrived. But the city was still overwhelmingly white and Protestant, as the bulk of newcomers hailed from Canada, Great Britain, and other white Protestant nations.[31]

The second Klan, which billed itself as the militant arm of Protestantism, was implicated in several violent attacks, largely against people of color, but its main targets in Oregon were Catholics. Portland hadn't experienced as great an influx of Irish immigrants as many other big cities of that era. But by 1920, more than one of fourteen Oregonians, and one of eleven Portlanders, was Catholic.[32]

As with anti-Semitism, agitations against Catholics were on the rise in the years before Callaway's arrival. Masonic lodges had passed resolutions calling for a ban on private schools. In the spring 1921 primary, anti-Catholic forces helped win a decisive victory in Portland School Board races, defeating a four-person slate endorsed by the establishment City Club of Portland and three of the city's four daily newspapers.[33]

A severe downturn after the war, termed the Depression of 1920–1921, likely made Oregonians, like other Americans, more receptive to the Klan's nativist or anti-foreigner message. Nationally, economic production shrank nearly a third, business failures tripled, and big corporate stocks in the Dow Jones Industrial Average fell nearly in half.[34] In Oregon, war's end slashed demand for the state's lumber, grain, and shipbuilding resources, rendering Oregonians more anxious about depressed farm prices, wages that hadn't kept pace with inflation, and competition from immigrants willing to work for less.

Portland was Oregon's dominant city, accounting for nearly a third of its population and fifteen times as many residents as Salem, the state capital and second-largest city. With 258,288 residents, Portland ranked as the nation's twenty-fourth biggest city, larger than Houston, San Diego, Dallas, and the Klan headquarters city of Atlanta.[35] Portland was by now riddled with the same urban ills afflicting other big cities: political corruption, bootlegging, prostitution, and dope peddling. Prohibition had worsened those afflictions by driving alcohol sales and related activities underground. Industrial Workers of the World unionists publicly identified thirteen illegal speakeasies and bootleg joints in Portland in 1919, in a stunt designed to take the heat off the embattled group.[36] Portland also had experienced occasional violence stemming from competition among *tongs*, the fraternal groups established by Chinese immigrants for mutual support, business, and social benefits.[37]

The Klan exploited that social and economic turmoil after Callaway arrived in the spring of 1921 and set up operations at the downtown Multnomah Hotel. Operating by the Klan playbook, Callaway acquired lists of fraternal lodge members to recruit.[38] By late June, the Texan inducted the first cohort of ninety recruits into the Klan, recruiting many prominent citizens, Masons, and other anti-Catholic lodge members, as well as a smattering of policemen.[39] Before being "naturalized" as Klan members, recruits filled in applications spelling out where they were born, along with details about their family, their education, political affiliations, and military experience. The Klan also demanded to know about their criminal records and whether they used alcohol or narcotics.

Though the Klan prided itself on operating in secrecy, word soon got out to a *Portland Telegram* reporter that Callaway was organizing in town. On June 17, 1921, a banner atop the scrappy newspaper's front page read "Portland Invaded by Ku Klux Klan." It was the first public announcement that the Klan had penetrated Oregon, published five days after Callaway arrived. Though the kleagle wasn't directly quoted, the article appeared to be based on leaked information, as the reporter uncovered details of Callaway's name, how he was identified on his business card, the literature he was using for recruitment, his goal of recruiting 2,500 Klan members in Portland, and his plans to stage a public parade once he reached his membership goal.

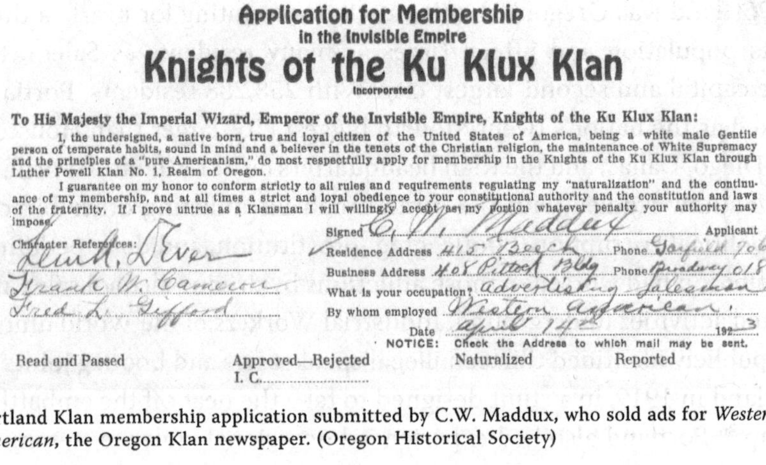

Application for Membership
in the Invisible Empire
Knights of the Ku Klux Klan
Incorporated

To His Majesty the Imperial Wizard, Emperor of the Invisible Empire, Knights of the Ku Klux Klan:

I, the undersigned, a native born, true and loyal citizen of the United States of America, being a white male Gentile person of temperate habits, sound in mind and a believer in the tenets of the Christian religion, the maintenance of White Supremacy and the principles of a "pure Americanism," do most respectfully apply for membership in the Knights of the Ku Klux Klan through Luther Powell Klan No. 1, Realm of Oregon.

I guarantee on my honor to conform strictly to all rules and requirements regulating my "naturalization" and the continuance of my membership, and at all times a strict and loyal obedience to your constitutional authority and the constitution and laws of the fraternity. If I prove untrue as a Klansman I will willingly accept as my portion whatever penalty your authority may impose.

Signed C. W. Maddux Applicant

Character References:
Frank W. Cameron
Fred L. Gifford

Residence Address 415 Beech Phone Garfield 7069
Business Address 408 Pittock Bldg Phone Broadway 0187
What is your occupation? advertising salesman
By whom employed Western American
Date April 14th 1923

NOTICE: Check the Address to which mail may be sent.

Read and Passed Approved—Rejected Naturalized Reported
I. C.

Portland Klan membership application submitted by C.W. Maddux, who sold ads for *Western American*, the Oregon Klan newspaper. (Oregon Historical Society)

The publicity likely helped Callaway with recruitment and earned him substantial commissions, but Klan headquarters in Atlanta wasn't happy. He was abruptly replaced by a more seasoned Klan recruiter making his way from Southern Oregon, Luther Powell.[40] Callaway and Powell may have quarreled over how to divvy up sales commissions earned from member sign-ups,[41] but it seems more likely that Callaway was bumped for disobeying instructions from Atlanta to operate in secret,[42] as he apparently had second thoughts after seeing news of his organizing

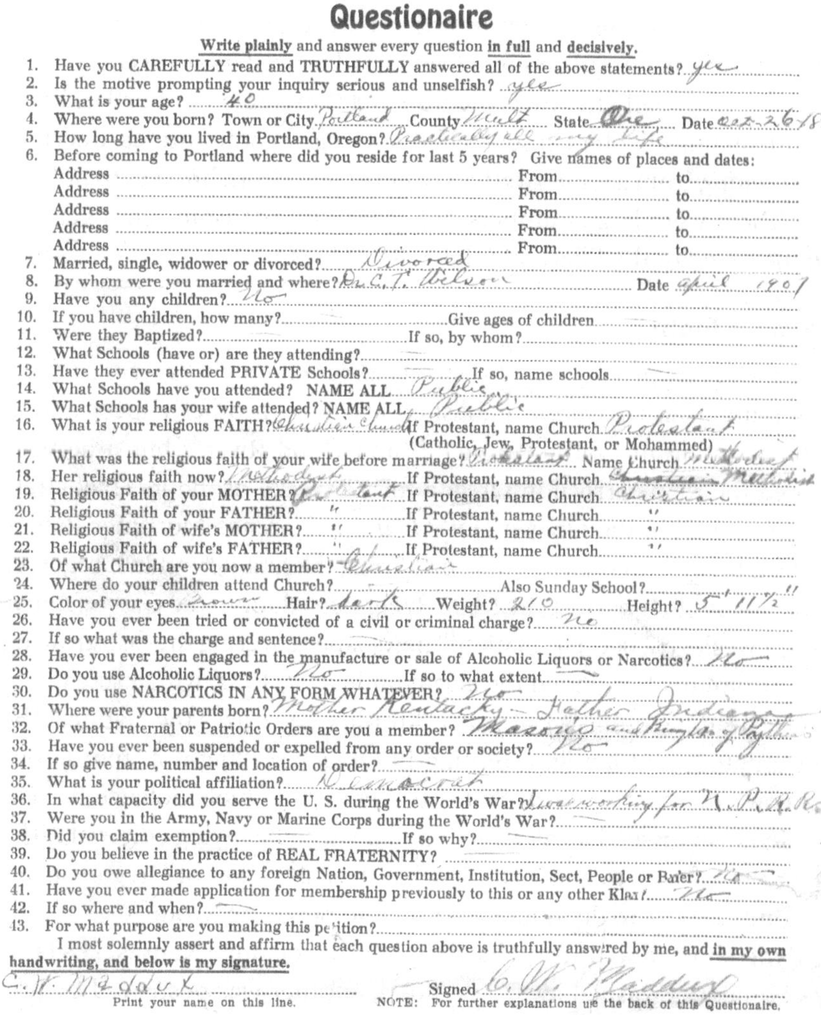

Questionaire

Write plainly and answer every question in full and decisively.

1. Have you CAREFULLY read and TRUTHFULLY answered all of the above statements? yes
2. Is the motive prompting your inquiry serious and unselfish? yes
3. What is your age? 40
4. Where were you born? Town or City Portland County Mult State Ore Date Oct 26 1882
5. How long have you lived in Portland, Oregon? Practically all my life
6. Before coming to Portland where did you reside for last 5 years? Give names of places and dates:
   Address ... From ... to ...
   Address ... From ... to ...
   Address ... From ... to ...
   Address ... From ... to ...
   Address ... From ... to ...
7. Married, single, widower or divorced? Divorced
8. By whom were you married and where? Dr. C. T. Wilson Date April 1901
9. Have you any children? No
10. If you have children, how many? ... Give ages of children ...
11. Were they Baptized? ... If so, by whom? ...
12. What Schools (have or) are they attending? ...
13. Have they ever attended PRIVATE Schools? ... If so, name schools ...
14. What Schools have you attended? NAME ALL Public
15. What Schools has your wife attended? NAME ALL Public
16. What is your religious FAITH? Christian Church If Protestant, name Church Protestant
    (Catholic, Jew, Protestant, or Mohammed)
17. What was the religious faith of your wife before marriage? Protestant Name Church Methodist
18. Her religious faith now? Methodist If Protestant, name Church Christian Methodist
19. Religious Faith of your MOTHER? Protestant If Protestant, name Church Christian
20. Religious Faith of your FATHER? " If Protestant, name Church "
21. Religious Faith of wife's MOTHER? " If Protestant, name Church "
22. Religious Faith of wife's FATHER? " If Protestant, name Church "
23. Of what Church are you now a member? Christian
24. Where do your children attend Church? ... Also Sunday School? ...
25. Color of your eyes brown Hair? dark Weight? 210 Height? 5' 11½"
26. Have you ever been tried or convicted of a civil or criminal charge? no
27. If so what was the charge and sentence? ...
28. Have you ever been engaged in the manufacture or sale of Alcoholic Liquors or Narcotics? No
29. Do you use Alcoholic Liquors? No If so to what extent ...
30. Do you use NARCOTICS IN ANY FORM WHATEVER? No
31. Where were your parents born? Mother Kentucky – Father Indiana
32. Of what Fraternal or Patriotic Orders are you a member? Masonic and Knights of Pythias
33. Have you ever been suspended or expelled from any order or society? No
34. If so give name, number and location of order? ...
35. What is your political affiliation? Democrat
36. In what capacity did you serve the U. S. during the World's War? I was working for N. P. R. R.
37. Were you in the Army, Navy or Marine Corps during the World's War? ...
38. Did you claim exemption? ... If so why? ...
39. Do you believe in the practice of REAL FRATERNITY? ...
40. Do you owe allegiance to any foreign Nation, Government, Institution, Sect, People or Ruler? No
41. Have you ever made application for membership previously to this or any other Klan? No
42. If so where and when? ...
43. For what purpose are you making this petition? ...

I most solemnly assert and affirm that each question above is truthfully answered by me, and in my own handwriting, and below is my signature.

C. W. Maddux
Print your name on this line.

Signed C. W. Maddux

NOTE: For further explanations use the back of this Questionaire.

Maddux had to prove he was proper Klan material by answering questions about his religion, values and other highly personal matters. (Oregon Historical Society) work blasted on the front page of the *Portland Telegram*. The next day, the state's largest newspaper, the *Morning Oregonian*, published a two-sentence brief based on information supplied by Callaway, who denied working for the Klan and claimed he was merely in Portland on vacation. "Mr. Callaway said that if such organization was being effected in Oregon, the movement would be conducted in secrecy."[43]

Despite the discord within the Invisible Empire, Portlanders were flocking to the Klan. The *Telegram* reported a week after Powell's arrival that scores of Portlanders were joining each day.[44] In a dig at its larger competitor, the *Telegram* noted that its first story was greeted with skepticism, but subsequent events had proved its story correct. By then, the Klan had already signed up 1,000 members in Portland and was organizing chapters in several other Oregon communities. Recruits were coming from a wide swath of occupations, from brokers to policemen. There were large numbers of Scottish Rite Masons, Orangemen, and members of the Elks and Odd Fellows lodges.[45]

Picking a Fight

After the *Portland Telegram* scoops, its larger competitors were surprisingly mum. The *Oregonian* published briefs from other papers noting Klan recruiting in Seattle,[46] Salem,[47] and Hood River,[48] but otherwise ignored the Klan's arrival in Oregon for six weeks, as did its chief afternoon competitor, the *Oregon Daily Journal*. Clarence Mortimer Rynerson beat them both to the punch, becoming the first person in Oregon to speak out publicly against the Klan. Rynerson, editor of the *Oregon Labor Press*, a weekly 12,000-circulation[49] newspaper covering the fast-growing union movement, sounded the alarm on July 22, 1921, with a screaming banner headline on his front page, "Ku Klux Terrorizes the Nation." The article noted the Klan was forming in Oregon, calling it a "murderous and cowardly organization" that was committing mob violence in Texas.[50] Rynerson issued a call to action in an accompanying editorial. "The Labor Press wants to know NOW what the authorities of Oregon and of Portland propose to do" about the threat to peace, he wrote.[51]

Rynerson had weathered hard times growing up in Kansas. His family's home was washed away in a flood, another was destroyed by fire, and his entire town was decimated by a grasshopper plague.[52] He was witty, affable, and gutsy. "He was used to speaking up," observed the editor's grandson, Robert Rynerson.[53] In its next issue, the *Labor Press* reported on a local union member who received a threatening letter from the Klan.[54] "One of the chief purposes of the Klan is said to be the maintenance of supremacy of the white race," Rynerson penned in an editorial. "If the white race must resort to such methods to maintain its supremacy, it is not entitled to supremacy."[55]

If Rynerson was picking a fight with the Klan, he succeeded. The next week, he published another critical front-page story, but now the subject was himself.[56] Luther Powell, calling himself King Kleagle of the Realm of Oregon, had written a letter to Rynerson criticizing the "scathing condemnation" in recent editorials. Powell's letter listed the Klan's stances, including white supremacy, protection of women, 100 percent Americanism, the "eradication of gamblers, grafters, parasites, thieves, and degenerates," limitations on new immigration, and a closer relationship between American labor and capital. If Rynerson didn't support that agenda, Powell warned, "then you would be a fit subject for a Vigilance Committee." Rynerson also received a threatening telephone call warning him to answer the letter "right."

Rynerson, who would go on to run for an Oregon House of Representatives seat the next year, didn't back down. He printed the Klan's

Oregon Labor Press editor Clarence Mortimer Rynerson, shown with his new bride Margaret, was the first Oregonian to openly challenge the Klan. After a burst of aggressive news coverage when the KKK first organized in Portland, Rynerson backed off when the Klan mounted a punishing boycott of the weekly newspaper. (Courtesy of Rynerson family)

letter in its entirety, along with a defiant, sarcastic response, referring to Powell as "your highness." Rynerson invited the Klan's vigilante group to his workplace and told Powell where to find him. "Tell the gang not to bother the girl in the front office...Just walk right into my private office," he wrote.[57] That edition included four articles about the KKK, including a sarcastic poem about Powell, plus another editorial. Over three weeks, Rynerson published three banner headlines on his front page and three editorials attacking the Klan, even as Klan vigilante actions mounted in other states.

But the Klan's intimidation tactics started to pay off, as Rynerson started carrying a gun for self-defense.[58] The Klan mounted a boycott of the *Labor Press*, and its circulation took a hit.[59] Rynerson, who had recently married and was starting to raise a family, likely felt financial pressure, said his grandson.[60] The *Labor Press* abruptly halted its attacks on the Klan.[61]

As Callaway and Powell made a splash stirring up controversy in Portland, fellow Kleagle C. N. Jones used a stealthier approach to organize Eugene. Residents of Oregon's fourth-largest city got wind of the Invisible Empire's arrival a month after the Klan surfaced in Portland, though there were scant details. "As mysteriously as it is quiet, the organization is being formed, gathering recruits from among the best people of the city," the *Eugene Guard* reported on July 16, 1921. "The *Guard* has reason to believe that if the Klan has not already been formed, it is in the process of formation and will have several hundred members within a week."[62] Jones reportedly enlisted about a hundred members in Eugene in slightly more than a month.[63]

The *Capital Journal* of Salem, which ultimately would track the Klan more closely than any other Oregon publication, first mentioned the KKK's arrival in the state capital the following week. As in Eugene, the Klan wasn't yet seeking to call attention to itself in the state's second-largest city. "Rumors have been circulating in the city concerning the activity here of a mysterious order of the Ku Klux Klan with the purpose of organizing a local Klan among responsible members of the community," the newspaper reported on July 21. "No one is willing to speak concerning the movement, but it is supposed to have aroused much interest in certain circles."[64]

Klan organizing efforts in Hood River and Marshfield (later renamed Coos Bay) also were reported that month by local newspapers. Yet the state's two largest and most amply staffed publications, which both covered statewide news, still hadn't weighed in with their own reporting. That was about to change.

The Klan's Coming-Out Stunt

The *Oregonian* finally conceded that the Klan, indeed, had penetrated the Portland market on July 31, though it failed to provide any local details.[65] The state's largest newspaper may have decided it couldn't dodge the issue any longer, after getting invited to an unusual press conference scheduled for the next day. Unidentified Klan representatives had contacted newspapers, as well as the mayor, police chief, and other city, county, and federal law enforcement officials. They were all invited to what turned out to be the Oregon Klan's coming-out presentation at the Multnomah Hotel.[66]

As the dignitaries and reporters arrived at the hotel suite, a masked and hooded Klansman greeted them, identifying himself as the "king kleagle." He turned out to be Powell, now the chief statewide organizer for the Klan. Powell introduced a second hooded Klansman as an exalted cyclops. Later he was identified as Fred Gifford, appointed to run the Portland klavern so Powell could focus on organizing other chapters around the state.

None of the invitees knew what to expect or why they had been summoned. They soon learned the Klan was trying to portray itself in a positive light and reassure those troubled by recent reports of Klan violence and law-breaking in Texas and other states. Powell removed his hood, announcing that the Portland Klan had already recruited 1,500 men, including one hundred fifty members of the city police force, and that other chapters had formed in Salem, Ashland, Medford, and Hood River. "In six to 12 months we will have no less than 100,000 members in Oregon," Powell boasted, though that would have been the bulk of the state's native-born white Protestant men.[67]

Powell relayed the Klan's standard mantras. They were patriotic, and they advocated 100 percent Americanism. They had formed to clean up Portland's morals and politics. "Ours is not an 'anti' organization of any kind," Powell insisted. "We are not anti-Japanese, or anti-Jew, or anti-Negro or anti-Catholic or anti anything else."[68] They were law-abiding, and they aimed to help law enforcement. "We uphold—not break the law," Powell said.

"I realize that you won't break the law in Portland," responded Portland Mayor George Baker.[69] But that claim was belied by the Klan's own press release handed out to reporters at the hotel. "As to the many stories and dispatches which have been circulated about tar-and-feathering activities in the Klan in other sections, some are true and some are not true," the statement noted.[70] In a frank admission of the Klan's penchant for vigilante actions, the statement went on to say the Klan sometimes decided that conditions warranted "direct action, or in other words the Klan takes up cases where the law leaves off."

It's unclear how law enforcement personnel in attendance reacted. But the Portland mayor and other distinguished invitees obliged the Klan organizers by agreeing to line up in front of a velvet curtain for

The Oregon Klan scored a public relations coup when the *Portland Telegram* published this photo, orchestrated by the Klan, of public officials and two Klansmen at the secret order's introductory press conference. From left: H. P. Coffin, National Safety Council; Portland police captain John T. Moore; Portland Police Chief Lee V. Jenkins; District Attorney Walter H. Evans; federal District Attorney Lester Humphreys; Oregon King Kleagle Luther Powell; Sheriff T. M. Hurlburt; Russell Bryon, US Justice Department special agent; Portland Mayor George Baker; P. S. Malcom, Oregon Scottish Rite Masons sovereign grand inspector general; and Frederick Gifford, exalted cyclops of the Portland chapter. (Oregon Historical Society)

a group photograph. Seconds before the camera flashed, the curtain opened and out stepped the two hooded Klansmen to join the assembled group.[71] The group photo, published by the *Portland Telegram* on August 2, shows nine well-dressed men, all but one wearing ties and sports coats. Sticking out in the foreground were two hooded Klansmen—Powell and Gifford.[72]

The presence of the lone private citizen among the depicted guests, Philip Schuyler Malcom, suggests he was already associated with the Klan. P. S. Malcom was the Oregon Scottish Rite Mason sovereign grand inspector general, and Powell and Gifford were Scottish Rite members.[73] The Klan would team up with the lodge the next year to enact a ballot initiative banning private schools in Oregon.

"Before many moons," Powell predicted, "there will appear on the streets of Portland a parade of many hundreds of men from not only the city, but throughout the realm."[74] Attendees then crowded around Powell to examine his elaborate costume. Powell wore a white mask with an eagle on the side embroidered in red, black, gold, and white. Over that he wore a hood and a full-length white robe. On his breast was a Ku Klux Klan cross, a white cross edged in black placed diagonally in a red circle surrounded by a yellow ring. In the center of the cross was a white square with a red crescent, representing blood shed by Jesus on the cross.[75]

The *Telegram*'s use of the staged photo turned out to be a public relations bonanza for the Klan. "The publication of the picture has given the idea to thousands of citizens that the officials are in league with the Klan," observed the *Labor Press* in its next edition.[76] That may not have been accurate at the time, but it certainly was true later for at least some of the gentlemen.

Governor Olcott Not Worried

Portland's Ku Klux Klan chapter had already made good on its threat to carry out vigilante actions by sending that menacing letter to Rynerson a few days before the press conference. Rynerson hired prominent left-wing attorney William U'ren, known as the father of Oregon's initiative and referendum system, to represent him. U'Ren brought a complaint about Powell's threatening letter to the district attorney, and Powell was soon summoned to appear before a grand jury.[77] Powell reportedly slipped out of town until the heat was off; he may have gone back to

Atlanta to consult with Klan headquarters. Callaway was put back in control, ensconced at the Multnomah Hotel, and by the end of August was calling himself the new king kleagle.[78] But Powell soon resurfaced in Portland and was back in charge, along with Gifford. It appears the district attorney didn't press criminal charges against Powell, as Multnomah County court archives don't include records of any such case.

That summer, new Klan chapters were springing up fast. Jones organized a chapter in Albany and then moved on to Corvallis.[79] Astoria, then Oregon's third-largest city, had a new chapter by August,[80] as did Roseburg.[81] Flush with success, the Portland Klan sent application materials to Governor Ben Olcott in Salem, inviting him to join the Invisible Empire.[82] Additional kleagles were hired in or dispatched to Oregon. In September, Kleagle T. A. Rogers stepped off the train in Pendleton and commenced organizing a klavern there.[83] That month, the Klan arrived in Oregon City.[84] In October, Kleagle C. C. Starr organized a chapter in Bend.[85] Another new chapter formed that fall in coastal Tillamook.[86]

Thanks to scores of kleagles dispatched by Clarke and Tyler, the Klan was experiencing spectacular growth across the nation.[87] But many Oregonians grew fearful after reading news of Klan vigilantism and violence in Texas and other states. Springfield resident J. E. Forbes sent a petition signed by 112 local residents to Governor Olcott on August 8, 1921, asking him to take action to suppress the Klan. "We, the undersigned citizens of Springfield, believing that a crisis has arisen in the civic affairs of this state, on account of the organization of a branch of the Ku Klux Klan which assumes for itself extralegal, judicial and plenary powers not granted by the constitution or the laws of the state, hereby wish to express horror of the cowardly methods wont to be used by this organization on defenseless people, and do hereby petition you to use your utmost executive powers, by proclamation, martial law or the calling of an extra session of the legislature, if need be, to suppress the activities of this anarchistic gang, that the fair name of Oregon may continue unbesmirched by lawless raiders who are trying to hide their guilt under the pretense of Americanism." Olcott responded the next day, assuring the citizens of Springfield they had no need to worry.[88]

Portland's Black community was the most alarmed, and it also sought action from the governor. On August 20, the NAACP Committee on

Legislation and Legal Redress, chaired by Cannady, sent the governor a similar letter, stating that the civil rights group "respectfully call your attention to the formation and rapidly spreading organization known as the Ku Klux Klan." The Klan made a pretense of supporting law and order, the NAACP wrote, but sought the "persecution of individuals who may incur their disfavor. And to the end that all citizens may have a sense of security in their homes at night, and peaceable protection in their places of business and employment during the day, we humbly pray you honor to prevent in our state any organization or public demonstration of the said notorious Ku Klux Klan under any pretext whatsoever."[89] Olcott responded two days later in a letter to Cannady. "I wish to commend the signers of the petition upon the attitude they have assumed, although I think they need not be apprehensive about the Ku Klux Klan becoming any very serious menace to our government," Olcott wrote. "I have a great faith in the sound sense of the people of our commonwealth, and I think our laws and our form of government requires no secret associations to assist them in properly functioning for the liberty and happiness of our people."[90]

Two months earlier, disgruntled Knoxville, Tennessee, Kleagle Henry Fry quit the Klan and decided to go public with his criticisms. Fry's revelations formed the basis of a gripping exposé of the second Klan by the *New York World* newspaper, which started running a twenty-one-part series on September 6. At least eighteen other newspapers published the series, including the *Seattle Times.* No Oregon papers ran it, but word spread nationally of its findings. *New York World* editor Herbert Bayard Swope sought a comment from Olcott while the series was running. The governor responded in a September 22 telegram much as he had to Cannady and the folks in Springfield. "Because of wholesome conditions in Oregon, with little discontent and a satisfied people," Olcott wrote to Swope, "the Ku Klux Klan, although endeavoring to invade the state, has made little or no progress and am informed it is now folding its tent like the Arab and silently stealing away. The Klan has been taken lightly here and because of the fact it has made practically no impression on our people or our institutions, the executive office of this state has deemed action or any particular comment unnecessary."[91]

Olcott would later regret those words.

President and Congress Step In

President Warren Harding's administration wasn't so nonchalant. He faced clamor for government action in response to the *World's* revelations of Klan violence and other illegalities. The US Justice Department and the US Postal Department soon commenced investigations. Then the House Rules Committee launched hearings starting October 11. Congressman Peter Francis Tague, an Irish Catholic from Boston who had pressed for the investigations, denounced the Klan as lawless and un-American for inciting race and religious prejudice. Atlanta Klan leader William Simmons was clearly making money from the Klan yet never reported it on his income tax filings, Tague said at the hearings. "The time has come when Congress should put out its hand and let the country know that the Constitution is not a scrap of paper and will be upheld at any cost."[92]

But the hearings wound up helping the Klan rather than hindering it. Simmons, a redhead with a "round, good-natured face," was able to charm the lawmakers with his disarming humor and folksy stories. "Nothing seemed to disturb his ever-present smile," wrote a *New York Times* reporter covering the House hearings.[93] Any violent acts attributed to the Klan were committed by outside troublemakers donning masks to avoid being identified, Simmons testified. "This is purely a fraternal and patriotic organization," he insisted. "Our mask and robe, I say before God, are as innocent as the breath of an angel."[94] Simmons kept his composure throughout the hearings, obliging photographers to help them capture good images of him. As the *New York World* stories revealed, the Klan had already recruited congressmen and senators to the Invisible Empire. One Klan-friendly congressman was Atlanta Democrat W. D. Upshaw. To thwart the Congressional probe of the Klan, Upshaw introduced a bill calling for similar investigations into the prominent Catholic fraternal lodge, the Knights of Columbus, and other secret societies.[95] Lacking consensus, the House committee abruptly ended its hearings a week after they began, issuing a report while calling for no enforcement actions.

The hearings and Simmons's performance proved a boon for Klan recruitment. Kleagles collectively reported new enlistments running at five thousand a day.[96] Within four months, two hundred new klaverns formed. Within a year, total membership grew tenfold, from an estimated 100,000 to almost one million.[97]

Powell called the first meeting of the Portland klavern in October, the same month as the Congressional hearings. Standing near the door of the Woodmen of the World Hall adorned in his Klan robe, Powell congratulated newly initiated members while an organist played "You're Going to Leave the Old Home, Jim."[98] Two months after that inaugural klavern meeting, Portland Klansmen learned they no longer needed to conduct vigilante activities outside the law. The city of Portland presented its 1922 budget for approval by the tax supervising commission as required. That panel lopped off $72,000 from the police budget, requiring a cut of about 10 percent. Facing an unexpected loss of twenty-nine to thirty-seven police officers, Mayor Baker announced a stopgap plan on December 22.[99] "Such a reduction at this time when crime is rampant is a serious thing," Baker said. "To make up for the men who will have to be laid off, I am going to organize a committee of one hundred responsible citizens who will be on call for emergencies." Under pressure to fill the gap before the new budget cycle took effect in less than ten days, Baker said he'd turn to the American Legion, a conservative veterans group, as well as other organizations that stand for law and order, and ask them to contribute names to serve.[100] Within days, dozens of Portland Klansmen would become part of the city police department's official vigilante force. Though there was little time for training, the men were given official badges and guns. Gifford, exalted cyclops of the Portland klavern, reportedly had to approve the Klansmen who would join the new vigilante squad, forwarding their names to the police department. "At the start all were Klansmen under Gifford's orders, with possibly one or two exceptions, and always under his dictation," wrote former Klan publicity chief Lem Dever after he defected in 1924. The arrangement made Gifford an "invisible super chief of police."[101]

Whipping Up Portlanders' Prejudices

Three days before Christmas 1921, the biggest show in Portland was a coming-out party for the Oregon Ku Klux Klan, with the Reverend Reuben H. Sawyer as its leading showman. Sawyer had tried his hand as a newspaperman, pastor of Portland's East Side Christian Church, and, most recently, as a pitchman for a group that believed Anglo-Saxons descended from the lost tribes of Israel and thus were among God's "chosen people." Now Reverend Sawyer was a paid lecturer and organizer for the budding Ku Klux Klan, his first big break.[102]

A reported six thousand Portlanders filled the city's new Municipal Auditorium, shelling out fifty cents during the holiday season to attend Sawyer's lecture titled "The Truth about the Invisible Empire of the Knights of the Ku Klux Klan," and to watch the Klan-friendly film, "The Face at your Window."[103] Municipal Auditorium, now called Keller Auditorium, opened in 1917, and remains one of Portland's largest entertainment venues.[104] The Oregon Klan was busy organizing klaverns across the state, but this was its first event open to the public. Many people who'd seen *Birth of a Nation* were curious about, if not outright supportive of, the revived white-supremacist group. Dignitaries in the audience that night included Mayor Baker, who graciously accepted two free tickets mailed by Sawyer. Governor Olcott wrote Sawyer expressing appreciation for a similar ticket offer but gave his regrets.[105]

Sawyer, dressed in Klan regalia, greeted the audience on behalf of the Klan's 200,000 members and Imperial Wizard Simmons. Deflecting criticism of the KKK that surfaced during Congressional hearings that fall, Sawyer blamed the "prejudiced press" and said the Klan stood for a "purified Americanism where law-abiding Americans will be respected."[106] Blacks had nothing to fear from the Klan, Sawyer claimed, as many of their brethren understood from living in Southern homes for many years—an apparent reference to house servants. However, he warned, the Klan will oppose those who are "sowing the seeds of discontent and racial hatred among the Negroes of this country by preaching and teaching social equality." Then he amplified that by explaining the Klan's core belief in white supremacy: "We hold it is obligatory upon the Negro race, and upon all the other colored races in America, to recognize that they are living in the land of the white race, and by courtesy of the white race, and that the white race cannot be expected to surrender to any other race, either in whole or in part, the control of its vital and fundamental governmental affairs."[107]

Klansmen didn't see Jewish people as their enemies, Sawyer claimed, except those who rejected the teachings of Jesus. In other words, Jews had to convert to Christianity. And the Klan wouldn't fight the Catholic Church, he added, unless the church injected itself into state affairs. Then he bashed Catholic groups such as the Knights of Columbus, which, he charged, sought to control politics, close public schools and Protestant churches, and destroy Masonic and other fraternal organizations.

In addition to being a skilled orator, Sawyer had an entrepreneurial bent. When he was hired as a Klan speaker, he was earning money lecturing, writing, and selling books for the *Watchman of Israel*. The Boston publication was part of the multinational British Israelism movement, which aimed to demonstrate the superiority of Anglo-Saxons based on their blood ties to ancient Hebrew tribes. In a December 19, 1921, resignation letter to his *Watchman* editor, Sawyer said he'd signed a new contract as a regional lecturer for the Klan, starting two days before his big Portland lecture. His new duties would also take him to Washington, Idaho, Montana, and Wyoming, he wrote.[108]

Simmons was making a great living profiting from the privately owned Klan, and Sawyer followed his lead. He published a version of his Portland lecture in a booklet and secured ownership rights via a copyright. Sawyer soon began crisscrossing the state, repeating his Portland lecture in Eugene, Ashland, La Grande, Pendleton, Tillamook, and elsewhere. Through his lectures and correspondence, Sawyer promoted sales of his booklet for fifty cents apiece—thirty cents if purchased in blocks of fifty or more.[109] As a newly named king kleagle, Sawyer also stood to earn a share of the initiation fees paid by new members he recruited, on top of his lecture fees. By March 1922, Sawyer boasted of finally being able to buy a "little gray home" with a yard full of roses in Northeast Portland's Rose City Park neighborhood, where he lived with his wife and two daughters.[110]

In April of 1922, Simmons wrote Sawyer, praising the booklet and asking him to speak at a national Klan anniversary celebration the following month. Sawyer wrote back saying he could do the lecture if paid $1,000 plus expenses, or more than $18,000 in mid-2020s spending power. That speaking gig never panned out.[111] Sawyer soon latched onto a new idea to expand the Klan's reach and earn him more money: bringing women into the Klan fold.

3
Bridgehead of Bigotry in Portland

I have seen men of Portland, Oregon who are, individually, as fine a type of man as the country affords, duped, bamboozled and made party to political villainies that would make a ward heeler blush—for the glory and power of a few men who have gained control of their patriotic emotions and have warped and distorted them to unpatriotic ends.

—Ben Titus, former Portland Klansman[1]

"There is only one way... to convert a Catholic priest ... kill the son of a gun."

—Reverend James R. Johnson, exalted cyclops of Portland Klan[2]

1922: Portlanders Flock to Klan

Kleagles found receptive audiences for the Klan message from Astoria to Roseburg to La Grande. In Tillamook and other smaller communities, the Klan enlisted a greater share of the population than in Portland. But the Rose City was Oregon's dominant population center, and the sheer number of recruits there dwarfed other klaverns. From his perch as Portland exalted cyclops, Fred Gifford dominated the state Klan.

Early 1922: Portland's Luther I. Powell Klan No. 1 becomes Oregon's first nationally chartered klavern.

May 9–10: Klan attracts five thousand people a night to two Portland lectures; thousands more are turned away due to lack of space.

June: Oregon Klan leaders form Royal Riders of the Red Robe, an auxiliary for white male Protestant immigrants.

July: Lem Dever establishes *Western American* as Oregon Klan newspaper.

July 1: Four Portland Klan leaders incorporate Ladies of the Invisible Empire, a women's arm of the Klan.

October: Fred Gifford, exalted cyclops of the Portland klavern, is named grand dragon of Oregon Klan.

November 2–6: Ben Titus exposé published by *Portland Telegram*.

November 28: Hiram Evans supplants William Simmons as national KKK imperial wizard.

Cannady's Humiliation

Beatrice Hulon Morrow dreamed of becoming an opera singer while growing up in the small Black community of Littig, Texas, and managed to study voice for two summers in Chicago.[3] So it was a fitting honor when she was invited to sing two solos at Northwestern College of Law's May 24, 1922, graduation ceremony at the Multnomah Hotel Ballroom.[4] Morrow had moved to Portland ten years earlier, at age twenty-three, to marry Edward Daniel Cannady,[5] and was now Oregon's leading civil rights activist and manager of a Black weekly newspaper. Cannady was doubly honored that day because she was one of twenty-two law-school students slated to receive their diplomas—making her the first Black woman in Oregon to graduate law school. Her brother Almus Morrow also was among the twenty-two graduates.[6]

The Honorable Robert Tucker delivered the commencement address to the cohort of future Portland attorneys, then handed the microphone to Cannady. Accompanied by pianist Olga Rull, Cannady rose to sing "By the Waters of Minnetonka," a 1917 love song by Thurlow Lieurance and James Mulloy Cavanass, and "To You," a 1919 piece by J. C. Rodenbeck.[7] After finishing her solos, Cannady was shocked and humiliated when law school dean J. Hunt Hendrickson unceremoniously asked all the Blacks in attendance—Cannady, her brother, their families and guests—to leave the elegant hotel. Hendrickson, who'd be elected a county judge four years later, proceeded to hand out diplomas to the remaining graduates, before a closing benediction by the Reverend William Eliot.[8]

Though Cannady was Oregon's best-known Black citizen, the state had just experienced a tumultuous primary election. Five days earlier, the newly emboldened Ku Klux Klan won numerous county and

Hundreds of Oregon Klansmen fill auditorium, possibly in Portland, in the early 1920s. (Oregon Historical Society)

legislative races and nearly defeated a sitting governor, becoming the dominant political force in Oregon.

Attracting Mainstream Folks

Oregon Klan recruitment continued at a feverish pace long after the publicity bump from the *New York World* series and Congressional hearings, and Portland was the epicenter.

Fraternal lodge members and police officers weren't the only people flocking to join. Kleagles successfully recruited businessmen, politicians, professionals, firefighters, and streetcar conductors. They devoted special attention to Protestant clergy, offering them free membership in the Klan. That was national KKK policy, helping the Invisible Empire enlist an estimated 40,000 Protestant ministers across the country.[9] "The backbone of the Klan movement is not the fanatics, the bigots or other elements of the 'lunatic fringe,'" concluded C. Easton Rothwell, the budding Reed College scholar, after interviewing several original Portland Klansmen. Many people erred, he said, by assuming the second version of the Klan attracted the same type of followers as the openly terrorist Ku Klux Klan of the Reconstruction Era.[10]

That doesn't mean the second Klan wasn't racist in its attitudes toward Blacks, Chinese, and Japanese residents, or that Klansmen didn't loathe Catholics, Jews, and other immigrants. "They were bigoted, but this was the basic viewpoint of most white Protestants," said Oregon Klan historian David Horowitz.[11] "Nationwide, it was more of an anti-immigration movement and also a purity crusade." The Klan spoke out against political corruption and supported Prohibition, which had been championed by Protestant ministers and women to stem the degrading effects of alcohol abuse on the family. That played well in a Western city such as Portland, Horowitz said.

Woodrow Wilson, US president from 1913 to 1921, was considered a political progressive but also was openly racist. The first Southerner elected president since the Civil War, Wilson imposed racial segregation in the US military and hosted a White House screening of *Birth of a Nation* so all his staff could view it. Many fraternal lodges at the time barred Blacks and Jews from joining, and some Klan recruits saw the Invisible Empire as just another lodge. In January 1922, the Portland Klan moved its meetings from one fraternal lodge building to another, from Woodmen of the World Hall to the Pythian Temple.

Around that time, the klavern became Oregon's first to earn a prized charter from the Atlanta Klan headquarters, officially becoming the Luther I. Powell Klan No. 1.[12] So many people were now rushing to join the Portland klavern that it held new-member initiations at the spacious Municipal Auditorium, which seated 5,500 on its ground floor. At a February 27, 1922 ceremony at the city-owned hall, the *Oregonian* reported more than eleven hundred Klansmen were inducted. "There were doctors, lawyers, businessmen of all kinds, railroad men, clerks and citizens from other professions and employments."[13] Two months later, more than twelve hundred were inducted, in "one of the largest initiatory ceremonies of its kind ever held in the United States."[14]

By spring 1922, Portland exalted cyclops Fred Gifford claimed his chapter had grown to nine thousand men, the lion's share of the statewide Klan's fourteen thousand members.[15] The Klan was highly visible, often erecting fiery crosses atop Mount Tabor and Mount Scott on Portland's east side that could be seen for miles. Klansmen staged public car rallies called klavelkades, where men in full regalia would drive around Portland, often passing by Catholic schools in a not-so-subtle form of harassment.[16]

Two weeks before the May 1922 primary election, some one hundred fifty Klansmen dressed in full regalia fanned out to Portland Protestant churches, passing out flyers at the doors and inviting churchgoers to two more lectures by Reverend Reuben Sawyer at Municipal Auditorium. Representatives of sixteen churches called the police to complain about the unwanted intruders, though no arrests were made.[17]

At the first lecture on May 9, thousands of people were turned away for lack of seats, noted Cicero Hogan, an army captain in the Great War who testified the next day before the City Council. Hogan publicly appealed to Mayor George Baker to deny Klan use of the city-owned facility for a second Sawyer lecture that evening. Several veterans, including Catholics, Jews, and immigrants, had remarked about verbal abuse they'd received from Klansmen, Hogan said, and he feared violence might break out. "Let me repeat, these men are all ex-servicemen and have proved they are 100 percent loyal Americans. Could they give greater proof of their loyalty to this country? And yet because of their creed, religion, color, ancestors or personal beliefs, they are reputed not to be 100 percent."[18]

Baker, who had enrolled dozens of Klansmen as armed police vigilantes five months earlier, responded that people attending Klan lectures believed in law and order. Besides, it wasn't practical to deny them use of the city building. "What would have been the effect had I called out the police and attempted to suppress that meeting?" Baker asked Hogan. "You have said there are 8,000 to 10,000 members here in Portland. Do you think you can suppress that kind of organization with a handful of policemen? To attempt such suppression would only stir up riots worse than anything this town has ever known before."

However, based on the esteemed veteran's warning, Baker and Police Chief Jenkins ordered a "riot squad" to provide public safety for Sawyer's second lecture that night, made up of eighty-three city policemen and fourteen county sheriff deputies.[19] The Klan packed the auditorium again that night, and a crowd of those turned away formed outside. "Several thousand persons unable to get seats in the building surged about the outside and up and down Third Street during the early part of the lecture," the *Oregon Daily Journal* reported the next day. "Blue-coated policemen were stationed at every entrance to the building and around the wall of the interior."

Many of those cops likely were Klansmen. In addition to the unpaid vigilantes, an estimated 60 percent of the Portland police force reportedly joined the Klan at one time or another.[20] Sawyer, in a letter the next month to two British associates, bragged that thousands of people were turned away from his two speeches. Fortunately, he added, "There are hundreds of police officers who are members of our great order."[21]

Political Opportunist

Mayor Baker, like so many men of his era, was a joiner. "He joined every club and organization he could," wrote his friend, *Oregonian* reporter Frank Sterrett. "He used to say, 'If you want to get elected to any public office, join 'em all, those votes are all in the bag.'"[22] One lodge Baker

Portland Mayor George Baker openly allied with the Klan after it began organizing in his city. (Oregon Historical Society)

joined was the Shriners, which, like other Masonic groups of that period, tended to be anti-Catholic. At the June 1920 Shriners convention, the Portland mayor introduced a resolution calling for mandatory public schooling, which would shut down Catholic and other private schools.[23] When the Invisible Empire expanded into Oregon the following year, it was perhaps inevitable that a politician like Baker would cozy up to the anti-Catholic white supremacist group. Former Klan propagandist Lem Dever would later write that Baker joined the Klan, though Baker denied that and it was never corroborated. "My sense is he was just an opportunist," Horowitz said.[24]

Born in The Dalles, Baker quit school at age nine to support his family, then turned to shining shoes and hawking newspapers. After moving to Portland, Baker wound up owning and managing downtown theaters.[25] He took office as Portland mayor in 1917, the same year the United States entered the Great War and Bolsheviks prevailed in the Russian Revolution. Baker would host breakfasts at Municipal Auditorium for young enlistees bound for overseas military duty.[26]

The war intensified patriotic feelings and fears of foreigners. Baker and other Portlanders grew increasingly nervous about the loyalties of ethnic Germans in the city, as well as other Catholic and Jewish immigrants. Thousands of people migrated to the city during wartime to work in ten shipyards now humming around the clock to churn out cargo ships for the war effort, and some of those workers became regular patrons of the city's illegal alcohol joints. The great flu pandemic of 1918–1920 added to the social anxiety. As a result of the pandemic, Portland's Standard Insurance Co. reported its highest losses from deaths in the company's history.[27]

Baker ordered attacks against the militant Industrial Workers of the World, known as the Wobblies, shortly after Seattle unions shut down that city's waterfront in the February 1919 general strike. Portland police raided the IWW hall in Portland, smashing furniture and carting off literature and union records.[28] On the November 11 anniversary of the armistice ending the Great War, American Legion members marching eighty miles north of Portland in Centralia, Washington, attacked the IWW hall. In the ensuing melee known as the Centralia Massacre, four veterans were killed and IWW member Wesley Everest was lynched. Klansmen that Baker had enlisted as Portland police vigilantes would later take credit for rounding up four boxcar loads of Wobblies and riding them out of town on the rails.[29]

Baker's refusal to bar the Klan from using Municipal Auditorium, as requested by Cicero Hogan in May 1922, telegraphed his political sympathies. The year before, he'd denied access to the same building for a speech by muckraking journalist Lincoln Steffens, who had earned fame exposing urban corruption and had just returned from Russia with glowing reports about the revolution.[30] If not an outright Klan member, Baker aligned politically with the group. *Oregonian* reporter Stewart Holbrook recalled watching a Klan parade in the early 1920s when ten thousand people marched west across the Morrison Bridge into downtown Portland, with Baker and other dignitaries waving to onlookers from cars.[31] Baker later would seek political support from the Klan for his 1924 US Senate bid.

Riding the Fundamentalist Wave

As it mushroomed in size, the Klan worked hand-in-glove with Protestant ministers, paying orators like Sawyer twenty-five dollars a pop to deliver introductory lectures about the Klan around Oregon.[32] Of twenty-nine regular Klan lecturers deployed in all the states, two-thirds were Protestant ministers.[33] One common Klan tactic in Oregon and other states was bestowing money on ministers, which bolstered the Klan's image and helped build strategic relationships. On April 22, 1922, the Portland Klan sent an unsolicited letter, apparently from Sawyer, to fellow Reverend James R. Johnson, pastor of Sellwood Christian Church, enclosing a sum of money for his "personal needs."[34] The next January, Reverend Johnson replaced Gifford as exalted cyclops of the Portland chapter after Gifford was elevated to Oregon grand dragon.[35]

On May 7, 1922, when Klansman were passing out flyers outside churches promoting Sawyer's upcoming lectures, some went inside the places of worship in full regalia. In one visit, the audience cheered as three robed Klansmen gave $50 to evangelist John Wood Anderson.[36] In other churches, the Klan wasn't so welcome. A Protestant man complained the unannounced Klan visits led to conflicts at many congregations.[37]

A Klan ceremony, probably in Portland, illustrates the secret order's cultivation of close ties to Protestant clergy. (Oregon Historical Society)

The Klan's visceral disdain for Catholics, combined with its vocal support of Prohibition and other morals crusades, gave it broad appeal to Protestants of that era. Reverend Johnson, who was paid $400 a month to run the Portland Klan, was known for his inflammatory remarks about Catholics. "There is only one way in God's almighty world to convert a Catholic priest...kill the son of a gun," Johnson told Oak Grove Community Church congregants, in the Milwaukie area.[38]

The nation was undergoing a religious revival, as a growing number of Protestant ministers preached returning to what they termed "fundamental" beliefs in the Bible. "The Klan overlapped with, and helped feed, the larger upsurge of fundamentalism in the 1920s," wrote historian Nancy McLean. "Indeed, the very term fundamentalist only came into use in 1920."[39] Yet mainstream and evangelical congregations provided the Klan's core base of support among Protestants.[40] In Oregon, the evangelical denomination known simply as the Christian Church was particularly attracted to the Klan. The La Grande chapter secretary referred to it as the "Klan church" because so many Klansmen were members. There also were clusters of La Grande Klansmen identifying as Methodists, Episcopalians, Presbyterians, and Baptists.[41]

Founded by a former minister, the second Klan made rich use of Christian symbols, from the burning cross that became its insignia to the symbolic drop of Jesus's blood on Klan robes. Klan meetings typically began with Christian prayers, and Protestant ministers paid to deliver lectures served as the Klan's public face. Klansmen were urged to attend church and follow the apostle Paul's guidelines for living, in Romans 12 of the *New Testament*.[42] The Klan was in effect a "religious order," which was a big part of its appeal, argues Kelly Baker, a religion professor and author of *Gospel According to the Klan: The KKK's Appeal to Protestant America, 1915–1930*. "The Klan . . . was not just an order to defend America but also a campaign to protect and celebrate Protestantism."[43]

In contrast, many liberal Protestants, including leading writers and those on national governing bodies, condemned the Klan for distorting the teachings of Jesus and Christianity.[44] Other Klan critics, including former Kleagle Henry Fry, dismissed the Invisible Empire as a money-grubbing enterprise operating under a cloak of Christianity.[45]

Both perspectives had a ring of truth. While the Klan undoubtedly attracted many true Christian believers, its leaders cynically manipulated public opinion by, for example, sending robed Klansmen to deliver donations of money at church services.

The Oregon Klan newspaper, *Western American*, frequently highlighted the Klan's socially conservative and moral stances that were consistent with Protestant clergy's views. The newspaper, owned and edited by Lem Dever, criticized state prison officials for allowing penitentiary inmates in Salem to play baseball on Sunday while other prisoners attended church.[46] Dever, who lived in Astoria, criticized the Clatsop County court for being a "divorce mill" because it was so lenient in granting divorces and welcoming divorce petitions from Portlanders.[47] Other articles promoted censorship of motion pictures, vacation Bible schools for children, and Protestant orphanages proposed in Portland and Corvallis. In a sign that Klan racism apparently trumped its support for evangelical Christianity, though, *Western American* directed Klansmen and their wives to boycott Cannady's upcoming talk at a Vacation Bible School in the Arleta neighborhood of Southeast Portland.[48]

Professional Propagandist

As a child growing up in Pulaski, Tennessee, Dever frequently stole Ku Klux Klan costumes from his father's old war chest, which he and his buddies then wore in what he described as "nighttime excursions" to scare people.[49] Dever was born nine years after the original KKK was founded in his hometown, shortly after it had disbanded and Klansmen put away their sheets and other regalia.

Dever deployed his talent for writing during the Great War, serving with the American Committee on Public Information in Vladivostok, a Pacific Ocean port in far southeastern Russia.[50] The committee, led by George Creel, produced wartime propaganda to win public support for the US war effort.[51]

Dever's experience producing that propaganda proved useful later in building the Oregon Klan. Dever moved to Oregon after the war to take a job as an Astoria newspaper editor. In that capacity, he established contact with Klan organizers in Portland in 1921. He joined the Klan in early 1922, later saying he was attracted by the lure of good fellowship and the chance to gain influence in politics and civic reform efforts.[52] Around that time, Dever sought the names and addresses of 1,000 Klan members to promote a newspaper he was planning.[53] He also led the robust Astoria Klan's political work, including a successful 1922 campaign to recall the Clatsop County sheriff.[54] Dever later confessed to engaging in dirty tricks in Astoria campaigns, such as placing a stink bomb that cleared the hall during a speech by a Klan opponent.[55]

In the summer of 1922, Dever unveiled his newspaper, the *Western American,* to serve as the Oregon Klan's official propaganda organ. Dever initially produced the paper in Astoria, filling its pages with articles about Clatsop County politics and supporting it with ads from Astoria merchants.[56] But soon he reached an agreement with Gifford and moved the operation to Portland. Dever claimed he never bought a Klan mask or robe and was never on the Klan's payroll.[57] Yet his role as owner, publisher, and editor of *Western American* made him the mouthpiece of the Oregon KKK and one of its best-known leaders.

Dever ran pieces promoting Klan ventures in electoral politics, its ballot initiative to ban Catholic schools, and its tirades against Catholics, Blacks, Jews, Chinese, Japanese, and other immigrants. "The Roman Catholic Church is alien in its practices, heretical in its teachings, tyrannical and despotic in its practices..." Dever wrote in an editorial.[58] He promoted Portland Klan leaders' creation of a group for women, the Ladies of the Invisible Empire, and a similar one for immigrants, The Royal Riders of the Red Robe. Dever lauded Gifford's efforts to create a national Klan auxiliary for young boys, claiming credit for the idea.[59]

As the Klan opened events to the public to gain more support, Dever ran news briefs promoting public initiations of new members, barbecues, and marches. Dever published regular lists of companies for Klansmen to boycott, such as the *Portland Telegram*[60] and Meier & Frank, the Jewish-owned Portland department store headed by Julius Meier.[61] It was sometimes hard to distinguish official Klan positions from Dever's personal views, such as when his paper urged the recall of Oregon Governor Walter Pierce, or when it praised Clatsop County Sheriff Harley Slusher.[62] He frequently dismissed Klan controversies as meaningless lies published by the mainstream media. When Gifford faced a mutiny by Klan chapters outside Portland, Dever sang his praises. Gifford was the "bravest, whitest and best man in the state," Dever assured readers. "Naturally, since his constructive work began with the Klan, he became the target of wicked and cowardly slanderers, but their efforts have been futile."[63]

Coup in Atlanta

Money flowed freely into Klan leaders' pockets after Simmons placed recruitment and management into the hands of marketing whizzes Clarke and Tyler in June 1920. In the first sixteen months of the new commission scheme, Simmons earned $170,000 in commissions and Tyler and Clarke netted $212,000 after covering expenses.[64] They earned $4.50 in profits from each $6.50 robe sale after Klansmen were ordered to buy their regalia from the Klan-owned Gates City Manufacturing Co. in Atlanta.[65] Clarke's real estate company earned commissions for handling the purchase of an Atlanta house for Simmons and a Klan headquarters, dubbed Imperial Palace.[66]

In the spring of 1922, Clarke and Tyler brought in blue-eyed dentist Hiram W. Evans, the Klan's star organizer from Dallas, to help with membership recruitment in Atlanta.[67] By this time, Simmons had a diminished role in Klan operations. He was a drunkard and in ill health,

Hiram Evans conspired with other Klan leaders in the fall of 1922 to oust Klan founder William Simmons from power. Evans, shown marching in a 1926 Washington, DC, parade, replaced Simmons as imperial wizard. (Library of Congress)

and his wife feared he was on the verge of a nervous breakdown. Simmons was persuaded to take a six-month leave of absence, starting in May.[68] While Simmons was away on leave, the others schemed to wrest control of the Klan.

Clarke, who was business-minded and more concerned about making money, took over as interim imperial wizard. Evans, who was keen on turning the Klan into a political force, conspired to supplant Simmons. His fellow conspirators included Indiana Klan leader David (D. C.) Stephenson, Clarke aide Fred Savage, and regional Klan leaders.[69]

The plotters rousted Simmons from bed at 4 a.m. the night before leadership elections at the Klan's first national klonvocation (convention) during Thanksgiving week of 1922. They told him violence might break out on the convention floor, but it could be averted if he agreed to support Evans as the new imperial wizard, while Simmons maintained his other position as emperor. "I saw visions of a bloody shambles among the one thousand delegates the next day," Simmons explained later.[70] Through trickery and deception, the plotters persuaded Simmons to accept a largely ceremonial role for himself as Klan emperor for life.

Unbeknownst to Simmons, a revised Klan Constitution to be voted on the next day would strip the emperor of much of his power. "I didn't know at first that my interests had been harmed in any way," Simmons said later.[71] Evans, the primary coup instigator, became the new imperial wizard, while co-conspirator Stephenson gained control of an empire of Midwestern states.[72]

In the leadership struggle, Oregon Grand Dragon Gifford threw his support to Evans.

Upwardly Mobile Klansman

Gifford was "practically penniless" when he became exalted cyclops of the Portland Klan in August 1921, but within six months he bought a house in Portland's affluent Irvington neighborhood, where he lived with his wife and three daughters.[73] By October 1922, when he became Oregon grand dragon, Gifford was believed to have amassed a personal fortune worth roughly three-quarters of a million dollars in mid-2020s currency.[74] Gifford also bought a summer home along the Washougal River in Washington, thirty miles from Portland.[75]

Gifford's family had arrived in Portland from Minnesota in 1888, when he was ten. He attended Couch School in Northwest Portland, and then the Lutheran Academy, before launching a career as a telegraph operator on the Southern Pacific railroad line. Gifford was put in charge of line and repair gangs and wrecking crews between Portland and Dunsmuir, California. He then switched to the telephone company, doing construction and maintenance. Gifford demonstrated his appetite for money and power in 1919, when he abandoned a labor union he had once led to side with management during a bitter telephone workers strike. (See Gifford in League with Big Utilities, Chapter 5, p. 112.) He moved to Northwestern Electric Co., where he was a middle manager upon joining the Klan.

Of iron-gray hair and average build,[76] Gifford attended an Episcopalian church and joined the Scottish Rite Masons,[77] whose members were closely aligned with the Klan. Fellow Scottish Rite lodge member Luther Powell made Gifford exalted cyclops of the fledgling Portland chapter during the Klan's initial recruitment phase. That freed Powell, the king kleagle for Oregon, to earn money organizing new chapters.

Frederick Gifford was appointed exalted cyclops of the Portland klavern in the summer of 1921 by Oregon Klan King Kleagle Luther Powell. Gifford, shown near his prized automobile, leveraged that post to dominate the Oregon Klan. (Courtesy of family member related by marriage)

In December 1921, local Klansmen formally elected Gifford to the exalted cyclops position.[78] According to Rothwell, the Reed College scholar, Gifford maneuvered to avoid the annual re-election required for Klan officers.[79] Instead, he had local bylaws drafted to grant himself the exalted cyclops position for five years.[80] It was an ominous sign of Gifford's ruthlessness and willingness to skirt the rules to get ahead.

Bring on the Silver Showers

The lights were dim as Ben Titus stepped inside Portland's Municipal Auditorium the night of February 28, 1922. Titus gazed out at the audience of about three thousand men and recognized some of Portland's most prominent citizens. He and several hundred of them had paid their ten-dollar initiation fee and eagerly awaited the ceremony inducting them into the Luther I. Powell chapter of the Ku Klux Klan. "The solemn and beautiful language of the ritual form a memory that I shall always cherish as one of the most inspiring moments of my life," Titus wrote later, in an anonymous four-part series published by the *Portland Telegram* on the eve of the November 1922 election.[81]

After the ritual, up stepped a man of medium build in full Klan regalia, his hood thrown back to reveal his face and curly hair. Fred

Gifford, the exalted cyclops of the Portland Klan, paced back and forth as he addressed the crowd. "His voice was powerful and resonant, with a quality that tingled on the emotions of men already stirred to a high pitch of fervor by the impressive ceremonials that had gone before," Titus recalled.[82] Gifford spoke of Klan principles and his plans for the chapter, demanding members' unquestioning obedience. If they failed to carry out his orders, Klansmen risked being "taken out some dark night and beat over a stump," Gifford told the audience, adding an obscenity. "I was startled to realize that scores of Klansmen and initiates, carried away by the speaker's vigor, were roaring with pleasure," Titus wrote.

Sessions led by Gifford rarely featured rituals at the beginning and close of meetings that were required by the national Klan, and Titus was convinced Gifford never even learned those rituals. Minutes never were read from prior meetings, but the exalted cyclops made sure there was a recitation of all the new members the chapter recruited. Sometimes Gifford offered new recruits a drink from a flask, though the Klan supposedly was a devout Prohibition backer.[83] Gifford often worked up the crowd's fervor via "raw meat in the form of religious and racial agitation." He'd rant about public officials who hired too many "foreigners" on their staffs, and how Klansmen needed to register their disapproval.

As the spring 1922 primary approached, Gifford devoted much time in the chapter meetings to his strategies and progress in electing friendly politicians. Gifford named committees of Klansmen to vet candidates, yet Titus never heard of them reporting their findings. To gain more political influence, Gifford commanded Klansmen to join or infiltrate fraternal lodges that had become increasingly influential in local and state politics, especially Orange and Masonic groups that were part of the Federation of Patriotic Societies.[84]

One ritual that *was* commonplace at meetings during Titus's tenure as a Klansman was known as the "silver shower." A Gifford henchman would step up and direct members to "decorate the mahogany" by tossing coins onto the stage near Gifford. Titus observed hundreds of dollars showered on Gifford, though he wasn't clear if the proceeds went for chapter use or into Gifford's pockets.

The Klan's Anti-Semitism

For someone who proudly claimed to descend from an ancient tribe of Israel, Reverend Sawyer seemed filled with hatred toward their modern-day Jewish descendants. "Their influence as a whole is pernicious and antagonistic to the ideals of white Christian Americans, and their power is growing to an extent that threatens control of the American government," Sawyer declared in a typical Klan lecture. "In some parts of America, the Kikes are so thick that a white man can hardly find room to walk on the sidewalk."[85] Gifford reinforced the hate group's anti-Semitic stance when in December 1921 he lobbied the legislature to deny Portland businessman Julius Meier's appointment to a panel working to secure a 1925 world trade exposition in Portland. "So far as Mr. Meier was concerned, the agitation against him was on the ground of race and not on the ground of alleged unfitness for the honor," wrote *Oregon Voter*, a respected journal covering state politics.[86]

Portland's Jewish community was treated better than in many other parts of the country. In contrast to other cities around the country in that era, Portland's newspaper articles about Jewish subjects typically didn't see a need to mention their faith, even in obituaries.[87] But anti-Semitism was on the rise. Many analysts concluded that the well-publicized lynching of Jewish businessman Leo Frank in 1915 helped precipitate the second Klan's revival a few months later. In the early part of the century, amid a wave of violent attacks known as pogroms against Russian and Polish Jews, a document emerged called the Protocols of the Elders of Zion. It was a fabricated text outlining supposed Jewish plans for world domination. Detroit automobile magnate Henry Ford highlighted the bogus document in a series of rants in his newspaper, the *Dearborn Independent*. Starting in 1920 and running for many months, the *Independent* published a regular feature called "The International Jew: The World's Problem." Ford's newspaper widely circulated conspiracy theories blaming Jews for the Great War and a host of other social and economic maladies.[88]

The Klan eagerly took up the anti-Semitic cudgel. Eastern European Jews were maligned for retaining their native Yiddish language and failing to be properly Americanized as Protestant immigrants had. Imperial Wizard Evans bashed them as "Judaized Mongols" who had little hope of being assimilated into American society.[89] Jews were reviled for being exploitative capitalists dominating banks and world finance, as well as for leading the main movement challenging capitalism: communism. "Jews are either Bolshevists, undermining our government, or are shylocks in finance or commerce who gain control and command of Christians as borrowers or employees," thundered Sawyer in a Klan lecture.[90] When someone hearing such remarks asked Sawyer to clarify his views on Jews, he responded that Anglo-Saxons like himself were "direct descendants" of the tribes of the northern kingdom of Israel. "So how can anyone accuse me of being a Jew hater?" he wrote.[91]

Though Portland's Jewish population was relatively small, it was better-placed and more powerful than the city's Black, Chinese, or Japanese minorities. There wasn't a large Jewish working class in Portland toiling away in sweatshops as in other big cities.[92] Several Jews were considered leading pioneers and builders of the city.[93] Former Portland Mayor Joseph Simon was elected to the US Senate in 1898, becoming one of the most powerful politicians in Oregon. "That made Jews a very different type of target," observed Darrell Millner, the emeritus Black history professor for Portland State University.[94]

Gifford appeared to soft-pedal the Klan's hatred for Jews in a March 1922 interview with *Oregon Voter*. Unlike Catholics, who, the Klan argued, took their marching orders from church leaders in Rome, "the Jews have no such foreign allegiance, and we are not anti-Jew as so often reported."[95] But there was no let-up in vitriol from Sawyer or the *Western American*. A cartoon run by the Klan newspaper featured a bald man with an oversized nose, labeled a "Kike lawyer."[96] The newspaper called for Klansmen to pack a June 7, 1923, meeting of the Motion Picture League to protest "filthy" films that featured "race equality" and sex. "It is the Jews who are doing the dirty work in the movies," the article stated, topped with a sub-headline castigating "evil Sheeny producers."[97]

Boycotts were a common Klan tactic deployed to punish Jewish and Catholic merchants or others deemed as foes. *Western American* ran reminders to boycott Meier and Frank for months. La Grande Klansmen were ordered not to patronize a grocery store in their town because "they are 100 percent Jews."[98]

The Klan also urged members to patronize businesses owned by fellow Klansmen. In Portland, that took the form of the "100% American Directory," a thirty-page booklet listing hundreds of Klan-friendly retailers and service providers in the city.[99] Compiled by S. C. Berry, who dubbed himself "100% Berry," the booklet guided Klansmen and Klanswomen where to spend their money. Readers could find a like-minded attorney, doctor, dentist, or insurance agent, or places to buy cigars, groceries, jewelry, office supplies, and car tires. They could find Klan-supportive ways to shine their shoes, eat out, take a taxi, open a savings account at Lumbermans Bank, go to the movies, or buy oil stocks. The booklet even listed "the only Spanish-American War veteran undertaker in Portland" and the city water bureau. Someone strolling along Southeast Foster Road and Sixty-Seventh Avenue could find a bonanza of Klan-friendly businesses within a two-block radius: Phoenix Pharmacy, Pfund's butcher shop, Black Cat Variety Store, Fred G. Gilstrap's barber shop, Hansen Sheet Metal Works, Sixty-Seventh Street Garage, and Francis Feed Co.

Getting listed in the "100% American Directory" wasn't always beneficial, as it could give the Klan's adversaries reason to shop elsewhere. Jews, Catholics, and foreigners reportedly shied away from doing business at the St. Nicholas Café, which an arsonist later set aflame. The owners blamed the fire on their listing in the Klan directory.[100]

Capitalizing on Women

As the 1920s dawned, state and national Klan leaders took notice of the possibilities afforded by the upsurge in women's social and political roles outside the home and church. Simmons, after contracting out day-to-day operations of the Klan in 1920 to Clarke and Tyler, soon asked Tyler to oversee creation of a women's organization.[101] "We plan that all women who join us shall have equal rights with that of the men," Tyler announced.[102] But that plan was put on hold as Simmons, Clarke, and Tyler became enmeshed in factional and legal battles for control of the Atlanta-based Klan.

In Oregon, entrepreneurial minister Sawyer and his cohorts saw an opening, and seized the opportunity. On July 1, 1922, six months after his first stirring lecture at Municipal Auditorium, Sawyer joined with three other Oregon Klan leaders to establish a new private corporation, the Ladies of the Invisible Empire.[103] Sawyer, then the Klan's chief lecturer for the Northwest, originated and led the effort.[104] He was joined by Powell, then king kleagle for the Northwest; Gifford, then exalted cyclops of the Portland chapter; and Rush H. Davis, a friend of Simmons who had moved to town from Shreveport, Louisiana, also serving as a king kleagle. The four men named themselves the Supreme Grand Council of the Ladies of the Invisible Empire, which quickly became known by its LOTIE acronym.

By opening the Klan universe to half the population that previously was excluded from membership, the foursome saw an opportunity to expand the Klan's influence and collect more money from initiation fees, dues, and robe and literature sales. A news item about the LOTIE founding was headlined "Ku Klux Promoters Turn to More Fertile Fields; Women May Now Donate."[105] Money collected from LOTIE stayed in Oregon, unlike revenues from regular Klansmen that had to be shared with the Imperial Palace in Atlanta. A surviving balance sheet for the month of October 1922 shows payments made to Sawyer, Gifford, Powell, Davis, and Davis's wife. The balance sheet also lists $2,750 paid out in salaries, likely to Sawyer and Davis, but no payments going to the Klan in Oregon or Atlanta. LOTIE was a lucrative start-up business, reporting $9,567 that month in income.[106]

Sawyer's correspondence makes it clear he was running LOTIE, assisted by Davis. Sawyer named himself the new group's supreme grand counselor, and he wrote and copyrighted *The Red Book*, an instruction manual for chapter leaders. It's akin to the *Kloran* that Simmons wrote for the national Klan, detailing officer titles, meeting procedures, rituals, prayers, and dialog to read during initiation ceremonies. One excerpt from the start of the initiation ceremony: "The Senior Advisor proceeds to altar, thence to station of the Junior Counselor, gives two raps with staff. Junior Counselor: Who comes there? Senior Adviser: The Senior Adviser with a message of importance from the West."[107]

Sawyer also secured a copyright for the LOTIE constitution, designed for national use.[108] Though LOTIE was based in Portland, Sawyer and his cohorts quickly expanded the privately owned enterprise into other cities and states. Ten days after LOTIE was incorporated, Gifford boasted that 1,300 members were about to be inducted, and chapters were sprouting in Portland and six other cities.[109] Soon, women wearing the distinctive LOTIE uniforms—white robes with red, white, and blue sashes—were a fixture at Klan parades, initiations, and fund-raising events.

From the start, the Klan had conflicting notions about the role of women. Stemming from its Southern, Reconstruction-era roots, the Klan often spoke of its chivalrous role in supposedly protecting white women's honor. But the Oregon Klan aggressively moved into politics starting in early 1922, and women now were voters. The second Klan's approach to women sometimes had a feminist flavor. Though Tyler wasn't granted a Klan officer's title like the one bestowed on her male partner Clarke, dissident Klansmen testifying before Congress in 1921 depicted her as the real power behind the throne.[110] When a bill was introduced in the Texas Legislature calling for men to pay child support to their abandoned wives, the Klan there endorsed it.[111]

Oregon Klan leaders claimed LOTIE was not just a women's auxiliary of the Klan but a kindred group of like-minded people, run by its women members. "Klanswomen embraced the KKK's racist, anti-Catholic, and anti-Semitic agenda and symbols of American womanhood, but they used these to argue as well for equality for white Protestant women," wrote historian Kathleen Blee.[112] LOTIE members often wound up doing fund-raising events or cooking food for the men at joint events. Nevertheless, hundreds of women eagerly joined LOTIE and shelled out five dollars for the initial membership fee. Sawyer soon realized he could double that to ten dollars. LOTIE chose officers with titles prescribed by Sawyer and followed his rituals. The founding chapter in Portland hosted orientation classes for upwards of five hundred potential recruits for three weeks in a row in August 1922, Sawyer claimed.[113] Several hundred members were regularly attending LOTIE meetings at Portland's Redmen's Hall, led by Maybelle Jette, their energetic mother counselor. When Jette, a thirty-three-year-old grandmother, was being attacked for her supposed pro-Catholic sympathies, an Aurora man who had bought hops from her Champoeg farm disputed that in a letter to Sawyer, saying the single mom was raising her three children as "real Americans." He called Jette a strong-willed woman who was clever, courageous, and capable.[114] Bents went on to marry Jette in 1924.

Sawyer wasted little time expanding the venture, putting an ad in the *Searchlight* to hire Klan organizers in other states to work on commission. While Davis ran operations in Portland, Sawyer hit the road to interview organizers and meet with national Klan leaders in Atlanta. He hoped to get exclusive rights from Klan headquarters to organize a national Klan women's group, having written to Tyler in August 1922 saying he thought she'd be particularly interested in the idea. LOTIE applications were pouring in from as far away as Illinois and Missouri and Southern states, Sawyer wrote, and he hoped to expand LOTIE into Great Britain and perhaps other countries. "I was told that the Imperial Palace would offer no objections to a ladies organization originating in this domain," he wrote Tyler.[115] By which he meant the state of Oregon.

Oregon Klan leaders likely supported Sawyer's expansion plans, as Gifford and Powell stood to share in the revenues LOTIE earned. But national Klan leaders grew concerned that LOTIE and other women's Klan groups were popping up around the country, beyond their control. A power struggle was under way at the Imperial Palace. Evans, now scheming to supplant Simmons as imperial wizard, tried to get Sawyer and Davis to cease organizing LOTIE. "As I have already written to you in a former letter," Sawyer responded to Evans on August 18, 1922, "we have already launched the Ladies of the Invisible Empire, and it is spreading rapidly throughout a dozen or more states." Sawyer stressed that he wanted to continue doing his LOTIE organizing under Klan auspices. He sent a September 1 telegram from Atlanta, notifying Davis back in Portland that his meeting with interim Imperial Wizard Clarke went well, but Evans wanted to combine the various Klan-affiliated women's groups under one umbrella.

In October, Simmons dealt Sawyer another blow. Sawyer and Davis must refrain from using the words "invisible empire" in the name Ladies of the Invisible Empire, Simmons wrote them, as that was "a direct infringement on our name." Simmons also ordered them to stop using the image of a fiery cross with LOTIE material, as that was an official symbol of the KKK through "established usage."[116] Simmons apparently viewed LOTIE as competition for a women's group he was organizing.

As Sawyer's hopes were dashed for a national Klanswoman empire, he grew alienated from the Klan. Sawyer's relationships with Gifford and Powell also deteriorated. At a large LOTIE rally held November 18, 1922, at Portland's Municipal Auditorium, which women paid fifty cents to attend, Sawyer claimed he was no longer connected to the Klan, and that LOTIE was now an independent group.[117]

On November 28, 1922, Evans was formally named the new imperial wizard after outmaneuvering Simmons for the top job in the

Invisible Empire. Gifford, who sided with Evans in that battle, shared the bad news with Sawyer after returning from the klonvocation. The Klan passed a motion commending the various ladies organizations, Gifford wrote, but none would be recognized as official Klan groups. Clarke, the former interim imperial wizard, was assigned to bring all the women's organizations into one new group.[118]

In January 1923, Sawyer and Davis offered to transfer their ownership interests in LOTIE to Clarke for $7,000 apiece plus twenty-five cents for each member they'd recruited. They claimed to have 1,940 LOTIE members in Oregon plus 595 in other states and 540 new applicants.[119] That offer went nowhere. The next month, Sawyer resigned his post as supreme grand counselor and told Davis he was severing his connection to LOTIE.[120] Davis agreed to buy out Sawyer's ownership stake in LOTIE for $1 and pay off the group's $4,783 in debts. If Davis was able to sell LOTIE, he pledged half the proceeds to Sawyer.[121]

Increasingly bitter about the Klan, Sawyer took ill and was confined to his home for several weeks. "I have lost all confidence in the leaders of this organization and believe it is destined to do more harm than good," he wrote his brother. "They have nearly ruined me in their dishonest attempt concerning the ladies organization."[122] In late April 1923, Sawyer notified Reverend Johnson, now exalted cyclops of the Portland chapter, that he was quitting the Klan, and bluntly warned he'd communicate his ill feelings about the Klan to others. Johnson, in a note to fellow Klansmen, expressed fears that Sawyer might share his critique with the *Portland Telegram*. He asked that "a score or more" Klansmen call or visit the sickly Sawyer at his home.[123] By summertime, though, Sawyer had rebounded enough to open a new church in Portland.

4
Klaverns Blanket the State

> *"Nearly every community was infected by Klan propaganda and bigotry, and prejudice that had lain dormant for years or had never existed was exploited by the Klan leaders and propagandists."*
>
> —Eckard Toy[1]

1921–1924: Violence, Intimidation, and Statewide Expansion

As Portland exalted cyclops Fred Gifford built a political base beholden to him in the Rose City, Powell and other kleagles organized more than five dozen klaverns across the state. In short order, the Klan became a dominant political force in Astoria, Eugene, and Tillamook, and a force to be reckoned with in Salem, La Grande, and other communities. The Klan playbook relied on threats, intimidation, and sometimes violence to win converts and fend off critics who might impede its rise to power.

June 1921: Salem Klan holds first meeting.

October 22: Two men in white robes and masks leave note threatening Marion County judge at Salem's Deaconess Hospital.

January 11, 1922: Eugene Klan holds first public event, a Reverend Reuben Sawyer lecture.

March 14: Black shoe shiner Arthur Burr abducted by masked mob in first of three threatened lynchings in Jackson County, dubbed Southern Oregon Outrages.[2]

March 17: Piano salesman Joseph F. Hale abducted and strung up by masked mob in Medford.

April 9: Henry Johnson, a person of color from Jacksonville, kidnapped by masked Medford men and strung up.

May 13: Federal authorities abandon investigation of Southern Oregon Outrages.

May 14: Jackson County Sheriff Charles E. Terrill alerts Governor Ben Olcott that violence is spinning out of control in Medford.

May 15: Medford Mayor Charles Edwin "Pop" Gates admits he joined the Klan.

June 1–2: Perry Ellis, Black man from Oregon City, victimized by lynching party.

July 6: Governor Olcott orders state attorney general to take over investigation of Medford near-lynchings.

July 29: Sheriff Terrill fends off Klan-supported recall campaign.

August 4: Six Medford-area Klansmen arraigned by grand jury for three threatened lynchings in the spring.

November 7: Astoria Klan takes control of city, electing mayor and four city commissioners.

November 21: Two hooded men enter home of Tillamook woman and brand her left breast with hot metal cross.

February 25, 1923: Trial begins in three Medford near-lynching cases.

Spring: Eugene mayor, police chief, and city attorney resign due to conflicts with the Klan.

July: Gifford orders aide to confiscate Salem klavern's funds, records, and regalia.

November 5–9: Tell-all series by anonymous Salem Klansman published by *Capital Journal*.

December: King Kleagle Luther Powell says there are now fifty-eight KKK chapters in Oregon, with seven more provisionally chartered.

May 26, 1924: Thousands of Klansmen stage ten-block parade in Tillamook; mayor presents Klan with ceremonial key to the city.

"Necktie Parties" Rattle Medford

When Black porter and shoe shiner Arthur Burr was released from county jail in Jacksonville on March 14, 1922, after serving time for public intoxication, the jailer told him a car was waiting outside to give him a lift home to Medford.[3] Instead, the car's occupants kidnapped Burr and forced him on a harrowing journey into the Siskiyou Mountains. There, he later testified, a mob of fifteen to twenty robed and masked men put a noose around his neck and strung him up a tree,

Klansmen march down Ashland's East Main Street, possibly during the city's July 4 parade in 1922. (Oregon Historical Society)

demanding to know where he procured the moonshine he'd been drinking that landed him in jail. Though he told them, the men lifted Burr's body so his feet dangled in the air. After bringing him back to the ground, the kidnappers asked if Burr had been annoying white girls in Medford. Burr denied that, and the mob once more yanked him into the air. After being hoisted off the ground three times, the masked men released Burr and told him to leave Medford and never return, firing pistol shots near him as he fled on foot.[4] It was the first of three abductions and threatened lynchings by masked and hooded nightriders in Jackson County in less than a month. The public came to call the crimes the Southern Oregon Outrages; Klan vigilantes called them "necktie parties."

Three nights later, about ten carloads of masked men believed to be Klansmen reportedly gathered on Medford's east side, where an unmasked accomplice lured former piano merchant Joseph F. Hale from his home on a pretext. The mob placed a gun to Hales's chest, forced him into a car, and drove him to an isolated area outside Medford called Table Rock. There they placed a rope around Hales's neck and threatened to hang him unless he agreed to drop a $150 lawsuit against B. M. Bunnell, a Medford man who was a reputed Klansman. Hales pretended to faint, scaring the kidnappers into releasing him. They threatened to kill him if he divulged what had transpired.[5]

Three weeks later, Henry Johnson, a twenty-two-year-old person of color, was driving his truck home to Jacksonville when he was halted by seven masked men in two cars, one of them pointing a revolver.[6] The apparent Klansmen accused Johnson of stealing chickens, which had been reported in Jacksonville. He denied it, and they placed a rope tautly around his neck. The men asked if he had peddled booze and associated with any white women, which he also denied. After firing gunshots near Johnson's feet, the men let him go, telling him to run fast into the nearby forest.[7]

Medford Klansman Edison Marshall soon quit the klavern, saying he and other early recruits had been misled into thinking it was a patriotic order, not one devoted to mob violence and religious bigotry.[8] After its hasty early-1921 founding by Kleagle Powell, Oregon's first Klan chapter had faded from the public limelight. But by mid-1921 the social turmoil it had first exploited—rampant Prohibition violations—degenerated into an "open war" between law enforcement and bootleggers, marked by a series of raids, drunken brawls, and shootings.[9] Sensing opportunity amid the upheaval, the Klan dispatched Kleagles John H. Hoogstraat and H. E. Griffith to rejuvenate the Medford chapter in January 1922.[10] The two kleagles recruited local business leaders, the Medford police chief, a deputy district attorney, and the county jailer to join the Klan.[11] Klan lecturers and the gubernatorial campaign of state Senator Charles Hall, a Republican from Marshfield backed by the Klan, also whipped up support for the Invisible Empire that spring. After the three near-lynchings blamed on Klan vigilantes, Medford residents began packing guns around town, and hardware stores reported they'd exhausted their supplies of revolvers.[12]

Barely a month after the necktie parties, Medford Mayor Charles Edwin "Pop" Gates admitted he too had been initiated into the Klan. "The obligation and oath was one that no Christian man could take exception to," Gates explained in a newspaper letter to the editor. "When all the masks were removed, and I looked around the room into the faces of over 200 men present, men from every walk of life in the community, I could not help but wonder why the packing of so many guns in Medford?"[13]

With the mayor and Medford police in league with the Klan, the city balked at investigating the three abductions and near-hangings. The federal Justice Department stepped in to investigate, but on May 13 it pulled out. United States Attorney General Harry Daugherty telegrammed Governor Olcott, saying the cases were best prosecuted by the state, and he offered to hand off results of the federal investigation to state authorities.[14]

One local law enforcement leader willing to criticize the Klan was Jackson County Sheriff Charles Terrill. Worried that Klan violence was spinning out of control, Terrill wrote of his concerns to Governor Olcott on May 14. "I fear that some innocent person or persons are going to be killed if it is not stopped," he wrote.[15] The Klan accused Terrill of going easy on bootleggers. It teamed with Ashland and Medford ministers plus Woman's Christian Temperance Union volunteers to gather signatures and force a voter recall of the sheriff.[16] The two kleagles and other Klansmen ran the campaign, and the man they put up to become sheriff in the event Terrill was recalled was reputed Klansman D. M. Lowe.[17] Terrill managed to stave off recall in a July 29 special election by a slim margin of about three hundred votes.[18]

Salem a Thorn in Gifford's Side

While Kleagle Bragg Callaway was stirring up publicity in Portland, an unpaid Klansman was quietly organizing a chapter in Oregon's second-largest city. The state capital became one of the first Oregon cities the Klan penetrated, yet one of the last to win official blessing from Klan headquarters in Atlanta. The reason: Salem Klansmen were more independent-minded than their comrades elsewhere in Oregon, which didn't sit well with Gifford, now grand dragon at the helm of the Oregon Klan.

"Unlike any other Klan in the state, the Salem Klan was not founded by an imported professional organizer, and was organized without the inspiration of artificially inflamed religious and racial prejudices," wrote an unidentified Salem Klansman in a revealing five-part series in the *Capital Journal* in November 1923.[19] The chapter was organized not by a kleagle, the anonymous Klansman wrote, but by a Salem city employee who had single-handedly recruited twenty-eight members, including several prominent businessmen and professionals. The founders conceived the chapter as akin to a traditional fraternal lodge and never cottoned to Gifford's dictatorial leadership style, he said. That appears to explain why the chapter had to wait more than two years for its official charter, despite enrolling several hundred members.

Salem residents got their first inkling the white supremacist group was active in town in late-July 1921, when the *Capital Journal* reported rumors of the Klan's arrival.[20] The rival *Oregon Statesman* confirmed the Klan was organizing in Salem the following month, saying it had "the first actual proof" of the Klan's presence there.[21] A chapter founder later divulged that the Klan actually held its first Salem meeting in June, the same period when Callaway began recruiting in Portland.

The Salem klavern first stirred up controversy in October 1921, when two men dressed in white robes and carrying torches arrived late at night and kicked at the doors of Deaconess Hospital, frightening nurses and patients.[22] The intruders left a note threatening Marion County Judge J. M. Bushey, who had recently committed two young girls to the hospital in the care of an official there. A recent newspaper article had suggested one of the girls was only eleven years old and was held at the hospital as a virtual prisoner.[23] "You better let those girls loose," the note read. "What the Ku Klux Klan starts it finishes."[24] Whoever penned the note provided no reason why they objected to the judge's decision.

In response to the negative publicity, Callaway came to town, marking the first time the Klan went public in Salem. He claimed to have investigated the Deaconess incident and concluded the hooded men were Klan imposters, a frequent alibi recited by Klan leaders. A kleagle accompanying Callaway, L. C. Pilkington, divulged that the Klan had just inducted twenty new Salem members, and now claimed one hundred fifty Klansmen in the city.[25] Chapter membership doubled in the next three months, rising to three hundred by February 1922. Many of the members were recruited from the ranks of Scottish Rite Masons, who were attracted to Senator Hall's campaign after he endorsed the fraternal lodge's proposal to shut down private schools.[26] As the Salem klavern gravitated into electoral politics, chapter membership doubled again to about six hundred by the fall 1922 general election.

Many original members objected to Gifford's cunning tactics and the harsh anti-Catholic rhetoric spewed by the Reverend James R. Johnson, a Portland Klansman who became its second exalted cyclops.

C. C. Starr, a Klan organizer whom Gifford dispatched from Portland, tried to recruit new members at the Oregon Hospital for the Insane by warning doctors they must join the Klan if they wanted to keep their jobs.[27] Salem klavern members opposed that strategy and also criticized Gifford's dubious fundraising schemes.[28]

Klan headquarters in Atlanta repeatedly promised to grant the Salem klavern its official charter, but it kept delaying a formal ceremony, for unexplained reasons. When members challenged Starr about the delays in a June 1923 meeting, he responded: "There will be no charter as long as this criticism of Gifford continues." The dispute came to a head the following month, when Starr confiscated the funds, records, and regalia held by the Salem chapter.[29] Gifford later appointed Starr to reorganize the chapter, accepting only members who swore allegiance to Gifford's regime.[30]

Evolving Beyond Lynchings

The original Ku Klux Klan was a violent terrorist group bent on restoring white supremacy after the Civil War. Historian David Chalmers estimated those Klansman killed one thousand Blacks and their white Republican allies.[31] A more recent and exhaustive analysis by the Montgomery, Alabama-based Equal Justice Initiative documented more than two thousand lynchings and other murders of emancipated Black people during the Reconstruction Era of 1865 to 1876.[32] It's difficult to know how many of those victims were murdered by Klansmen, since nightriders wore masks and were rarely held to account for their crimes. But the Klan set the table for the post-Civil War wave of terror against Blacks and their white defenders.

The second version of the Klan that formed a half century later portrayed itself as law-abiding and peaceful. But that was a myth that could be argued only in comparison to the original version, as the Klan never shed its penchant for intimidation and vigilantism. "It threatened, boycotted, banished, tarred and feathered, flogged, mutilated and, on occasion, murdered," Chalmers concluded.[33] The *New York World*'s twenty-one-part series in September and October 1921 documented a slew of violent incidents in the prior year attributed to the second Klan: four murders, five kidnappings, forty-one floggings, twenty-seven tar-and-featherings, and other crimes.[34]

Violence blamed on the Klan continued despite the media spotlight and subsequent Congressional hearings, though it varied from state to state. In northern Georgia, a series of racist attacks in 1922 followed a resurgence of lynchings from 1917 to 1921, propelling hundreds of Blacks to flee their homes.[35] In August 1922, masked shotgun-wielding Klansmen blocked a road in Mer Rouge, Louisiana, yanking two people out of cars and lynching them. The Louisiana governor sought help from the FBI to restore law and order. From 1921 to 1923, Klan-inspired vigilantism in Oklahoma led to hundreds of floggings and other violence. To address the wave of violence, Governor Jack Walton declared martial law in Oklahoma, but that was overturned when the Klan-influenced state legislature impeached him and turned him out of office in November 1923.[36] Klan violence also erupted in Carnegie, Pennsylvania; Inglewood and Kern County, California; and communities in Virginia, Florida, Ohio, Illinois, Colorado, and Michigan. The Dallas, Texas, klavern, led by Hiram Evans, was implicated in a brutal kidnapping and near-lynching of a Black bellhop, among other violent incidents.[37] Later, Evans claimed he quelled Klan violence after supplanting William Simmons as imperial wizard in late 1922. "One result of this is to be seen in the decrease of lawlessness in Klan territory," Evans wrote in 1926. "We can justly claim credit for the remarkable improvement as regards lynching in the last two years."[38]

Klan Violence in Oregon

Klan violence resulting in bloodshed was relatively rare in Oregon during the 1920s, when compared to other states. But Reverend Reuben Sawyer openly incited violence against Blacks in his inaugural Portland speech, later distributed statewide in brochure form. "We control madmen, mad dogs and other mad beasts," Sawyer thundered to the crowd of six thousand on December 22, 1921. "The Negro in whose blood flows the mad desire for race amalgamation is more dangerous than a maddened wild beast and he must and will be controlled."[39] The Southern Oregon Outrages were the most widely publicized violent acts attributed to the Oregon Klan. But they weren't the only ones. The victims usually were people of color.

On April 2, 1922, Roseburg Klansmen mobilized after hearing complaints about Black shoe shiner Sam Jackson's supposedly insulting remarks to a young white woman working at a confectionary store. Klansmen mobilized twenty-five to thirty members to conduct a manhunt around Roseburg for Jackson, who managed to elude capture and a potential lynching.[40] Such incidents, along with the necktie parties, instilled tortuous fear of the Klan without any actual bloodshed. "I'm not convinced the Klan didn't like that kind of publicity," observed Darrell Millner, a longtime scholar of Oregon Black history who studied the Klan.[41]

Oregon City car wash operator Perry Ellis received a telephone call just before midnight on Friday, June 1, 1923, asking him to rescue people whose wagon broke down outside of town on Abernathy Road. Ellis, the community's lone Black resident, saddled up his horse and rode several miles, accompanied by his white friend Ira Thrall. They halted when six men wearing Klan robes, hoods, and masks emerged from two parked cars, threatening to shoot Ellis and ordering Thrall to leave and take Ellis's horse with him, according to accounts the two men later shared with Beatrice Cannady's newspaper, the *Advocate*.[42] The masked men blindfolded Ellis and forced him into a car. Then they drove to an isolated spot and placed a noose around his neck, demanding that Ellis confess to charges recently brought by a white woman against him, though the charges had been dropped a week earlier. Ellis refused, denying the allegations as the men tightened the noose and slung the end of the rope over a tree branch. Eventually he was released and commanded to leave Oregon City. Ellis walked home to Oregon City, shared his account with the *Advocate*, then fled to Tacoma, Washington.

On July 6, 1924, Black veteran Timothy Pettis was reported missing in Marshfield (present-day Coos Bay). His mutilated body, with his testicles removed, later washed ashore in the bay. Police were slow to investigate, so the NAACP pressed authorities to find the culprits. "Marshfield is infested with the Ku Klux Klan and we are of the opinion, and so are the colored people who live in Marshfield, that all efforts are being made to cover up the crime," the Portland NAACP wrote to its national office.[43] There's no proof the Klan was to blame, as the perpetrators never were identified.

La Grande Klansman Dr. Ellis O. Willson was indicted in February 1924 for raping his clerical assistant and then committing manslaughter by performing an abortion on her.[44] In Portland, a Black woman named Elise Reynolds claimed she was branded with acid on her cheek by a masked man, after a threatening letter signed "KKK" was posted on her front door. Police detectives dismissed the woman's charges and claimed the branding was likely self-inflicted,[45] though brandings, like necktie parties, were common tactics of the second Klan, and the Portland police department was riddled with Klansmen.

Klansmen also were accused numerous times of making violent threats, often via anonymous letters. In August 1922, a note signed KKK threatened the Marshfield mayor with a necktie party.[46] Other Klan-linked threats were leveled against the *Oregon Labor Press* editor in Portland,[47] the *Heppner Herald* editor,[48] a Medford judge,[49] a Black shoeshine shop owner in Salem,[50] Judge Bushey in Marion County,[51] two Black men in Klamath Falls,[52] and a Black Portland minister.[53] Even if the targets weren't physically injured, the threats provided vivid reminders of the Klan's power and potential for violence.

Woman Branded in Tillamook

Two nights before Thanksgiving in 1922, two men wearing Klan regalia entered A. M. Standish's home in Tillamook and attacked the white woman, branding her left breast with a hot metal cross. Standish shared her account of the violent attack with her parents when she went home to Portland for Christmas, and they both reported seeing her scar.[54] Tillamook police investigated Standish's claim, and a doctor examined her. They reported that it appeared to be a self-inflicted injury caused by an iodine burn.[55] Amid a wave of news coverage, Standish changed her story. The two hooded men were not Klansman after all, she said, now claiming she knew their identities but wouldn't divulge them. "The Ku Klux Klan is not responsible," she insisted.[56] "No Klansman had anything to do with it," declared the Klan's newspaper *Western American*, blaming the unfounded claim on the *Portland Telegram* and other "unreliable newspapers owned or controlled by Catholics and Jews."[57]

But the branding had everything to do with the Klan. The Tillamook police department was controlled by the Klan, and the doctor who examined Standish was a Klansman. Her father was a Klansman, as was her husband, Nevada Standish. The victim and her mother were members of the Oregon Klan women's group, Ladies of the Invisible Empire. A week after *Western American*'s denial of Klan involvement,

Grand Dragon Gifford fessed up at a closed meeting of the La Grande Klan. Gifford explained the branding was a case of the Klan policing its own member for illicit activities. "The woman had been a bootlegger, and had trouble with the authorities," Gifford told La Grande Klansmen. The authorities "desired to get rid of her and that is the means they used," he said, acknowledging the branding was committed by the police chief and his assistant, who were fellow Klansmen.[58]

Klan organizers signed up their first Tillamook members in November 1921, the same year local dairy farmers obtained a copyright for their primary product, Tillamook Cheese.[59] Of Tillamook County's 8,810 residents in 1920, there was only one Black person, twenty-eight Native Americans, and seven people each from China and Japan. The bulk of the county's 1,010 immigrants were from Switzerland, Germany, Sweden, and Canada.[60] "The Klan seemed to grow most rapidly in areas with the least cause for civic alarm, and where opposition to its principles was slightest," observed historian Eckard Toy Jr., who studied the Klan in Tillamook and elsewhere in the state. "Yet one must not underestimate the appeal of anti-Roman Catholicism and anti-Jewish feeling during a period of militant evangelical Protestantism."[61]

Kleagles in Tillamook drew heavily from local Mason, Odd Fellows, and Elks lodges, and members of the Nazarene, Baptist, Christian, and United Brethren congregations. The county fair board offered free showings of *Birth of a Nation*, spiking interest in the Klan. Several ministers joined, including United Brethren pastor W. O. Woolever, who became exalted cyclops. The chapter soon attracted six to eight hundred members, including forty-two dairy farmers, twenty-four retailers, six fishermen, two school principals, two hotel owners, the city clerk, the city marshal, a deputy sheriff, and the publisher and editor of the *Tillamook Headlight*, one of the community's two newspapers supporting the Klan.[62]

By the time of the fall 1922 election and for several years afterwards, a majority of elected officials in Tillamook were Klansmen, including the mayor, city councilors, a state representative, and the county sheriff. Sometimes elections pitted one Klansman against another.[63] The Klan-supported ballot measure aimed at closing Catholic schools passed countywide in 1922 by a resounding two-to-one margin.[64] On Memorial Day in 1924, thousands of area Klansmen from three counties, including members of the immigrant and women's auxiliaries, staged a ten-block-long parade, marching from Tillamook's city center to the county fairgrounds. The Tillamook mayor, a Klansman, presented the Klan with a ceremonial key to the city.[65]

While the Klan dominated Tillamook as much as any Oregon community, the klavern there served more like a traditional fraternal lodge, which may explain why it continued meeting until 1929, long after most other Oregon chapters faded away. In October, 1924, the mayor welcomed a new Knights of Columbus Hall to town, a sign the community's anti-Catholic fervor had eased.[66] By July 1926, the chapter still counted one hundred ninety-six members in good standing, though thirty-eight members were suspended in the second quarter of that year for failure to pay dues, while only one new Klansman was recruited.[67] Only nine Klansmen attended the regular meeting of August 2, 1928, shortly before the chapter fizzled. The Klan brought a "flourish of excitement to the socially and geographically isolated city," concluded University of Oregon history professor William Toll in his study of the Tillamook klavern, but the Klan no longer served its purpose as a fraternal lodge or political force.[68]

Astoria Klan conducts nighttime ritual with lighted cross at the Columbia Club ball fields, possibly on September 1, 1924. (Clatsop County Historical Society, photo 3503-540, detail 1)

Burning Crosses Surface Around the State

It took seven sticks of dynamite and a 360-foot-high wooden cross atop Baldy Mountain to herald the Klan's presence in Southern Oregon's Rogue River Valley on May 23, 1922. John J. Hoogstraat and H. E. Griffith, a pair of kleagles organizing a klavern in nearby Grants Pass, bragged that their pyrotechnics could be seen thirty miles down the valley that night.[69] Two months later, Roseburg Klansmen lit a 380-foot cross on Mt. Hebo Summit, plus a second fiery cross on nearby Reservoir Hill emblazoned with the letters KKK.[70] Such fiery crosses attracted attention and commanded respect for the Klan's bravado, becoming a frequent sight in Oregon during the early 1920s.

Americans associated burning crosses with the Ku Klux Klan ever since *Birth of a Nation* premiered in 1915. The giant flaming crosses struck fear among Blacks, Catholics, and Jews and other immigrants, undoubtedly part of the Klan's intent. But the ritual was largely used as a sophisticated public relations stunt, akin to searchlight beams that once heralded Hollywood movie premieres. Burning crosses called attention to the Klan's arrival and presence in a community, and they alerted the community to the Invisible Empire's initiations and rallies.

In a move from Klan public-relations whiz Elizabeth Tyler's playbook, the Klan hired airplane pilots to fly a fiery cross (or a cross adorned with electric lights) over the state fairgrounds after a massive parade and member induction in Salem. Crosses lit up Portland's Mount Scott and Mount Tabor during Klan initiations, as well as Eugene's Skinner Butte. The La Grande chapter lit a cross to celebrate Klan victories in the 1922 gubernatorial race and anti-Catholic schools campaign, and again when the chapter secured its official charter in March 1923.[71] Burning crosses also were reported in Albany, Astoria, Baker, Beaverton, Bend, Corvallis, Cottage Grove, Enterprise, Hood River, Independence, Klamath Falls, Lebanon, Medford, Pendleton, Scio, Springfield, St. Helens, Tillamook, and Vernonia.

Annunziata Merlo, a Catholic immigrant from Italy, ran a boarding house in Beaverton in the early 1920s, where she served guests home-cooked Italian food, including a traditional glass of wine with the evening meals. The wine part didn't sit well with Beaverton Klansmen, who held their meetings across the street, recalled Merlo's grandson, Richard Botteri.[72] Local Klansmen showed up at Merlo's door one day and demanded she stop serving wine. She refused, according to family lore. In response, angry Klansmen erected a burning cross outside her front door. Merlo didn't back down.

While growing up in the boarding house, Merlo's daughter Louise would peer out a second-story window to get a glimpse inside the neighboring Cady Building, where Klansmen held their meetings. She could spot them "parading around in their sheets," recalled Botteri, Louise's son. His mother vividly remembered the day Beaverton's St. Cecilia Catholic Church closed down its school, after Oregon voters approved the Klan-backed measure aimed at shutting down Catholic schools. Her pastor walked Louise and her classmates across town to enroll them in a public school.

Attacking Vice and Catholics in Astoria

No Oregon city experienced a greater takeover by the Ku Klux Klan than Astoria, despite having the state's largest concentration of immigrants. More than one in three Astorians hailed from abroad, many from Finland and other Scandinavian nations.[73] Wisely, the Klan didn't trumpet its anti-immigrant stance in the port city.

Astoria was the world leader in salmon canning, attracting many Finns who worked seasonally, often returning home after fishing season. Single men were known to frequent scores of taverns that lined Taylor Street, in open violation of Prohibition. One anti-vice campaigner counted sixty-eight "roaming houses" in Astoria, where one might find alcohol, prostitution, and sales of cigarettes to minors.[74] Growing calls to take action against vice in Astoria, including from Finnish Protestant churches, provided an opening for the Klan, which positioned itself as an avid supporter of Prohibition. The Klan also found a fertile audience for its anti-Catholic message among Scandinavian Lutherans.

Agitation against Catholics spiked after the Astoria School Board approved the temporary use of a public-school classroom by Catholics in June 1920, after a Catholic school burned down.[75] Anti-Catholic citizens then lobbied the school district to stop hiring Catholic teachers, and they unseated Catholic school board member James Hope when he sought re-election in June 1921. A leader of that campaign, Ernest Hawkins, became exalted cyclops of the Astoria Klan when it formed two months later, and his fellow activists became the core of the new chapter.[76]

Astoria Klansmen lower a casket into the earth to bid farewell to a comrade. Astoria was then Oregon's third-largest city and home to one of the most potent Klan chapters in the state. (Clatsop County Historical Society, photo 3503-540)

When the chapter appeared to stagnate, the Portland Klan dispatched two kleagles and Reverend Sawyer to Astoria.[77] On January 26, 1922, the newly invigorated chapter hosted a public meeting at Astoria's municipal auditorium, where twelve Klansmen dressed in regalia lined up on stage next to a burning cross.[78] Five days later, the newly formed Astoria Law Enforcement League held an inaugural meeting at the Methodist Church.[79] The group formed to address rampant vice in town, and decried the mayor and police chief for coddling bootleggers. Participants included Klansmen as well as Hope, the former school board member they'd unseated. "Chief Carlson and the police force are protecting vice here," Hope said at the meeting, a sign that some Catholics and Protestants had common ground on the matter. But then Hope criticized the Klan for stirring up religious animosity and dividing the community, and he was promptly rebuked. "You can't say anything against the KKK from the rostrum. You know this church is anti-Catholic," declared Reverend Wire, the meeting host.[80] Around the same time, the Catholic president of the Astoria Chamber of Commerce, W. P. O'Brien, resigned, saying he wanted to be free to refute the Klan without entangling the business group.

Rampant charges of vice and municipal corruption spurred a May 1922 ballot initiative to scrap Astoria's commissioner form of municipal government and hire a city manager. That would put city affairs under control of a professional administrator and limit commissioner meddling in city operations. The Klan opposed the measure, though voters passed it. But the klavern was building a potent political machine, under the direction of local resident and *Western American* editor Lem Dever.

Chapter membership grew that fall to about eight hundred men. After there were two fatalities associated with drunks leaving the Whistle Inn tavern, the Klan issued a threatening letter to Clatsop County Sheriff Ole Nelson, demanding he stem liquor use at the tavern or it would take action. Two days later, it did. Fifty armed men mobilized by the Klan showed up at the tavern on June 19, 1922. The proprietor was subsequently arrested, but it came too late to save Nelson's job, as the Klan spearheaded a recall campaign. In August, voters tossed out Nelson and elected Klansman Harley J. Slusher as the new sheriff.[81]

Klansmen took control of the Astoria Port Commission in the September 1922 elections, sweeping all three seats. That promised lucrative business opportunities for Klan-connected businesses.[82] Then, in the November 7, 1922, general election, the Klan had a clean sweep, electing Klansman O. B. Setters as mayor and four city commissioners. As the Klan rose to dominate city politics, Merle Chessman, editor of the *Astoria Evening Budget*, grew increasingly critical of the divisive group. The Klan demanded that Chessman be fired. Failing to achieve that, it launched a boycott of the paper. Then the Klan sought to buy the paper outright, but it was rebuffed.[83]

Tragedy struck Astoria in December 1922, when a fire left much of downtown in embers. It was a perfect time to bring in a professional manager to run the corrupt city government. Conveniently, the voter-approved charter amendment required such a manager be hired to start the new year. Mayor Setters and the Klan-controlled City Council hired O. A. Kratz, a Klansman who was La Grande city manager, to fill the new post in Astoria.[84] But then a curious thing happened.

As Dever and Grand Dragon Gifford started directing Kratz to hire and fire managers and staff of their choosing, Kratz asserted his independence. "Under the city charter most of the city appointments are mine, but when I arrived I found many of them had been agreed upon," Kratz said in a public statement issued in March of 1923.[85] Kratz fired the police chief, and accused the mayor of trying to go around him in appropriating a large public-works contract. He singled out Dever for meddling and threatening him with negative stories in the *Western American.* Kratz also complained to a Seattle reporter that Gifford was pressing city officials to "go easy" on liquor violators, contradicting the Klan's public embrace of Prohibition.[86] Dever sought to have his fellow Klansman replaced as city manager, but the four city commissioners propelled into office by the Klan resisted, coming to Kratz's defense.[87] The messy split within the Klan, along with opposition from Catholics and the *Astoria Evening Budget,* caused its influence and membership to wane. Hawkins soon resigned as exalted cyclops.[88]

Warring Factions in Baker

At age fourteen, Walter Lee Lansing fled his home in rural Baker County after his father broke Walter's arm in a drunken rage. Lansing made his way to Baker, a bustling city on the eastern edge of Oregon near the Wallowa Mountains.[89] A Klan chapter formed in Baker in July 1922, when King Kleagle Powell came to town along with a La Grande-based kleagle. The two paid organizers recruited fifteen members, including the Baker police chief.[90] Lansing, now in his mid-twenties and building a career in law enforcement, signed up. It's unclear why he joined, but the Klan targeted police officers in its recruiting, and Lansing's wife harbored lifelong resentment against the Catholic Church stemming from horrible childhood memories of attending Catholic school.[91] Lansing was not religious, but he later was a proud member of the Scottish Rite fraternal order, which often was closely aligned with the Klan. Most Oregon Klansmen eventually destroyed records of their involvement with the group, but Lansing's membership card and other Klan records remained in the family, discovered nearly a century later by his grandson and donated to the Oregon Historical Society.

By October 1922, five men attracted a crowd in downtown Baker by erecting a burning cross outside the offices of the *Baker Democrat,* which had been critical of the Klan.[92] On January 31, 1923, the Baker Klan initiated 155 new recruits, a cohort likely including Lansing. The Baker Klan now boasted of having several hundred members, and about five hundred of them joined a public parade in the city that summer.[93]

The lone surviving minutes from a Baker klavern meeting show that eighty-four members attended the September 12, 1923, session, when members approved six new recruits and an eight-dollar ad in the local newspaper to publicize their next open-air member induction.[94] Despite its sizable membership, the Baker klavern, as elsewhere in Oregon and the rest of the nation, was wracked by warring factions and allegations of corruption. Some members aligned with Imperial Wizard Evans, while others remained loyal to the man he ousted, Simmons. Lansing stuck with Simmons, and he was one of many Oregon Klansmen who started raising questions about where members' dues and fees were going. The controversy came to a head when Lansing was summoned for a cursory Klan "trial" in January 1924.[95] After an internal investigation overseen by Klansman C. T. Godwin, Lansing and fellow dissident O. F. Coulter were accused of "circulating false and scandalous reports" and falsely charging officers with misappropriating chapter funds. In addition, both were charged with recruiting Baker chapter members to a Klan rival, apparently a splinter group created by Simmons. Lansing left no records of his involvement with the Klan or the splinter group after 1924, so he likely left both organizations.[96]

In 1931, Lansing was hired to join the newly created Oregon State Police, where he expanded a school traffic-safety patrol effort he'd pioneered in Baker into a statewide program. In 1958, Lansing was elected grand master of all Oregon Masonic lodges. Godwin, a former Baker County district attorney and one of three Klan investigators who had "prosecuted" Lansing, was named grand dragon of the Oregon Klan in 1926, after Gifford resigned.

Insider View of La Grande Klavern

One St. Patrick's Day, the Ku Klux Klan burned a fiery cross halfway up Table Mountain, directly above La Grande's residential area. "We assumed the timing was meant to be somewhat of a threat to Catholics," recalled Sister Margaret Meyers, who grew up in La Grande.[97] Decades later, the nun learned that March 17 was chosen because it was the date the La Grande klavern had received its charter.

Her parents sought to shield Sister Margaret and her siblings from the KKK, but the Klan was highly visible in the Eastern Oregon community. "Several times I saw Klan members, their identity concealed under full regalia, riding horseback about our streets in broad daylight," Meyers wrote in her personal reflections about that era. "Though there was a strong anti-Catholic element behind the Klan's actions, we—or I—never felt any anxiety or concern at this sight, simply mild surprise and curiosity." But to her parents, the Klan posed a real threat. The Klan sought to get her father, Fred L. Meyers, fired from his cashier job at La Grande National Bank because of his Catholic faith. The Klan backed off when it realized the bank could lose too much business as a result.

When Simmons created rituals and titles for the resurrected KKK in 1915, he borrowed or adapted them from original Klan practices and fraternal lodges. There were Klan hand grips, coded acronyms, and oaths, which he published in the *Kloran*. A Klansman trying to flesh out a comrade in public might ask, "AYAK" (Are You A Klansman?). The proper affirmative answer was "AKIA" (A Klansman I Am). Simmons was fond of creating insider terms starting with the letter k, such as kleagle (paid recruiter); klavern (space where meetings are held, or a Klan chapter); kligrapp (chapter secretary); klaliff (vice president); klokard (lecturer); kludd (chaplain); klabee (treasurer); klokan (investigator); and klonklave (meeting).

The La Grande klavern presents the best case study for how the second Klan operated, because it's the only klavern in Oregon and one of the few nationwide whose meeting notes were well-preserved. Then-Portland State University history professor David Horowitz published the minutes, adding historical context, in his important book *Inside the Klavern.*[98]

Before entering La Grande klonklaves, members typically recited a secret password to the night hawk (curiously, the only position that Simmons didn't start with the letter k). Opening ceremonies sometimes began with a "100 percent" orchestra leading Klansmen in song, or members singing a patriotic song. Later, at the command of Grand Dragon Gifford, they added recitation of a Biblical passage, such as Romans 12. Chapter members were urged to arrive decked out in official KKK robes.

In combing through the chapter notes, Horowitz tallied references to 326 individual Klan members.[99] That's the same number who donned masks and robes to march in a July 25, 1923, parade through La Grande's business district, before seventy-five Klansmen were inducted into the klavern.[100] Several thousand reportedly witnessed the ceremony, in a city of only 6,913 residents.[101]

One factor in the second Klan's popular appeal was an explosion of fraternal order membership at the time, which some called the era of joiners. By 1924, one out of every fourteen Americans belonged to a fraternal order.[102] Many belonged to multiple lodges; Klansmen often belonged to the Scottish Rite Masons, American Legion, and other fraternal groups. Some Oregon klaverns, such as in La Grande, Tillamook, and Mill City, were closer in style to the fraternal order that Simmons initially conceived. Members sought companionship, community service, and networking, which they called Klannishness, akin to the ethnic solidarity practiced by new immigrants. Those pursuits are amply illustrated in the La Grande minutes.

When Clyde Bunting's wife took ill, the chapter voted to send her flowers and wishes for a speedy recovery. The day after Christmas in 1922, when the chapter learned J. W. S. Johnson might have to sacrifice his cow due to a lack of feed, members voted to send him a ton of alfalfa. At other meetings they pledged $25 for a needy minister, Stanton Lapham; $50 to the Red Cross; and $25 for a Japan relief fund after an earthquake. Another aspect of Klannishness was helping chapter members get jobs or customers, especially when their competitors were Catholics, Jews, or other immigrants. An announcement went out that Perkins Motor Co. had a job opening for a "100 percenter," the Klan's oft-used term for a kindred spirit who was white, Protestant, and US-born. At the February 6, 1923, meeting, members voted to make a list of La Grande businesses owned by the "right" people, "thus keeping Klansmen's money in Klansmen's pockets."[103]

Members encouraged a boycott of a Jewish-owned grocery store, which competed with the Klansman-owned Holm's grocery, and the klavern asked members to take their money out of La Grande National Bank in favor of its competitor. Some members were criticized for still patronizing a Greek shoe shiner and Herman's Lunch Counter, owned by a Catholic German immigrant. The chapter pressed the local school district and bank to fire Catholic employees such as Sister Margaret's father, and pushed the Red Cross to fire its secretary.[104] Sometimes the chapter pushed back against national mandates from Klan headquarters, which dictated that all robes had to be purchased from the Klan-owned plant in Atlanta. Members argued they should continue buying their robes from a local tailor because his competitors were all Jewish-owned.[105] The chapter also pushed Governor Walter Pierce to appoint its members to state posts. At the chapter's urging, Pierce named James E. Reynolds to the Union County Tax Supervising & Conservation Commission, and promoted Robert Hugh Baldock in the state highway department.[106]

The minutes also reveal klavern stances on what were deemed moral issues. The chapter vowed to take action against a local man who reportedly was neglecting his three children.[107] An investigation into John Hodgins revealed that he believed in evolution: "that is, he means to say, that he firmly believes that man and monkey are true kindred."[108] Ten chapter members volunteered to be deputized by police to help uproot Prohibition violators. The chapter circulated a petition asking the city to "clean up" alleged drunken and disorderly behavior in the Black side of town near the railroad. Police promptly responded by arresting fifty people, and convicting forty-three of them for liquor-related charges.[109] Some applicants for chapter membership were rejected because the candidates were fond of moonshine, had gone bankrupt, or were living "in sin" with someone not their wife. But concerns about adultery only went so far. "If you married Klansmen insist on going out with another man's wife, be sure she doesn't belong to a Klansman," the minutes reflected.[110]

Though Klan membership patterns evolved over the years, the list of recruits in the minutes for December 5, 1922, and February 23, 1923, reveal a broad mix of La Grande's population: high school coach, beekeeper, oil company worker, railroad brakeman, produce dealer, dry goods merchant, insurance salesman, taxi driver, hotel proprietor, meat cutter, grocery clerk, railroad inspector, sheriff's deputy, insurance man, game warden, three mechanics, and two farmers.

The La Grande chapter was first organized in the spring of 1922 when kleagles from Portland and Pendleton came to town. The chapter grew quickly, giving the Klan significant political clout. Members bragged about distributing flyers promoting the anti-Catholic-school initiative on every resident's doorstep in November 1922. Membership surged after the klavern recruited Sister Lucretia, a disgruntled former nun, to speak in town, and after winning its coveted charter from the national Klan. In June 1923, two Klan members won seats on the local school board, giving the Klan three of five votes. A Klansman was elected to the La Grande City Council in November 1924.

But the chapter was already losing its footing by late 1923, when minutes start to show the required complement of officers failed to show up for meetings. The chapter's demise also seemed to coincide with a sensational prosecution of Dr. Ellis Willson, the member indicted in February 1924 for raping his assistant and committing manslaughter by performing an abortion on her. Dr. Landis, a fellow La Grande Klansman, testified against Willson in the trial. Willson initially was sentenced to three years, but he ultimately prevailed on appeal due to legal technicalities.[111] By April 1924, minutes show the chapter meetings still attracted fifty to sixty people, but the activities seemed tame compared to its prior work. That month, the chapter's exalted cyclops, C. W. Jones, resigned his post.

Town and Gown and White Robes in Eugene

The Klan rose to power in Eugene on the strength of its anti-Catholic agitation, targeting municipal affairs in Oregon's fourth-largest city and at the University of Oregon, the state's flagship college and city's hub. Kleagle C. N. Jones arrived in town sometime before July 1921, the same time Callaway showed up in Portland.[112] Jones recruited several dozen war veterans and younger members of fraternal lodges and service clubs.[113] The Klan first announced its presence in Eugene with a public lecture by Reverend Sawyer on January 11, 1922, a reprise of his Portland appearance a few weeks earlier. Residents packed the Eugene Theater, paying fifty cents to hear Sawyer discuss "The truth about the KKK" and watch the films *The Face at Your Window* and *The Knights of the KKK Ride Again*. Hundreds of residents were turned away due to lack of capacity.[114]

Before the Klan came to town, anti-Catholic forces were alarmed by the early successes of a dynamic young priest who had relocated from Portland. The Reverend Edwin Vincent O'Hara arrived in 1920 to take charge at St. Mary's Catholic Church, a Eugene congregation of 125 families. He soon added a Catholic high school, and created a vacation Bible school and correspondence courses to expand religious education in outlying rural communities.[115] (Also see Oregon's Activist

Priest in chapter 6, p. 116.) O'Hara proposed an interfaith dialogue on religious education and public schools to Henry Davidson Sheldon, the University of Oregon's dean of education and a leader of Eugene's Unitarian congregation. Sheldon mentioned the idea in a letter to a Portland Unitarian minister, suggesting the Rose City might be a more appropriate place for such dialogue. "It seems to me inadvisable to attempt anything of this sort in Eugene, as Father O'Hara's arrival has created considerable stir," Sheldon wrote, a few months before the Klan's arrival in town.[116]

That stir may have been over the Newman Hall project, one of O'Hara's many initiatives. O'Hara hoped to provide a physical space for the campus Newman Club, which served the university's 130 Catholic students and was launched by his brother John O'Hara when he taught history at the university. Father O'Hara envisioned a physical space where Catholic club members could socialize, soak up culture and religious teachings, and gain mutual support, with some dorm space for women.[117] O'Hara chose a site on Thirteenth and Kincaid Streets, two blocks from campus, and a building design and fundraising campaign emerged a week after Sheldon's letter.[118]

Two months later, the Klan began organizing in Eugene, and by May 1922, Sheldon heard rumors that Frederick S. Dunn, head of the university's Latin Department, was leading the Eugene chapter. "Several of the members of our august faculty have joined its ranks," Sheldon wrote a former UO colleague in Wisconsin. "A large number of faculty members are supposed to be Jesuits in disguise," he scoffed. "The whole thing is very silly and yet is likely to have considerable influence in the next year or so."[119] Sheldon's allusion to Jesuits, a prominent Catholic order, referred to the Klan's focus on weeding out Catholic influence at the university. Dunn subsequently went public as the Eugene klavern's exalted cyclops, and he mobilized Klansmen to oppose O'Hara's Newman Hall initiative. The Klan claimed O'Hara had a "sinister motive" and wanted to replace Protestant faculty and regents with Catholics.[120] The Klan also attacked Eugene's Catholic-run Mercy Hospital.

The attack on Newman Hall proved unsuccessful. The university administration and student newspaper openly opposed the Klan, which never made significant inroads recruiting on campus.[121] "Klansmen increasingly regarded the university as an enemy rather than a potential ally," wrote Eckard Toy, who wrote his UO master's thesis on the Oregon Klan and later taught at the university.[122] Aside from Dunn, the Klan's biggest recruit on campus was football coach C. A. "Shy" Huntington, who was quarterback of the beloved UO team that won the Rose Bowl in 1917.[123]

The Klan enlisted some bigger fish outside the university.

Shortly before the pivotal fall 1922 election, the *Capital Journal* published the names of the Eugene klavern's first eighty-three members, obtained from a police raid on the Klan in Southern California. The list included Eugene *Guard* publisher Joseph E. Shelton; A. O. Waller, commander of the local American Legion, and W. G. White, local commander of the Oregon National Guard.[124] While embarrassing, the revelations proved only a modest brake on the chapter's growth. The Klan eventually attracted four hundred to four hundred fifty members in Eugene.

The Invisible Empire had far greater success with its anti-Catholic agitation outside the university. In the 1922 general election, Eugene Klansmen waged a highly effective campaign for the Klan-supported ballot initiative aimed at shutting down Catholic schools. In Lane County, 69 percent of voters supported the initiative, the highest margin of any Oregon county.[125] In the same election, Klan candidates won a majority of the seats on the Eugene City Council.[126]

The Klan successfully pressured the Eugene school board to dismiss three Catholic teachers. When school board member L. L. Ray objected and supported those teachers, the Klan unseated him at the next election.[127] E. F. Carleton, superintendent of Eugene schools, resigned in March 1923, shortly after being reappointed for a third year. His unexpected departure likely was due to opposition from the Klan.[128]

After the Klan took control of the City Council, Mayor O. C. Peterson braced for future clashes. The Klan then turned its attention to attacking him and two of his appointees, City Attorney O. H. Foster and Police Chief Chris Christensen. Klansmen complained about lax enforcement of Prohibition and prostitution laws, but Christensen's Catholic faith may have been the bigger factor. Facing intense criticism from the Klan, the major, city attorney, and police chief all resigned in May 1923, giving the Klan its biggest victory in the city. "Eugene now appears to be one of the thoroughly Ku Kluxed cities of Oregon," remarked *Oregon Voter* after the trio of resignations.[129]

More Than Five Dozen Klaverns

By some measures, the Invisible Empire made a bigger splash in Eugene, Tillamook, Astoria, and other communities than in Portland, despite the Rose City klavern's far-larger membership and domination of the statewide Klan. Some smaller cities also enrolled a higher proportion of the population. Here are some other cities where the Klan drew sizable crowds or recruited hundreds of members:

Albany: The Globe theater was filled to capacity to hear Reverend Sawyer lecture in April 1922.[130] After a nine-block-long parade, three thousand Klansman from around the state attended a May 1923 ceremony to see charters awarded to the Albany, Corvallis, Lebanon, and Mill City klaverns.[131]

Ashland: Large crowds attended two Reverend Sawyer lectures at Vining Theater on May 23 and 24, 1922.[132] Two months later, 110 Klansman marched in full regalia in the city's annual July 4 parade.[133] Ashland voters provided strong support for the Klan in 1922 elections, more so than Medford voters.[134]

Bend: The chapter quickly grew to more than two hundred fifty members, enrolling the mayor, police chief, and county sheriff.[135] Klansmen in cars paraded before a ceremony on Pilot Butte in September 1923.[136] The chapter was declared defunct in April 1925 after shedding more than three hundred members in the past year.[137]

Dallas: Thousands reportedly attended an open-air lecture by the Reverend Virgil "Bearcat" Allison in August 1923.[138] An estimated two thousand Klansmen from multiple klaverns paraded, including two hundred women, before Gifford presented the chapter its charter in April 1924.[139]

Grants Pass: Several hundred marched in a June 1923 parade.[140] The women's chapter had 135 members.[141]

Hood River: A cohort of two hundred fifty recruits was slated to be initiated in February 1923.[142]

McMinnville: A Reverend Johnson lecture attracted 2,500 people in 1923.[143]

Oregon City: Willamette Falls Klan No. 6 reportedly enrolled 1,280 members.[144]

Roseburg: An estimated two thousand people attended a July 1922 ceremony, billed as the largest Oregon Klan gathering to date.[145]

Springfield: More than five hundred attended the initiation of one hundred to one hundred fifty new Klansmen in July 1922.[146]

Vernonia: Some five hundred people attended a lecture by Reverend Allison in 1923.[147]

Luther Powell bragged in December 1923 that the Klan had by then chartered fifty-eight chapters in Oregon, with seven more in the works.[148] Though Klansmen claims were often wildly overstated, Powell made his living organizing Klan chapters, and he wasn't exaggerating in this case. A review of contemporary newspaper accounts, surviving documents, and other published sources revealed evidence of sixty-six klaverns during the second Klan's heyday in Oregon, close to the number Powell cited. There also were reports of clusters of KKK members, or Klan organizing and other activities, in twenty-eight additional Oregon cities and towns. In addition, there were at least eighteen chapters of the Ladies of the Invisible Empire or its successor, the Women of the Ku Klux Klan, plus at least four chapters of the Royal Riders of the Red Robe, the auxiliary for white Protestant immigrants. Of the fifty-three Oregon cities with one thousand or more residents in 1920, all but five had documented Klan chapters or other organizing activities. The author was unable to find references to Klan activities or chapters in Burns, Clatskanie, Lakeview, Oswego, and Prineville.

Seven months after Powell's assertion, the Klan's new chief lecturer in Oregon, the Reverend C. R. Mathis, crowed that the group just formed its hundredth Oregon chapter, in the tiny coastal community of Mapleton.[149] He may have been exaggerating, or may have included all the women's and immigrants' auxiliaries as separate Klan chapters. By then the Klan was scrambling for operating funds and may have loosened its requirements, so newer chapters may have quickly faded without leaving much of a mark. See map on pages viii–ix and appendix A, page 223, for a list of all the documented klaverns and other communities where the Klan organized in the 1920s.

5
Grabbing Political Power in Oregon

"We woke up one morning and found the Klan had about gained political control of the state."

—Governor Ben Olcott

"The Klan in Oregon represents the capitalization of religious prejudice and racial animosity by public service corporations as the means of sidetracking the public mind from economic issues. With the people foolishly fighting over religion and fanning the fires of fanaticism, they have forgotten all about the agitation against eight-cent streetcar fares, high telephone and other service rates and reduced wage scales, that before the advent of the Klan threatened the profits of big business."

—*Capital Journal*[1]

1921–1922: The Klan Moves into State Politics

Portland exalted cyclops Fred Gifford proved a master at political manipulation, stampeding opponents inside and outside the Klan and wielding power like a big-city machine boss. Less than five months after first emerging as a Klansman, Gifford started throwing his weight around Salem in a special legislative session. Less than a year later, he and the Klan reached the pinnacle of state power.

December 19–24, 1921: Oregon Klan makes first foray into politics when Fred Gifford lobbies special legislative session, reportedly inducting some lawmakers into Klan.

February 1922: Governor candidate Charles Hall, a Republican state senator from present-day Coos Bay, endorses compulsory public schooling, securing backing by the Federation of Patriotic Societies and the Klan.

Spring: Hand-picked group of Scottish Rite Masons approves ballot initiative requiring all Oregon students to attend public schools.

May 13: Governor Ben Olcott issues proclamation attacking Klan days before primary.

May 19: Olcott narrowly defeats Hall in GOP primary; Klan candidates sweep all but one Oregon House district primary in Multnomah County.

June: Scottish Rite Masons file petitions to qualify November ballot initiative banning private schools.

September 10: Hall announces run for governor as independent.

September 12: Senator Walter Pierce, winner of Democratic gubernatorial primary, announces support for mandatory public-school initiative, gaining Klan backing.

September 16: Hall scraps independent bid for governor, endorses Pierce.

October 13: Striking Longshore and Marine Transport unions shut down Portland waterfront. Mayor George Baker declares Portland in "throes of revolution"; claims 25,000 Wobblies descending on city.

November 7: Oregon voters elect Pierce governor, approve initiative banning private schools, and ensure Klan control of state House of Representatives.

November 21: Pierce introduced as honorary Klansman at La Grande klavern meeting.

November 28: Dallas, Texas, dentist Hiram Evans elected imperial wizard of national Klan, forcing out founder William Simmons.

Gifford Becomes Political "Boss" of Oregon

Fred Gifford set his sights on state politics just four months after emerging as a Klansman in the summer of 1921. The week before Christmas, when the Portland Klan staged its massive coming-out event at Municipal Auditorium, the chapter's exalted cyclops slipped down to Salem to lobby a special session of the Oregon Legislature, booking a room at the Marion Hotel. Gifford made waves at the State Capitol trying to thwart Julius Meier's appointment to a panel promoting Portland's bid

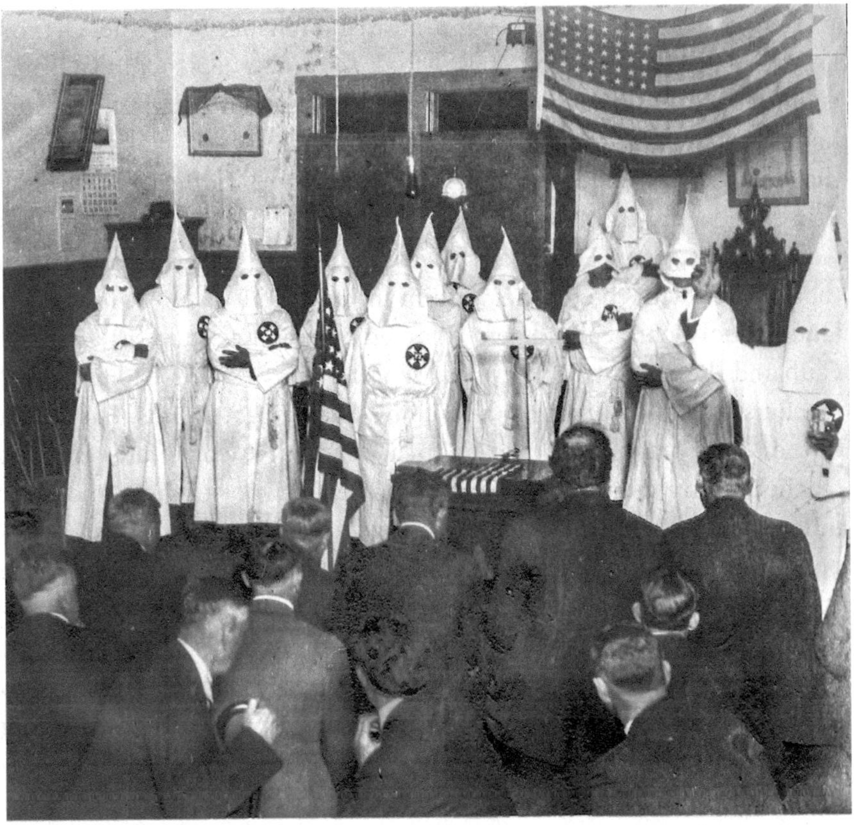

A cohort of new Oregon Klansmen undergoes initiation on June 1, 1923. (Oregon Historical Society)

to host a 1925 trade exposition on Hayden Island, apparently because of Meier's Jewish faith.[2] Blocks from the Capitol, in the boiler room of his hotel, Gifford allegedly inducted some state lawmakers into the Klan, in a makeshift ritual in clear violation of Klan rules. Dissident Klansmen later claimed one of those lawmakers was Senator Charles Hall, the Marshfield Republican whose gubernatorial bid was blessed by Gifford two months later.[3]

A few weeks later, in January of the new year, Gifford was back at his office in Portland's Pittock Block, vetting local and state political candidates. Aspiring office-holders were angling for face time with the exalted cyclops, hoping to win his blessing for the spring 1922 primary.[4] The Portland Klan was expanding like prairie fire, and *Oregon Voter,* a respected newsweekly focused on state politics, called Gifford the "reputed boss of Oregon politics."[5]

Gifford also was cementing a strategic alliance with the Oregon Federation of Patriotic Societies, which ostensibly represented a broad coalition of Protestant fraternal lodges. The anti-Catholic group, known as FOPS, wielded political influence by circulating yellow tickets listing its endorsed "patriotic" candidates. In the 1916 Oregon primary, twenty-eight out of thirty-three FOPS-endorsed candidates won nominations.[6] FOPS likely was among the anti-Catholic forces that teamed with the teachers union in June 1921 to defeat four Portland School Board candidates endorsed by the powerful Portland City Club and the city's major newspapers. The four winners had endorsed teachers' rights to unionize and enjoy tenure protections.[7] In a sign of the Klan's pragmatism and political acumen, it would later endorse teacher tenure and higher teacher salaries to woo teachers and their union. It also supported a state motor vehicle licensing law to win support from the automobile association.[8] That pragmatism led Gifford to court FOPS, whose leaders claimed their yellow tickets listing endorsements could deliver 40,000 votes in the Portland area.[9] Gifford foresaw immense political benefits of allying with another anti-Catholic group and piggybacking on its yellow tickets. FOPS, which had little funding and minimal presence outside Portland, was able to expand its reach by teaming with the Klan.[10]

Gifford began working hand-in-hand with FOPS while ordering Klansmen to infiltrate its component Protestant lodges so he could gain control over it. On two occasions, Gifford sought to place two of his top aides into FOPS leadership but was rebuffed.[11] Gifford revealed his scheme to take over the Protestant group at a closed-door meeting of his Portland klavern in the spring of 1922. "We will support the FOPS and its ticket in the primaries," Gifford reportedly said, "but from then on the Ku Klux Klan is going to dominate politics in Oregon."[12] *Oregon Voter* reported in early March that Gifford was now widely believed to be the primary political boss of both groups.[13]

The May 1922 primary came two years after a regional body of Scottish Rite Masons called for mandatory public schooling for all children. The idea that all youth should be educated in the same classrooms had broad appeal in an era when immigrants speaking multiple languages were flocking to the United States. But it also was a ploy by militant Protestants to shut down Catholic schools, which were viewed as building blocks to expand the Catholic Church in Oregon. (See chapter 6 for a fuller discussion of the initiative's origins, its backers, and the campaign to enact it.)

Senator Hall stressed his support for mandatory public schooling in February 1922, two months after he was allegedly inducted into the Klan. Around the same time, FOPS endorsed his bid to challenge incumbent Governor Olcott in the GOP primary.[14] Gifford initially considered backing other candidates but soon came around to support Hall, who, like the exalted cyclops, worked for a private utility.[15] Hall was president and part owner of the Coos and Curry Telephone Co. Hall's candidacy benefited from anti-Catholic sentiments being whipped up by the Klan and FOPS, and by talk of shutting down Catholic schools. *Capital Journal* editor and publisher George Putnam lamented that Hall's candidacy meant a divisive religious issue had entered the governor's race. "The election promises to be the bitterest and hardest fought in years and to create a new alignment in politics," he editorialized.[16]

A Carefully Manufactured Myth?

G. Davidson Buchanan, a Welshman and former Presbyterian minister from South Africa, conceived the idea of a secretive anti-Catholic society after settling in Portland in the early 1910s. Buchanan's idea was to harness the votes of Protestant fraternal lodge members typically opposed to Catholics.[17] His creation, the Oregon Federation of Patriotic Societies, or FOPS, claimed to represent Masons, Orangemen, Knights of Pythias, Redmen, Odd Fellows, and other lodges. Each lodge would select two delegates, who would jointly select a slate of anti-Catholic political candidates for the self-described patriotic forces to endorse.[18]

Buchanan suffered a stroke and receded to the background, and Portland streetcar employee W. C. Elford arose to run FOPS from his position as secretary. He was a Portland labor leader and foreman in charge of washing streetcars. Elford also was an Orangeman, a militant fraternal society originating in the north of Ireland that had a long history of conflict with Catholics there. Orange lodges had supported mandatory public schooling since the 1890s.[19]

FOPS operations remained secretive, with Elford declining to publicly name other leaders or divulge when and where they held meetings.[20] "It should be understood that the Orange Lodge is the very backbone of the FOPS...since its inception," *Oregon Voter* wrote.[21] Historian Malcom Clark Jr., in a comprehensive study of anti-Catholic groups in Oregon, concurred that FOPS was largely tied to militant Orange lodges, and alleged that it was actually controlled by a self-appointed council of five men "speaking only for themselves."[22] A major reason FOPS remained so secretive, Clark wrote, was that the Orange lodges included immigrants, who retained strong ties to England, Scotland, and Northern Ireland, and were periodically replenished by newcomers from those lands.[23] "The FOPS was, in short, a carefully manufactured myth," Clark concluded.[24]

Two days before the 1922 primary, a *Capital Journal* reporter unearthed evidence to back up that assertion. Yellow tickets listing FOPS endorsements were distributed door to door in Salem, outside FOPS' primary political base of Multnomah County. Marion County representatives of the Scottish Rite Masons, Shriners, Knights of Pythias, and Odd Fellows told the newspaper they had no hand in devising the local endorsements, contradicting FOPS' claim to represent them. So the newspaper simply called the list of candidates the "Klan ticket."[25]

By mid-March, the *Catholic Sentinel* warned in an editorial that anti-Catholic forces were preparing a ballot initiative that would shut down all private schools in Oregon, calling it "the Ku Klux Klan proposal."[26] A week later, Gifford publicly endorsed compulsory public schooling in an interview with *Oregon Voter*. "By that, I mean that no child should be permitted to be educated in the primary grades at any private school," Gifford said. The Klan opposed denominational schools run by religious groups, he said, as well as "select" schools, which he called "snobbish."[27]

The Klan's growing political role and increasing talk of closing Catholic schools would dominate primary campaigns throughout the state. "The public school is one of the most fundamental factors in our system of government," Hall stated on the campaign trail. "I favor compulsory attendance in the primary grades."[28] Hall told a Medford reporter he was endorsed by the Federation of Patriotic Societies and wanted to gain the Klan's backing as well. "I hope the K.K.K. will support me," he said, "for I hear there are thousands of them, and such support will make my nomination certain."[29] With crucial support from both secretive groups, Hall turned a crowded Republican primary into a fierce two-man battle with Olcott. In heavily Republican Oregon, GOP primary winners typically waltzed to victory in November.

Governor Condemns Klan

Olcott had boasted just eight months earlier that the Klan wasn't making any headway in his state. Now he changed his tune. Six days before the May 19 election, in what the *Oregonian* billed as the first of its kind in the nation, the governor issued an official proclamation condemning the Klan.[30]

"Dangerous forces are insidiously gaining a foothold in Oregon," Olcott's proclamation began. "In the guise of a secret society, parading under the name of the Ku Klux Klan, these forces are endeavoring to usurp the reins of government, are stirring up fanaticism, race hatred, religious prejudice and all of those evil influences which tend toward factional strife and civil terror." The statement, issued just weeks after the Medford string of near-lynchings, took particular aim against nightriders and marauders' use of masks to disguise vigilante violence. "Danger lurks when masked men parade the streets on missions of a character known to none but themselves," the statement read. Olcott directed all law enforcement arms of state and local government, including police, sheriffs, and judges, to maintain order and enforce the laws, including a statute known as Section 2046 that barred the use of disguises to commit crimes.[31]

In response to the proclamation, Hall emphasized his support for mandatory public schooling. "I would rather be defeated on this platform than elected on any other," he declared.[32] Gifford, identifying himself as exalted cyclops of the Luther I. Powell Klan No. 1 in Portland, issued a stinging written rebuttal, dismissing Olcott's statement as a political stunt by a struggling candidate. "I have only to say that the Ku Klux Klan is a law-abiding organization, based on the maintenance of white supremacy and the Christian religion," Gifford stated. The Klan permitted the public use of masks and robes only for parades or ceremonies, he said, and bore no responsibility for any "outrage of any kind."[33]

Portland Mayor Baker responded to the proclamation by vowing to bar the use of masks in public demonstrations in the city. The *Oregonian*, which had remained curiously silent about the Klan, responded by issuing a questionnaire to five Republicans and four Democrats running for governor, challenging them to share their views on the Klan, as well as on Olcott's contentions and whether they sought the Klan's endorsement. Hall responded to the questionnaire saying he barely saw any Klan presence on the campaign trail.[34] That was clearly a lie, as became evident when Klan supporters, incensed by Olcott's condemnation of their secret order, flocked to Hall's candidacy. The anti-Klan vote, in contrast, was split among Olcott and other candidates from both parties.

The incumbent governor managed to squeak past Hall in the GOP primary. But Klan-backed candidates won twelve out of thirteen primaries for Multnomah County seats in the Oregon House of Representatives, positioning the Invisible Empire to take control of the chamber in the 1923 legislative session. Klan candidates Dow Walker and John J. Rankin also won seats on the Multnomah County Board of Commissioners.

The Klan prevailed in one statewide primary: O. P. Hoff's bid for state treasurer. But the Klan/FOPS slate didn't fare so well in Marion County and elsewhere outside of the Portland area. Nevertheless, the Invisible Empire emerged as Oregon's new political powerhouse, only eleven months after first surfacing publicly in Portland. "May 19 may pass into history as the Dawn of the Nightshirt Era in Oregon politics," *Oregon Voter* observed. "Endorsements by other organizations and semi-political associations seemed to have little or no effect."[35]

Sour Grapes from Hall

Despite a final tally showing Olcott won the GOP primary by 521 votes, Hall declared that *he'd* actually won by 4,123 votes.[36] Hall blamed Catholic priests for unlawfully swaying their parishioners' votes, especially in the heavily Catholic towns of Mt. Angel and St. Paul in Marion County. "Hall's opponents have stolen the nomination for a candidate whose every recent act has borne the indelible stamp of the Catholic Pope in Rome," the Salem Klan argued in a letter to members seeking donations to pay for a recount. The solicitation ended: "Read the contents of this letter, then BURN it."[37] The *Catholic Sentinel*, the Oregon Archdiocese's weekly Portland newspaper, scoffed at the accusation that the church told its flock how to vote, as it didn't even issue political endorsements. "It is a notorious fact that Catholics have never voted as a unified force," the newspaper lamented in an editorial.[38]

The Pendleton klavern pledged to put up two dollars per member for the recount after meeting with Hall, and Salem Klansmen said they expected to raise fifteen dollars per member.[39] With ample financial backing from the Klan, Hall filed for a recount. However, he sought an official recount only in specific areas won by his opponent, usually precincts with relatively large numbers of Catholic, Jewish, and Black voters. Olcott issued a three-page response on July 15, saying $50,000 pledged by the Klan should have enabled Hall to hire twenty investigators to pore through results of every precinct. "As a matter of equity, justice and right, if any recount is to be had, it should include all the precincts of the state properly counted and not merely a small portion of the precincts hand-picked."[40] Hall dropped his recount bid on August 10, after initial results confirmed Olcott's victory. Instead, Hall began plotting to run for governor as an independent, which would require him to legally challenge the Oregon law barring such candidacies for those who had lost partisan primaries.[41]

A month after the primary, the Scottish Rite ballot initiative requiring compulsory attendance at public schools qualified for the November ballot, assuring the issue would dominate fall campaigns.[42] Hall had been the chief politician backing compulsory public schooling, and FOPS and the Klan initially supported his run as an independent. Gifford indicated he backed Hall's effort but secretly pursued a Plan B.

Oregon was solidly Republican, and the Klan usually worked through the GOP in the Beaver State. But the 1920s Ku Klux Klan was opportunistic, not wedded to either political party. In the South it supported the dominant Democrats, longtime advocates of white supremacy. State Senator Walter Pierce, a La Grande Democrat well known as a progressive, had secured his party's 1922 nomination after losing a 1918 run for governor with only 42.8 percent of the vote. Given that loss and Democrats' dismal track record in statewide races, it might take a miracle for him to unseat an incumbent Republican in 1922. The Klan was that miracle.

Faustian Deal

After Hall lost the GOP primary, Gifford journeyed to Eastern Oregon to seek Pierce's public support for the compulsory public-school initiative. Pierce may have seemed an unlikely bedfellow for the Klan. The Umatilla County hay farmer and former schoolteacher had earned a

(*Left*) Republican Governor Ben Olcott survived a bruising May 1922 primary in his quest for a second term, after issuing a proclamation denouncing the Ku Klux Klan; (*right*) Liberal Democrat Walter Pierce struck a deal with Gifford to win Klan support in the fall 1922 governor's race. Pierce agreed to endorse the compulsory public-school initiative and reward the Klan with patronage appointments. (Oregon Historical Society)

progressive reputation in the legislature, supporting liberal causes such as public ownership of utilities and a graduated income tax to aid beleaguered farmers chafing under burdensome state property taxes. He cast the lone Senate vote against a 1919 syndicalism bill that aimed to cripple militant unions.[43]

Yet on some matters Pierce and the Klan saw eye to eye. While teaching school in the Northeastern Oregon town of Milton, Pierce was dismayed to see his students drawn to the town's three saloons and pool halls instead of their studies. So the twenty-two-year-old teetotaler led a successful 1883 drive to persuade the county to deny liquor licenses to saloonkeepers. That turned Milton into a "dry" town, spawning the creation of a new "wet" town next door named Freewater, where alcohol ran freely.[44]

Pierce also was a strong nativist, supporting the rights of native-born Americans over immigrants, and he was disdainful of Blacks, voting against a measure urging Congress to ensure Blacks had the right to vote. "In modern terms, Pierce was a racist and remained so throughout his life," wrote his friend and biographer Arthur Bone.[45] In his 1918 run for governor, Pierce recorded a statement that foreshadowed his position on the dominant issue of his second run. "If elected governor, should the question arise as to whether I would support the public schools of this state or the Catholic Church, I will die fighting for the public schools."[46]

Nevertheless, Pierce initially balked at endorsing the 1922 ballot measure, for fear it would hurt his prospects in the governor's race.[47] Gifford used the threat of Hall's independent run for governor to nudge Pierce into the Klan's camp, according to Harry Crain, now reporting full time on the Klan for the *Capital Journal*.[48] On his trip to La Grande, Gifford swung a private deal with Pierce, promising Klan support in the governor's race in exchange for Pierce backing the school initiative. The Klan leader initially failed to disclose the deal even to his allies. "He did not inform the Klansmen at first that Pierce was friendly to the Klan or that in return for its support he was willing to play the Klan game right down the line," wrote former Klansman Ben Titus on the eve of the general election.[49]

The second Klan often bashed New York's Tammany Hall and other city political machines controlled by Democrats and tilted toward Catholics. Now Gifford was operating like the corrupt machine bosses the Klan often trashed. He created two front groups—the Good Government League and the Progressive Party—to advance Klan positions and give himself more clout.[50]

Gifford's political maneuvering appeared to do the trick. On September 10, Hall formally announced his expected independent bid for governor. Only two days later, Pierce came around, announcing he too would support the mandatory public-school initiative.[51] Pierce's statement of support was released to the press by none other than the Portland Klan exalted cyclops, Gifford. "I am a Protestant, the ninth generation in America," the press release quoted Pierce as saying. "I am in favor of and shall vote for the compulsory school bill sponsored by the Scottish Rite Masonic bodies of Oregon. I believe we would have a better generation of Americans, free from snobbery and bigotry, if all children up to and including the eighth grade were educated in the free public schools of America."[52] In his Faustian deal with the Klan, Pierce also promised Gifford a share of patronage jobs in state government, perhaps as many as 50 percent of all positions.[53] For its part of the deal, the Klan would press Hall to withdraw from the race. Four days after Pierce publicly supported the school initiative, Republican Senator Hall announced he'd withdraw and endorse the Democrat Pierce in the governor's race.[54]

Gifford and Pierce Prevail

FOPS initially balked at ditching Hall for Pierce because Elford distrusted the Democrat's commitment to the crusade against private schools. That suspicion proved correct. On the campaign trail, the veteran politician soft-pedaled the issue and made tax reform his central campaign plank. Oregon farmers had complained for years that state property taxes imperiled their livelihoods. Pierce, now working as a rancher, complained that owners of farmland, cattle, and hogs paid steep property taxes on those holdings while owners of stocks and bonds escaped state taxes, and that big utilities and timber companies were skirting their fair share. Pierce was a strong advocate for creating a graduated income tax, to broaden the pool of taxpayers and ease the burden on farmers.

When Pierce's brother Charles visited Pendleton, he told Protestant ministers that his brother was forced by political pressure to endorse the compulsory public-school initiative, and was really against it.[55] State GOP Chairman Walter L. Tooze Jr. accused Pierce of double-crossing initiative supporters by endorsing their measure until Hall dropped out of the race, and then avoiding the issue on the campaign trail "as a hot political potato."[56] But the Klan and its endorsed candidates kept the school initiative front and center in the campaign, even if Pierce largely stayed mum on the matter. "Between top and bottom is a complete ticket of Ku Kluxed candidates for every office," the *Capital Journal* reported.[57]

Olcott campaigned squarely against the Klan, though he also avoided talking much about the school initiative. Pierce made a strategic visit to a Portland Klan meeting, where he privately assured Klansmen of his support for the school initiative and also vowed to dump critics of the Klan from state posts.[58] "There can be little doubt that Pierce played 'footsy' with Klan leaders," Bone wrote later.[59]

Supporters of the mandatory public schooling initiative spread false rumors on the campaign trail that Olcott and his wife were closet Catholics and had sent their three children to a convent-run school in Salem. "I believe that two-thirds of the people of Oregon, despite all we could do to offset the malicious lies told by the Klan, believed that I was a Catholic," Olcott told fellow governors after the election.[60] Actually, it was Gifford's family that had ties to the Catholic Church and its schools, as revealed by news reports published in the final days of the campaign. Gifford's wife had been baptized a Catholic in St. Paul, and the couple sent daughters Marcella and Mary to St. Mary's Academy, Portland's well-regarded Catholic girls' school, from 1914 to 1916. Their son Fred Jr. was enrolled during the campaign at Hill Military Academy in Portland. Both schools would have been forced to close by the Klan-supported initiative.[61] Father John R. Laidlaw, a Portlander who later authored a history of the Catholic Church in Oregon, wrote confidently that the wife of the Klan's "exalted cyclops" was Catholic, referring to Gifford's wife without mentioning either by name. Laidlaw was in a position to know, because the priest had delivered last rites to Gifford's mother-in-law. Gifford had arranged for the funeral and was present during the last rites.[62]

Gifford took another body blow late in the fall 1922 campaign when Elford publicly accused him of sending out fake yellow tickets that were replicas of those used by FOPS. The yellow tickets listed endorsements of the Good Government League and the Progressive Party, which Elford accurately called "political aliases" of the Ku Klux Klan. "Why doesn't Grand Dragon Gifford sign indorsements in the name of the Klan instead of hiding behind other titles?" Elford asked publicly.[63] The only differences between FOPS and Klan endorsements were two candidates for the Portland City Commission. The FOPS-endorsed candidates placed first and third in those races, while both Klan-endorsed candidates lost, finishing fourth and eighth.[64]

Nevertheless, Gifford and the Klan scored huge wins in the general election, emerging relatively unscathed from the late-breaking controversies. The Klan's biggest plum was passage of the initiative barring private schools, which garnered nearly 53 percent of the vote. Pierce swept into office with 57 percent of the vote, the largest majority in an Oregon governor's race since 1858. He became Oregon's second governor from east of the Cascade Mountains, the first since Zenas Moody in 1882. While Pierce's win coincided with a national swing to Democrats in 1922 elections, other Republican candidates, particularly those blessed by the Klan, won strong majorities in both chambers of the Oregon Legislature.

Republican Charles M. Thomas, a Medford state senator supported by the Klan, won a circuit court judgeship with 70 percent of the vote.[65]

That would give Thomas jurisdiction over the Southern Oregon Outrage trials of Klansmen in Jackson County. In another upset, Democrat Elton Watkins toppled incumbent Republican Clifton McArthur in the Congressional district representing Portland, becoming the first Democrat elected to Oregon's US House of Representatives delegation in more than four decades. McArthur had been outspoken against the Klan. Watkins, a former FBI agent who had made a name as a union-busting attorney,[66] had endorsed the Klan school initiative. He went on to become a leading Congressional champion of immigration restrictions.[67] Klan-supported candidates also won statewide races for state treasurer and the Oregon Supreme Court.[68]

"Influence of the anti-Catholic vote was tremendous, especially in Portland," *Oregon Voter* concluded in its assessment of the 1922 election results. "In fact, the religious issue was the main issue of the election, and the anti-Catholic organizations carried pretty much every office in spite of bickerings and differences among themselves."[69] Klan leaders took credit for passage of the school initiative and Pierce's victory, among other wins. *Oregon Voter* cited other factors, such as farmer discontent over high taxes, but left no doubt about the Klan's new role as kingmaker. "The lesser or less-known candidates all owe their election to the KKK or the other anti-Catholic organizations, and they know it." The Klan did fall short trying to unseat the state's lone Catholic Congressman, Nicholas Sinnott, a Republican who retained his District 2 seat in Eastern Oregon.[70]

Pierce, dancing around his anti-Catholic stances, would later credit his win over Olcott to the "religious situation" that arose in Oregon.[71] Pierce's wife, Cornelia Marvin Pierce, was more explicit: "The proposed Oregon School Bill was the most bitterly contested issue and the deciding factor in the 1922 election."[72]

Another likely factor in the Klan's dramatic victories was a series of worker strikes. Oregon had recovered from the brutal post-war recession, and workers were better positioned to flex their muscles after suffering eroded wages due to the war. Portland longshore workers struck in May 1922, followed by railroad workers in the summer. In October, nearly one thousand striking members of the longshore union and its smaller rival, the Marine Transport Industrial Union, shut down Portland's waterfront, demanding the right to have a union-controlled hiring hall and higher wages.[73] The Marine Transport union had been organized by the militant Industrial Workers of the World, known as the Wobblies. Mayor Baker fomented public hysteria by claiming the Wobblies wanted to "take control of Portland" and that twenty-five thousand armed Wobblies were descending on the city to support the striking workers. Baker ordered police to raid union picket lines and arrest every known Wobbly in the city. Police hauled more than five hundred picketers off to jail.[74] No incident of Wobbly violence was ever reported, and the threatened invasion never occurred. But the hysteria fostered by the Klan-aligned mayor likely helped swing votes to the Klan, which claimed to support law and order.

Two weeks after the Klan triumphed in the November 1922 general election, the La Grande klavern welcomed a special guest: hometown hero and governor-elect Pierce. Pierce had bought a home in La Grande in 1907, and he and his wife spent summers on their ranch in Island City, two miles out of town.[75] Klansmen welcomed Pierce as an "honorary member" at their November 21, 1922, meeting, according to notes recorded by chapter secretary Harold Fosner.[76] Fosner's minutes also referred to their guest as "Klansman Walter Pierce, governor-elect of La Grande, Oregon," saying he was elected "by our combined efforts." The minutes summed up the visit, stating: "Let us bid Klansman Pierce God's speed in his new undertakings; to come and continue to support him as we have done in the past." After taking office, Pierce made a second, dramatic appearance before the La Grande klavern on June 5, 1923. "Just as the kligrapp had finished reading a letter from our Gov. that it would be impossible for him to attend our meeting, the door opened and in he walked," the minutes reflected. "That was the hour of great rejoicing."[77] Despite those references, there's no documentation proving Pierce was ever inducted as a Klansman, and he denied ever joining the order.

After his defeat, Olcott warned peers about the Klan at a national governors' conference in White Sulphur Springs, West Virginia. "Everywhere this movement goes, you will find strife," Olcott said. "This movement is founded on bitterness and hate." He was confident the anti-Catholic schools initiative would be declared unconstitutional, but he feared it would leave a long-lasting stain upon Oregon. "It has caused hatreds which may not be ironed out during this generation." If the Klan was allowed to fester, Olcott said, it could lead to another civil war.[78]

Gifford was sitting pretty after prevailing in what came to be known as the "Klan election" of November 1922. The Portland exalted cyclops was already the dominant Klansman in Oregon, but his position became official that month when he was officially named grand dragon of the state Klan.

Despite Gifford's rise to near-absolute power within the state Klan, there were ample signs of dissension in the ranks. Defecting Klansman Titus's four-part newspaper series in the final week of the general election had exposed Gifford's ruthless tactics, corrupt practices, and personal hypocrisy.[79] Leaders of smaller klaverns were raising serious questions about his leadership. Just days after the Klan helped elect a governor and passed a sweeping ballot initiative, Portland Klan leaders Reuben Sawyer and Rush Davis wrote a letter to second-Klan founder William Simmons, complaining that Gifford had lost the support of many Oregon klaverns and Klansmen. More than two-thirds of the men in the dominant Portland Klan were "dissatisfied and disgusted with the manner in which he has misinterpreted the sacred principles of Klannishness," the two Klansmen wrote. Gifford is "entangled in Catholicism," they wrote, likely a reference to revelations about his wife and daughters. They concluded that Gifford was "totally unfit for even membership in the KKK."[80]

Gifford in League with Big Utilities

One of the curious subplots of the Ku Klux Klan's meteoric rise to power in Portland was klavern leaders' links to the city's powerful private utilities. When Gifford was first named exalted cyclops of the Portland Klan chapter back in August 1921, he brought in Charles Hurd and W. D. "Ole" Quinn as his top aides. The threesome all worked for local telephone and electric utilities and were members of the Electrical Workers Union No. 25 during a bitter 1919 strike by its telephone operators and linemen. Hurd was then local president, and Gifford was the former president and business agent.[81] During the strike, Hurd was dispatched to San Francisco to represent workers in labor negotiations with out-of-state management. After returning to town, he mysteriously changed his tune, urging workers to retract their demands and settle without any pay raises. Union members were outraged and slapped a $1,000 fine on Hurd, deriding him as the "thousand-dollar scab."[82] Hurd, Gifford, and Quinn were booted out of the union for taking management's side in the strike.[83] Shortly after, Pacific States Telephone and Telegraph Co. promoted Hurd and Quinn to superintendent positions, while Northwestern Electric elevated Gifford to foreman of overhead construction.[84] After Gifford became exalted cyclops, he moved Klan headquarters into the Pittock Block in downtown Portland, the same office building where Northwestern Electric was based. He brought in Hurd and Quinn as his right-hand men, later dubbed his fixers or henchmen by dissident Klansmen. Gifford lacked the funds to pay Quinn and Hurd for their considerable KKK duties, but "they did not suffer as a result," wrote historian Malcolm Clark Jr. "Their employer continued them on its payroll, just as the Northwestern Electric Co. was to continue Gifford on its payroll long after he began to devote the whole of his time to Klan affairs."[85]

Throughout their Klan tenure, the threesome were dogged by criticism that they continued tending to utilities' corporate interests. In that era, political battles raged in Portland over transit fares and utility rates, as well as over public power—whether utilities, then known as public service corporations, should remain in private hands or convert to municipal or nonprofit utilities, as formed in Eugene, Tacoma, and other Northwest communities. Oregon Klan propagandist Lem Dever once bashed supporters of public power as delusional and "Communist minded."[86] But later, in his 1924 tell-all memoir, he confessed that Klan leaders had been in bed with the private utilities: "The ruling powers of the Klan, from the start until now, represented the public service corporations."[87] Gifford's thirteen-man kitchen cabinet for the 1924 election cycle included representatives from the electric and telephone companies and other utilities.[88] Private utility executives reportedly encouraged their employees to join the Klan because it opposed government ownership of utilities.[89] The utilities wanted to get the threat of publicly owned power off the table, observed historian Jeff LaLande.[90] Hall, the telephone company president initially backed by the Klan for governor, had been keenly interested in a planned November 1922 ballot initiative aimed at giving the governor power to appoint public utility commissioners who set utility rates.[91]

Pierce, ironically, was no friend of private utilities, as he actively supported the public power movement and higher property-tax assessments for utilities.[92] However, utilities had many reasons to maintain good ties with Pierce and seek influence in his administration. Utilities "flirting" with the Klan did so as a matter of "self-defense," a prominent political source told Pierce's biographer.[93]

One of the Oregon Klan's favorite punching bags was George L. Cleaver, ostensibly because the state Prohibition director wasn't aggressive enough in going after bootleggers and others flouting anti-alcohol laws. "The real reason was probably Cleaver's unacceptability to the public utilities," wrote Bone, the Pierce biographer who had access to his private papers. Cleaver had been secretary of the Hydro-Electric League of Oregon and had lobbied for a publicly owned hydro project in the Deschutes River canyon.[94]

Gifford's pro-utility stances figured prominently when the split deepened between the Klan and FOPS in 1923. Elford publicly accused Gifford of being more interested in promoting big utilities' interests than those of the Klan's supposed allies in FOPS.[95] In May 1924, voters recalled Klansmen John Rankin and Dow Walker from their posts as Multnomah County commissioners. Voters were dismayed by their support for higher utility rates, among other charges.[96]

6
Crusading Against Catholics

> *"The sole idea of the compulsory school bill is to strike at the Catholics and close their parochial schools and to serve as a rallying point for fanatics."*
>
> —*Capital Journal*[1]

> *"The Klan assault upon the foreigner is the acme of stupidity. We are all foreigners except the few Indians we have not killed."*
>
> —Thomas Dixon Jr., author of *The Clansman*[2]

Anti-Catholicism and the Oregon KKK

The Scottish Rite lodge, a prestigious wing of the mainstream Masonic order, selected Oregon as a test case to advance its goal of shutting down Catholic and other private schools. The Klan piggybacked on its effort, conducting much of the legwork in the ensuing ballot measure campaign. The ballot initiative campaign led to an upsurge of attacks on Catholic candidates and people of Catholic faith, featuring boycotts, wild conspiracy theories, and harassment. In one sign of the Klan's success in poisoning public opinion, a Medford war hero who dared to attack the Klan lost a judicial race to a former lawmaker who shielded Klansmen on trial for three abductions and near-lynchings.

November 29, 1847: Cayuse tribal members kill Protestant missionaries Marcus and Narcissa Whitman and eleven others at Walla Walla mission. Protestant clerics allege Catholic missionaries provoked the murders.

May 19, 1855: *Oregon Statesman* publishes exposé of fast-growing Know Nothing party in Oregon, crippling the nativist anti-immigrant group.

September 1893: American Protective Association leader William J. H. Traynor visits Portland on Western swing, launching the secretive anti-Catholic society in Oregon.

May 1920: Southern Jurisdiction of Scottish Rite Masons passes resolution supporting compulsory public schooling.

June 17, 1920: Grand Lodge of Oregon Masons endorses Scottish Rite resolution.

1921: Congress passes Emergency Quota Act to stem growing immigration from Southern and Eastern Europe.

January: Oregon Legislature debates three anti-Catholic bills.

June 15: Anti-Catholic forces win four seats on Portland School Board.

March 16, 1922: *Catholic Sentinel* reports ballot measure being prepared to ban Catholic and other private schools in Oregon.

June: Scottish Rite Masons file petitions to qualify state initiative banning private schools.

November 7: Compulsory public schooling initiative passes. Democrat Walter Pierce, who endorsed the measure, defeats incumbent Republican Ben Olcott in governor's race.

March 30, 1924: Federal district court rules compulsory public schooling initiative unconstitutional.

May: President Coolidge signs Immigration Act of 1924, establishing strict quotas for each country, sharply restricting Catholic and Jewish immigration.

June 1, 1925: US Supreme Court unanimously rules compulsory public schooling initiative is unconstitutional, tossing law before it takes effect.

Oregon's Activist Priest

Prominent socialist Tom Burns was whipping up a crowd from a soapbox on Seventh Avenue and Washington Street in downtown Portland, arguing that religion was the "enemy of the working man." It was Thanksgiving evening, 1912. "If all I say ain't true," Burns thundered, "why don't some parson get up here and answer me? I'll let him have a say."[3] Up stepped Edwin V. O'Hara, a young Catholic priest at Portland's Pro-Cathedral of the Immaculate Conception. "I will answer your questions," said the red-headed son of Irish immigrants. O'Hara remained

Father Edwin V. O'Hara helped shape a distinctly American brand of Catholicism in Oregon and led a campaign to secure a state minimum wage. O'Hara tangled with the Klan while serving Catholic students at the University of Oregon and overseeing Oregon Catholic schools. (Courtesy of Archdiocese of Portland in Oregon)

atop the soapbox for twenty minutes, highlighting his fight to improve workplace conditions and establish a minimum wage in Oregon. Keenly aware of the anti-Catholic views held by many Portland Protestants, O'Hara accused Burns of being both anti-church and anti-government. In contrast, he said, "Our church, the Catholic Church, believes in obedience to one's country, and the officials that are in power, even if we think them mistaken."

It's hard to imagine someone better-suited to counter anti-Catholic sentiments and Protestant charges that Catholics owed allegiance to the pope instead of Uncle Sam. O'Hara supported the "Americanizers" who sought to establish a distinctly American strand of Catholicism and preached that Rome had nothing to fear from democracy and separation between church and state.[4] He supported the Protestant-dominated temperance movement and counseled his flock to steer clear of taverns.[5] And O'Hara, a transplanted Minnesotan, brought a passion for social justice to daily work in his new home state. "A living wage shall...take precedence over profits and dividends," O'Hara said in an address to the Oregon Consumer's League.[6] He spearheaded the fight to establish a minimum wage in Oregon for women and minors, authoring a minimum-wage law that was legally challenged and then upheld by the US Supreme Court, becoming a model for twelve other states. Agitating against poor sanitation and "greedy landlords," he helped persuade the City of Portland to adopt a new housing code and inspection system.[7]

O'Hara would go on to write about Catholic contributions to Oregon, beginning with white settler John McLoughlin—dubbed the "father of Oregon"—and dispel the myth that Catholics were responsible for the murder of Protestant missionaries Marcus and Narcissa Whitman at their mission in Walla Walla.

Inevitably, when he became superintendent of Catholic schools in Western Oregon, O'Hara butted heads with the powerful Ku Klux Klan. Though he often worked behind the scenes, his work proved pivotal. On March 27, 1922, shortly after news broke of a planned ballot initiative to shut down Oregon's private schools, O'Hara wrote the National Catholic Welfare Council, asking for expert legal opinions on whether the initiative would pass constitutional muster.[8] Archbishop Alexander Christie, Oregon's leading Catholic churchman, later asked O'Hara for advice about how to fight the initiative. O'Hara counseled that arguing the measure was bigoted would be futile, given popular opinion against Catholics. Instead, he argued it should be portrayed as a violation of personal liberties. "The rights of parents to educate their own children and to choose the instructions for their own offspring is the most sacred of human rights," O'Hara said in a July 4, 1922, speech to Catholic educators.[9] "The exercise by the state of its police power to drag children from the homes of parents who are capable of and willing to perform their full duty in the education of their children would be an indelible stain on the fair name of a free country." That argument set the tone for the Catholic counterattack against the Klan, and eventually prevailed in the courts.

Centuries-Old Animosities

Bitterness between Protestants and Catholics arrived on American shores when Protestant England vied with Catholic Spain and France to colonize North America. In the British colonies, Protestants had the upper hand. "Throughout much of the colonial period, Catholics were harassed, discriminated against, denied the right to own or bear arms," wrote Oregon historian Malcom Clark Jr.[10] Puritans who formed the Massachusetts Bay Colony believed the pope was the Antichrist and those who followed him were in league with the devil.[11] Only thirty thousand Catholics lived in the thirteen British colonies, a little more than 1 percent of the population, when the War of Independence broke out in 1776.

George Washington, while leading rebel troops in the war, banned colonists' November 5 celebrations of Guy Fawkes Day, to help persuade Catholic France to support the revolt against the British. Fawkes was part of a failed Catholic plot to blow up the House of Parliament in London, and colonists often burned the pope in effigy that day.[12] When the US Constitution was drafted in 1787, Catholics had the right to vote in only three of the thirteen new states: Pennsylvania, Maryland, and Delaware.[13]

Rome did not help their cause. In 1832, Pope Gregory XVI's encyclical rejected the notion of separating church from state, making life more difficult for American Catholics. The Catholic Church's longstanding hostility to the Masonic lodge movement, which mostly attracted Protestants, further fueled tensions. Catholics also supported a ban on teaching the Bible in American public schools, because it likely would mean using the Protestants' King James version, not the Douay-Rheims Bible used by Catholics in that era.[14]

Newer waves of European immigrants brought longstanding hatreds with them, such as those between Irish Catholics and Scotch-Irish Protestants.[15] Surges of newcomers often led to heightened hostility to the foreign-born. The nativist American Party grew swiftly in the 1850s, after a wave of Catholic immigrants from Ireland and Germany. The watchword of its Protestant leaders was "America for Americans."[16] Members took secret oaths and adopted elaborate rituals and passwords. Critics derided them as Know Nothings because they were sworn to answer, "I don't know" if asked about their political organization. "When the Know Nothings get control," up-and-coming Illinois politician Abraham Lincoln warned in the 1850s, it will mean "all men are created equal except Negroes and foreigners and Catholics."[17]

Catholic immigration grew steadily in the latter half of the nineteenth century, enabling working-class Irishmen to gain political footholds in New York, Boston, and other cities. In 1887, Iowa lawyer Henry Francis Bowers formed the American Protective Association, another secretive anti-Catholic society whose members were bound by oaths. Bowers argued that the Catholic church was more of a political movement than a religious one, and that it had captured control of the federal government.[18] The American Protective Association, known as the APA, opposed Catholic political candidates and spread wild conspiracy

A dozen Sisters of the Holy Names of Jesus and Mary pose in 1863 at Portland's St. Mary's Academy, Oregon's oldest continuously operated high school. The nuns arrived from Canada four years earlier to establish Catholic schools in Oregon. (Archives of the Sisters of the Holy Names of Jesus and Mary, US-Ontario Province)

theories about Catholics stockpiling weapons in church basements. It promoted "Americanism" and non-sectarian public schools, mushrooming into a mass movement of more than two million supporters at its peak in the 1890s. The APA evoked comparisons to the Know Nothings, though it welcomed immigrants if they were Protestant.

Ensuing waves of immigrants, many of them Catholics and Jews, fueled another nativist upsurge in the 1920s, spearheaded by the second Ku Klux Klan. Newer immigrants from Southern and Eastern Europe often spoke in Yiddish, Italian, or other foreign tongues. They lived in ethnic enclaves, making them more isolated or distant from mainstream Americans. By 1920, one out of six Americans was Catholic, up from one out of twenty in 1850.[19] Imperial Wizard Hiram Evans told fellow Klansmen at a 1923 gathering that the bulk of new immigrants were from the "lowest strata" of Poland, Italy, and other Catholic nations. "The policy of the Klan is to stop the storm of undesirables and thus prevent the glutting of the labor market and the Romanizing and mongrelizing of the citizenship of the United States."[20] In interviews that historian John Mecklin conducted for his 1924 book on the second Klan, he found anti-Catholicism was the most compelling reason why people joined the Invisible Empire.[21] Those sentiments were strongest, he concluded, in Oregon, Georgia, and Texas, where Protestantism reigned supreme and the share of Catholics was lower.[22]

Anti-Catholicism Reaches Oregon Territory

Tensions between Protestants and Catholics arose in Oregon Territory in the 1830s, when dueling missionaries competed to educate children of white settlers and proselytize among indigenous tribes.[23] A full rupture occurred after 1847, when physician and Presbyterian missionary Marcus Whitman was murdered, along with his wife Narcissa and eleven others at their mission near present-day Walla Walla, Washington. Whitman was providing medical care to Cayuse tribal members, and some blamed him when a measles outbreak devastated the tribe while leaving white missionaries largely unscathed. Protestant evangelists Henry Harmon Spalding and John Smith Griffin later accused Catholics of inciting the Cayuse to commit the massacre in a bid to rid Oregon Territory of Protestants. "The Indians had declared that the Protestants be murdered but the Catholics spared," Spalding wrote.[24] There was no evidence for the allegation, but Spalding and Griffin's writings gained wide currency among Protestants.

US attorney Amory Holbrook, who prosecuted the Whitmans' alleged murderers, later introduced the upstart American Party (aka Know Nothings) to Oregon Territory in 1854. Holbrook organized its first chapter, known as a wigwam, in Oregon City.[25] The nativist party grew swiftly, attacking immigrants and the ethnically diverse, British-owned Hudson's Bay Company, which dominated Northwest fur-trading.[26] Asahel Bush, the influential *Oregon Statesman* editor in Salem and Democratic Party leader, felt threatened by the rapid rise of the secretive American Party. A Bush confidante infiltrated the Salem wigwam, sharing his findings with the newspaper. Bush, seeking to thwart the secretive group, published the names of its leading members and details of its secret rituals. "They are wolves in sheep's clothing," Bush wrote. "There is not a man of prominence or influence belonging to the damning conspiracy in Oregon whose connection with it will not be known in less than six months."[27] His newspaper reported there were twenty-eight wigwams operating in Oregon, with a membership of 1,218. The disclosures helped nip the fast-growing nativist movement in the bud before it made major political inroads.

Public schools were a perennial battleground between Catholics and Protestants. Though courts barred religious teaching in schools, some Catholics, beginning in the 1870s, began urging public funding of parochial schools, providing more fuel for Protestants' anti-Catholic attacks.[28]

The next outbreak of anti-Catholicism in Oregon began in September 1893, when newspaper publisher William J. H. Traynor, the second president of the American Protective Association, is believed to have journeyed to Portland on a Western swing to organize chapters of the anti-Catholic group.[29] Five months later, the *Portland Telegram* published a detailed account of an APA meeting in Portland, describing its rituals and the robes and turbans worn by members.[30] Major H. G. Mathies, the APA state secretary, claimed there were 3,100 members in Oregon. Salem members spread sensational charges that Catholics stored guns and ammunition in churches and trained paramilitary troops in the dead of night.[31] The Oregon APA, which was strongest in the Portland area, elected members to school boards in Portland, Roseburg, and other Willamette Valley towns. In 1894 legislative elections, the APA elected a handful of its members to the Oregon House of Representatives and one to the State Senate. The APA's lone achievement in the 1895 legislative session was a bill preventing the flying of foreign flags over public buildings. That was aimed at Irish Catholics who displayed Ireland's flag on St. Patrick's Day. The APA accomplished relatively little in Oregon before collapsing in 1897, though it provided a template for anti-Catholic agitation that the Ku Klux Klan copied a generation later.[32]

Oregon's "Escaped Nuns"

Anti-Catholic groups of the nineteenth century often spread titillating tales of nuns held against their will in convents, where they were kept as priests' sex slaves until managing to escape. The best-known "escaped nun," Maria Monk, showed up in New York City in 1836, claiming she had fled a Montreal convent after being impregnated by a priest. Monk authored a book sharing lurid tales of nuns sexually abused by priests. Her book was widely read and cited, even after journalists and scholars debunked her story as a hoax. It turned out Monk actually had lived in an asylum, not a convent.[33]

Oregonians got their first exposure to an "escaped nun" when Edith O'Gorman lectured there in 1872, charging fifty cents for admission.[34] Three decades later, Oregon got its first homegrown "escaped nun." On the evening of June 26, 1913, Mary Lasenan showed up at the Christian Church in the Marion County community of Silverton, wearing a nun's habit and asking to speak to minister Leon Myers. Lasenan said she'd just escaped from a drunken orgy of priests at Mt. Angel, five miles away, and begged to take refuge at the church. "About six months ago, having previously escaped from a convent in the East, I was kidnapped while walking home, on the streets of Portland, and taken as a prisoner and confined in the convent of Mt. Angel, Oregon," Lasenan reportedly told Reverend Myers.[35] Mt. Angel, now known for its annual Oktoberfest celebration, was settled by Swiss Benedictine monks in 1881, when they established a monastery and school known as Mt. Angel Abbey. Reverend Myers and three of his congregants signed a notarized statement attesting to Lasenan's comments. The notary public who signed the statement was John E. Hosmer, who also was publisher and editor of the *Silverton Journal,* which printed the statement in full.

Lasenan implied that while serving as a nun, going by the name Sister Mary Louise, she'd been subjected to unmentionable sexual abuse: "After I took the black veil they told me plainly that I was to be to the priests what the concubines were to Solomon and David and other men of old Bible times." Lasenan told Reverend Myers she feared being murdered if captured after escaping from Mt. Angel. "I have known several nuns to be murdered in this way, but I would rather die than submit myself any more to their licentious treatment." She also claimed she'd been poisoned, and that her family's home back East had been burned down by Catholics because of her defection. One of Myers's congregants asked Lasenan what happened to the children born to nuns raped by priests. "Many of them are murdered at birth, while many others are sent to the Catholics' orphan homes and there trained up to become nuns and priests."[36] Lasenan also volunteered that half the students taught at Catholic schools were Protestants, and that "she knew positively that the Roman Catholics had as their aim to secure the control of the United States government."

Reverend Myers was a leading recruiter in Oregon for the Guardians of Liberty, a secret anti-Catholic order formed after the demise of the APA.[37] Newspaper editor Hosmer was a strong Prohibition supporter and critical of Catholics' allegedly lax attitudes toward alcohol.[38] He also was a founder of Liberty University in Silverton, and opposed a bid by Catholic Archbishop Christie to buy the facility for use as a hospital.[39] Shortly after featuring Lasenan's account in his weekly newspaper, Hosmer published a twenty-page pamphlet detailing her story, along with a laundry list of other alleged Catholic atrocities, which he sold for ten cents.[40] Reverend Myers wrote the introduction.

It later emerged that Reverend Myers had planted Lasenan at the Mt. Angel convent in order to dig up scandalous material. She'd remained there for only one day and then was reported missing, according to convent officials.[41] Catholics in Mt. Angel, at Archbishop Christie's urging, sued Hosmer for libel, seeking $50,000 in damages. The state of Oregon then pursued criminal libel charges against Hosmer. When the criminal case came to trial, an all-Protestant jury found Hosmer guilty after Lasenan failed to show up to testify. A Tacoma lawyer hired to prove Lasenan's contentions came up empty-handed, concluding she was not the person she claimed to be.[42]

Hosmer, known around Silverton as an atheist, recanted his story thirty-three years later. On his deathbed at Silverton Hospital in 1946, Hosmer apologized for "all the things that I said which were in any way derogatory to the Roman Catholic Church." He said he was misinformed about the material he wrote in his pamphlet, and wished to state he now believed in God, asking forgiveness "for all the sins I committed against Him."[43]

The libel verdict quashed the use of Sister Mary Louise's fake story, but anti-Catholic forces in Oregon later seized on the case of a real nun, Sister Lucretia, who did leave the church after three decades of service. Elizabeth Schoffen, the disgruntled former nun, became a star lecturer for the Oregon Ku Klux Klan, drawing big crowds of people across the state, curious to hear her scandalous claims about Catholics. "The ex-nun technique was as old as the hills but it never failed to achieve its purpose," observed Father Wilfred P. Schoenberg, a Gonzaga University professor in Spokane who wrote widely about Northwest Catholic history. "Sister Lucretia had it all, the experience, the nun's habit, the poise, especially the bitterness."[44] To help recruit new members and promote the La Grande Klan, the klavern arranged to bring Sister Lucretia to town as a paid speaker in October 1922. The chapter secretary was pleased to report that her "firey talk" at the Star Theatre "did much to build up our membership."[45]

That same month, dressed in a nun's habit and presenting herself as an escaped nun, the former Sister Lucretia regaled a capacity crowd at Portland's James John High School during the heat of the Klan-led campaign to ban Catholic schools. In a two-hour lecture, she accused the Catholic Church of being un-American, teaching nuns to hate Protestants and maintain loyalty to the pope instead of the US government. Children in Catholic-run orphanages are subjected to cruelty, she said, blasting the care given by nuns at the Catholic-run St. Vincent's Hospital in Portland. Schoffen implied she had been raped by priests but was infertile. "I have been asked if I have borne children," Schoffen told the audience. "I have not, but that is not the fault of the priests."[46]

Catholics mobilized to counter Schoffen's sensational claims against St. Vincent's. Fifty-eight Portland doctors signed a statement denouncing her "malicious" allegations against the hospital and defended the good work of nuns there. "Our daily contact for years with the Sisters and their Hospital has thoroughly familiarized us with their lofty standards of personal morals, and their unimpeachable character and efficiency."[47] The signatures were vouched for by John P. O'Hara, editor of *The Catholic Sentinel* and brother of Edwin O'Hara, the activist priest then working in Eugene. When Schoffen lectured in Gresham on October 8, 1922, Portland haberdasher Michael P. Brennan stood outside, passing out circulars listing more than fifty non-Catholic doctors who disputed her claims against St. Vincent's Hospital. A mob formed, kicking Brennan and beating him unconscious.[48]

Schoffen's own words, penned in her 1917 book *The Demands of Rome,* reveal a rebellious nun who sometimes chafed at strict convent rules and her lack of freedom, but also contradict some of her outlandish claims. Born in 1861 into a large Catholic family, she joined the Sisters of Charity of Providence of her own volition at age twenty.[49] Early on, she was unhappy and complained that her letters home were censored to hide that fact from her parents. She didn't know where to go, she wrote, because her parents wouldn't welcome her back.[50]

Schoffen wrote of one priest who kissed her and tried to ply her with alcohol, though she was able to resist his advances. But readers seeking sensational stories about priests' sexual abuse had to look elsewhere, based on her experiences. "I have no tale of immorality to tell," she wrote.[51]

Sister Lucretia moved up the employment ladder at St. Vincent's, from doing the laundry to cooking to patient care, ultimately managing an entire hospital floor. After eighteen years there, she wrote, "I loved the work and had made hundreds of friends from every part of Oregon, administering to them in sickness."[52] Yet Sister Lucretia complained a lot, and her role as a squeaky wheel appeared to precipitate her transfer to a new assignment in Cranbrook, British Columbia. Once there, she complained about the bitter cold and begged to return to St. Vincent's. In a bold letter to Archbishop Christie, she wrote: "I was too successful and well liked, and no means could be found to break my influence except by taking advantage of my sacred vow of obedience to get me out of the way."[53] Unable to secure a transfer back to St. Vincent's, Sister Lucretia left the Sisters of Charity of Providence after thirty-one years. Now fifty-one years old, she sought a severance payment of $2,000 to help her start anew in the outside world, at a time when nurses earned $25 a week. The order worried that might set a bad precedent for other departing nuns and indicated it might pay $1,000. Sister Lucretia dug in, hiring an attorney who sued the Catholic hospital for $28,000. The two parties reached a settlement, with Sister Lucretia getting $3,000 plus $1,500 for attorney fees.[54] Schoffen refused the order's demand to relinquish her nun's habit, in order to pose as a nun to get free rides on the train. The habit would also come in handy for her later public speaking gigs for the Klan.

Schoffen opened a nursing home, but that was a financial flop. She blamed Catholic doctors and others for failing to refer clients to her, further embittering her toward the church. She left the church, converted to Protestantism, and began sharply attacking Catholicism. At Gladstone's annual Chautauqua festival in 1915, Schoffen became acquainted with Protestant leaders of the Woman's Christian Temperance Union, and was convinced she could begin public speaking about her experiences. By 1916, she was earning a living as a lecturer, then released her memoir the following year, which she sold for fifty cents. Five years later, she became a star lecturer for the Ku Klux Klan.

Shunned Catholics Form Fraternal Lodge

In 1881, American men were flocking to fraternal lodges, many of them hostile to Catholics. So Father Michael J. McGivney decided to found the Knights of Columbus for Catholic men. It was a mutual support group, designed to help families of deceased members and "prevent Catholic men from entering secret societies antithetical to Church teaching," according to the order.[55]

In the Klan's telling, the Knights of Columbus was an armed militant group preparing to do battle with Protestants. "It is reported that all good K. C. (Knights of Columbus) members carry a 32-automatic when they go out at night. Be careful, Klansmen," warned Harold Fosner, kligrapp (secretary) of the La Grande Klan.[56] One Klan speaker described the Knights of Columbus as storing two thousand rifles in a Catholic church.[57] The Oregon Klan newspaper, *Western American*, regularly published outlandish allegations against the Knights of Columbus, depicting the Catholic service group as the Klan's mortal enemy. The biggest whopper of all, circulated widely in Oregon, was the oath supposedly taken by members of the Catholic order, including this passage: "I do further promise and declare that I will, when the opportunity presents, make and wage relentless war, secretly and openly, against all heretics, Protestant and Mason, as I am directed to do, to extirpate them from the face of the whole earth; and that I will spare neither age, sex or condition and that I will hang, burn, waste, boil, flay, strangle, and bury alive these infamous heretics."[58] The bogus oath had emerged publicly in 1912 and was widely circulated during World War I. A committee of Masons investigated the oath in 1914 and concluded it was a fraud.[59] That didn't prevent it from being spread later by the Klan in Oregon and elsewhere.

In its own defense, the Knights of Columbus released its real oath to the public, which stated: "I swear to support the Constitution of the United States. I pledge myself as a Catholic citizen and Knight of Columbus, to enlighten myself fully upon my duties as a citizen and to conscientiously perform such duties entirely in the interest of my country and regardless of all personal consequences. I pledge myself to do all in my power to preserve the integrity and purity of the ballot, and to promote reverence and respect for law and order. I promise to practice my religion openly and consistently but without ostentation, and to so conduct myself in public affairs, and in the exercise of public virtue as to reflect nothing but credit upon our Holy Church to the end that she may flourish and our country prosper to the greater honor and Glory of God."[60]

Western American editor Lem Dever, when he left the Klan and published his memoir in 1924, expressed remorse about promoting the fake Knights of Columbus oath. "The 'K. C. oath' is a vile, monstrous and unspeakable fraud, like all the rest of the familiar propaganda which is kept in circulation against the Catholics and Jews," Dever wrote, now calling the Knights of Columbus a "patriotic organization."[61] Though the Knights of Columbus was not the devious political tool the Klan depicted, it did rise to become a formidable Klan adversary. When Oregon voters passed the anti-Catholic school initiative, the national Knights of Columbus offered to bankroll a legal appeal.

Medford War Hero Denounces Klan

"Big Ed" Kelly was the kind of guy who didn't back down, not to a Catholic priest, the enemy in two wars, nor the Ku Klux Klan in Medford. As a child, Edward once spat at a priest in his Catholic school, or maybe it was his twin brother Fred. When neither twin would confess to the misdeed, both were expelled.[62] The son of Irish Catholic immigrants would grow to six-feet-three-inches and 240 pounds, earning the nicknames Big Ed and Lantern Jaw. In his teens, Kelly joined the Army in 1898 to fight in the Spanish-American War. An experienced telegraph operator, he was assigned to restore communications during the American occupation of the Philippines. "He was the first man ashore in Manila, splicing the cable that the Spaniards had cut, under fire," according to a Medford newspaper account.[63] Working from a small boat, Kelly took two weeks to finish the job, braving the enemy, intense heat, sharks, and typhoons. Later he was cited for his gallantry by an act of Congress.

Kelly became a lawyer and moved to Medford in 1907, successfully defending then-*Medford Mail Tribune* editor and publisher George Putnam in a libel lawsuit that went all the way to the Oregon Supreme Court. Kelly was elected Jackson County district attorney in 1912. Five years later, he volunteered to serve again when the United States entered World War I. He was now fifty years old and suffering from varicose veins, which doctors feared would make trench warfare dicey. Yet Kelly managed to enlist and get sent into combat, enduring poison gas in the Battle of Argonne in France. Once, he was beset by a bursting shell and thrown fifty feet, losing his hearing for a month. When Kelly had departed Medford to join the war effort in France, he was already "one of the best known and most popular men in Southern Oregon," according to his hometown paper.[64] He emerged from the war with a purple heart, two silver stars, and three citations for distinguished service.[65]

When Kelly returned home to Medford in 1920, he joined the new American Legion post, a patriotic veterans group. But the Irish Catholic veteran was alarmed when some fellow American Legion members joined the Ku Klux Klan. In April 1922, after three Jackson County residents were strung up in near-lynchings traced to Klansmen, Kelly asked his American Legion post to pass a resolution condemning the violence and decrying the "mob rule" gaining strength in Oregon. The resolution failed to pass due to opposition from Klansmen in the veterans group, despite Kelly's stature as a local war hero. He and four other post members resigned from the American Legion, explaining the move in a biting letter to the editor. Kelly became one of the few Oregonians with the courage to publicly attack the Klan as it rose to power, writing: "I regard the Ku Klux Klan as the gravest menace to internal peace that has threatened this country since the Civil War."[66] Two weeks later, he came before the Medford City Council with a proposed ordinance that would ban people from wearing masks in public. Mayor Charles "Pop" Gates, who had publicly joined the Klan, was taken by surprise, but the city council took up Kelly's proposal anyway and passed it unanimously.[67] In the summer of 1922, as the Klan was spearheading a recall campaign against county Sheriff Charles Terrill, Kelly and two colleagues organized a public meeting at the Ashland Armory to clear spurious allegations against the sheriff. Terrill survived the recall, but just barely.[68]

Kelly next declared his candidacy for a soon-to-be-vacated seat as Jackson County Circuit Court judge, to be decided on the same ballot as the Klan-supported initiative to ban Catholic schools. Kelly won a high-profile political endorsement from General John J. Pershing, America's World War I hero. But the KKK's anti-Catholic agitation was making headway in Medford. Kelly's son later recalled the Klan circulating wild rumors about the Catholics' Sacred Heart Hospital in Medford: "The hospital sat up on a hill overlooking town, and the Klan was always talking about the guns being taken up to the hospital so they could cover the city of Medford with the fire power."[69] The judicial race took place after six Klansmen and sixteen John Does were indicted for the three near-lynchings, and the winner would preside over the trials. The Klan threw its support to Kelly's opponent, Republican State Senator Charles M. Thomas, who earned the Klan's loyalty by remaining silent on the three abductions and threatened lynchings. It became "the bitterest political campaign in the history of Jackson and Josephine counties," according to the local paper.[70] When the votes were cast, the Klan candidate defeated the Catholic war hero by more than two to one.

Oregon Chosen As Test Case

Many in Oregon and the rest of the country were puzzled as to how the state became a national test case for a tenacious battle against religious schools. After all, schools started by religious sects were some of Oregon's oldest and most prestigious. In 1842, nine years before Oregon's first public school opened,[71] Methodists founded the Oregon Institute in Salem, which later became Willamette University, the oldest university in the West. Congregationalists established Tualatin Academy in 1849, which became Pacific University in Forest Grove. The Sisters of the Holy Names of Jesus and Mary founded St. Mary's Academy in Portland in 1859, which remains an acclaimed Catholic high school for girls. Presbyterians founded the Albany Collegiate Institute in that city in 1867; it later relocated to Portland and was renamed Lewis & Clark College. Oregon law already required school attendance for students aged nine to fifteen, and it mandated that private schools offer the same curriculum as public schools. Oregon had an enviable literacy rate of 98.5 percent,[72] and the nation's top school attendance rate.[73]

Catholic schools *were* being added rapidly in Oregon, a top priority of Archbishop Christie, who also founded the University of Portland. There were twenty-six Catholic schools in Oregon at the dawn of the new century when Christie took charge, and forty-seven by 1923.[74] Yet the state still had a relatively small Catholic population, about half the

Archbishop Alexander Christie aggressively expanded Catholic schools in Oregon to build the church, also founding the University of Portland. (Oregon Historical Society)

national average. That may help explain why the Scottish Rite Masons pursued their initiative in Oregon. "In the East, the number of foreign-born and indifferent people is so overwhelming that such a bill as this could never be put through," explained Robert F. Smith, a Portland bank president who spearheaded the Scottish Rite signature-gathering drive in Oregon. "In accordance with the wishes of the Scottish Rite, therefore, we are beginning in Oregon, to set an example for the rest of the country."[75]

Actually, the Scottish Rite had previously supported a similar measure in Michigan, where the order was alarmed by a surge of Catholics migrating to Detroit for jobs in the booming auto industry. Michigan voters rejected the measure on the 1920 ballot.[76] Oregon, with its relatively small Catholic population, was an easier target.

Despite its racist history, Oregon had a national reputation for progressive innovations when the Klan arrived in 1921. That stemmed largely from a package of direct-democracy reforms enacted after the turn of the century. Dubbed the Oregon System, those enabled citizens, via the ballot, to write and approve their own laws (the initiative), to dump corrupt or unpopular elected officials (the recall), and to overturn measures passed by the legislature (the referendum). The initiative system had enabled Oregon voters to enact progressive reforms such as women's suffrage and an eight-hour day for workers on public works projects. Between 1902 and 1921, Oregonians cast votes on 196 initiatives and referenda.[77] In 1922, Masonic lodges and the Klan decided to exploit the initiative system to advance their measure banning all private schools.

Seeds for the attack on Catholic schools were sown before the Klan came to Oregon. In May 1920, the Supreme Council of the Scottish Rite Masons for the Southern Jurisdiction met in special session in Colorado Springs, Colorado, and adopted a resolution proclaiming the order's support for compulsory public schooling. The Southern Jurisdiction represented 260,000 members in thirty-three states in the South, West, and Midwest.[78] The resolution stated: "That we recognize and proclaim our belief in the free and compulsory education of the children of our nation in public primary schools supported by public taxation, upon which all children shall attend and be instructed in the English language only, without regard to race or creed, as the only sure agency for the perpetuation and preservation of our free institutions guaranteed by the constitution of the United States and we pledge the efforts of the membership of the Rite to promote by all lawful means the organization, extension, and development to the highest degree of such schools, and to oppose the efforts of any and all who seek to limit, curtail, hinder or destroy the public school system of our land."[79]

For centuries, the Roman Catholic Church was hostile to the Masonic movement, barring Catholics from joining the popular fraternal lodges. Scottish Rite Masons were an elite subgroup within the nation's 2.5 million-member Masonic movement. All Masons study lodge rituals, traditions, and self-improvement, earning up to three certifications, known as degrees. Scottish Rite Masons commit to continuing education and self-improvement, earning up to thirty-two degrees. The Southern Jurisdiction was "the most bitterly anti-Catholic wing of the Masonic order" and was then "openly allied with the Klan," according to Father Schoenberg, the Northwest Catholic historian.[80] Along with the Orange Lodges, Scottish Rite Masons proved to be "particularly rich hunting grounds" for Klan recruiters.[81] William Simmons, founder of the second Klan, was a Scottish Rite member,[82] as was his successor Hiram Evans.[83] So were Oregon Klan leaders Luther Powell,[84] Fred Gifford,[85] and Kaspar Kap Kubli,[86] among others.

Masons have a proud history of supporting public education, including their efforts to help land the University of Oregon in Eugene and serve in its top leadership posts.[87] At the Scottish Rite's 1920 convention in Colorado, Secretary General John H. Cowles depicted the mandatory public-school resolution in egalitarian terms, though the meeting minutes reveal the proposal also seemed aimed at thwarting religious schools. If all pupils attended public schools, Cowles stated, "the children of the very rich, the very poor and of all religions would rub elbows and become impregnated with that true democracy which is the foundation of our Republic." Later, he added, "If any of the church denominations opposed this on the ground of lack of religious training in the schools, the obvious answer would be that religious teaching properly belongs to the home."[88]

Lutherans and other Protestant denominations were devoted to building religious schools, but none matched the number of schools operated by Catholics. Meeting minutes reflect the Scottish Rite's anti-Catholic and nativist sentiments. Cowles also proposed that the Scottish Rite endorse the creation of a new public university in Washington, DC, in part because it would "militate greatly against the two very large Catholic universities now in the District of Columbia" (Georgetown University and Catholic University of America). Backers would have to take care that "sinister influences" did not seek control of the public university, such as "Romanists," Cowles warned. Cowles's proposal also urged the Scottish Rite to oppose the teaching of all foreign languages in public schools, and to guard against the introduction of "Roman Catholic propaganda" in public libraries.

Portland Scottish Rite leader P. S. Malcom, before his alliance with the Klan, was one of the officers attending the Colorado meeting, the minutes show. A month later, he also attended the seventieth annual convention of the Grand Lodge of the Ancient Free and Accepted Masons of Oregon,[89] the umbrella group for all Oregon Masons. Representatives from 121 of Oregon's 147 chartered Masonic lodges met at that convention on June 16–18, 1920, at Portland's Knights of Pythias Hall. Those attending were Oregon's elite Masons, not the rank-and-file "joiners" who flocked to fraternal lodges in that era to gain business contacts and comradeship. "They were the policy-makers, the hard core of Masonic believers," Schoenberg wrote.[90] Grand Master Earl C. Bronaugh presided over the three-day Portland convention. At least seven past grand masters attended, including Malcom and William C. Bristol.[91]

Masonry stands on "firm foundations," including illustrious alumni George Washington, Benjamin Franklin, and Alexander Hamilton, wrote former Oregon Supreme Court Justice Wallace McCamant in the grand orator address for the convention. "It has aways been a champion of civil and religious liberty," he wrote. "It has no Spanish Inquisition for which to apologize. It has persecuted no man for his religion."[92] Yet the day before, with little dissension, the convention passed a resolution supporting mandatory public schooling that had been submitted by a six-man committee.[93] It was almost identical to the one passed a month earlier by the Scottish Rite Masons: "Be it resolved, by the M. W. Grand Lodge of Oregon, A. F. and A. M., that we recognize and proclaim our belief in the free and compulsory education of the children of our nation in public primary schools supported by national taxation, upon which all children should attend and be instructed in the English language only, without regard to race or creed, as the only sure foundation for the perpetuation and preservation of our free institutions, guaranteed by the Constitution of the United States, and we pledge the efforts of the membership of this body to promote by all lawful means the organization, extension and development to the highest degree of such schools, and to oppose any and all efforts of any and all who seek to limit, curtail, hinder or destroy the public school system of our land."[94] On its face, the resolution sounded high-minded and egalitarian, but if successful it would mean the forced closure of dozens of Oregon's elite private and religious schools.

The Shriners, another elite wing of the Masonic movement, endorsed the Scottish Rite resolution the same month, after it was introduced by Portland Mayor George Baker at a June 1920 gathering in Portland of the Imperial Council of the A. A. O. Nobles Mystic Shrine.[95] Other Masonic bodies around the country followed suit.[96]

The year after Masonic groups endorsed the mandatory public-school resolution, anti-Catholicism reared its head in the 1921 Oregon legislative session that convened in Salem in January. Three bills attacking Catholics were introduced and hotly debated. One would bar public-school teachers from wearing religious garb, which was aimed at twenty nuns hired to teach in public schools, typically in heavily Catholic communities.[97] Another bill sought to replace the Protestant and Catholic chaplains ministering to prisoners at the state penitentiary in Salem with one pastor from the Protestant-dominated Salvation Army. A third bill would bar private colleges from granting teacher certifications. That was aimed at a teacher-training program founded a decade earlier by the Sisters of the Holy Names of Jesus and Mary in Marylhurst (present-day Lake Oswego), which trained and certified nuns to teach in Oregon Catholic schools. None of the three bills passed as proposed in the short 1921 session, but Catholic observers considered them a bad omen.[98] "Noon today witnessed the closing of a legislative session which has, since the opening day, given us great uneasiness," wrote a Catholic nun at the time.[99]

That legislative session took place before the first kleagles enlisted significant numbers of Oregon Klansmen in the early months of 1921. Those first Klan recruiters surely took note when anti-Catholic forces won four seats in the June 1921 Portland School Board election.[100]

Malcom's Pivotal Role

The Scottish Rite Lodge of Oregon was so shaky back in 1890 that it was on the brink of being dissolved. Instead, lodge members handed the reins to P. S. Malcom, practically a lifelong Mason, who was working at his father-in-law's clothing shop in downtown Portland.[101] Malcom turned around the lodge's fortunes so completely that by 1903 it opened the grand Scottish Rite Temple, which still stands on Portland's Southwest Morrison Street and Fifteenth Avenue. In 1907, President Teddy Roosevelt awarded Malcom, by then an insurance agent, the plum appointment of US Collector of Customs for the Port of Portland.

Masons had long been viewed as a prestigious fraternal order, claiming multiple US presidents as members and at least nine signers of the Declaration of Independence. Malcom, who hailed from Oswego, New York, was the grandson of President John Adams's secretary, and the great-grandson of George Washington's second-highest-ranking general in the Revolutionary War.[102]

So when Scottish Rite Masons teamed with the Ku Klux Klan to promote a ballot initiative requiring every Oregon youngster to attend public schools, newspaper editors gushed about the order's noble traditions. "No informed person will seriously question the sincerity or

Philip Schuyler Malcom revived Oregon's flagging Scottish Rite Masonic lodge, then teamed with the Klan to enact the lodge's compulsory public schooling proposal into state law. (Courtesy of Oregon Scottish Rite Masonic lodge)

patriotism of the motives of those who are behind this measure," wrote *Oregon Voter* editor C. C. Chapman.[103] "The compulsory school measure has behind it a great and highly honorable fraternal order," wrote the *Morning Oregonian* editorial board. "It is not necessary to say that so patriotic, respectable and influential an organization as the Masons (Scottish Rite) would not sponsor any measure without a conscientious desire to promote the public welfare."[104] But the Masonic movement, known for its secret oaths and secularism, had been condemned by a string of Catholic popes dating back to 1738. Over the centuries, Masons became hostile to Catholics.

When kleagles arrived in Oregon and other states, they gained credibility by enlisting Masons as members. "The Klansmen are for everything that Masonry stands for, and against everything that it opposes," crowed the Klan's Oregon newspaper.[105] Scholar Miguel Hernandez, after an exhaustive study of the relationship between freemasonry and the Klan in the 1920s, estimated that about one-third of Klan members nationally were also Masons.[106] Masonic lodges experienced major growth after World War I, leading to a faction of more-militant nationalists. "There are times when neutrality is disgraceful, when indifference is a mark of turpitude," thundered Wallace McCamant at the 1920 gathering of the Oregon Grand Lodge.[107] "In Oregon," Hernandez observed, "militant Freemasons found an ally in the Invisible Empire that would help them defend America."

As Senator Charles Hall was creating a stir in the 1922 primary election by championing compulsory public schools, the *Catholic Sentinel* broke the news that a ballot initiative was being prepared to ban all private schools in Oregon.[108] The newspaper may have gotten wind of a secret meeting that spring, when exalted cyclops Gifford and a group of Scottish Rite members reportedly hand-picked by Malcom approved the wording of a ballot initiative to turn the Scottish Rite resolution into law. "The majority of those present...were members of the radical faction of the Masonic order that fell in line with the Ku Klux movement from the first," according to the *Capital Journal*.[109] All the fourteen official co-sponsors of the ballot initiative were Masons. At least three also were believed to be Klansmen: one in the Medford klavern, another in the Pendleton klavern, and another in the Albany klavern.[110] Gifford was not an official sponsor, but his fingerprints were everywhere.

Oregon's Compulsory Education Law, since 1889, required all youths aged nine to fifteen to attend either public or private schools.[111] The proposed initiative made two basic changes to that statute: eliminating language allowing students to attend private schools, and expanding the age range to cover youths aged eight to sixteen. Sponsors also added a stiff new penalty if parents refused to send their children to public schools. Parents would be liable for a misdemeanor offense, fines of $5 to $100, and county jail sentences of two to thirty days. Each day parents were out of compliance would constitute a new offense. Exceptions were made for children physically unable to attend school, children who had already completed the eighth grade, and those living too far from public schools that didn't provide transportation.

On April 28, 1922, while Hall was duking it out with Olcott in the heated Republican primary, the Oregon secretary of state referred the proposed initiative to the attorney general. As required, he wrote the explanatory language to appear before voters, known as the ballot title. He called the measure the Compulsory Education Bill, because it amended that statute. That turned out to give a huge advantage to the Klan and Masons, as many voters thought they were being asked to require students to attend school, not realizing that mandatory attendance had been in force for decades. "The name of the law was a misnomer," Olcott told fellow governors a month after the election. "It was intended to deceive."[112]

But the effective start date for the new law turned out to be a blessing for Catholics and other opponents. The initiative wouldn't take effect until the fall 1926 school term, to give public schools time to provide added classroom space, textbooks, and other materials. That gave opponents time to challenge the initiative in court before it took effect. After receiving the favorable ballot title, Scottish Rite Masons organized a one-day blitz on June 15, 1922, to collect qualifying petition signatures. By circulating petitions at lodge meetings, they gathered an astounding 29,000 signatures in a day. State officials determined that more than 16,000 of the signatures were valid, exceeding the 13,000 needed to put the proposal on the November ballot.[113]

Mom, Apple Pie, and Public Schools

The surge of US immigrants in the early twentieth century coincided with growing numbers of rural Americans moving to cities to take jobs in industry. Schools became crucial gathering places for a great multiethnic "melting pot," where children of farmers and immigrants sat side by side, learning to read and write in English and rubbing shoulders to help newcomers get Americanized. Initiative backers argued that requiring every child to attend public schools in such conditions was a necessary and progressive reform. "The public school is DEMOCRATIC," Scottish Rite Masons argued in a campaign pamphlet promoting their ballot measure. "It receives and treats all alike; wealth does not count, poverty does not hinder. The knowledge and the books are there for ALL."[114] Backers also depicted the measure as patriotic. "One Flag–One School—One Language," declared a newspaper ad sponsored by the Eugene Compulsory Education League.[115] Portland School Board member William F. Woodward, arguing for the initiative in a campaign debate, cited the example of Atkinson School in the northwest part of Portland: "Over 300 children there; 26 nations, and there they are learning first the lesson of toleration through association."[116]

At the time, 134,216 youngsters were enrolled in Oregon's public schools. An estimated ninety-two private schools would be forced to shut down, with their 12,031 students forced to switch to public schools.[117] Catholics operated the lion's share of the targeted schools, thirty-nine of them, with 9,190 students. The bulk of those students were in Portland's eighteen Catholic schools.[118] Seventh-Day Adventists, Lutherans, Episcopalians, Mennonites, and Christian Scientists also offered religious schools, mostly in larger cities such as Portland and Eugene. A smaller number of independent nondenominational schools, often billed as college-preparatory academies, also were in jeopardy. Those included Hill Military Academy, a boarding school in Northwest Portland that closed in 1959, and Miss Catlin's School, which later merged with Portland Academy to form Catlin Gabel School, still one of Portland's premier private schools. The academies boasted of having one teacher for every twelve students, compared to one teacher for every forty students in public elementary schools.[119] By including college-prep schools, the initiative sponsors were able to campaign on a populist, class-based message with wider appeal. "We do not believe in snobbery, and are just as much opposed to private schools of the so-called 'select' kind as we are to denominational private schools,"

Hill Military Academy cadets in October 1922. The Portland private school, faced with closure due to the compulsory public schooling initiative, joined with Catholics to challenge the measure's constitutionality in court. (Oregon Historical Society)

Gifford said in a rare media interview in March 1922, the same month the initiative reportedly was being hatched.[120]

Hiram Evans, elevated to Klan imperial wizard in late 1922, called for closing all religious schools because they "very readily become agencies of propaganda."[121] Instead, the Klan joined Protestant calls to bring back use of the Bible for teaching in public schools, which had been barred by courts. "One of our purposes is to try to get the Bible back into the schools, such as it was in the old days," Reverend Reuben Sawyer said on the campaign trail.[122] By "Bible," Klan leaders meant the King James version used by Protestants and eschewed by Catholics. The Klan also joined with Masons and public-school teachers in the National Education Association to lobby for the Towner-Stirling bill pending in Congress, which would create a federal Department of Education. "This great measure will promote Americanization en masse through all schools," explained the Klan's Oregon newspaper.[123]

Gifford wasn't the only campaign leader who cynically argued for closing private schools while sending his children to one. Lark Bilyer, who led a Eugene campaign committee promoting the initiative, sent

THE KLAN

Believes the Free Public School is a fundamental American doctrine.

* * *

Advocates the adequate education of all future citizenship through the Free Public School.

* * *

Declares the Public School is the most essential of all American institutions.

* * *

Insists that the young be taught *how to think, not* what to think.

* * *

Favors a Department of Education with a Cabinet Secretary at its head. The Catholic Hierarchy opposes this.

* * *

Believes that the agencies and objects of education should be publicly controlled—that such is the fundamental function of the State.

Maintains that Public School education is Democratic education. The fight against this system is being waged by and for Catholic parochialism, which is the essence of monarchy.

* * *

Challenges Rome to submit our differences to democratic education in a Public School System as an educated electorate, and is willing to wait the required generation to impanel the jury.

* * *

"Promote, then, as an object of primary importance, institutions for the general diffusion of knowledge."—*George Washington.*

* * *

"The national safety—can be obtained only through Free Public Schools, open to all, good enough for all, and attended by all."—*HORACE MANN, Sponsor of the American Public School.*

A Klan campaign flyer promoting the compulsory public-school initiative makes the Klan's anti-Catholic motivations clear. (Oregon Historical Society) his children to private and Catholic schools, as did Woodward, the Portland School Board member.[124]

There was no doubt that Catholics strategically used schools as building blocks to grow their congregations. Archbishop Christie made that clear soon after his appointment as Oregon's leading Catholic cleric in 1899. "I shall build schools first, or I shall have an empty cathedral 20 years from now," he declared.[125] There also was no doubt among many observers that the initiative was conceived to attack Catholics. "The sole animus of this bill is anti-Catholicism; we may as well admit it and discuss it candidly," stated a campaign flyer produced for the independent schools.[126] The Klan and other anti-Catholic forces made wide use during the campaign of "escaped nuns" to promote the initiative measure. They made political hay by circulating photos of nuns teaching school while dressed in their habits. One photo depicted nuns teaching in a spare classroom at Astoria's Shively Public School that was made available by the public-school superintendent after the Catholic school burned down. That arrangement was retracted after an outcry from Protestants who saw the photo.[127]

Fissures in the Masonic movement arose amid charges their initiative was squarely aimed at religious schools. A newspaper ad headlined "Attention, Mason," and signed by Malcom, stated that "Nothing is further from the real truth. No other organization is so free from religious prejudice or so opposed to religious intolerance as the Masonic fraternity."[128] Yet some Masons were having second thoughts as the campaign devolved into a bitter fight over religion. George G. Brown, a top officer of the Oregon Grand Lodge of Masons, told the *Capital Journal* that the Grand Lodge had never endorsed the initiative.[129] That may have been technically true, though the minutes show he attended the Grand Lodge convention that endorsed the Scottish Rite resolution that spawned the initiative. William C. Bristol, another former grand master who attended that 1920 convention, went public a week after Brown and declared that the initiative ran counter to Masonic principles. "Masonry, by its teachings, endeavors to refrain men from the commission of injustices and acts of wrong and outrage," Bristol said. "Masonry alone preaches toleration, the right of man to abide by his own faith."[130] Scottish Rite Mason A. F. Flegal spoke out against the initiative in a campaign event at a Portland-area courthouse. "This bill was conceived in hate and intolerance...using false and misleading statements," he said. Flegal said Malcom later called and informed him that their order's Supreme Council had backed the initiative. "He replied he would report me to the Supreme Council and I told him to report and be damned," Flegal said.[131]

Some initiative supporters made their anti-Catholic motivations clear. One full-page newspaper ad, topped with the provocative headline "The Roman Monopoly," stated that "our country is in danger." The ad explained that "Nine thousand children are now being fitted to promote un-American ideals and many of them will become subjects of a foreign prince."[132] The Klan typically sought to camouflage its involvement in the campaign and let Masons do most of the public-facing work. One pro-initiative newspaper ad didn't mention the Klan but in small print named the ad sponsor as the Committee on Americanization of Public Schools, Fred Gifford, secretary.[133] The Klan clearly supplied much of the people power for the campaign. The night before election day, twenty Klansmen in the La Grande klavern placed leaflets listing the Klan's endorsements, plus copies of the school initiative, on every doorstep in town.[134] In a confidential July 1922 letter sent to Klan members, Gifford described the initiative as "our school bill" and depicted Catholic opponents of the measure as "the enemy." He commanded Klansmen to pony up $1 each for the Klan's political work, and recruit five friends to do the same. His letter said all members were "seriously summoned" to attend a Klan meeting at Portland's Municipal Auditorium on July 17. "It is expected that at that time, your contributions will be at hand and turned over, or ready to report."[135]

Catholics Mobilize

At what might have been the same meeting, a priest and a few other Catholics snuck inside Municipal Auditorium where Klansmen gathered. Outside the building, sons of Knights of Columbus members scurried among parked cars, jotting down license plate numbers. When police accosted them, the boys claimed in faux outrage that "some Catholics got into that meeting," which they knew to be true. The police moved on.[136] Later, Catholics checked those license plate numbers against public records to obtain a list of suspected Klansmen. Sister Mary Flavia, the mother superior at St. Mary's Academy, organized volunteers to look up the identified Klansmen in the phone directory. She proceeded to call Klansmen whom she knew to be businessmen selling to Catholic customers, suggesting they steer clear of the initiative campaign. Others on the list received personal letters. "Our business relations for many years have been most pleasant and beneficial," she wrote them, "and in the hour of our trial...may we not appeal to you, yours, your people and friends to vote down this bill?"[137]

Catholics, much like the Klan, tried to stay under the radar in the campaign. Early on, Catholics decided that asserting their religious rights to offer private schools would be counterproductive and only inflame more bigotry.[138] Instead, Catholics relied on a campaign message of defending parents' rights to guide their children's education. In a campaign speech at a Catholic church in Corvallis, Father O'Hara depicted the initiative as "intolerance trying to disguise itself under the veil of patriotism."[139] He stressed that Oregon private schools already taught in English and were required to use state-mandated textbooks and curriculum.

Despite conspiracy theories spread by the Klan, American Catholics were not accustomed to taking marching orders from Rome or any church leaders when it came to politics. "Our Catholic people have never united, nor has it ever been seriously suggested that you should unite on questions of a purely political character," Archbishop Christie wrote his flock in a three-page pastoral letter about the ballot measure. Catholic schools, he stated, provide youths with vital moral guidance, educating "the heart as well as the mind."[140] The *Catholic Sentinel*, his Archdiocese's official news organ, had in the spring 1922 primary merely urged Catholic readers to vote, without making any endorsements.[141] But when the school initiative came up for a vote in November, the newspaper broke its "custom of many years standing" by making endorsements, citing the unprecedented attack on Catholics.[142]

Christie created a separate campaign arm, the Catholic Civil Rights Association of Oregon, which concentrated on organizing his parishioners. Christie summoned Dudley G. Wooten, a Catholic convert and former Texas congressman, to temporarily relocate from Seattle to lead the campaign committee. Wooten lamented after the campaign that Catholics remained politically weak and divided. He complained they were able to raise only $200 in campaign contributions from outside Oregon—even from well-funded national Catholic organizations.[143] But under Wooten's direction, Catholics at the parish level functioned like a well-oiled political machine. Each of the state's one hundred thirty Catholic parishes established two executive committees, composed of ten men and ten women. Volunteers organized churchgoers to canvas registered voters in their communities. Canvassers who were able to assess neighbors' views on the initiative jotted their findings on color-coded index cards: white cards for Catholics, blue ones for undecided non-Catholics, and yellow cards for what were termed "bigots," whose minds were made up to support the initiative.[144] Wooten's committee distributed Christie's pastoral letter to parishioners, and produced and disseminated a half-million copies of a campaign flier—more than one for every Oregon family.

The committee also circulated materials produced by Seventh-Day Adventists and the two other major campaign committees, the Protestant and Non-Sectarian Schools Committee and the Lutheran Schools Committee.[145] Lutherans hadn't been on the best of terms with Catholics ever since founder Martin Luther split from Rome in the early sixteenth century. Now they were uneasy allies in fending off a measure that would gut both denominations' schools. Lutherans, who set a goal of opening one religious school for each congregation, operated Concordia Academy, a Lutheran high school in Northeast Portland, plus other schools in Oregon. Concordia later evolved into Concordia University, which operated until 2020. Unlike Catholics, Lutherans were able to marshal significant political and financial resources from outside Oregon.[146] Two years earlier, Lutherans had mobilized to oppose the Scottish Rite initiative on Michigan's 1920 ballot, gaining valuable political experience. Lutherans also had spent decades defending their use of German language, the tongue spoken by many new Lutheran immigrants, in the face of campaigns to require English-only instruction in schools. The Lutheran Schools Committee, managed by the Reverend R. G. Messerli, paid for newspaper ads and produced its own campaign flyers, including one titled "The Truth about the So-Called Compulsory Education Bill." "Its purpose is not to compel all children in the state to go to some school," the flyer stated. "Its sole purpose is to outlaw private and church schools."[147] The committee printed enough flyers to distribute one to every Oregonian. Young volunteers at Lutheran churches in Portland addressed and mailed the pamphlets to 329,000 voters. Messerli, in a private assessment of the initiative campaign sent to church leaders in Nebraska, shared his take on the origins and goals of the initiative backers. The initiative was "a unified effort on the part of Scottish Rite Masons and the Ku Klux Klan to exterminate the Catholic schools," he wrote. With less than a month to go before the election, Messerli cited two major obstacles: Oregonians who mistakenly thought the state didn't already require students to attend school, and "the bitter antagonism which has been worked up against the Catholics by the Ku Klux Klan."[148]

Many if not most Protestant clergymen openly backed the initiative. Methodists, who were busy raising money to support Willamette University in Salem, officially remained neutral during the campaign.[149] The influential Portland Ministerial Association hosted a debate on the initiative but didn't take a position on the measure. Twenty-five Presbyterian pastors signed a Voters Pamphlet statement opposing the initiative.[150] Other Protestant clerics teamed with the college-prep academies to oppose the measure via the Protestant and Non-Sectarian Schools Committee. That group argued that the initiative would drive up taxes. Public schools would have to bulk up to take on more than twelve thousand additional students, a 9 percent increase. The committee also operated a speakers bureau consisting of some forty clergymen from Presbyterian, Methodist, Baptist, Jewish, and Christian Science congregations.[151]

One of those speakers, Rabbi Jonah Wise of Temple Beth Israel in Portland, lamented that the initiative was reigniting a centuries-old religious battle among Christians. "The wars which soaked Europe in blood are being transferred to the soil of this state by a movement so unscrupulous and dense as to baffle belief," he told a gathering of the B'Nai B'rith Jewish service organization.[152] Wise also served as editor of *The Scribe*, a Portland Jewish newspaper that ran multiple articles and editorials bluntly critical of the initiative. "To vote for it is to support reaction and tyranny; not to vote at all is to stand idly by the destruction of one's own house," Wise editorialized.[153] Jewish youngsters in Portland learned Hebrew and studied Jewish scripture at private facilities, but those were not directly threatened because students attended outside their time in public schools. Still, Jewish leaders were concerned about the attack on others' religion. "This weapon is not at present aimed at the Jews, but we feel that all Jews are deeply concerned in the promotion of religious freedom and jealously interested in its promotion," read one advertisement in *The Scribe* signed by several Jewish community leaders.[154]

Harassing Catholics

Sister Mary Ethelind gathered up her girls at St. Mary's Academy to walk them to Sunday Mass at a nearby church in downtown Portland. As they reached the Park Blocks, two hooded Klansmen suddenly appeared on horseback. In menacing fashion, they moved their horses to block the girls' pathway on the sidewalk.[155] "Good neighbor turned against good neighbor in that strange time," wrote Sister Christine Mary, reflecting on the incident during the dark days for Catholics when the Klan was on the rise in Oregon. A quarter-century later, her haunting memory was of childhood insults hurled by Protestant schoolmates. "The taunt 'Cat-likker, Cat-likker' as we walked home from school remains for many our only memory of those historic issues," the former Catholic school teacher recalled in 1958.[156] Sister Margaret Meyers had a different trauma embedded in her memory sixty-five years after the Klan's heyday in Oregon. The ten-year-old attended Sacred Heart Academy in La Grande and feared her school would have to close after Oregonians voted to ban Catholic schools in 1922. Her school was spared, but her aunt Evelyn was fired as a public-school teacher because she'd sent her twin sons to Sacred Heart.[157]

When an initiative supporter sought to get a qualifying petition signed by a man at the Portland YMCA who turned out to be a Knights of Columbus member, a heated argument resulted in both men getting arrested.[158] When Sister Lucretia spoke at Portland's James John High School, fisticuffs broke out between two women attendees, both of whom were arrested.[159] Frank Leo Smith, a Portland native who turned twenty-one when the Klan arrived in Oregon, recalled that fellow Catholics weren't so worried about Klansmen's attacks on his brethren until they went after parochial schools, when things got noticeably worse for Oregon Catholics.[160] Smith remembered how a Catholic personal-injury lawyer felt compelled to warn clients that, should their case go to a jury, he was liable to find one or two anti-Catholic jury members who might side against him merely because of his faith. Catholic-owned businesses such as Albers Brothers Milling Company suffered due to a Klan boycott, Smith said. His sister-in-law was advised to lie on her application for a teaching job at West Linn School District by writing "Christian" instead of "Catholic" where it asked her religion. "He said 'You put down Catholic, you won't get your job.'" Portland Public Schools also was notorious for its reluctance to hire Catholic teachers in those days, Smith recalled.

Initiative Passes

Walter Pierce did his darnedest to focus on tax reform in his fall 1922 campaign for governor, but he found that religious discord swamped all other voter concerns. Opponents of the measure spent nearly four times as much money as supporters,[161] yet the Klan and its Protestant allies won 53 percent of the vote.[162] "That the school bill carried was a surprise," *Oregon Voter* observed in its election wrap-up, crediting the "anti-Catholic vote."[163]

Voters in Multnomah County accounted for half the statewide victory margin, with the strongest support coming from working-class neighborhoods. It passed with more than 67 percent of the vote in North Portland, and more than 56 percent on Portland's east side. Jewish voters, which included many in the working class, proved the exception. Two heavily Jewish precincts on Portland's west side voted overwhelmingly against the initiative.[164] Portland's well-to-do neighborhoods also opposed the initiative, including a majority of voters in the affluent West Hills, Irvington, and Alameda neighborhoods.[165]

Lane County voters approved the school measure by a margin of more than two to one. The measure also was soundly approved in Coos, Clackamas, Clatsop, Linn, and Douglas Counties.[166] Voters in Marion, Washington, and Umatilla Counties opposed the measure, as did those in Jackson County, site of the three near-lynchings. There were no Catholic schools in Medford, and Catholics likely retained some voter sympathy from operating Sacred Heart Hospital, the lone hospital in town, said historian Jeff LaLande. Sacred Heart had opened its top floor to serve victims of the flu epidemic.[167]

Klan propagandist Lem Dever said chief credit for the victory should go to Malcom and his Scottish Rite lodge, with backing from the Klan and the Federation of Patriotic Societies.[168] But there was considerable overlap in the membership of the three secret groups. Luther Powell, the KKK's leading recruiter in the Northwest, had no such modesty, claiming the Klan "put over" the school bill in Oregon. Soon after the election, Powell announced he'd launch a similar initiative campaign in Washington, where, as in Oregon, Catholics made up a relatively small share of the population.[169]

Private-school opponents hoped their Oregon success would spark similar campaigns elsewhere, and they threatened to file initiatives in twenty other states unless lawmakers in those states enacted similar laws.[170] The Klan supported a bill in Congress to require every child to receive a "common school education."[171] The Scottish Rite and other anti-Catholic forces qualified a second ballot initiative in Michigan, and efforts commenced in California, Missouri, and several other states. But the momentum started shifting. Supporters failed to gather enough signatures to qualify a California measure modeled after Oregon's initiative. State legislators turned down similar measures in Mississippi, Wyoming, Iowa, Arkansas, Ohio, Texas, and Alabama.[172] In 1924, voters in Washington, Michigan, and Missouri rejected ballot measures to ban private schools. In the end, Oregon stood alone, and that turned out to be a short-lived victory for opponents of Catholic schools.

Father O'Hara was among those who championed a court challenge. The alternative—asking voters to rethink their decision via a 1924 ballot initiative—would not settle the question once and for all, he argued.[173] Catholics and their allies decided their best course was to file in federal court. Any judge opposing the initiative in a state court risked a recall campaign organized by the Klan and its allies.[174] On August 22, 1923, a team of attorneys hired by Catholics filed suit in the federal district court for Oregon, on behalf of the Society of the Sisters of Holy Names of Jesus and Mary.[175] The nuns, who had arrived in Oregon in 1859, were deemed to have a contractual relationship with the state, and thus would provide the best chances of prevailing in court.[176] When the initiative passed, two hundred eleven nuns in the order were instructing nearly two thousand students in a dozen Oregon Catholic schools.[177]

The National Catholic Welfare Council, now clearly understanding the threat posed to Catholic schools in other states, agreed to foot the legal appeal. The national Knights of Columbus offered to fund the Catholic appeal but was pushed aside in a turf battle with the National Catholic Welfare Council. Instead, the Knights of Columbus agreed to fund the Hill Military Academy's attorney fees when it joined the case to ensure a non-religious school was part of the legal challenge.[178] The plaintiffs challenged the constitutionality of the initiative under the Fourteenth Amendment, arguing the measure deprived them of property without due process of law.

In January 1924, when the case went before a panel of three federal judges in Portland, five attorneys represented the Sisters of Holy Names and a sixth represented Hill Academy. Named defendants in the lawsuit were Governor Pierce, Oregon Attorney General Isaac H. Van Winkle, and Stanley Myer, Multnomah County district attorney. The lead defense attorney, Wallace McCamant, said he primarily represented his lodge, the Scottish Rite Masons, along with Governor Pierce.[179] On March 31, 1924, the three-judge panel ruled the initiative violated the Fourteenth Amendment by effectively taking the sisters' school properties without due process, and that the initiative deprived parents of the right to "direct the education of children by selecting reputable teachers and places." The court granted an injunction, restraining the state from enforcing the initiative. That set up a dramatic final decision by the US Supreme Court.

In 1925, former President William Howard Taft was chief justice of the US Supreme Court. The Taft Court was a conservative panel known for being unfriendly to Progressive Era reforms adopted earlier in the century. Its unanimous decision in the case known as Pierce v. Society of Sisters of the Holy Names of Jesus and Mary was monumental. "The child is not the mere creature of the state," the court held on June 1; "those who nurture him and direct his destiny have the right, coupled with the high duty, to recognize and prepare him for additional obligations."

Many Catholics were embittered by Pierce pursuing the appeal to the Supreme Court. After the court ruled, Pierce made his personal support for the initiative clear in a private letter: "It is too early to say what will be the next move but I am sure we who believe in educating our children in the public schools will continue to fight for...what many of us regard as the very bulwark of American institutions."[180]

7
Ensuring a Docile Media

> *"Loss of respect for the public press seems to have stimulated numbers of Americans to react by joining the Klan when the organization was attacked in the newspapers. Condemnation has failed. Ridicule has failed."*
>
> —C. Easton Rothwell, 1924[1]

During the early 1920s, Americans learned what was going on in their world from newspapers. The new medium of radio devoted little airtime to news, and "talkie" newsreels shown at movie theatres didn't become popular until 1927, the same year television debuted.[2] Oregon had three large daily newspapers, the *Morning Oregonian/Sunday Oregonian,* a staid morning paper allied with establishment Republicans; the *Oregon Daily Journal,* its afternoon competitor that leaned toward Democrats; and the smaller, scrappier, and politically independent *Portland Telegram.* The *Telegram* had more than twice the readership of Portland's fourth daily paper, the *Portland News,* and ten times the circulation of Oregon's next-largest daily, the *Capital Journal* of Salem.[3] Competing newspapers engaged in fierce rivalries in Portland, Salem, Eugene, Astoria, Medford, and elsewhere, making them more vulnerable to Klan boycotts.

Newspapers Cowed

Six months after voters approved a Klan-backed governor and the initiative to close private schools, the Oregon Klan showed its appreciation for news coverage bestowed by the state's leading newspaper. Meeting in a state klonklave (convention), the Klan adopted a resolution: "In view of the fair treatment accorded the Klan by the *Morning Oregonian* in all press items, and its desire to print only the facts in its news columns, that this convention extend to the *Morning Oregonian* our thanks for its fairness and impartial policy." A copy of the resolution was forwarded to editor Edgar Piper.[4]

Though there were notable exceptions, the dominant news media of the era largely failed to fulfill their watchdog role in covering the Ku Klux Klan's swift rise to power. The Klan was the overriding issue in Oregon in 1922, *Medford Mail Tribune* editor Robert W. Ruhl told peers at a March 1923 Oregon News Editors conference in Eugene. "And yet during all this time, in at least 80 percent of the newspapers of Oregon, there was not the slightest editorial reference to this amazing development," Ruhl lamented. "With the school issue, as with the Klan issue, outside of a pitiful minority, the newspapers of the state as a whole expressed no opinion at all."[5]

Newspaper editors did condemn religious strife in the midst of the 1922 campaign, but they neglected to mention the cause of such strife. "We deplore the fact that religious issues have been injected into Oregon politics," the Oregon State Editorial Association stated in a vague resolution passed at a Corvallis gathering.[6] George Putnam, the *Capital Journal* editor and publisher, lambasted his peers for that timid and misleading statement. "In passing resolutions instead of vigorously combating a sinister movement, the press of Oregon is failing to function," he charged.[7] Putnam was especially critical of Portland newspapers, accusing them of "cowardly and shameful silence" due to fears of lost subscribers and advertisers if they dared challenge the Klan. Smaller newspapers outside of Portland, equally vulnerable to Klan boycotts, also buckled under pressure. As Klan support fueled Democrat Walter Pierce's unusually strong challenge to incumbent Republican Ben Olcott, the *Corvallis Gazette-Times* noted that only five of the twenty-five daily newspapers outside Portland endorsed Olcott, though "all but three of them parade themselves as Republican papers."[8]

Feisty *Telegram*

Putnam really meant the *Oregonian* and *Oregon Daily Journal*, not the *Portland Telegram*, when bashing his Portland competitors for their lackluster coverage of the Klan. But the *Telegram*, the first newspaper to document the Ku Klux Klan's penetration into Oregon, paid a dear price for its aggressive reporting. "The *Telegram* was an early and vocal opponent of the Klan in Portland" and "consistently exposed and attacked the Klan and its activities," observed scholar Francis Paul Valenti, who analyzed Portland press coverage of the Klan in the 1920s.[9] During the crucial final weeks of the 1922 general election campaign, Valenti counted two to four *Telegram* stories per day attacking the Klan, its anti-Catholic school initiative and its choice for governor, Walter Pierce.[10] In response, the Klan orchestrated a multi-pronged campaign against the *Telegram*. "Ad cancellations, threats against employees and their families, and destruction of *Telegram* papers and property were among the methods," Valenti wrote.[11] The newspaper lost five thousand subscribers in one month.

The *Telegram*, founded in 1877, prospered after lumbermen John and L. R. Wheeler purchased it in 1914. The newspaper moved into spanking-new quarters at the stately Telegram Building on Eleventh Avenue and Washington Street in downtown Portland on October 16, 1922.[12] Despite economic pressure from the Klan, the newspaper continued its aggressive reporting, coming out strongly against the initiative aimed at banning Catholic schools. The ballot measure was dividing residents along religious lines, the newspaper argued. "The school bill is not only a religious question," the *Telegram* editorialized on November 2, 1922. "It strikes at the very foundation of American liberty and it is wholly at variance with the teachings and the spirit of Christ. It is wholly un-American and it should be defeated." In the final days of the campaign, the *Telegram* published a riveting four-part series titled "I Was a Klansman." It was a highly revealing insider's account by an anonymous former Klansman, later identified as Ben Titus.

But the paper suffered from sagging revenue due to Klan attacks, including ongoing threats in the *Western American*. "Those who advertise in the *Portland Telegram* are not on your list of friends" and "are going to get what's coming to them," warned the Klan paper.[13] The Klan campaign propelled the *Telegram* into a downward financial spiral from which it never recovered. The newspaper eventually was forced to vacate its new colonial-style building.[14] In 1931, the paper ceased publication.

Wimpy *Oregonian*

First the *Oregonian* ignored the Klan. Then it used sarcasm while minimizing the Klan's impact. Then it buckled under Klan pressure. In June 1921, when the *Telegram* documented the arrival of the first kleagle in Portland,[15] that was followed in July by accounts in smaller papers such as Eugene's *Morning Register,*[16] the *Eugene Guard,*[17] the *Capital Journal,*[18] and *Oregon Labor Press.*[19] The *Oregonian* stayed mum during that formative period for the Klan in Oregon. The state's largest and most prestigious paper broke its silence only after receiving an invite to the Klan's coming-out press conference in Portland, though it buried the story on page fourteen.[20] The *Oregonian* then covered the press conference in a dismissive and sarcastic fashion, calling it "theatrical claptrap" and a "sheet-and-pillowcase masquerade," while relegating the story to page fifteen.[21] The *Oregonian*'s campaign to ridicule and dismiss the Klan continued in late September, when it reported that several hundred Portlanders, including many policemen and other "unsophisticated suckers," had spent ten dollars to join the Klan "before the ridiculousness of the Ku Klux began to sink in."

"The *Oregonian* viewed the Klan as more of a nuisance than a threat," Valenti wrote, "and did not appear to take them seriously."[22] In December 1921, when the Klan planned its first big public event at Municipal Auditorium, the *Oregonian* previewed the pivotal event in a one-paragraph brief.[23] When the Klan event attracted some six thousand attendees during the busy Christmas season, the newspaper's coverage also consisted of one paragraph.[24]

The Reverend Lawrence Saalfeld, who wrote a detailed history of the Oregon Klan for his 1950 master's thesis, blamed the media's softball coverage for the KKK's rapid expansion: "In Oregon, it was precisely the lack of opposition that gave the Klan full reign."[25] *Capital Journal* editor Putman had expressed a similar view during the Klan's rise to power, citing the example of Asa Bush, the former editor of Putnam's Salem competitor: "Had the Portland newspapers of today handled the Ku Kluxers as fearlessly and courageously as Bush handled "Know-Nothings" of sixty-eight years ago, their lawless organization would never have secured a foothold in the state, and have attained a prominence whereby they threatened dominance of state affairs by electing a governor and Legislature pledged to their bidding."[26]

It was an understandable yet dubious assertion. In September and October 1921, the *New York World*'s nationally syndicated twenty-one-part series on the second Klan, and the resulting Congressional hearings, spurred surging interest in the new version of the Klan and a massive spike in membership. The *Oregonian's* strategy of ridiculing or downplaying the Klan may have been a reasonable *political* strategy for the time, even if it didn't meet contemporary standards for objective journalism. We'll never know, though. The *Oregonian*, fearing a loss of subscribers due to pressure from the Klan, backed down from its "tirade of ridicule."[27]

"Consequently, the *Oregonian*'s approach seems to have been to make every effort to avoid antagonizing anyone on any side of the issue," Valenti observed.[28] The *Oregonian* stepped up its Klan coverage when it asked gubernatorial candidates to respond to Governor Olcott's May 1922 proclamation condemning the Klan, and published their remarks.[29] Salem editor Putnam then lashed out at the *Oregonian* for asking candidates' views on the Klan without stating its own. "The *Oregonian* itself has side-stepped the issue that it raised," Putnam editorialized. "The *Oregonian* has miserably played the coward in its duty to the party, to the public and to the state."[30] In the fall, Putnam fumed that the *Oregonian*, the state's leading Republican paper, stood silently while the Klan seized control of the GOP.[31]

The *Oregonian* did provide serious coverage of the Klan-supported ballot measure—in its editorials. Its weeklong series meticulously addressed several aspects of the initiative and the newspaper's perspectives. However, the actual viewpoints expressed in the editorials resembled wishy-washy rambling rather than clear-cut opinions. One piece explained that Catholics, Lutherans, and people of other faiths viewed the initiative as an assault on religious liberty. "It is not entirely clear to the *Oregonian* that this is strictly so," editors wrote. "If a parent wishes to impart religious instruction to his child, he may freely do it elsewhere."[32] One of the editorials declared that the Scottish Rite Masons' motives and patriotism should not be questioned.[33] Another complained the measure would result in unnecessary expense, because public schools would be forced to duplicate classroom space and school buildings serving private-school students.[34] In another piece, editors praised the initiative's mandate to close college-preparatory academies and thus level the playing field for all students. "Conceived in that spirit and having that effect, it is a great and noble idea."[35]

The newspaper concluded its lengthy editorial series by stating its position on the initiative in just one sentence: The *Oregonian* "believes it to be unconstitutional—an infringement upon parental rights and property rights."[36] Throughout its exhaustive editorial series, the

Oregonian avoided linking the initiative to the Klan or defending religious liberty. "The *Oregonian's* editorial approach," Valenti concluded, "while mildly disapproving, reflected an ambivalence toward the issues involved and a reluctance to take a strong position."[37] It was hardly a surprise, then, when the Klan lavished praise on the *Oregonian* with that resolution after the election. In March 1923, the Klan described Edgar B. Piper as the "distinguished editor" of the paper and called the *Oregonian* "one of the world's greatest newspapers."[38]

Oregon Daily Journal Tilts to Klan

If the *Oregonian* was weak-kneed in covering the Klan, the *Oregon Daily Journal* was downright sympathetic. Like its morning competitor, the *Daily Journal* ignored the Klan until the August 1, 1921, press conference, then sarcastically depicted the secretive group: "Hope for the white race took on a violent turn for the better Monday afternoon when the old King Kleagle . . . showed the law enforcement agencies of Portland and Oregon that the Ku Klux Klan aspires to purify impure politics, put the fear of God into the lawless . . . protect American womanhood and simplify spelling."[39] The paper then shifted to cover the Klan in a straightforward, dispassionate manner for several months.

By the spring of 1922, the *Oregon Daily Journal* seemed to become a willing accomplice to a Klan charm offensive. Newspapers across the state were providing continuing coverage of three kidnappings and threatened lynchings in the Medford area blamed on Klansmen, occurring March 13, March 17, and April 9. The Oregon Klan appeared to be devolving into a violent vigilante group, in the mold of its Reconstruction Era predecessor. The Klan chose at that time to bestow a series of money donations, taking pains to notify the news media of its sudden burst of generosity. The *Daily Journal* obligingly rewarded the Klan's PR campaign with a string of puffy news briefs, two of them appearing on its front page: "Spokane Evangelist is Given $50 by Klan," March 16; "Pervert Reward is Increased by KKK," March 17; "Klan Carries Food to Needy Families," March 18; "Klan Gives Pastor of Portland $50," March 21; "Klan Aids Salvationists," March 28; "Klan Gives $50 to Dr. Anderson, Gospel Crusader," April 21; "Klan Pays Visit to Revivals, Pastor is Presented with $75," April 25. When the abduction and near-lynching defendants came up for their first trial, *Daily Journal* stories minimized the allegations against the Klan and seemed to affix more blame on victim Joseph Hale: "As matters stand now at the end of the trial, the evidence is largely the story of Hale, denounced as a 'moral leper and untrustworthy,' against the stories of the defendants, admittedly prominent and trustworthy men of the community."[40]

As the compulsory public schooling issue intensified bitterness between Protestants and Catholics, the *Daily Journal* urged Oregonians not to get divided over religion, while failing to point out who started that fight. In one editorial, the newspaper blamed the media—not the Klan nor the Scottish Rite Masons—for raising the religious issue.[41] In another opinion piece, it accused Catholics, Jews, and other targets of the Klan's wrath of overreacting. "The Ku Klux Klan cannot harm the Catholic Church, cannot extinguish the Jewish race or limit its numbers by one single person, cannot change the status of the foreign-born, cannot disenfranchise the colored citizen."[42]

"The *Journal* was willing to support the Klan," Valenti observed of Oregon's second-largest newspaper. It depicted the controversial initiative as "an irrelevant squabble over a religious issue and generally refused to discuss it at all."[43] As the election drew near, the *Daily Journal* insisted "the bill is no encroachment on religious liberty," and said claims of increased public spending that would be needed were exaggerated.[44]

One month after the ban on Catholic and other private schools passed, the *Daily Journal* insisted that the newspaper wasn't a Klan supporter, and that the school initiative was the work of the Masons, not the Klan. "There is not the slightest possibility that the people of Oregon are going to be led by the Klan into any wicked or disreputable action to 'blight' the state."[45]

Putnam reserved his harshest media criticism for the Klan-friendly newspaper. "The *Journal* has never once told its readers what the Klan really was and what its sinister intent and baleful purpose are," he editorialized. "Does the *Journal* approve of the Ku Klux Klan? If not, why does the *Journal* ooze Klux pus about Catholics and anti-Catholics, echo Klan propaganda and play the Klan game?"[46] Months later, *Western American* bestowed the Klan's appreciation for the *Daily Journal* and its editor, Benjamin Irvine, saying thousands of Klansmen purchase and read the paper. "Our people frequently praise and applaud Editor Irvine's brilliant writings, as found on his editorial page."[47]

The Klan secured docile treatment from many newspapers after demonstrating its clout early on with the *Oregon Labor Press.* After editor Clarence Rynerson's initial flurry of sharply critical stories about the Klan in August and September 1921, mentions of the Klan vanished from the *Labor Press* for the next two years. Rynerson surely knew of the Klan's rapid rise to the pinnacle of state political power, as he was a candidate for a state House of Representatives seat in the 1922 election. Yet his newspaper never wrote about the Klan's rise as a political force. In its wrap-up story about Oregon's 1922 general election, the *Labor Press* totally ignored the Klan's role. "In Oregon, the victory of Pierce for governor...is largely due to local issues," the newspaper wrote.[48]

In Eastern Oregon, *Pendleton Tribune* editor Harry Kuck also tangled with the Klan. He was particularly offended by its anti-Catholic rhetoric. In an open letter published March 11, 1922, Kuck

Oregon Labor Press

VOLUME XX | PORTLAND, OREGON, FRIDAY, AUGUST 5, 1921 | Number 32

KLAN AFTER LABOR PRESS EDITOR

OFFICIAL THREAT IS SENT THROUGH MAILS

Activities of Outlaw Organization in Portland Assuming Threatening Proportions

THE THREAT OF THE KLAN AND OUR ANSWER

FRISCO WILL HAVE NO GENERAL STRIKE

P. H. McCarthy Is Storm Center Both Within and Outside the Ranks of Organized Labor

FOOD PRICES WENT UP IN LAST MONTH

Special Notices

Oregon Labor Press mounted an aggressive response to a threatening letter from Klan recruiter Luther Powell, but stopped mentioning the Klan after the secret order's boycott sliced circulation and ad sales. (Courtesy of *Northwest Labor Press*)

acknowledged a Klan boycott was costing him money. Nevertheless, he called Klan orator and evangelist "Three-Fingered Jack" Godwin a liar, offering $100 if Godwin could prove the accuracy of the fake Knights of Columbus oath he'd recited from the pulpit of a church.[49]

The Klan grew to an estimated eight hundred members in Pendleton by the summer of 1922.[50] It was so powerful by year's end that newly elected Mayor James Fee felt compelled to say his administration was not run by the Klan.[51] S. B. Sanderson, nephew of Oregon Grand Dragon Gifford, sought to buy the *Pendleton Tribune* on behalf of the Klan, but was rebuffed. Instead, Kuck went down swinging, ultimately shutting down his paper in May 1923. "Not only was a personal campaign of malignant hate and vindictiveness carried on against the *Tribune* editor, but a boycott against his paper was instituted, advertising was withdrawn, subscribers dropped away, and finally after a year of struggle, the *Pendleton Tribune* is gone," lamented the *Medford Mail Tribune*. "The result was catastrophic."[52]

Standing up to Klan

No man stood up to the Oregon KKK more than *Capital Journal* editor and publisher George Putnam. His newspaper, while much smaller in daily page count than its Portland counterparts, devoted more ink to the Klan than any other Oregon publication, in both its news coverage and its editorials. When the Klan proposed that students must attend public schools in the name of "pure Americanism," Putnam countered that was a blatant attack on Catholic schools by the "apostles of intolerance."[53] When the Klan mailed him an application for membership, he scorned the group's "ill-conceived and sinister appeal to racial prejudice and religious intolerance."[54]

Putnam was fearless in his criticism, no matter the target. He slammed Portland newspapers for imposing a "conspiracy of silence,"[55] the Salem Ministerial Association for failing to condemn the Klan as unchristian,[56] and Republicans for ignoring the elephant in the room when adopting their 1922 platform. He even faulted fellow Democrats for pretending the 1922 election was about tax reform while failing to acknowledge the overriding issues of the Klan and its assault on Catholic schools.

Putnam initially made his mark as editor and owner of the *Medford Mail Tribune* from 1907 to 1919. In Medford he was "the epitome of the fighting editor," wrote former Northwest journalist and professor Floyd McKay. "His battles with an entrenched political machine in Medford cost him a night in jail, a libel conviction, and physical assaults."[57]

Putnam sold the *Mail Tribune* in order to buy the *Capital Journal* in 1919 and relocate to Salem. He was still relatively new in town when the Klan threatened his investment, mounting a boycott against the *Capital Journal* in the spring of 1922. The Klan had by then enlisted several hundred Salem members, and they threatened merchants with boycotts unless they stopped advertising in Putnam's newspaper. Putnam didn't back down. Instead, he pulled together a meeting of his major advertisers, arguing that he'd loyally supported them and even declined to accept ads from their Portland competitors. Salem merchants voted to ignore the Klan boycott.[58]

Later that year, the *Capital Journal* put reporter and managing editor Harry Crain on full-time assignment covering the Klan. Crain churned out a stream of scoops on the Klan's origins in various Oregon cities and its continuing political shenanigans. Crain wrote multiple revelatory stories each week on the Klan while Putnam was churning out editorials. When Pierce endorsed the Klan's anti-Catholic school initiative in a blatant deal to win Klan campaign support, Putnam, a lifelong Democrat, switched to support Republican Ben Olcott. Putnam ultimately penned thousands of editorials over six decades in the business, frequently championing the cause of liberty.

Robert Ruhl bought the *Medford Mail Tribune* from Putnam shortly before the Klan arrived to town, and he sustained the paper's reputation for aggressive and independent news coverage. Ruhl, a Unitarian, was educated at the elite Phillips Andover Academy in Massachusetts and Harvard College, where he served on the staff of the *Crimson* campus newspaper alongside Franklin Delano Roosevelt.[59] While his newspaper failed to notice the Klan's surreptitious arrival in Medford in the first half of 1921, the *Mail Tribune* later provided extensive and impartial reporting of the three near-lynchings and subsequent trials, the Klan's efforts to recall county Sheriff Charles Terrill, and related events. After the Southern Oregon Outrages, Ruhl wrote in an editorial that the Klan "prides itself upon assisting, in a perfectly legal and lawful way, the local and state authorities in bringing law violators to justice. And yet the authorities have apparently received no assistance from this organization in bringing

Oregon's ten largest daily newspapers in 1920

Paper	Daily circulation
Morning Oregonian	76,390
Oregon Daily Journal	63,531
Portland Telegram	57,020
Portland News	27,462
Capital Journal (Salem)	5,061
Morning Register (Eugene)	4,511
Oregon Statesman (Salem)	3,748
Astoria Evening Budget	3,430
News-Review (Roseburg)	3,350
Eugene Guard	3,293

Source: *N. W. Ayer & Sons American Newspaper Annual & Directory*, 1921

to justice these unknown citizens, armed and masked, who on three distinct occasions have violated every principle of good citizenship and turned the Constitution of the United States into a scrap of paper."[60]

Faced with Klan attacks on his newspaper, Ruhl withstood lost subscribers and advertisers and a "fear of sabotage in the printing press," said historian Jeff LaLande.[61] In 1921, attorney William Phipps founded the *Medford Clarion*, which quickly became a rival, pro-Klan newspaper. The two Medford papers engaged in a classic newspaper war. "While Robert Ruhl and the *Mail Tribune* rallied anti-Klan forces, Phipps made the *Clarion* into Jackson County's KKK mouthpiece," LaLande wrote.[62]

Corvallis Gazette-Times editor Claude Ingalls also withstood Klan attacks that resulted in cancelled advertising, threats to his family, and personal slanders.[63] "Is there any reason under heaven why the Catholics should not be permitted to continue their schools? Were the Catholics less loyal in the late war, did they not fight as readily and fight as valiantly as did the Protestants?" Ingalls's newspaper editorialized.[64]

The Klan also boycotted the *Astoria Evening Budget* and unsuccessfully sought to get editor Merle Chessman fired.[65] Klansmen accused *Heppner Herald* editor Sam Pattison of being a Catholic because they didn't like his stances. He was Scottish-American and not Catholic.[66] The *La Grande Evening Observer*, published by Republican State Senator Bruce Dennis, also was known as a Klan adversary. "Dennis condemned the 'mob rule' and secrecy of the KKK and viewed its members as 'breeders of trouble,'" wrote historian David Horowitz.[67]

8
Yanking the Reins of Power

"European and Asiatic civilizations cannot amalgamate and we cannot and must not submit to the peaceful penetration of the Japanese and other Mongolian races."

—Governor Walter Pierce, opening message to 1923 Oregon Legislature

"A member of the Ku Klux Klan cannot be convicted in Oregon at the present time. The evidence does not matter, if a Klansman sits on the bench or Klansmen are on the jury placing allegiance to the 'Invisible Empire' above allegiance to the blind goddess" (of justice).

—George Putnam, *Capital Journal*[1]

1923: The Klan Takes Control in Salem

The Oregon Klan reached the zenith of its power in 1923. It dominated the biennial state legislative session in Salem, while a grateful Governor Pierce, beholden to the Klan for helping him get elected, dutifully appointed Klansmen to state positions. Leading politicians paid tribute to Grand Dragon Gifford at a well-publicized banquet, and Klansmen were acquitted in two Southern Oregon Outrage trials. Unbeknownst to the public, though, the Klan was fracturing behind the scenes. It failed to achieve much of significance in the legislative session and bickered with Pierce, threatening to recall him from office.

January 8: Kaspar Kap Kubli selected as Oregon House Speaker.
January 8–February 22: Oregon legislators convene in Salem.
February 25: Trial begins for first Southern Oregon Outrage abduction and near-lynching case.

February 26: Governor Walter Pierce signs Alien Land Bill, barring Japanese and Chinese nationals from owning or leasing land in Oregon.

March 3: Pierce, Portland Mayor George Baker, and other politicians fete Oregon Grand Dragon Fred Gifford at banquet.

March 10: Jury takes forty minutes to acquit three Klansmen accused of kidnapping and near-lynching in first Southern Oregon Outrage trial.

March 15: State dismisses remaining charges in second trial after deciding a conviction would be impossible.

April: Klansmen complain Pierce not providing them enough patronage jobs that he promised.

April: William Simmons wins court order reinstating him to lead KKK; Hiram Evans agrees to buy off his predecessor instead with financial settlement.

May: Evans appoints Gifford as his imperial representative, overseeing all klaverns west of Rockies.

June: Oregon Klan elects school board members in districts across state.

June: Klan leaders, still fuming about lack of Pierce patronage appointments, begin circulating recall petitions.

June 11: Portland Klan inducts two thousand members at Mt. Scott Cemetery.

July 28: Portland Klan inducts one thousand white Protestant immigrants into Royal Riders of the Red Robe at Mt. Tabor Park.

October 10: Pierce recall drive fizzles.

Gaining Keys to the House

Kaspar Kap Kubli, born with the initials KKK, was fated to be associated with the Ku Klux Klan. As it turned out, he and the Klan would share political perspectives as well. Recognizing the marketing potential behind his name, the Oregon Klan granted legislator Kubli free membership, which he gladly accepted.[2] Kubli then exploited Klan strong-arm tactics to become Speaker of the Oregon House of Representatives in 1923—the highest-ranking confirmed Klansman ever elected in Oregon.

Kubli was born in 1869 with a political pedigree. His grandfather was a delegate to the sixty-man convention that drafted the Oregon

Kaspar Kap Kubli, center, parlayed his leadership in the Elks lodge into a seat on the Portland City Council and then the Oregon House of Representatives, where he became House Speaker and the highest-ranking confirmed Klansman in Oregon elected office. (Oregon Historical Society)

Constitution. His mother was a childhood friend of Abraham Lincoln in Illinois; his father was elected Jackson County treasurer in Southern Oregon.[3] Kubli grew up in Jacksonville, Oregon, then attended the University of Oregon and Harvard Law School. He moved to Portland in 1901, where he rose to prominence as a leader of the Benevolent & Protective Order of Elks. As the fraternal group's exalted ruler in Portland, Kubli helped land and then host the Elks' 1912 national convention in the Rose City, which enabled Kubli to gain a seat on the Portland City Council. Then he won election to the Oregon House of Representatives in 1916.

Kubli made his name in Salem as the prime sponsor of an anti-syndicalism bill. The Industrial Workers of the World were the foremost backers of syndicalism, which called for workers and their unions to take ownership of the means of production. The militant union's members, dubbed Wobblies, were organizing workers in lumber camps and other Oregon worksites, and they supported the Seattle General Strike that shut down that city's port operations. Kubli's anti-syndicalism bill was enacted by the 1919 legislature around the same time as that general strike, and business leaders feared the strike would spread to Portland's waterfront. The bill made it illegal to advocate violence to gain industrial or political change.[4] Unions hotly opposed the bill, fearing it would be used to clamp down on strikes and picketing. "There is no such thing as peaceful picketing," Kubli declared in promoting an early version of his bill. "The men who are building up the shipping industries in Portland ought to have protection."[5] Six days after his anti-syndicalism law took effect, on February 9, 1919, Portland police arrested five men for distributing radical brochures. Later that month, federal agents and local police raided the Portland Wobblies hall, arresting twenty-two men and trashing the offices.[6]

When the Ku Klux Klan rose to become Oregon's leading political force in 1922, Kubli endorsed the compulsory public schooling initiative during his re-election bid. In November, when Oregon voters handed the Klan majority control of the Oregon House for the upcoming 1923 legislative session, Kubli tossed his hat into the ring to become House Speaker. The Klan used its newfound political muscle to ensure that Kubli prevailed. Two coastal lawmakers publicly complained of being "pestered" or threatened by the Klan if they didn't endorse Kubli's bid for Speaker.[7] As Speaker, Kubli controlled the House agenda for the session beginning January 8, and he led a faction of like-minded Portland-area House members dubbed the Kubli Klan. The KKK-backed delegation included D. C. Lewis, a Portland attorney and Federation of Patriotic Societies officer; William F. Woodward, the Portland school board member; Cyril G. Brownell, a Portland insurance agent; Fred J. Meindl, a Portland attorney; Rollie W. Watson, a Tillamook Realtor; Ben F. Keeney, a Eugene poultry farmer; and H. C. Wheeler, a Pleasant Hill farmer.[8]

Gifford was now commonly acknowledged to be the political boss of Oregon.[9] Governor Pierce owed his election to the Klan, and Gifford figured the governor would be beholden to him. The Klan held sway in the House via the Kubli Klan. And the Klan backed Jay Upton's successful bid for Senate president. Upton had sided with Gifford's effort to kill a world's fair bill in the December 1921 special session.[10] But Upton was not a Klansman, and the Klan lacked a controlling majority in his chamber, narrowing its window to pass bills.

Bashing Japanese Immigrants

The stage was set for a legislative assault on immigrants, particularly those from Japan. Oregon had long been ambivalent about whether to welcome newcomers, distinguishing between "desirable and undesirable" immigrants, said Bob Bussel, an emeritus University of Oregon history professor and editor of a collaborative study of the history of immigration to the state.[11] An 1887 report by the State Board of Immigration concluded that "Germans and Scandinavians make up the best of foreign-born immigrants," as they brought useful skills to the farming sector.[12] A 1912 report by the Oregon State Immigration Commission panned unskilled immigrants from Southern and Eastern Europe because they often landed in cities and undercut wages there.[13] However, Irish, Italian, and Jewish immigration to Portland wasn't as big a phenomenon as in East Coast cities, Bussel said.

West Coast states, located on the Pacific Rim, were most attractive to Chinese and Japanese immigrants. They fared the worst of all immigrants in Oregon and had the most difficulty assimilating into majority culture. Their appearance, culture, and languages set them apart, and Oregonians' racist attitudes made them feel unwelcome. Back in 1870, businessman Ben Holladay had contracted to bring shiploads of Chinese laborers to Oregon to help extend his Oregon & California Railroad south along the Willamette Valley.[14] Chinese immigrants also worked in Oregon's mining industry, and many opened laundries and other small shops in Portland. A financial panic in 1873 triggered a long depression, leading to a backlash against Chinese laborers, especially on the West Coast, where labor leaders attacked them for taking scarce jobs. Many Chinese returned home after Congress approved the Chinese Exclusion Act in 1882. That was followed by a series of violent attacks against Chinese workers in Seattle, Tacoma, Hells Canyon, and Portland's Albina, Mount Tabor, and Guilds Lake neighborhoods.[15]

By the 1910s, much of the nativist agitation in Oregon shifted to Japanese immigrants. The 1907 "Gentleman's Agreement" between the United States and Japan restricted new immigrants but made an exception for the wives of resident Japanese. An estimated 769 single Japanese men in Oregon then selected "picture brides" from Japan, choosing future wives from afar via photographs, with the help of

Japanese matchmakers.[16] Nativists bashed the practice as an evasion of immigration restrictions. A 1920 report commissioned by the governor found "strong antipathy against the Japanese among small farmers, mechanics, laborers and salaried classes in general."[17] Fewer than five thousand Japanese lived in Oregon, but some white farmers were nervous about the growing number of Japanese families operating orchards and other farms in Multnomah and Hood River Counties, especially when some of those farms were acquired while Oregon-born soldiers were off fighting in World War I.[18]

The American Legion had lobbied since at least 1920 for an Oregon bill to strip Japanese and Chinese immigrants of the right to buy or lease farmland.[19] California passed such a law in 1913, and Washington followed suit. Olcott and Pierce, while running against each other in the 1922 governor's race, both endorsed passage of a similar Alien Land Bill in their platforms. The Klan jumped on the bandwagon for the Alien Land Bill in the 1923 legislative session, taking more credit for its quick passage than it properly deserved. The American Legion did more of the heavy lifting for the bill. "We want to see the state remain white and American," testified Ben Dorris of the American Legion when the bill came up for a hearing. The Portland Chamber of Commerce, not wanting to damage business ties to Japan, led the opposition. "The 1920 Census shows that one-half of one per cent of the population of the state is Japanese," countered W. D. B. Dodson, the chamber's secretary. "A serious menace does not exist."[20] The bill was signed into law by Pierce, along with two companion nativist bills. One required county assessors to list all property that Chinese and Japanese owned or operated; the other barred aliens from operating certain businesses. All three bills were introduced by members of the Klan-dominated Multnomah County delegation.[21]

Enactment of the Alien Land Law was a clear sign of Oregon's turn toward nativism, but its actual impact was muted. Despite the ominous implications for Japanese farmers, they were able to evade the law's stated objective by transferring land holdings to their Oregon-born children who were granted citizenship. Multigenerational families carried on running their farms and orchards as before, and the law was seldom enforced prior to the anti-Japanese upsurge during World War II.[22]

Going After the Nuns

The other major 1923 law pushed by the Klan was the religious garb bill, which barred teachers in public schools from wearing religious symbols or attire in the classroom. The bill was aimed at twenty nuns who wore habits while teaching in public schools, mostly in the largely Catholic communities of Sublimity, St. Paul, and Mt. Angel. A Senate amendment watered down the original House bill and eliminated provisions to fine and imprison offending nuns.[23] After the bill was signed, sisters teaching in St. Paul schools quit rather than comply with the law.[24]

A handful of other new laws responded to the upsurge of patriotism championed by the Klan. One required schools to teach about the US Constitution. Another required patriotic content in school curriculum, stipulating that "no textbook shall be used in our schools that speaks slightingly of the founders of the republic, or of the men who preserved the union, or which belittles or undervalues their work."[25] A third new law imposed a literacy test before people could register to vote in Oregon. Applicants had to read from among several passages in the Oregon Constitution and then write at least ten words about it in English.[26] The legislature also passed two advisory memorials to Congress that expressed lawmakers' nativist sentiments. Lawmakers asked Congress to restrict immigrants from Southern Europe and Asia, and to enact new immigration quotas to boost the share of "Anglo-Saxon and Teutonic races" while limiting others. Both measures passed nearly unanimously.[27]

In the most significant policy bill of the session, Governor Pierce persuaded legislators to approve the state's first income tax, a referral sent to the ballot so voters could make the final call. The Klan-dominated legislature couldn't wrangle enough votes to pass several of the order's other bills, including some targeting Catholics. The House passed bills to end the state celebration of Columbus Day, a holiday close to the heart of Italian Catholics, and to tax hospitals, including ones run by nuns in Portland, Eugene, and Medford. Another House-passed bill would tax sectarian hospitals, colleges, and schools.[28] Other Klan-supported bills passing the House would ban employment of aliens on public works projects,[29] require business owners to disclose their nationalities,[30] and revert to having only a Protestant chaplain serve all prisoners at the state penitentiary. Those six House bills all died in the Senate.[31] Other bills aimed at Catholics couldn't pass muster even in the Klan-controlled House. One would impose a tax on all church properties; another would ban the import of wines used in sacramental rituals.[32]

Catholics breathed a sigh of relief at the close of the forty-five-day session, concluding that the Klan's clout and effectiveness had been overstated. "The fair-minded people of the state," wrote the *Catholic Sentinel*, "have reason to congratulate themselves upon the defeat of nearly every attempt to place upon the statute books measures that were prompted by bigotry and hatred."[33]

"Love Feast" for Gifford

If the 1923 legislative session was a bit underwhelming for the Klan, the Invisible Empire scored a public relations coup shortly after the session ended, with an assist from Governor Pierce and Portland Mayor Baker. Some five hundred people filled the Portland Chamber of Commerce ballroom on Saturday evening, March 3, for an event billed as a patriotic banquet but derided by the *Portland Telegram* as a "love feast" for Gifford.[34] The governor and mayor sat at the head table with Gifford and others. It was a vivid public display of the Klan's political clout that made national news, including in the *New York Times*.[35] Also attending were Salem Mayor John Giesy, Astoria Mayor O. B. Setters, and Clatsop County Sheriff Harley Slusher.[36]

The Reverend T. Gallagher, minister at Portland's Sunnyside Methodist Church and toastmaster for the event, assured guests that neither the governor nor the mayor knew who was sponsoring the banquet when they accepted invitations to speak. But that was a dubious assertion. Reverend James R. Johnson, the recently named exalted cyclops of the Portland Klan, made it clear the whole purpose of the banquet was to honor Gifford. "We are not here under false pretenses," agreed Mayor Baker, closely allied with the Klan. "We have gathered here as a group of patriotic American citizens, and we need not apologize for that."[37] Pierce's friends told reporters he had been misled and didn't realize he was to speak at a Klan event.[38] But that also appears to be untrue. One reporter asked Pierce in advance if rumors were true that he was to speak at a Klan rally. "Well, I think I shall probably address them," Pierce responded.[39] Pierce, a teetotaler and Prohibition supporter, spoke to the crowd about the need to enforce liquor laws, to reduce alcohol consumption and illegal trafficking.

The banquet honoring Gifford came at a delicate time for the Oregon Klan and the grand dragon's leadership. Oregon newspapers were rigorously covering trials of Klansmen for the Southern Oregon Outrage abductions and threatened lynchings. Local and national papers were reporting on two gruesome Klan-linked lynchings in Mer Rouge, Louisiana. Less than six weeks earlier, while the legislature was in session, thirty disgruntled Oregon Klan chapters had voted to discontinue paying their dues until Gifford was removed as grand dragon.[40] The negative publicity and challenges to Gifford's leadership might explain why the banquet was scheduled, and why some political leaders might have shied away from it. Oregon Secretary of State Sam Kozer and Scottish Rite leader Malcom reportedly turned down invitations, while House Speaker Kubli said he couldn't attend because he was ill.[41]

Gifford, when his turn came to address the crowd, insisted the masked and robed kidnappers who strung up three Medford-area men were not Klansmen, and that allegations of Klan responsibility for the Mer Rouge lynchings were simply propaganda. "Oregon is the battleground," Gifford added, changing the subject. "It is here that we are going to prove what the standards of true American citizenship as espoused by this organization can accomplish."[42]

Oregon's most outspoken Klan critics were flabbergasted that Pierce and Baker would help shine the Klan's tarnished image while the state was prosecuting Klansmen for the Medford-area violence. "The theme, outside of fulsome flattering of the 'Grand Dragon,' was the white-washing of the blood-stained garments of the klan," wrote Putnam, the Salem editor.[43] The *Portland Telegram* was equally blunt: "The incident shows to what base depths public men will descend in order to secure votes."[44]

Evans Reshapes Klan Priorities

As internal dissent loosened Gifford's grip on the Invisible Empire in Oregon, he had crucial backing from the Imperial Palace in Atlanta. Hiram Evans, a round-faced, pudgy dentist from Dallas, reportedly joined other Texas Klansmen in the 1921 kidnapping and torturing of young Black bellhop Alex Johnson.[45] But after his elevation to imperial wizard in November 1922, Evans worked to shift the Klan from its roots as a fraternal lodge with a penchant for violence into a modern political machine.[46] "I took the job when there were whippings around the South. I had to run around and stop those," Evans said later.[47]

In late 1923, Evans relocated his headquarters from Atlanta to Washington, DC, to be closer to the seat of national power.[48] Evans's emphasis on electoral politics meshed with Gifford's passion and skills. In 1922 the Oregon Klan was one of the Invisible Empire's top political success stories, inspiring other states to emulate its ban on Catholic schools. In May 1923, Evans awarded Gifford a national title as deputy imperial wizard, in charge of one of three imperial districts. Gifford was now the biggest power in the Klan west of the Rocky Mountains, a reflection of how important Oregon had become to the Invisible Empire.[49]

Evans claimed to be weeding out corruption in the Klan, which he blamed largely on his predecessor William Simmons's thirst for profits and Edward Clarke and Elizabeth Tyler's incentive-based commission structure for kleagles. Under that scheme, Evans acknowledged later, kleagles were motivated to "sell hate at $10 a package" and reap the economic benefits of "inflaming prejudices."[50] Evans canceled Clarke's membership recruitment contract in March 1923 and shifted some of the staff overseeing kleagles to fixed salaries, conveniently enabling KKK headquarters to collect a greater share of membership fees.[51] "He had a gold mine," Evans said of Clarke. "There were some weeks when he took in as much as $30,000."[52] That would be valued at more than half a million dollars in mid-2020s currency. Some klaverns, such as La Grande, also took on their own recruitment.[53]

Scholar Miguel Hernandez concluded that Evans engaged in a "superficial facelift" of the incentive system, permitting kleagles on the ground to continue working on commission because it was so effective.[54] Oregon Klansmen who were expanding the Ladies of the Invisible Empire to other states also continued to seek recruiters paid via commission. Four months after firing Clarke, Evans agreed to pay organizer Daisy Barr four dollars of each five-dollar initiation fee paid by new recruits to the Women of the Ku Klux Klan.[55] Oregon Klan propagandist Lem Dever later wrote that Evans was merely adopting modern sales techniques for kleagles but compensating them the same way. "Think of the hordes of scientific salesmen, the high-powered type that delivers the goods, going after members on a rich commission basis! That is the purpose of Wizard Evans's training school."[56]

Klan leaders continued to joust for control of the for-profit corporation and its money-making potential. Simmons won an April 1923 court order reinstating his authority atop the Klan. Evans, rather than relinquish the top post, agreed to an out-of-court settlement granting Simmons $1,000 a month for life, plus a ceremonial title as Klan emperor if he bowed out. Simmons insisted on preserving his ownership of the Klan charter, rituals, and regalia, which he'd copyrighted.

Factional fights continued to plague the order. In November 1923, Evans's publicity chief Phil Fox, who edited the Klan newspaper *Imperial Night Hawk*, shot and killed Simmons's lawyer, William S. Coburn. The trial, which made national news, resulted in a life sentence for Fox.[57] Evans later tangled with Indiana Klan chieftain D. C. Stephenson, who was amassing power and money overseeing a vast recruitment operation in several Midwestern states. "Almost from the beginning," wrote historian Chalmers, "Klansmen were fighting Klansmen, and the prize was clearly loot rather than principles."[58]

Southern Oregon Nightriders Go Free

Despite Gifford's insistence on Klan innocence in the Southern Oregon abductions and near-lynchings, investigators turned up plenty of evidence linking the crimes to known Klansmen. But bringing the culprits to justice proved elusive in a county where the Invisible Empire had taken hold. From the start, Jackson County prosecutors failed to pursue perpetrators of what were dubbed the Southern Oregon Outrages, prompting federal authorities to step in. After launching an investigation, US Attorney General Harry M. Daugherty determined no federal statutes applied, so he handed the fruits of the federal probe over to the state.

On July 6, 1922, Governor Olcott instructed Oregon Attorney General Isaac H. Van Winkle to take charge of the prosecution, and to form a grand jury.[59] The grand jury subpoenaed kleagles and other Klansmen, hearing testimony from seventy-five people over the course of eleven days. Based on the grand jury's work, six known Klansmen were indicted, along with sixteen unidentified "John Does."[60] The Klansmen included an orchardist, a chiropractor who was a former minister, an auto dealer who was the former police chief, the former county jailer, a garage proprietor, and the janitor at the jail.[61]

By the time the cases went to trial in March of 1923, a newly elected judge presided: Klan-supported Charles M. Thomas, who appeared to reward the Klan for backing his fall campaign. During jury selection for the kidnapping and simulated hanging of J. F. Hale, Thomas ruled that the prosecuting attorney, Assistant Attorney General Liljeqvist, couldn't ask potential jurors if they were Klan members, though Klansmen were bound by secret oath to support each other.[62] The man chosen as jury foreman, John Norris, was a cousin of Alexander Norris, one of the accused nightriders.[63] During jury selection, one of the state's key witnesses, US Department of Justice agent Tom Word, was mysteriously arrested in Salem for public drunkenness.[64] The federal agent claimed he was framed to discredit his upcoming testimony. At the trial, a former Klan member testified that a defendant told him he burned fellow Klansmens' robes upon learning agent Word was in town investigating the threatened hangings. In the final day of testimony, Hale testified that he couldn't quite identify former Medford police chief Jesse F. Hittson as one of his abductors because he was masked, but said the masked man was addressed by other assailants as "chief" and "J. F."[65]

After two weeks, the most sensational Klan trial in Oregon ended with a whimper. The jury met for only forty minutes, returning innocent verdicts for Hittson, Jouett Bray, and orchardist Howard Hill. "Acquittal of the night-riders at Medford surprises no one—but it emphasizes the fact that a member of the Ku Klux Klan cannot be convicted in Oregon at the present time," opined Putnam of the *Capital Journal*. "The evidence does not matter."[66] State prosecutors reached the same conclusion. Three days later, in the early stages of the second trial, prosecutor Liljeqvist moved to drop the case. The state determined it would be impossible to win a conviction, given the circumstances.[67]

The trial results were further evidence the Oregon Klan was winning the PR battle despite a simmering internal rebellion and limited accomplishments in Salem. New recruits continued to sign up in droves, though there were signs the Oregon Klan was also shedding members. In November 1922, King Kleagle Luther Powell, the chief recruiter in the Northwest, boasted that the Portland chapter had twenty-two thousand members.[68] Two months later, Powell claimed Portland had more than twenty thousand members.[69]

At its peak, the Portland klavern was the nation's sixth-largest city chapter, counting women in Klan auxiliaries, according to historian Kenneth Jackson.[70] Portland enlisted more members than Atlanta, where the second Klan got its start and was headquartered, as well as Los Angeles, New York, Seattle, and Dallas. Only klaverns in Chicago, Indianapolis, Philadelphia, Detroit, and Denver signed up more members. Portland also ranked among the top handful of big-city klaverns on a per-capita basis.[71]

Klan membership in smaller Oregon towns was bolstered by public talks delivered by the Reverend Virgil "Bearcat" Allison, now the Klan's leading lecturer in the state. From October 1922 to September 1923, Allison delivered twenty-eight lectures in twenty-three Oregon communities.[72] "The Klan is proportionately stronger in Oregon than in any other state in the nation," wrote a Seattle newspaper reporter dispatched to Oregon for an in-depth 1923 series about the Oregon Klan.[73] Later, the Indiana Klan would lay claim to that honor.

US cities with the most Klan members

City	Members*
Chicago	50,000
Indianapolis	38,000
Philadelphia	35,000
Detroit	35,000
Denver	23,000
Portland	**22,000**
Atlanta	20,000
Akron	18,000
Los Angeles	18,000
Pittsburg	17,000
Youngstown	17,000

*Includes male and female members from 1915 to 1944
Source: *The Ku Klux Klan in the City, 1915–1930*, Kenneth T. Jackson

After Gifford's elevation to Oregon grand dragon in late 1922, the Portland klavern elected Dr. James R. Johnson, pastor of Sellwood Christian Church, to replace him as exalted cyclops. Johnson took the Klan's anti-Catholic rhetoric to a new level. In one lecture, he thundered, "I charge tonight that every Catholic priest and every Knight of Columbus in the city of Portland and the state of Oregon is guilty of treason." At another, he said priests ask questions of parishioners in confessionals to satisfy their lust. That was ironic, given Dever's later claim that Reverend Johnson was a Peeping Tom.[74]

Johnson addressed a large crowd of 2,500 at Portland's Municipal Auditorium on May 2, 1923.[75] Then, in a major show of strength on June 11, he presided over the Portland klavern's first big outdoor initiation ceremony, inducting a reported two thousand new members on Mount Scott. Without permission or advance publicity, Klansmen trooped up to the Mount Scott cemetery ten miles southeast of downtown Portland, in a section reserved for deceased soldiers. Two thirty-foot-high burning crosses flickered upon the tombstones and four American flags fluttered in the breeze as Klan oaths were administered in front of several thousand spectators in a four-hour event commencing at 7:30 p.m.[76] Johnson later insisted the *Oregonian* printed lies about the event and that the ceremony hadn't taken place inside the cemetery.[77] Johnson didn't convince the KKK's former allies in the American Legion, whose auxiliary issued a statement denouncing the Klan for using the site: "We believe the use of Mount Scott Park cemetery was an outrage and a desecration of the graves of our heroes, who are of every color and creed."[78] The Klan had lost influence in the veteran's group. After Gifford's men gained control of Portland's American Legion post in 1922, they were "overwhelmingly defeated" in 1923, Rothwell wrote in his Reed College thesis released the next year.[79] Critical coverage of the dust-up in Portland's pro-Klan newspaper, the *Oregon Daily Journal*, was another sign the Klan was losing its ability to intimidate critics.[80]

After coaxing voters to close private schools and persuading lawmakers to ban public-school teachers from wearing religious garb, the Klan turned to seeking outright control of public schools. In June 1923, the Klan fielded candidates in school board elections across the state. In Grants Pass, several hundred Klansmen marched in a parade four days before the election to promote their two school board candidates.[81]

A. M. Heston, backed by the Klan, won 594 votes, enough to win a seat while finishing slightly behind a candidate backed by anti-Klan forces, Minnie Tufts, who earned 610 votes. It was a record turnout for a Grants Pass school board election, rivaling the number of voters who had cast ballots in past presidential races.[82]

Albany voters elected two Klan-backed school board candidates, V. L. Calavan and Ben Bartcher, in what was billed as "the most hotly contested election ever held" there.[83] A total of 1,011 votes were cast in the school board contests, compared to a measly thirty-two in a similar election the prior year. At least one hundred additional voters arrived to polling stations too late to cast votes and were turned away. The Klan's biggest victory in June 1923 school board races was in La Grande, where it elected Lyman Weeks and Dr. R. P. Landis. They joined Klansman Colon Eberhard on the five-person school board, giving the Klan majority control. Turnout was fifty percent higher than for any previous school board election there.[84] Turnout in the Portland School Board election also broke a record, as incumbents Frank L. Shull and William F. Woodward won re-election to three-year terms. The Klan supported Woodward, a vocal advocate of the anti-private school initiative. But the Klan's other favored candidate, William C. North, finished out of the running in third place.[85] There were other signs the Klan was losing some of its clout. In Pendleton, turnout was very high, but Klan candidate J. E. McCormmach fell far short of winning, attracting less than half the votes of the two winners.[86] Klan-backed candidates also lost in Astoria, an ominous sign for the Klan after taking over local politics in the city in late 1922.[87]

Immigrants Inducted atop Mount Tabor

The following month, thousands of Portlanders headed to Mt. Tabor, an extinct volcano three-and-a-half miles east of downtown, for an open-air spectacle promised by the Klan. Many rode the streetcar, disembarking at Belmont Street and Sixty-Ninth Avenue before walking up to the Mount Tabor Park picnic grounds. Others drove cars. Many attendees wore flowing crimson robes, the regalia of the Royal Riders of the Red Robe, a new Klan auxiliary.

At 9 p.m., under the glow of six burning crosses visible across town, about one thousand new members were inducted into the Royal Riders

The Royal Riders of the Red Robe, the Portland Klan's auxiliary for white Protestant male immigrants, assemble in the Portland area. The immigrant group helped expand the Klan's presence and revenues. (Oregon Historical Society)

before more than two thousand family members, friends, and spectators.[88] Unlike the regular Klan, the Red Riders accepted immigrants, but only those deemed the "good" kind—white, male, Protestant, English-speaking types from Canada, the United Kingdom, and Scandinavia. Immigrants from Greece and the Balkans weren't eligible.[89] "There are two menaces facing the country today, which we must meet standing together as one man," Reverend Johnson told the assembled crowd. "These menaces are rum and Rome, and we have gotten rid of one and will get rid of the other."[90]

Portland Klan leaders conceived of an auxiliary for immigrants after the May 1922 primary, upon realizing they missed the chance to attract thousands of votes from folks turned off by the Klan's harsh anti-immigrant stance.[91] So in June 1922, the Portland Klan, without permission from Imperial Palace in Atlanta, created a first-of-its-kind Klan auxiliary for select immigrants.[92] Grand Dragon Gifford was well-connected at Klan headquarters, but he had a habit of hatching schemes to raise money independently and keep it for local operations—or for himself. The Klan gained a new revenue source by charging wanna-be Klansmen $12.50 to join the Royal Riders.[93] "In reality, the program was simply another means for collecting dues by targeting a population that had previously gone untapped," wrote Ben Bruce in an academic paper for Chapman University.[94] Local physician Martin W. Rose was named imperial regent, nominally in charge of the Royal Riders. But Gifford and his aide Ole Quinn were the powers behind the throne.[95]

Aside from the new revenue they earned for the KKK, Royal Riders amplified the Klan's public presence. They marched in Klan parades, attended initiation ceremonies, and helped stage a variety-show fundraiser in Portland, among other activities.

Despite billing itself as a secretive Invisible Empire, the Klan turned to public spectacles to build its brand, as modeled by public relations whizzes Tyler and Clarke. By mid-1923, as the national and Oregon Klans were embroiled in internal bickering and power struggles, more and more Oregon chapters began organizing such spectacles. The events boosted flagging morale among members and bolstered public support. They also conveyed an impression the Klan was unified and strong at a time when it was increasingly neither. The Klan promoted the Mt. Tabor Park initiation ceremony in advance to Portland newspapers. It was billed as a rare chance for the public to see Klansmen wear their regalia in public without masks shielding their identities. Operating out of downtown Portland's Morgan Building, the Royal Riders of the Red Robe, known as the 4Rs, expanded into Astoria, Pendleton, Baker, and other Oregon communities. Then it expanded to Washington, Maine, New Jersey, Montana, and other states, attracting an estimated seventy-five thousand men.[96]

But, as occurred with the Portland Klan's effort to form a women's auxiliary, national Klan leaders soon cracked down on the klavern's efforts to create a new immigrants' auxiliary—and independent funding source—outside Atlanta's control.[97] In August 1924, the 4Rs was dissolved in Oregon, and forcibly merged into the American Krusaders, a new group under Klan headquarters control.

The Portland Klan also hatched the idea of an auxiliary for boys aged twelve to eighteen. Gifford, in a sign of his national profile, pitched the idea at a July 1923 meeting of grand dragons in Asheville, North Carolina. "The average boy's mind is like a plate of putty, in which impressions easily are made," Gifford told fellow state Klan chieftains. Conceived as an alternative to the Boy Scouts, the YMCA, and church groups, his proposed Junior Order of the Ku Klux Klan would instill "godlike character in the rising generation of boys," Gifford said.[98] Dever later claimed he had written Gifford's speech and persuaded the grand dragon to promote the idea, as "he probably saw financial possibilities in it."[99] Luther Powell boasted that fall that the Rose City chapter would soon get authority to launch the national junior order, and that "national headquarters undoubtedly will be established in Portland."[100] But Gifford's dream of controlling another nationwide auxiliary went up in smoke. The Klan did create a Junior Ku Klux Klan along the lines he proposed, with its own rituals and tentative constitution, and by 1924 there were chapters in fifteen states. But the auxiliary was directed from an office in Atlanta and served by a magazine published by the editor of the Indiana Klan newspaper.[101]

Shootout in Condon

In the fall of 1922, Condon was a small, peaceful town off the beaten track in north-central Oregon, near the John Day River. Then Condon Congregational Church recruited G. A. Chaney of Pasco, Washington, as its new pastor, offering him $2,000 a year. "For a while he did very well," organizing a church boys club, said church trustee G. W. Parman.[102] Then Reverend Chaney picked up a side gig, unbeknownst to church leaders. Sometime around May 1923, Chaney began quietly organizing a new Ku Klux Klan chapter.[103] When congregation leaders learned Chaney was a Klan recruiter and their parsonage was doing double duty as a Klan meeting hall, they tried to fire him. But new church members outvoted the church leaders, Parman said. The newcomers were Klansmen that Chaney had recruited.

Leaders of the Gilliam County community of 1,127 mobilized, with some creating an anti-Klan organization called the Minutemen. In a show of strength, fifty-two Klan critics marched in a parade on July 21, 1923, headed by Sheriff Elmer Montague. "They were trying to start something," the Klan newspaper reported, protesting that Chaney was a "sincere, earnest Christian, and practicing the Golden Rule."[104] On

Friday, July 27, Chaney was summoned to a meeting at First National Bank, where he faced seven of the town's leading citizens, including a local judge, the bank director, a doctor, a jeweler, an attorney, master of the local Masonic lodge, and a leading Irish Catholic. The group's spokesman, Circuit Court Judge D. R. Parker, warned Chaney he was headed for trouble. "Everything was peaceful in this community until you came here," Parker said. "We are not now threatening violence, but for your own good and the good of the town, get out!" Chaney made it clear he wasn't leaving.[105] Less than forty-eight hours later, around 3:30 a.m. Sunday, people from moving cars reportedly fired guns at the parsonage. "Outlaws shoot up Klan Hall" read the banner headline of the August 3 *Western American*. The paper confidently predicted that justice would be served.

Governor Pierce, elected the prior November with Klan support, later divulged that Chaney approached his staff in July for help, saying his life was threatened by the Minutemen and his home was shot up. He asked Pierce to send a militia to Condon.[106] Pierce said he tried to console Chaney and thought the pastor left satisfied after the meeting. Then Chaney returned to Salem in early August and asked to be appointed a special state law enforcement officer, as some other Klansmen had been anointed. Pierce declined, instead promising to send his private secretary to Condon to investigate. After getting reports from the field, Pierce said the whole situation had been exaggerated and was a "tempest in a teapot."[107] Pierce predicted there'd be no further outbreaks of violence in Condon.

With no further law enforcement response, local vigilantes took matters into their own hands. On September 1, Condon resident Frank Smith, suspected of shooting up the Klan headquarters, was apprehended by a group of men and taken to the jail in Pendleton.[108] Upon learning that, Sheriff Montague went to the Pendleton jail, rescued Smith, and escorted him back to Condon.

The Congregational Church soon learned that Chaney was not an ordained minister and replaced him. A grand jury later charged Chaney and a group of other men with conspiracy to kidnap Smith. Chaney's attorney sought to move the trial to Umatilla County, claiming his client could not get a fair trial due to adverse publicity about the case in Gilliam County.[109] If one Minutemen got on the jury, said Chaney attorney

Barge E. Leonard, "he would furnish the rope with which to hang the preacher."[110] The district attorney opposed moving the case to Umatilla County, home of La Grande. He told the judge almost seven hundred Klansmen plus three hundred and fifty sympathizers lived there, over half the city's voting population. In the entire county, he said, there were 1,600 Klansmen, including the district attorney and the "whole county court."[111] So Judge Parker, the same man who had earlier warned Chaney to leave town, agreed to move the case to remote Wheeler County instead. No records could be located by Wheeler County clerks to determine the ultimate resolution of Chaney's kidnapping charge.

Whining About Patronage Jobs

Governor Pierce's even-handed response to the Condon violence illustrated the juggling act he'd performed since his election the previous fall with Klan support. "The opinion prevails in political circles that the governor owes his election to the Klan vote, and the Klan no doubt shares that belief," Black newspaper editor Beatrice Morrow Cannady wrote in June 1923.[112] A week earlier, on June 5, Pierce made his second appearance before his hometown klavern in La Grande, hailed by the chapter secretary as an occasion of "great rejoicing."[113] But by then Pierce's relationship with the Klan was fraying. In a private letter sent to his brother Charles Pierce on June 20, Pierce made that clear: "The Klan is pretty mad at me these days. I haven't appointed all the officials they demand and they are now talking of recalling me."[114]

In exchange for Klan support of his candidacy, Pierce had promised the Klan would get a major voice choosing appointments to state positions. But the precise terms of his deal with Gifford were fuzzy. Gifford privately bragged to Portland Klansmen that Pierce had granted him the right to "dictate most of the political patronage of the state if elected," according to defecting Klansman Ben Titus.[115] In the heat of the campaign, rumors circulated that Pierce promised Gifford fifty percent of the statehouse patronage.[116] Pierce also pledged to oust anti-Klan people from state positions if elected.[117] Gifford had spent the early weeks of 1922 vetting political candidates to endorse from his office in downtown Portland's Pittock Block. After Pierce's election, he held court at the same locale, now screening applicants seeking state appointments.[118]

Early in his term, Pierce appointed a large number of state special security officers nominated by Gifford, according to Dever.[119] Akin to the Klansmen appointed as unpaid police vigilantes by Portland Mayor Baker in December 1921, the special officers patrolled state highways, ostensibly enforcing state liquor and narcotics laws. The state granted them badges and the power to make arrests and carry concealed weapons.

A week after the 1922 general election, an Astoria Klansman wrote to Portland Klan leader Reuben Sawyer asking for Gifford to "put in a good word for him" to get a position in the new Pierce administration. "There are several Clatsop County boys after positions...to land them in some fat job," the Klansman wrote.[120] In the midst of the early-1923 legislative session in Salem, a *Catholic Sentinel* reporter detected a surge of job-seekers at the governor's office in the Capitol. "Gov. Pierce is harassed day and night by a small army of seekers after appointments, the most insistent being the young Ku Kluxers who supported him..." One Pierce hire at the state Corporations Department replaced "an accomplished Catholic gentleman," but the appointee quit after one day when he realized the job was over his head.[121]

While Pierce obliged the Klan with numerous appointments, sometimes he balked. Fellow Democratic leaders, who felt they should play a major role in the governor's appointments, complained Pierce was appointing too many Klansmen.[122] Pierce refused Klan entreaties to fire Dr. Robert E. Lee Steiner as head of the Oregon State Hospital, a priority for the Salem klavern.[123] He also resisted persistent Klan lobbying to fire his old friend George L. Cleaver as state Prohibition director. Pierce attended a meeting in Salem with a Klan committee that pitched a candidate for secretary to the Board of Control. The board, made up of the governor, state treasurer, and secretary of state, had considerable sway over state purchasing. The Klansmen "openly stated that they expected to collect a commission from wholesalers who sold goods to the State of Oregon through the Secretary of the Board of Control," Pierce wrote in his memoir, adding that the Klan hoped to net $1 million annually to maintain its newspaper and Portland office. Pierce, saying he preferred not to serve time in the penitentiary, appointed someone else to the post.[124]

Whispers of a Klan effort to recall Pierce began just four months into his term.[125] Applying political pressure on the governor, the Klan newspaper ran a series of one-sentence blurbs in June, 1923, asking its readers: "Do you want to recall Pierce?"[126] It was unclear whether editor Dever was acting independently of Gifford on the talk of recall, or the two were playing good cop-bad cop to manipulate the governor. A week after *Western American* posed that provocative question, Gifford said the Klan was calling off the recall effort.[127] Then four days later, a Dever editorial said Klansman were "rarin' to go in every city" to carry recall petitions.[128] "The victory of November went to his head," Dever wrote, calling Pierce a "parasite" who won his post on the back of the Klan campaign for the compulsory public-school initiative. By late July, *Western American* reported that Gifford finally put a stop to the Klan recall effort after returning from an East Coast business trip.[129] In August, Dever publicly apologized to Pierce in an editorial: "We are human and made some mistakes. We're sorry for hitting him so hard."[130]

But Pierce was not out of the woods. The next month, a new, well-funded recall campaign emerged. At least one hundred petitioners reportedly were hired to gather signatures full time, earning ten cents per signature.[131] Pierce and his allies believed this drive was not being led by the Klan, but by major businesses opposed to his policies: private utilities, timber and fishing interests, irrigation district bondholders, bankers, and wealthy Oregonians alarmed by the new state income tax he had advanced. In his memoir, Pierce wrote that the recall drive was restarted after he met with a banker and a utility executive, who offered him a $100,000 bribe to change some of his policies. Pierce was in financial straits then, and his wife was dying with cancer, but he claimed to have turned down the bribe.[132] Pierce allies then threatened to go to the press with some damning information about the recall forces, which reportedly put a stop to their campaign. By October 10, three days before the deadline for submitting signatures, the campaign was still 12,000 signatures short of the required number.[133] Oregonians would have to await the 1926 governor's election to toss Pierce from office.

9

Oregon Klan Self-Destructs

> *"The death of the Klan in Oregon was not brought about by its opponents. The Klan died by its own hand, the suicide of its own weapons."*
>
> —Reverend Lawrence Saalfeld[1]

> *"The Klan is a war-time product. It was born of psychopathic hysteria and religious delusion."*
>
> —Lem Dever[2]

Corruption, Splits Lead to Klan's Demise

In 1923 and 1924, Fred Gifford's audacious money-making schemes unraveled and he lost his political Midas touch. Klansmen in Portland and other klaverns tired of his tyrannical leadership and incessant demands on their pocketbooks. The Ladies of the Invisible Empire and the Royal Riders of the Red Robe, which showed great promise after expanding into new states, were forcibly shut down. Imperial Wizard Hiram Evans ordered both enfolded into newly created national auxiliaries under his thumb. Gifford brawled openly with rival Luther Powell, parallel to national KKK leadership jousting between Evans, William Simmons, and D. C. Stephenson. From Salem and Eugene to Washington, DC, the Klan sought to bolster its image and popularity via showy parades and ceremonies. Such spectacles fooled much of the media and the public, but the state and national Klans were rupturing.

September 18, 1922: Portland Klansman Carl F. Lemke shouted down at chapter meeting while reciting thirty-four allegations against Fred Gifford.

November 27: Anti-Gifford factions send delegate Carl Green to the KKK's first klonvocation in Atlanta, but he's unable to secure audience to share Oregon grievances.

January 7, 1923: Thirty Oregon klaverns vote to discontinue paying dues until Gifford is removed from office.

May 11: Rush Davis storms Ladies of the Invisible Empire meeting in Portland in brutish bid to seize its written charter.

July 4: More than 100,000 people attend D. C. Stevenson's inauguration as Indiana grand dragon.

October 8: American Federation of Labor, at national convention in Portland, unanimously adopts resolution condemning KKK.

November 5: Hiram Evans's publicity officer Philip Fox murders William Coburn, William Simmons's lawyer.

November 10: Seven hundred Klansmen initiated at state fairgrounds in Salem, before audience of nearly four thousand.

December: Dever resigns as *Western American* editor.

December 17: Three thousand dissident Klansmen gather outside Oregon City, vow to withhold 1924 membership dues until their accusations against Gifford are investigated.

December 21: Fox gets life sentence for murdering Coburn.

February 1924: Gifford banishes chief rival Luther Powell from Klan.

February 12: Evans agrees to final financial settlement with Simmons, paying him $146,000 for his interests in Klan.

March: Federal court declares Oregon's compulsory public-school initiative unconstitutional.

Spring: Dow Walker and John Rankin, Klansmen on Multnomah County Commission, implicated in corruption scandal over bridge construction contracts.

May: Stephenson breaks away from national Klan to create splinter group.

May 16: Oregon's US Senator Charles McNary easily wins GOP primary after Klan factions back three different candidates.

May 16: Multnomah County voters recall Walker and Rankin.

May 24: President Coolidge signs Johnson-Reed Act (aka Immigration Act of 1924), sharply restricting Catholic and Jewish immigration and banning newcomers from Asia.

June: Klan has major presence at Republican National Convention in Ohio.

June 27: Thousands of spectators watch Eugene parade of four hundred Klansmen and Klanswomen, in one of Oregon Klan's last big events.

July: Damaging split emerges at Democratic National Convention when motion to condemn KKK fails by one vote.

August 14: Portland Klan immigrants' auxiliary, Royal Riders of the Red Robe, is dissolved.

October: Dever publishes devastating exposé, "Confessions of an Imperial Klansman."

November: George Baker easily wins re-election as Portland mayor, defeating Klan-backed rival.

June 1, 1925: US Supreme Court rules compulsory public-school initiative is unconstitutional, tossing law before it takes effect.

July: Gifford resigns as Oregon grand dragon.

August 8: In show of strength, Evans leads march of thirty thousand robed Klansmen and women in Washington, DC.

November 14: Stephenson convicted of second-degree murder of twenty-eight-year-old school superintendent aide Madge Oberholtzer.

September 13, 1926: Klan stages another march in Washington, DC, with fewer attendees than prior year.

Scandals Engulf Gifford

The Oregon Klan remained an intimidating and potent political force to the outside world, cowing politicians and the media and striking fear among Catholics, immigrants, Blacks, and Jews. But mounting scandals and internal fissures were tearing the group apart. Rebellious chapters first conspired to topple Fred Gifford before the Klan's triumphs in the 1922 elections, blaming him for corruption and iron-fisted rule. Critics accused Gifford of hypocrisy after revelations that his wife was raised Catholic and the Giffords sent their three children to private schools. Many of the critiques stemmed from Gifford's money-making pursuits, such as the "silver showers" of coins that members obligingly tossed to him in klavern meetings that never seemed to make it into the chapter treasury.[3] Ben Titus's anonymous series in the *Telegram* charged that

Gifford never accounted for funds the Klan raised to pass the compulsory public schooling initiative.[4]

In the midst of the fall 1922 campaign, Portland dissidents prepared a list of thirty-four allegations against Gifford. Their spokesman Carl F. Lemke stood up at the September 18, 1922, klavern meeting to recite the charges,[5] but Gifford loyalists shouted him down and threatened violence against the dissidents. When Gifford defenders demanded Lemke be banished from the Klan, Lemke and fellow Klansman Ray Caldwell set down their Klan membership cards and walked out. "There followed a riot in which one member of the minority group was forced to draw a gun to escape," C. Easton Rothwell wrote in his 1924 Reed College thesis.[6]

Gifford disregarded Klan constitutional requirements for annual officer elections so he could stay on as Portland exalted cyclops.[7] He fended off critics by allying with Evans, which paid off handsomely. Gifford overpowered his main rival, Luther Powell, who remained wedded to William Simmons. With Evans's backing, Gifford was named Oregon grand dragon in October 1922, formalizing his dominant position in the state Klan.[8] In late November 1922, Gifford set off to Atlanta for a showdown at the KKK's first klonvocation (convention). The anti-Gifford faction in Portland, allied with klaverns from Salem, Eugene, Pendleton, Roseburg, and Coos Bay, raised money to send delegate Carl Green to the klonvocation, in hopes of unseating Gifford. The dissidents reportedly represented thirty-seven votes at the convention, dwarfing the seventeen votes allied with Gifford. But Green couldn't secure an audience with national Klan leaders and couldn't get any floor time at the convention. Gifford, backed by newly named Imperial Wizard Evans, emerged unscathed.[9]

One of Gifford's pet projects was a proposed ten-story Klan headquarters in downtown Portland, projected to cost up to five million dollars.[10] The Skyline Corp. of Oregon secured an option to buy the Failing Block, bounded by Salmon and Taylor Streets and Fifth and Sixth Avenues. Skyline sold stock to finance the development, soliciting Klansmen to buy shares.[11] Unbeknownst to members, Skyline promised Gifford and Powell could each pocket three percent of the proceeds, Dever wrote later. "Thousands of dollars were collected from

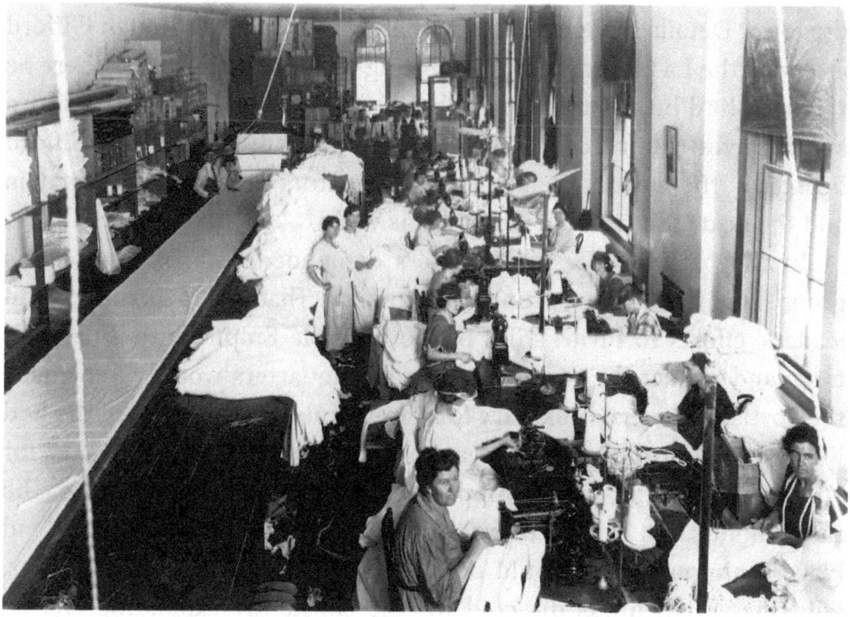

Women textile workers sew robes for members of the second Klan. Klansmen were obliged to buy regalia from the Klan-owned sweatshop in Atlanta at a steep markup. (Alabama Department of Archives and History)

deluded members for this worthless stock," he wrote.[12] The project fell apart by December 1922.[13]

Gifford's vote of confidence from Evans didn't quell restive opposition in his Oregon realm. Portland School Board member George B. Thomas decided to speak out publicly when a man claiming to represent Masons, T. F. Drake, protested the board's hiring of a Catholic-owned firm to design Washington High School. Disregarding his oath of secrecy, Thomas divulged that Drake was a fellow Klansman. "You have violated a solemn obligation…you are not a Klansman," an enraged Drake complained in front of the school board. "No, and I never will be again," Thomas declared, publicly quitting the Klan.[14]

A few days later, on December 11, 1922, Eugene Klansman S. S. George sent a letter to other chapters, inviting delegates to a meeting at Portland's Multnomah Hotel to gather data aimed at prosecuting Gifford.[15] Rebellious klaverns also met in Salem on January 7, 1923, to form a new splinter group to be called Associated Klans, Realm of Oregon. At that gathering, representatives from thirty klaverns voted to discontinue paying Klan dues until Gifford was removed as grand dragon.[16] Details are spotty about what happened next, though Gifford attended the La Grande klavern meeting on January 26, 1923. There he reported he'd been put "on trial" before the Portland klavern and by a special investigator from Atlanta, and he was duly acquitted.[17] Gifford boasted at the meeting that sixteen US senators were fellow Klansmen, and the next US president would be as well.[18]

In May 1923, KKK headquarters demanded control of women's groups that had formed around the country. That ended Portland Klan leaders' efforts to turn Ladies of the Invisible Empire into a national force and pocket the women's dues. Headquarters would later quash the Portland klavern's auxiliary for immigrants, Royal Riders of the Red Robe, and Gifford's plan to create a locally run national auxiliary for youngsters. Gifford never stopped plotting ways to raise money. The same month that it lost control of its women's auxiliary, the Portland klavern announced it would double initiation fees for new recruits, with the added funds directed to "the constantly expanding charity work of the local Klan."[19] The Portland klavern already billed members $1 a month to fund the Klan Kommunity Kit, the chapter's version of Community Chest charities that were sprouting up around the country. Dever later dismissed the Klan alternative as a "money-making scheme." The Portland klavern also created the Klan Komfort Insurance Fund, "formed ostensibly to provide protection for members," he wrote, "but really to enrich the promoters."[20]

Gifford's home klavern felt compelled to issue a vote of confidence in the grand dragon after some critical coverage in the *Portland Telegram.* In June 1923, when Gifford returned from an East Coast swing on Klan business, the chapter reportedly greeted him with a standing ovation and unanimously approved a fawning resolution affirming its support for him. "As of old, as always, he was the hero, the pride of the great Portland Klan, in whose leadership all hopes are centered," *Western American* gushed.[21]

Gifford assured Klansmen after his trip to KKK headquarters that Evans had eliminated all graft within the organization. But that proved illusory. Portland Klansmen later questioned why Gifford used $10,000 of klavern funds to purchase stock in Crown-Willamette Pulp and Paper Co. but have it issued in his name rather than the Klan's.[22] Dr. Martin Rose, leader of the Royal Riders of the Red Robe, pitched members of the immigrant auxiliary to invest in an oil venture. One member, Frank Spencer of La Center, Washington, later said he invested $5,000 based on promises he'd earn 5 percent a month in dividends. Backers told him three oil wells were ready to churn out oil once a pipeline was finished. The venture never produced any oil, and Spencer and the other investors associated with the Klan never got a dime.[23]

Gifford earned the Klan good will by promising to donate $50,000 to the Woman's Christian Temperance Union home for children planned in Corvallis. Gifford boasted the home would provide a Protestant-run orphanage, apparently as an alternative to the Catholic-run St. Mary's Home for Boys in Beaverton and Christie Home for Girls in Oswego.[24] In an *Oregonian* story headlined "Klan Gives $50,000 to Children's Home," Klan leaders assured the reporter that the funds were at hand and would soon be delivered.[25] That seemed reasonable, as each Klansmen was dinged $3 to cover the obligation.[26] But five months later, temperance union president Ada Wallace Unruh divulged that less than $100 of the Klan pledge was ever paid to her group. That prompted questions from Klansman about what happened to the rest of the money they'd donated.[27]

LOTIE Implodes

Reverend Reuben Sawyer was one of the first Klansmen to capitalize on women recruits by forming Ladies of the Invisible Empire, known as LOTIE, but he soon had competition. Simmons launched Kamelia, a Klan-like women's group, after he was pushed out of national leadership in the fall of 1922. That group expanded to twenty states by mid-1923. D. C. Stephenson formed the Queens of the Golden Mask to add women to his Midwestern Klan fiefdom. He initially recruited Daisy Douglas Barr, a popular evangelist, to lead it.[28] Evans made it clear he wanted to consolidate all the Klan women's groups into one national entity that he'd control.

Rush Davis, who had purchased Sawyer's interests in LOTIE in February 1923, realized its days as a locally controlled group were numbered. However, LOTIE leaders, who attracted several hundred women to meetings and were promised a semblance of independence from the men, had their own ideas. The conflict came to a head when Davis arrived unannounced at the May 11, 1923, LOTIE meeting at Redman's

Hall in Portland, demanding the women hand over the group's written charter. Davis was accompanied by a man armed with a six-shooter and known as The Rattlesnake.[29] The women refused Davis's request, apparently believing Klan promises that LOTIE would be run by its female members. Several of the chapter honor guards surrounded Maybelle Jette, their mother counselor, to shield their petite, thirty-three-year-old leader from Davis. According to one account, Davis managed to get his hands on the charter and tore it, but Jette wouldn't back down.[30] Davis grabbed Jette's arm and "savagely twisted it, causing her to writhe in pain." Then one of the honor guards bashed Davis over the head with her umbrella, while several others "kicked him where it hurts most." The attack on his crotch sent Davis out the door screaming for help. Jette then serenely led the women in singing the "Star-Spangled Banner."[31]

Portland Klanswomen won that skirmish but ultimately lost the fight to run their own affairs. Davis headed east to confer with Evans and other national Klan leaders. In June, the national Klan formally chartered the new Women of the Ku Klux Klan. That group, known as the WKKK, was based in Little Rock, Arkansas, but was firmly under Evans's control. LOTIE was forced to merge into the WKKK, under a deal negotiated with Davis and Gifford. Davis scored a lucrative job with the Klan in the South, and in June 1923, sold his interest in LOTIE to the WKKK. His wife Lucien Trigg Davis was named WKKK treasurer, while the grand dragon's wife Mae Gifford was named imperial commander for the Western states.[32] Jette kept her local leadership role, now as exalted cyclops of the new Portland chapter of the WKKK. The struggle for control of LOTIE caused some women to leave the Klan group in disgust. To goose up membership, Gifford issued an order commanding every Oregon Klansman to recruit a new member to the WKKK: "Let no Klansman shirk his duty of bringing in the application of at least one woman—his wife, daughter, mother, sweetheart or friend."[33] But the WKKK never gained much traction in Oregon after the LOTIE debacle.

Defections and Revolts

As klaverns resisted Gifford's dictatorial grip, the grand dragon tightened the screws. He arbitrarily suspended the Pendleton klavern's top three officers in July 1923 and replaced them with his own loyalists. The power play alienated what had ranked among Oregon's five largest klaverns the prior year.[34] The Pendleton Klan secretary defiantly handed back the chapter's hard-earned charter to Gifford, issuing a July 25 letter ordering the grand dragon's operatives to stay away from the klavern. Chapter members then reinstated the three suspended Klansmen.

As the Oregon Klan split apart, it staged more showy public events to bolster its sagging image and exaggerate its strength. On July 6, 1923, Klansmen hosted a fundraising ball in Seaside to support brethren harmed by a huge fire in Astoria. The Klan newspaper boasted that thousands of people were expected.[35] In August, some five hundred Klansmen participated in a public parade in Baker.[36] In a sign that the Oregon Klan wasn't the only realm bleeding members, the Atlanta headquarters announced new financial incentives to boost local recruitment. Chapters could now keep a greater share of membership fees and dues, and the cost of buying robes from headquarters was reduced.[37]

In October, the Klan newspaper announced a klonvocation in Corvallis billed as "the greatest gathering of Klansmen ever held in Oregon." Special trains would bring Klansmen from Portland, Forest Grove, McMinnville, Salem, Albany, Eugene, and Roseburg to the college town for a parade and initiation ceremony.[38] Corvallis exalted cyclops H. E. Walter bragged that three thousand Klansmen would attend the October 18 parade and ceremony, making it the biggest-ever event of its kind in the city. "The Klan is growing by leaps and bounds all over the country," Walter blustered.[39] But the event was overhyped. The local newspaper reported the next day that two hundred twenty-five Klansmen marched in the parade, walking only three abreast to make the line seem longer. A reporter counted eighty-five carloads of Klansmen and spectators venturing to the ceremony one mile outside of town, estimating that only five hundred Klansmen attended.[40]

There also was evidence of sagging attendance at Klan meetings. Not enough officers attended the October 9, 1923, La Grande klavern meeting to conduct business, so substitutes were appointed. Nearly all the officers failed to attend the December 4 meeting.[41] The Klan also was losing its power to intimidate critics. The mayor of Gervais, a small town in Marion County, denied the KKK's request to use its City Hall for a lecture in early 1923. The Klan complained the mayor was Catholic.[42] A bigger example, with national import, occurred in

Portland when the American Federation of Labor staged its national convention in the Rose City in October 1923. The AFL, led by Jewish cigar-maker Samuel Gompers, was often hostile to accepting Black and immigrant members.[43] So there was little surprise when *Western American* published a warm front-page welcome to labor federation delegates before they arrived to town.[44] But once assembled, the AFL delegates unanimously approved a resolution denouncing the "usurpation of government" by the Ku Klux Klan and declared it a menace. "We condemn this secret conspiracy, this hideous and sinister movement that proudly calls itself the 'invisible empire,' cloaking itself in masks and mummery while it eats at the heart of our institutions."[45]

Two weeks later, several hundred Klansmen were forced to withdraw from an Armistice Day parade in Roseburg after veterans lining up to march protested the Klan's presence. The mile-long parade proceeded after Klansmen pulled out.[46] In another embarrassing incident, one hundred fifty Klansmen strutting through downtown Forest Grove in a November 27 parade were bombarded by eggs tossed by a group of boys. "The eggs appeared to come from all directions and the white robes of the hooded knights who were within range were spattered with the eggs' contents," reported the *Oregonian*, now bold enough to put the story on its front page.[47]

In the summer of 1923, the simmering feud between the state's two leading anti-Catholic forces boiled over, another sign the Klan was losing its power to silence critics. The Oregon Klan initially supported the Federation of Patriotic Societies' yellow ticket of endorsed candidates in the spring 1922 primary, but then Gifford set out to infiltrate and take over the group. The two groups maintained their uneasy alliance in the fall 1922 election, teaming to elect Walter Pierce as governor and pass the anti-Catholic school initiative. But Gifford angered his ally by copying FOPS' yellow ticket, issuing it under the guise of a Klan front group, the Good Government League. The Klan yellow ticket endorsed the same candidates as FOPS, with one exception. It listed a different candidate for public service commissioner, a state utilities regulator. Their dispute came to a head at a July 22, 1923, FOPS meeting, when secretary W. C. Elford refused to seat Gifford's two lieutenants on the group's executive committee.[48] In August 1923, Elford submitted a blistering critique of the Klan in a letter to *Oregon*

Voter.[49] He accused Gifford of fostering alternative Orange lodges to gain influence over FOPS's political base. Rival FOPS factions loyal to Elford or Gifford duked it out in court, with both sides seeking legal control of FOPS and the right to use its yellow tickets.[50] In November, Elford issued another public statement, describing Gifford's past efforts to take over FOPS. Elford accused the grand dragon of being a tool of the big utility companies, saying Gifford's endorsement of a different public service commissioner was designed to help elect the utilities' candidate.[51]

Powell's Not-So-Triumphant Return

It was at this point that Luther Powell made a dramatic return to Portland. Powell had been nudged upstairs in late 1922 when Gifford consolidated power as Oregon Grand Dragon. Powell, a masterful salesman, was put in charge of member recruitment for Oregon, Washington, and Idaho, plus the territories of Alaska and Hawaii. He set up shop in Seattle in January 1923 and amassed a team of one hundred kleagles, who recruited heavily from Masonic lodges and other anti-Catholic groups.[52] Powell established a Klan newspaper for Washington, *The Watcher on the Tower,* and chapters of LOTIE and Royal Riders of the Red Robe. Within a few months, Powell claimed there were forty-eight Washington klaverns.[53] The largest was in Seattle, which claimed to have enlisted two thousand members, though the Washington realm's strongest base of support came in the smaller cities of Bellingham and Mt. Vernon.[54] By the summer of 1924, the Klan attracted an estimated twenty thousand or more people to two "Konventions" in Issaquah and Yakima.[55] Powell also launched an initiative campaign to ban private schools, aiming for Washington's 1924 ballot.

Despite Powell's organizing prowess, the Klan never grew as strong in Washington, attracting half as many members.[56] The dominant *Seattle Times* and *Seattle Post-Intelligencer* newspapers were more critical of the Klan than their Portland counterparts. Portland remained the Klan's center of power west of the Rockies, with Gifford in command.

In September 1923, Gifford named C. C. Curtis of Vancouver, Washington, as the provisional grand dragon for Washington, which may have precipitated Powell's move back to Portland the following month.[57] Powell announced he would hand over recruitment to Curtis on November 1, in order to organize a massive membership drive in Portland.[58] The Washington realm suffered when Powell left, and the newspaper fizzled. The following year, more than 58 percent of Washington voters rejected the mandatory public-school initiative modeled after the one Oregon voters passed two years earlier. Membership in the Washington Klan quickly plummeted.

Upon Powell's return to Portland in the fall of 1923, he partnered with Gifford by signing a contract with the Portland klavern, setting an audacious goal of boosting membership in the klavern to 50,000 by February 1, 1924.[59] That would have made Portland's Klan chapter just about the largest in the nation in only four months. Powell took the campaign seriously, issuing $10,000 in Klan Frolic Kurrency for member recruitment incentives. New recruits could redeem the currency at "100 percent White Merchants," whose names would be announced later. Powell boasted that the membership drive would culminate in an enormous parade of 25,000 Klansmen and four hundred horsemen.[60] A massive Klan Frolic, lasting three to six days, would be staged at Portland's Municipal Auditorium sometime after Christmas. Similar spectacles were being offered by Klans in Eastern states.[61]

Before Powell could bring his campaign to fruition, the Klan turned its attention to a grand public spectacle in the state capital. The Salem event, staged November 10, 1923, proved to be the Oregon Klan's greatest spectacle ever, featuring fifteen hundred to eighteen hundred robed Klansmen marching in a mile-long parade, followed by an extravaganza at the state fairgrounds.[62] To thousands of curious onlookers lining downtown Salem streets, the Oregon Klan appeared as formidable as ever. In reality, the Klan was riddled with internal conflict, mass defections, and eroding political influence, on a steady downward spiral from which it never recovered.

Despite chilly weather, spectators seated in cars or on curbsides waited up to four hours for the parade to commence at 8:45 p.m.

Hundreds of carloads of Klansmen headed to Salem from outlying chapters. Others filled two chartered trains arriving from the north and the south. After assembling at the fairgrounds, robed Klansmen marched down North Capitol to Court Street, site of the State Capitol. Powell, in prime position, walked or rode in cars along with other Klan officers, behind a US flag and a fiery cross. Gifford, who often avoided big public events, was a no-show.[63] Klansmen from Salem and several other chapters trailed, along with the Scottish Kiltie and Shrine bands from Portland, the Odd Fellows band from Eugene, and Royal Riders of the Red Robe in their colorful garb.[64]

The parade made its way to State Street, then Commercial, and east on Court to North Summer. Despite the spectacle, "the crowds on curbings were very quiet and there were few cheers," reported the *Capital Journal*, the state's leading anti-Klan paper.[65] Then the crowd filled the main grandstand at the state fairgrounds to hear Klan speakers and see the local chapter receive its long-awaited official charter. Sometime after 11 p.m., as visitors settled into their seats, Reverend Virgil "Bearcat" Allison, the fiery pastor from the Christian Church in Lebanon, Oregon, took the stage as keynote speaker.[66] While an immense, illuminated cross glowed behind him, Allison explained that Anglo-Saxons were preordained to lead the world. He called for a halt to new immigrants from Southern Europe and Asia, and bashed newspapers for failing to depict the truth about the Klan. Two airplanes circled above the fairgrounds, towing an electric-lit cross and a banner reading "Join KKK."[67] Next up was Tom Akers, head of intelligence at the Klan Imperial Palace in Atlanta. Akers trashed Simmons and two other former leaders who were clashing with Evans, then praised Gifford, assuring onlookers that the Oregon grand dragon would have been there if not for illness.[68] Next came the ceremony, when a large group of recruits was formally initiated into the Klan. Then Klan officials formally bestowed the long-awaited charter on the Salem chapter. Salem had been among the first chapters organized in Oregon back in July 1921, but was finally honored as the twenty-ninth klavern chartered in Oregon.

Salem residents had been reading about the KKK's series of broken promises to award the charter in a six-part series ending that day in the *Capital Journal*. An unnamed Klansman identified as a chapter founder was reported to have penned the series, providing a richly detailed insider history.[69] The anonymous Klansman said the chapter once had more than six hundred members, but fewer than one hundred were left after a mass defection of two hundred who had vainly sought to unseat Gifford. The newspaper estimated that only about eighty of those in the parade that day were from the Salem chapter, and the rest were directed by Gifford to attend from other chapters throughout the Willamette Valley.[70]

Messy Leadership Spats Go Public

It didn't take long for Powell's uneasy alliance with Gifford to collapse, along with the grand plan to recruit tens of thousands more Portland Klansmen. Gifford rescinded Powell's recruiting contract less than two weeks after the Salem spectacle. With Powell now out of work, the Northwest's two leading Klansmen waged their messy power struggle in public.[71] Powell blasted Gifford in a statement to the *Portland Telegram*, accusing him of being a "Klan Keizer" who had unfairly banished hundreds of loyal Klansmen from the invisible empire. He called for a "cleanup" to rid the Klan of the "autocratic grand dragon and his henchmen." Powell courted support from dissident Klansmen alienated by Gifford, arranging a meeting with a Salem faction.[72]

Gifford responded to the attacks via his chief publicist, Dever, who delivered a statement to the *Telegram* saying Powell was fired from his contract because he had failed to deliver and no longer held any formal positions within the Klan. "Mr. Powell, like every other man whose only interest in the Klan movement is represented by the dollar mark, now has turned upon the hand that fed him the moment he was disconnected from his gravy train," Dever wrote. He accused Powell of being disloyal to Imperial Wizard Evans and still allied with Simmons.

Gifford didn't stop there. His lieutenants notified Powell he'd be put on trial within the organization for three unnamed counts and banished from the order. "This is to notify you officially that you are suspended from all rights, benefits and privileges in the Knights of the Ku Klux Klan," the letter stated. "This suspension order prevails, pending your trial by a regularly selected tribunal upon charges preferred against you under the constitution and laws of the Knights of Ku Klux Klan on three or more separate counts."[73]

Dever was correct that Powell was in dire need of income and still loyal to Simmons. Powell initially sought to earn money by creating a new magazine, *Klansman's Progress*, with a hefty $1 cover charge. He formed a rival organization called the Allied Protestant Americans, conveniently using the same acronym as the anti-Catholic group that preceded the Klan, the American Protective Association.[74] Neither venture caught on, and Powell soon dropped them both. In February 1924, he emerged with a new job as an organizer for Kastle Knights Kamelia of the K-Duo, a new Klan rival formed by Simmons.[75] Mimicking the early Sawyer lectures, Powell organized a talk at the Salem Armory, billing it as "The Truth about the KKK" and charging fifty cents to attend.

As expected, a five-man tribunal met on February 3, 1924, and upheld Gifford's banishment order against Powell.[76] Meanwhile, other Klansmen were leaving the Invisible Empire of their own accord. An estimated three thousand dissidents from klaverns around the state gathered in the hills outside Oregon City on December 17, 1923. As a fiery cross lit the hills, the Klansmen adopted a resolution opposing Gifford's rule. They vowed to withhold their membership dues for 1924 until an investigation was mounted into their accusations against Gifford.[77]

The Oregon Klan's split into warring factions mirrored ongoing leadership battles in the national organization. In June 1923, eleven Klansmen loyal to Simmons filed a receivership petition against the Klan in Atlanta, asking a court to hand over control of the company.[78] Now Evans was fending off bids for control of the Klan on two fronts: the old guard led by Simmons, and the Indiana upstart who helped him unseat Simmons, D. C. Stephenson. In July 1923, Evans lured famed evangelist and recruiter Daisy Barr to defect from Stephenson's women's auxiliary, Queens of the Golden Mask. She agreed to undertake recruiting for the Women of the Ku Klux Klan controlled by Evans.[79]

More and more, the Klan's internal fights made it into newspapers. In November 1923, Evans's publicity officer and Klan newspaper editor Philip Fox shot and killed William Coburn, Simmons's lawyer. Fox was convicted of murder and sentenced to life imprisonment.[80] Ousted Klan leader Edward Young Clarke sent a letter to President Calvin Coolidge in the waning days of 1923, warning of future Klan violence. "The Klan today, on the inside, is a seething mass of animosity, strife and hatred," Clarke wrote, "and unless something is done to change the situation there will be practical feudal warfare."[81]

Evans got some breathing room in February 1924, ending a messy series of court battles by agreeing to a revised financial payout to Simmons. The founder received a lump sum of $145,500, replacing an earlier agreement that granted him $1,000 a month.[82] Simmons also agreed to halt organizing the Knights Kamelia, cease all opposition to Evans, and resign from the Klan.

Klansmen were by now abandoning the order in droves, prompting a mandate from Atlanta to mount state campaigns to reinstate lapsed members. Montana Grand Dragon Lewis Terwilliger lamented in mid-1924 that more than a fifth of his members "were allowed to drift off and perhaps become forever separated from the organization." That was *after* his realm was recognized for having the second-best results among state Klans at bringing lapsed members back into the fold.[83]

Dever Defects

When Klan lecturer and LOTIE founder Sawyer was souring on the KKK in late 1922, *Western American* editor Lem Dever sought to coax Sawyer back into the fold. "I know you aren't supporting the few filthy scoundrels who are trying at this critical time to undermine" Gifford, Dever wrote to Sawyer.[84] A year later, Dever became one of those filthy scoundrels. In a huge blow to the embattled organization, he resigned as *Western American* editor and publisher in December 1923, announcing he was leaving the Klan.[85] He was one of the Oregon Klan's most colorful, most influential, and best-known figures.

Dever's bigger bombshell came ten months later, when the guilt-ridden former journalist released his forty-eight-page exposé, *Confessions of an Imperial Klansman: Hot Tar and Feathers.* Copies of the self-published memoir sold for fifty cents. "For two and a half years, I have been miserable, reckless and wicked," Dever wrote. "I give my heart and hand to the effort, repairing as far as possible, the wrong I committed unintentionally in promoting this giant fraud instead of opposing it."[86] Curiously, he maintained his reverence for the original terrorist Klan while bashing its more-restrained successor. "In the name of the sublime old Klan of the (1860s), I hold the Fiery Cross on high," he wrote, then went on to criticize the 1920s version of the Klan as money-grubbing, corrupt, violent, and bigoted.

Dever depicted the Reverend James Johnson, Gifford's successor as Portland exalted cyclops, as a Peeping Tom who used binoculars to spy on waitresses changing clothes across the street.[87] Dever saved most of his venom for one-time ally Gifford, depicting him as a front man for public-utility companies who bragged about throwing "raw meat" to his followers in the form of racist, anti-Catholic, and anti-Semitic rants.[88] Dever acknowledged using his newspaper to cover up for Gifford by "playing upon the pathetic credulity of our honest but deluded followers."[89] He described Gifford becoming an "invisible super chief of police" when, with Mayor Baker's blessing, the grand dragon handpicked one hundred Klansmen to serve as Portland police vigilantes in 1922.[90] Gifford hired private investigators in order to keep personal files with "many dark and sinister secrets" about prominent Portland businessmen and other leaders, Dever alleged.[91] He provided damaging new details on Gifford efforts to raise money from fellow Klansmen for dubious schemes, including the downtown Portland high-rise, and Gifford's behind-the-scenes manipulations of Klan political endorsements. The Oregon Klan was far tamer than its more violent counterparts in the South and elsewhere, Dever wrote. Though his memoir focused on corruption and self-dealing among Oregon Klan leaders, Dever said he reached similar conclusions about defects among national Klan leaders. "I did not know then that they are interested solely in hate promotion and wildcat enterprises exclusively under their own control for their own personal enrichment."[92]

In the book's final page, Dever alleged that Simmons had expropriated Josiah Gilbert Holland's 1873 poem, "Wanted," to use in Klan recruitment. Dever then offered his own cynical version of the poem. Instead of Holland's first line of "God give us men!" Dever substituted "God give us TEN!" a reference to the $10 application fee collected from Klansmen. A month after the release of his exposé, Dever was arrested for public drunkenness in Portland and sentenced to fifteen days in jail.[93] In 1925 he released a slightly revised edition of his tell-all, titled *Masks Off!: Confessions of an Imperial Klansman*, which also sold for fifty cents. *Western American* limped along under new management after Dever left, but it shrank in size and suspended publication in March 1925. The following month, the company that printed the newspaper sued it for $18,942 in unpaid bills.[94]

Gifford Bungles Senate Race

Nineteen twenty-four was the year Gifford lost his political mojo, though not for lack of trying. The grand dragon clumsily maneuvered to win the biggest political plum on Oregon's ballot, the US Senate seat held by Republican Charles L. McNary. Though Gifford ultimately got what he wanted, he alienated his own members and two pro-Klan contenders for McNary's seat. The Klan, riddled with dissension and member defections, also suffered a string of defeats in other statewide and local races, further evidence of its lost political clout.

Back in the summer of 1923, Klansmen around the state were hyping Gifford as the best candidate to topple McNary in the GOP Senate primary.[95] Dever wrote a fawning editorial in the Klan newspaper, headlined "The People Want Gifford."[96] Gifford claimed he wasn't interested. He reportedly was grooming Mayor George Baker, a strong ally of the Portland klavern, to challenge McNary. But many klaverns outside Portland supported Kaspar Kubli, the Klansman serving as Oregon House Speaker.[97] Baker and Kubli adopted campaign platforms echoing Klan positions, and at various times they were led to believe they'd get the Klan's endorsement.[98] Republican Clifton McArthur added more intrigue when he entered the race in November, vowing to run on an anti-Klan platform. The former Portland congressman had lost his 1922 re-election bid when the Klan backed his Democratic opponent. Now he set about boldly attacking the Klan as no one else had in Oregon politics. "I feel that Mr. Gifford's power as a political boss should be broken and that his Ku Klux Klan machine should be relegated to the political scrap heap," McArthur stated publicly.[99]

Gifford won a reprieve when the forty-four-year-old McArthur died unexpectedly on December 9, just as the race was heating up. But the grand dragon still faced two Klan-aligned contenders in the GOP primary courting support from different factions of Klansmen. Gifford then shocked his members when he announced in January 1924 that the Klan front group wouldn't endorse anyone in the race, leaving the field clear for incumbent McNary.[100] McNary never openly courted the Klan, but he had named Gifford's nominee, Earl McFarland, to head the customs office at the Port of Portland, among other Klan-friendly patronage appointments. McNary also agreed to support the seating of Klansman Earle Mayfield to the US Senate after the Texas Democrat's election had been challenged. The Oregon Klan included Democrats among its members, and they wanted the Klan to endorse a Democrat in the Senate primary. But Gifford told members of the Portland klavern he'd received a letter from Evans directing the Oregon Klan to lay off McNary and not oppose him.[101]

Early in the race, Harry Crain reported that some seventeen klaverns critical of Gifford were "refusing to 'play ball' with the grand dragon on his political maneuvering.[102] As a result, the Klan vote split three ways between McNary, Baker, and Kubli, and the incumbent easily won the May 16 Republican primary. It was a hollow victory for Gifford, as he lost credibility and political capital. The bungled Senate endorsement wasn't the only setback for the Klan that spring. A month before election day, a federal court ruled the 1922 initiative banning private schools was unconstitutional.

Gifford's bitter feud with the Federation of Patriotic Societies also spilled into the primary election, when FOPS secretary W. C. Elford won a temporary court injunction barring the Klan from sending out copycat yellow-ticket endorsements. "We want forever to take the stain and smell of the Ku Klux Klan from the Oregon Federation of Patriotic Societies," a FOPS representative declared.[103] Then the Klan defied the judge's order, flooding the mail with thousands of yellow tickets made to look like FOPS tickets.[104]

In the primary, the archdiocese issued political endorsements for the first time, which likely helped some Catholic candidates.[105] The Klan and other anti-Catholic groups lost an aggressive effort to unseat Catholic incumbent Congressman Nicholas J. Sinnott, a Republican representing Eastern Oregon. Prominent Catholics John B. Coffey and Frank Lonergan also won primary races for Oregon House seats.[106]

The Portland Klan suffered an embarrassing defeat in the primary when Multnomah County voters recalled two Klansmen from the county commission, Dow Walker and John Rankin, plus a third commissioner endorsed by the Klan, Charles Rudeen. That came after they were implicated in gross irregularities when awarding construction contracts for the Burnside, Sellwood, and Ross Island Bridges. "Multnomah County apparently marked the passing of the Ku Klux Klan as a dominant political force in this community," the *Catholic Sentinel* observed after the election results were in.[107] Klan losses spread beyond its Portland power base. Several Klan candidates for legislative seats lost primary races, indicating the Klan would have dwindling influence in the 1925 legislative session.[108]

In statewide races, Klan-endorsed candidates for state treasurer and public service commissioner were defeated. FOPS-endorsed candidates for state treasurer, public service commissioner, attorney general, and the Oregon Supreme Court also lost.[109] "Everywhere that the Klan was victorious two years ago, it met disaster in the primary," observed Salem newspaper editor George Putnam. "The wave of hysteria that swept the country as an aftermath of the war is subsiding, and common sense is reasserting itself in a return to reason."[110] The Klan limped out of the primary in political decline.

It was time for another spectacle to convince the public the order remained a mighty force, this time in Eugene. Klan leaders boasted that two to four thousand Klansmen would parade through the city on June 27, prompting local police to recruit thirty special traffic officers from Portland to help handle projected crowds.[111] Fireworks flared and a giant cross flamed atop Eugene's Skinner's Butte as four hundred robed Klansmen marched three miles from downtown to the Lane County Fairgrounds. A Klan drill team and marching bands from the

States with the most Klan members

State	Members*	Population	Share of pop.
Indiana	240,000	2,930,390	8.2%
Oregon	50,000	783,389	6.4%
Florida	60,000	968,470	6.2%
Oklahoma	95,000	2,028,283	4.7%
Texas	190,000	4,663,228	4.1%
Ohio	195,000	5,759,394	3.4%
Louisiana	50,000	1,798,509	2.8%
Alabama	55,000	2,348,174	2.3%
Georgia	65,000	2,895,832	2.2%
Michigan	70,000	3,668,412	1.9%
New Jersey	60,000	3,155,900	1.9%
Pennsylvania	150,000	8,720,017	1.7%
Illinois	95,000	6,485,280	1.5%
California	50,000	3,426,865	1.5%
New York	80,000	10,385,227	0.8%

*Male and female members, 1915–1944
Source: *The Ku Klux Klan in the City, 1915–1930*, Kenneth T. Jackson; US Census

city and the Independent Order of Odd Fellows entertained onlookers, who included "practically all the population of Eugene, together with several thousand visitors from neighboring valley towns," a local reporter gushed.[112] After the march, Klansmen and Klanswomen fed five hundred guests at a banquet in the National Guard Armory. Later, families and friends gathered at the fairgrounds to witness dozens of new recruits from the Eugene area get inducted into the Klan.[113] In a special treat during the late-night initiation, Reverend Allison officiated at a marriage ceremony between a Klansman and Klanswoman. The bride and groom dispensed with the usual wedding dress, suit, and tie. Instead, they tied the knot in full Klan regalia.[114]

The impressive display camouflaged the Klan's withering strength in Oregon. To mobilize four hundred marchers, the Klan summoned members from Portland, Salem, Grants Pass, Ashland, Medford, Roseburg, Corvallis, Albany, and McMinnville to converge on Eugene. Organizers had promised two to four thousand marchers—five to ten times the number that actually showed up. It turned out to be the last major spectacle of the 1920s-era Klan in Oregon.[115]

Indiana Realm Rises and Falls

When a Klan lecturer warned a small-town Indiana audience the Catholic pope might pass through town the next day, more than one thousand riled-up residents showed up at the North Manchester train station. But the lone person disembarking from the Chicago-bound train was a corset salesman.[116] Such was the Invisible Empire's sway over Indiana in the 1920s, the only state that topped Oregon in per-capita Klan membership. More than one in fifteen Oregonians joined the Klan, versus more than one in twelve Hoosiers, according to the best estimates.

D. C. Stephenson, the dynamo behind the Indiana realm, rose to prominence after conspiring with Evans and others to topple Imperial Wizard Simmons in the fall of 1922. Evans rewarded Stephenson with the exclusive recruitment franchise for more than twenty Northern and Midwestern states.[117] More than one hundred thousand people flocked to Kokomo, Indiana, on July 4, 1923, to witness Stephenson's formal inauguration as Indiana grand dragon. By then, his Indiana realm was already the largest in the country.[118] By May 1924, Stephenson maneuvered to make his fiefdom independent of the national KKK.[119] Evans expelled him from the Klan in October, and Stephenson announced he was forming a Northern Klan, naming himself its grand dragon.[120] By that time, the Indiana, Illinois, and Ohio realms—Stephenson's home base—accounted for a whopping 40 percent of total Klan membership, leapfrogging the Invisible Empire's former strongholds in the South and Southwest.[121]

Stephenson's weakness for booze and sex proved his undoing, dealing a body blow to the entire Klan. The Indiana Klan leader took a fancy to twenty-eight-year-old Madge Oberholtzer, an aide to the state school superintendent. One March evening in 1925, Stephenson forced Oberholtzer to drink alcohol and board his private train car bound for Chicago, where he assaulted, mutilated, and raped her. At one stop, Oberholtzer managed to slip away to buy poison and swallow it.[122] She survived long enough to share her harrowing ordeal, and Stephenson was arrested on murder charges.[123]

As Stephenson was forging his splinter group that could split the Klan in two, the KKK claimed its biggest policy victory—passage of the Johnson-Reed Act, also called the Immigration Act of 1924. Evans had complained in an October 1923 Klan Day speech at the Texas State Fair that the 1921 immigration quotas enacted by Congress were ineffective. Of the half-million new arrivals in 1922, Evans claimed, 60 percent were Catholics, 10 to 15 percent were Jewish, 5 percent were "Balkan types," and 2 percent were Blacks.[124] In response to pressure from the Klan and other nativists, the 1924 law sharply restricted such immigrants. Named after its co-sponsors, Klan-friendly Representative Albert Johnson from Hoquiam, Washington, and Senator David Reed of Pennsylvania, the law stifled Catholic, Jewish, and Asian immigration for the next four decades. Newcomers were capped at 2 percent of each nationality's share of the US population in 1890. The year was deliberately set before the recent wave of Catholic and Jewish newcomers, largely closing the spigot of newcomers from those groups. New immigrants from Asia were barred entirely. A *New York Times* headline declared the law meant the end of the American melting pot.[125]

Evans and Representative Johnson bragged that the Klan had long pushed for such restrictive immigration and deserved credit. However, it was the culmination of a series of laws clamping down on immigration that began during wartime, before the second Klan's rise. Plenty of other groups joined the nativist push, including the American Federation of Labor. Few lawmakers opposed the 1924 bill in Congress, a sign that it reflected mainstream Americans' views. If the bill was a crowning Klan achievement, its passage crimped the KKK's ability to keep whipping up support by bashing immigrants. "I think that takes the wind out of its sails," said David Horowitz, the Portland historian who has written widely about the Oregon Klan. "That was the biggest item on its agenda."[126]

A better gauge of the Klan's political influence came when the nation's two major parties gathered for presidential nominating conventions in the summer of 1924. The Republican Party convention in Cleveland was a tame affair compared to the Democrats' later fiasco in New York City. Gifford helped lay the groundwork by securing Klansmen as GOP delegates representing Oregon and ten other states. The Klan had such a strong presence that *Time* magazine dubbed it the Kleveland Konvention and placed Imperial Wizard Evans on the cover of its June 23 issue.

When Democratic delegates arrived at New York City's Madison Square Garden for their convention in late June, the party was heavily divided. Northeast Democrats, including many Catholics and others opposed to Prohibition, wanted to nominate popular New York Governor Alfred E. Smith for president. Southern Democrats and all of Oregon's ten delegates opposed Smith largely because he was Catholic. They rallied around William Gibbs McAdoo, a former treasury secretary and son-in-law of President Wilson. During an early roll call, the mere mention of the Ku Klux Klan provoked a near riot. "Fights occurred in two delegations," according to a wire service dispatch published by Portland's Catholic newspaper. "It appeared that 600 to 700 of the total 1,100 delegates in their chairs were howling, whistling, cheering, fighting, throwing their hats in the air—in the cry against Klanism."[127] The convention was bitterly divided over a proposed resolution condemning the Klan as a threat to religious and political liberty. Politicians were so afraid of the Klan, said Maine Governor William R. Pattangall, that US senators feared they couldn't be re-elected if they opposed the secretive group. Another attendee complained that three hundred forty-three Klansmen serving as delegates were dictating the actions of the other eight hundred delegates who were not in the Klan.[128] All Oregon delegates opposed the resolution, which failed by just one vote on the initial count, highlighting the deep schism in the party.[129] When it came time to select a presidential candidate, delegates were hopelessly split between Smith and McAdoo, repeatedly failing to muster enough votes to nominate either man. Finally, on the 103rd ballot, delegates chose a compromise candidate, little-known John W. Davis, a former West Virginia congressman and ambassador to Great Britain.

Oregon Klan Fades Away

Despite the KKK's heightened national political profile, its dismal showing in Oregon's spring 1924 primary revealed sagging influence in one of its strongest outposts. The flagship Portland chapter was beset with money woes that were crimping operations. Klaverns in Salem, Newberg, Tillamook, Bend, Eugene, Oregon City, The Dalles, Corvallis, Pendleton, Roseburg, Grants Pass, Medford, Klamath Falls, and a half a dozen others were "refusing to pay tribute" to Gifford's ruling clique, wrote reporter Harry Crain in late-1923.[130] Dissident Klansmen evidently made good on their pledge to withhold 1924 dues. Jacques De Nyse, the Portland chapter kligrapp, sent members a plea to pay delinquent 1924 membership dues, which he noted were still $6, the same as in 1923. "You will want your 1924 dues card to avoid being temporarily suspended for non-payment of dues," De Nyse wrote.[131]

In March 1924, the Portland klavern was forced to move into cramped new office quarters at the Odd Fellows Lodge.[132] Two months later, the klavern voted by a three-to-one margin to oust Reverend Johnson as exalted cyclops and replace him with R. H. C. Bennett, a business-minded attorney who worked in the bond department of Ladd & Tilton, one of Oregon's biggest and oldest banks. Bennett campaigned on a pledge to reduce klavern operating expenses and eliminate officer salaries.[133] In a show of the Portland klavern's concern and still-sizable membership, more than eleven hundred Klansmen showed up at that May meeting to elect the new exalted cyclops. And thousands of Klansmen attended a Memorial Day rally that month in Tillamook.[134]

But the Oregon Klan continued on its downward spiral. In mid-August, the Royal Riders of the Red Robe was dissolved. The immigrants' auxiliary pioneered by Gifford was supplanted by a national replica controlled by Evans. Later that month, the once Klan-friendly *Oregon Daily Journal* published a scathing letter from a Grants Pass

Klansman announcing his resignation due to Gifford's dictatorial style. "When I was solicited to become a member of the Ku Klux Klan, it was represented to me as an American organization founded upon the traditions and principles of our American forefathers, and I naturally joined it," wrote W. H. Leonard, whose ancestor had arrived on the *Mayflower* ship in 1620. But Leonard came to see the Klan was ruled by "one-man power," a reference to Gifford.[135] Americans had the right to a jury by their peers, he said, but not inside the Klan, where they lost the ability to express their opinions. The final straw, Leonard wrote, came when he was chastised for supporting Robert La Follette's 1924 presidential bid under the Progressive Party banner. "The Cyclops and the Grand Dragon said that I would have to denounce Bob La Follette and swear not to vote for him, or quit the Knights of the Ku Klux Klan," Leonard wrote. "I want to say, once more, that my ancestors fought, bled and died on the battlefields of this country to establish for you and for me that political liberty of which we are so justly proud, and I will not allow one man to take that liberty from me."

Dever continued to pen embarrassing revelations about the Klan for the *Spectator*, Portland's liberal weekly newspaper. Many ministers, including leading Klan lecturer Allison, quit the KKK, Dever wrote, characterizing remaining members as "dangerous fanatics."[136] But he warned that the Klan was far from dead, and that it was still influential in Portland municipal affairs.

Indeed, with many of its endorsed candidates defeated in the May 1924 primary and outlying klaverns going their own way, Gifford's machine focused on its strength, the race for Portland mayor, in the fall general election. Mayor Baker, who severed ties with the Klan after the KKK failed to endorse his primary race for US senator, decided to seek re-election to a third term. Baker's chief rival was W. N. Gatens, a Catholic former Circuit Court justice who the Klan had unseated in 1922 due to his faith. The Klan opted to back one of its own for mayor, discredited Klansman John Rankin, who voters had dumped from the Multnomah County Commission six months earlier due to corruption charges. Baker easily defeated Gatens, 41,810 votes to 21,579. Rankin got only about sixteen hundred votes, a huge embarrassment for the Klan.[137]

The Klan fared well in November 1924 elections in Indiana and some other states. But in Oregon, the Invisible Empire's political heyday was over. Quantifying membership in a secret society is tricky. Historian Kenneth Jackson, relying on internal Klan records and a variety of other sources, estimated that 50,000 men and women joined the Oregon Klan and its women's groups at one time or another, with 22,000 of them joining the Portland klavern.[138] But there was frequent turnover. Rothwell, the budding Reed College scholar, wrote that membership peaked in May 1922, when there were an estimated 15,000 to 16,000 Klansmen statewide, 5,000 to 7,000 of them in Portland.[139] Those numbers were close to Gifford's claims.[140] By 1924, Rothwell calculated that statewide membership had fallen to 5,000 to 7,000, and the Portland klavern was down to 1,165. Some klaverns, particularly in smaller towns, left the Klan that year en masse but stuck together as Orange lodges.[141] In Astoria, eight hundred Klansmen reportedly defected to join an Orange lodge.[142]

By February 1925, the once-mighty Portland klavern was down to fewer than four hundred dues-paying members, Dever wrote.[143] That month, a demoralized Gifford announced he planned to step down from his Klan leadership post. As klaverns closed up shop, many, like the chapter in Coos Bay, destroyed their written records.[144] In a final indignity, the US Supreme Court unanimously ruled in June that the Klan-supported initiative banning private schools was unconstitutional. On July 15, 1925, Gifford officially quit his post.[145] M. S. Belser was dispatched from Atlanta as an interim replacement. Cecil Thomas Godwin, the former district attorney from Baker, was named the new Oregon grand dragon in 1926. Some Klan members remained in the Oregon Legislature, but the KKK lost its ability to shape policy in the 1925 and 1927 legislative sessions.

Remnants of the Klan functioned more like fraternal lodges. In the last recorded major Klan gathering in Oregon, the Gold Hill klavern hosted four hundred Klansman from Southern Oregon in a January 1926 "get-together" at the Odd Fellows Lodge.[146] The Tillamook klavern was Oregon's last surviving major klavern, likely because it functioned more like a traditional lodge. In mid-1926 there were still 196 members in good standing in Tillamook, with forty-five still attending monthly klonklave gatherings, on average.[147] Undated chapter financial records tallied 481 members who had stopped paying dues and were suspended. By the first quarter of 1928, average monthly attendance at

Tillamook klonklaves fell to twenty-five. Only nine Klansman attended the August 8 meeting that summer. The klavern finally shut down in 1929. Oregon's last operating klavern was in Cottage Grove, which continued meeting until the mid-1930s.[148]

Final Spectacles in Nation's Capital

The presidential conventions and 1924 immigration law highlighted the Klan's continuing political relevance but camouflaged its declining popularity in much of the country. Oregon voters weren't the only ones souring on the Klan in 1924; the Klan also was on a downward slide in Texas, Oklahoma, Arkansas, Louisiana, California, Kansas, and even Georgia.[149] Anti-Klan candidates swept into power in Texas in 1924 elections.[150] Voters in Michigan, Washington, and Missouri rejected 1924 ballot measures to ban private schools.[151] Other attempts to enact Oregon-style bans on private schools fizzled in Mississippi, Iowa, Wyoming, California, Arkansas, and Alabama.[152] In 1925, the KKK's Midwest membership base began to unravel after Stephenson's arrest and trial for the Oberholtzer kidnapping and murder. The young victim's ordeal made compelling national news, tarnishing the KKK's image. As the Stephenson trial was scheduled to begin,[153] Evans organized another Klan spectacle—an audacious, military-style march in the nation's capital.

On August 7, 1925, Klan members from numerous states streamed into Washington, DC, by car and train, filling all the city's hotel rooms and boarding houses.[154] Starting at 3 p.m. Saturday, more than thirty thousand Klansmen and Klanswomen began marching, with Evans at the lead in his flowing purple and gold robe.[155] Klansmen and Klanswomen marched in formation in their white robes and conical helmets, up to fifty abreast. They wore no masks, enabling their faces to be exposed to cheering onlookers. For three hours they marched through the seat of American political power, down Pennsylvania Avenue to Fifteenth Street before settling in to hear speeches on the grounds of the Washington Monument.[156] The *Washington Post* depicted it as "one of the greatest demonstrations this city has ever known" in a gushing story the next day headlined "White-Robed Klan Cheered on March in Nation's Capital."[157]

Despite the public show of strength, members continued to abandon the Invisible Empire, and the public closely followed news of

Stephenson's sensational trial. In November 1925 he was convicted of second-degree murder and sentenced to life imprisonment, but the controversy lingered. Stephenson hinted from prison that he might release damning information about the Klan's nefarious acts, in what some viewed as a way to pressure the corrupt Indiana governor into pardoning him.[158] "The Stephenson scandal was the last straw for many Klanspeople," concluded historian Linda Gordon in her study of the second Klan.[159]

By 1926, Evans's home klavern of Dallas, Texas, was in receivership, along with those in Houston, San Antonio, and Fort Worth.[160] The *New York Times* dispatched reporters around the country to survey the status of Klan realms and found the Invisible Empire was "on the wane." Some states retained tens of thousands of members in early 1926, while others, like Oregon, didn't merit any mention. Reporters found varying causes for the decline of state realms, largely based on local circumstances. "The conclusions of the survey show that internal dissensions have contributed much to the defeat of this cause."[161]

Evans decided to repeat his successful march in Washington. On September 13, 1926, Klansmen and Klanswomen were mustered again to show off the KKK's strength. This time, they marched only four abreast, and observers noticed wide spaces between clusters of participants. Police estimated there were 15,000 to 20,000 marchers, roughly half the prior year's turnout, and about one-third of them were women and children.[162]

In an eerie repeat of the Oregon Klan's clumsy handling of the 1924 GOP Senate primary, the Indiana Klan split into factions over which candidate to support in a 1926 Senate race. That dispute cost the Indiana Klan thousands more members.[163] In the summer of 1927, Stephenson released his confidential files while in prison, and he began speaking freely about the Klan's role in Indiana's corrupt politics.[164] By 1928, estimated national Klan membership shriveled from a one-time peak of more than three million to several hundred thousand.[165]

Once the Great Depression hit in 1929, the second Klan shrank to fewer than fifty thousand members, largely concentrated in the South.[166] By 1936, deteriorating finances caused the Klan to sell off its headquarters, which had shifted back to Atlanta in 1929. The new owner subsequently sold the Klan building to the Catholic Church, which used it as a home for its Atlanta archbishop.[167]

10

White Robes and Masks Come and Go

> *"I don't think the Klan really ever went away. The Klan philosophy never went away. Klan behavior never went away."*
>
> —Darrell Millner, emeritus Portland State University professor of Black studies.[1]

Klan Disappears, Then Re-emerges in New Forms

Not long after Fred Gifford resigned as Oregon grand dragon, the man he had propelled into the governor's seat lost a bid for a second term. In ensuing decades, Oregonians would take halting steps to reckon with their state's bigoted history. Voters elected the state's first Jewish governor in 1930, then state lawmakers chose a Catholic man as House Speaker. Congress voted in 1965 to reopen the gates to immigrants regardless of religion, color, or race, leading to a more diverse American populace. The Klan re-emerged in new forms, and other white supremacist groups took up its mantle in Oregon. In the late-2010s and 2020s, a powerful nationwide backlash against immigrants fueled another far-right upsurge, capturing the White House and Congress.

November 1926: Governor Walter Pierce loses re-election bid.

1937: Fred Gifford and Lem Dever try to revive Oregon Klan but effort fizzles.

1944: Second Klan disbands nationwide.

1949: Oregon Supreme Court rules Alien Land Law of 1923 is unconstitutional.

Mid-1950s: Eldon Lee Edwards leads third version of Klan in South, which commits terrorist acts to thwart racial integration and Black voting.

1965: President Lyndon B. Johnson signs Immigration and Nationality Act, abolishing 1924 quotas that discriminated against Southern and Eastern Europeans and barred Asians.

1970s: Young, media-savvy David Duke leads a fourth version of KKK.

1988: Mulugata Seraw, young Ethiopian immigrant in Portland, murdered by members of White Aryan Resistance.

The Second Klan's Swift Decline

The Klan's speedy fall from political power in Oregon was nearly as remarkable as its rapid ascent. It catapulted to political dominance in just a year and a half after Luther Powell's arrival in Medford. A mere two years after the order helped unseat a governor and Congressman, ban Catholic schools, and seize control of the Oregon House and several local governments, the Klan's star burned out. Along the way, it inflamed bigotry and prejudice in every corner of the state. Once-peaceful towns were torn apart by strife, from church congregations to schools to neighborhood clubs.[2] In communities large and small, damaging fissures arose inside fraternal lodges, American Legion chapters, and chambers of commerce. "There is not an important organization, civic, fraternal, or social, that has not been adversely affected by the entrance of the Ku Klux Klan into the city's business and politics," observed a Seattle reporter on special assignment in Portland.[3]

Governor Olcott reflected on the Klan's impact in a speech to fellow governors after his re-election defeat: "We have seen class arrayed against class, neighbor against neighbor. We have seen families divided, communities split. We have seen cities where for years nothing but peace and amity had existed between neighbor and neighbor torn into contending factions, where men went armed with guns, where deeds of violence were perpetrated under the guise of law enforcement, and where all had once been peace, harmony and trustfulness, turned into suspicions and hatred."[4] Oregon's reputation as a progressive state was battered after the anti-Catholic schools initiative passed. Catholics were reluctant to move to the state for fear of encountering religious intolerance.[5]

Historians differ on why the second Klan fell so far and so fast. Some cite the grisly murder trial of Indiana Klan leader D. C. Stephenson

Klanswomen march down Pennsylvania Avenue in Washington, DC, in 1926, the second Klan's final spectacle. (Library of Congress)

as the tipping point.[6] But the Klan was already tottering by then, especially in Oregon and other early strongholds. When Stephenson abducted and raped Madge Oberholtzer in March 1925, the Oregon Klan was in freefall and Fred Gifford was poised to resign his state and national posts. Voters had swept Klansmen out of office in Texas and rejected private-school bans in Washington, Michigan, and Missouri. Americans were turning away from the Klan in Oklahoma, Louisiana, Arkansas, California, and elsewhere.[7] Even in Indiana, Stephenson had already begun to sever his Midwest empire from the national Klan.

One conclusion all analysts share is that the second Klan's demise was largely self-inflicted. In Texas, California, and elsewhere, Klan violence spurred a public backlash. Klansmen tired of hearing tales of corruption, infighting, and hypocrisy among Invisible Empire leaders. And they resented paying for it. Perhaps inevitably, a privately owned business doing double duty as a social movement grew tarnished by missteps of leaders out to pad their own pockets. The for-profit nature of the second Klan made it ripe for internal splinters and incessant fights for control of potentially lucrative revenues. "The leaders of the Klan were out for money and ruled irrationally and dictatorially in its pursuit," Klan historian David Chalmers concluded. "The fight over the spoils wrecked the organization in nearly every state and practically every community."[8] Klan leaders directed the first wave of kleagles to seek respectability for the order by signing up business leaders, professionals, and politicians. But many of those early recruits drifted away from the Klan, which began to tilt toward lower-skilled, less educated and more easily persuadable members. Klan recruiter incentives were designed to produce dues-paying Klansmen, not men of high prestige and skills. Once kleagles pocketed their $4 share from a new member's $10 initiation fee, they moved on to the next potential recruit, with no follow-up services.[9] "I think it was a parody of itself and destined to fall from its own weight," concluded Portland historian David Horowitz.[10]

The second Klan flourished in large measure due to anti-immigrant sentiments exacerbated by World War I. But the hooded order didn't fare so well when social conditions changed. Americans enjoyed greater access to radio, movies, cars, and romance. Men had less desire to congregate in fraternal lodges and little desire to give up alcohol.[11] Post-war recessions eased and the economy prospered. Catholic, Jewish, and Asian immigrants continued to assimilate into mainstream society.

Two Steps Forward, One Step Back

Oregon's 1926 governor's race made it clear the Klan's heyday was over. Walter Pierce ran for a second term but was soundly defeated by Republican Isaac Patterson. The depleted Klan was a non-factor in the race.[12] Pierce later acknowledged the anti-Catholic backlash made all the difference in his 1922 win, in a gracious letter of reference he wrote for his predecessor when Olcott sought a banking job in 1927: "I was able to defeat him owing to a very peculiar religious situation that arose in this state," Pierce wrote diplomatically. "Had he been a candidate against me in 1926, he would have beaten me as badly as I beat him in 1922."[13] In the same election, Oregon voters finally removed the state Constitution's rarely enforced ban on Blacks and mulattoes living in Oregon, which was rendered obsolete by the post-Civil War passage of the Fourteenth Amendment to the federal Constitution but remained a stain on the state's reputation.

Two months after the 1926 governor's race, forty-one eighth-graders from Northeast Portland's Fernwood School went to Imperial Skating Rink to celebrate their graduation. The rink denied entrance to one student, thirteen-year-old George E. Cannady, because he was Black. George was the son of newspaper editor Beatrice Morrow Cannady, known for her diligent efforts to bridge Portland's racial divide. Rather than celebrate without him, George's classmates left the rink en masse and put a quick end to their party.[14] Later in 1927, Oregon voters agreed to remove another antiquated yet embarrassing provision of the Oregon Constitution that denied Blacks, Chinese, and mixed-race citizens the right to vote. Despite such modest signs of progress in race relations, it would take Oregon twenty-six more years to outlaw segregation in public places, when the legislature, pressed by Black leaders and prodded by young Republican lawmaker Mark Hatfield, passed the Public Accommodations Act of 1953.

There was concrete evidence that Oregonians' bigotry toward Catholics and Jews eased after the Klan's demise. In 1930, when the Oregon Klan had dwindled to one minor klavern in Cottage Grove, Oregonians voted in the state's first Jewish governor, Julius Meier, whom the Klan had vilified because of his faith and whose retail chain endured a Klan boycott. Shortly afterward, Catholic attorney Frank Lonergan, a key member of the archdiocese legal defense team that jousted with the Klan, was selected by peers as Oregon House Speaker. The Klan's primary moral crusade lost steam when the Twenty-First Amendment to the Constitution was ratified in late 1933, ending Prohibition and the nation's disastrous attempt to ban alcohol.

Lem Dever, whose memoir condemned the second Klan and former cohort Fred Gifford, did another about-face. Dever reconciled with Gifford, and the pair went public in 1937 with a campaign to relaunch the Oregon Klan. They claimed new chapters were forming in The Dalles, Bend, Medford, Toledo, and St. Helens, but their effort never gained traction and soon fizzled.[15]

Scattered remnants of the Klan survived elsewhere during the Great Depression, reverting to the intimidation and terrorist tactics of the original Klan. Now they demonized Communists, labor organizers, and New Dealers, as well as Southern Blacks.[16] In a sign of the changing times, the US Bureau of Internal Revenue filed a lien against the Invisible Empire in 1944, seeking $685,000 in back taxes from profits earned during the 1920s.[17] "We had to sell all our assets and hand over the proceeds to the government and go out of business," said then-Imperial Wizard James A. Colescott. "The Klan is dead; the whole thing is washed up."[18]

The Japanese attack on Pearl Harbor in December 1941 renewed hysteria against Japanese immigrants on the West Coast. After declaring war on Japan, President Franklin Delano Roosevelt ordered the roundup and imprisonment of an estimated 120,000 Japanese nationals and American-born citizens of Japanese ancestry. Families living west of Highway 97 in Western Oregon were uprooted and incarcerated at prison camps in Minidoka, Idaho; Tule Lake, California; and Heart Mountain in Wyoming.[19]

Fairview farmer Etsuo Namba and his family of seven were among the Oregonians imprisoned at Minidoka. His son Kenji Namba won release in 1943 by volunteering to serve in the US military. Kenji Namba, fighting in Italy, was wounded by a German hand grenade, spending forty days recovering in a hospital and earning a Purple Heart and Bronze Star. When the government closed the internment camps after the war, the Namba family returned home to find others had taken over their Fairview farm. They sought to lease a sixty-two-acre farm near Gresham, but they were prevented from doing so by the 1923 Alien Land Law. The Nambas, in cooperation with the landowner, agreed to join a test case to challenge the law. Their lawsuit was denied by a Multnomah County judge in 1947, but they appealed. In a landmark 1949 decision called Kenji Namba v. McCourt, the Oregon Supreme Court ruled that Oregon's Alien Land Law was unconstitutional. The signature legislative achievement claimed by the Oregon Klan was no longer valid.[20]

The burgeoning Civil Rights Movement and US Supreme Court's 1954 Brown vs. Board of Education decision banning school segregation gave new hope to Blacks that the nation was turning away from racial discrimination. But white supremacists alarmed by the changing racial climate were motivated to create a third version of the Klan. Led by Eldon Lee Edwards, the new version was similar to the original

Klan, confined to the South and deploying bombings, lynchings, and other intimidation to thwart the movement for Black voting and other civil rights. Despite perpetrating considerable violence and mayhem, it never grew anywhere near the size or influence of its predecessors. That third Klan faded by the late-1960s, in part because President John F. Kennedy prodded the Federal Bureau of Investigation to aggressively target the Klan for the first time.[21] FBI director J. Edgar Hoover estimated Klan membership fell from forty thousand in 1965 to fourteen thousand three years later, and continued dropping after that.[22]

Kennedy, the nation's first Catholic president, proposed a 1962 bill to overturn the 1924 immigration quotas that had long restricted new Southern and Eastern Europeans, Asians, and other nationalities. That bill became the Immigration and Nationality Act, which was signed into law in 1965 by Kennedy's successor, President Lyndon B. Johnson, heralding a broader racial and ethnic mix in the country. That same year, Congress passed the Voting Rights Act, which aimed to restore Black voting rights in the South.

In the 1970s, young, media-savvy David Duke helped lead another KKK revival. The fourth version of the Klan welcomed Catholics but vilified new groups, including gays and lesbians, Mexican Americans and Vietnamese immigrants.[23] Tom Metzger, the fourth Klan's grand dragon in California, left to form the White Aryan Resistance. Americans now largely viewed the Klan and its white robes and hoods as comical relics, but its ideology survived in new forms.[24] In 1988, two members of Metzger's white supremacist group murdered Mulugata Seraw, a young Ethiopian immigrant in Portland. Southern Poverty Law Center leader Morris Dees, in a precedent-setting legal strategy, sued Metzger and won a $12.5 million judgement for Seraw's family, bankrupting the group.

In the late-1980s and 1990s, Oregon experienced a major backlash against the growing gay rights movement. The Oregon Citizens Alliance, led by Lon Mabon, organized a 1988 referendum campaign that overturned Governor Neil Goldschmidt's executive order banning discrimination based on sexual orientation within state government. Mabon's group returned with a 1992 initiative that would amend the state Constitution and declare homosexuality "abnormal, wrong, unnatural and perverse." Oregonians rejected that measure, though the anti-gay group persuaded voters in twenty-six Oregon municipalities to enact similar measures. Those were later overturned by the Oregon Legislature and the Oregon Supreme Court.[25]

Historical Reckonings

Many Oregonians have sought to re-examine the Klan's legacy and draw lessons from the state's bigoted history. After a rigorous review, the University of Oregon agreed in 2016 to rename a dorm that had honored Frederick Dunn, the university's former Latin professor and exalted cyclops of the Eugene Klan.[26] The residence hall subsequently was named after DeNorval Unthank Jr., the first Black man to earn an architecture degree from the university. The university also agreed to rename Deady Hall, its oldest building, because of racist views held by namesake Matthew Deady.

Portland civil rights activist Taylor Stewart launched the Oregon Remembrance Project in 2018. The nonprofit creates community coalitions to foster remembrance, repair, and redemption in places with unsavory racist histories. Stewart and supporters formed coalitions in Coos Bay, where Alonzo Tucker was murdered in 1902 in Oregon's most widely documented lynching; and in Grants Pass and other "sundown" towns that informally barred Blacks from being seen in town after the sun sets.[27]

In 2021, the State Library of Oregon removed a plaque honoring Cornelia Marvin Pierce, the first state librarian and spouse of Governor Pierce, because of her advocacy of eugenics and her husband's Klan affiliation and support for the Alien Land Law.[28] In 2022, the Oregon Department of Transportation agreed to rename the Baldock Freeway, the stretch of Interstate 5 between Portland and Salem, and a freeway maintenance facility, because both were named after Robert "Sam" Baldock, the Klansman Governor Pierce had appointed as state highway engineer at the urging of the La Grande Klan. Portland General Electric followed suit and renamed Baldock Solar Station, a solar panel array alongside the freeway.[29]

A month later, the *Oregonian* published a deep, soul-searching review of its past coverage of racial minorities. Titled "Publishing Prejudice," it openly acknowledged what it called the "racist legacy" of the state's dominant newspaper, citing a host of passages it now deemed objectionable. "The now 161-year-old daily newspaper spent decades reinforcing the racial divide in a state founded as whites-only, fomenting the racism that people of color faced," the newspaper wrote in its mea culpa. "It excused lynching. It promoted segregation. It opposed equal rights for women and people of color. It celebrated laws to exclude Asian immigrants. It described Native Americans as uncivilized, saying their extermination might be needed."[30] The package included an official apology from the editor.[31]

Was the second version of the Ku Klux Klan an evil manifestation of the nation's longstanding sentiments of racism and other forms of bigotry? Or was it patriotic and mainstream, as its leaders and members proclaimed? Both could be true. To many Oregonians in the 1920s, joining the Klan was righteous, as routine as joining a lodge or trade union, groups that also deployed racial and religious exclusions. Harold Fosner, secretary of the La Grande klavern, called the Klan "the most noble band of men ever assembled and for the noblest cause in the world." There is no evidence in his voluminous meeting notes to suggest Fosner didn't believe that.[32] Sister Christine Mary, who shielded young girls from Klan attacks while teaching at Portland's St. Mary's Academy, held the opposite view. The Klan was a "mob pressure group," she wrote. "Its existence depended on violence, fear, lies and bigotry. Its tactics called for clandestine meetings, anonymous threats."[33]

Many Americans will deny it, but prejudice and discrimination are a continuing saga in our national story, starting with settlers' brutality against indigenous tribes and enslavement of Black people. Yet Americans also have generously welcomed tens of millions of newcomers from around the world, proudly calling our country a nation of immigrants.

Backlashes against immigration are a recurring theme in our nation, typically after waves of newcomers who look differently, talk differently, or pray differently than those who came earlier. Such backlashes fueled the Know Nothing movement of the 1850s, the American Protective Association of the late-1880s and 1890s, the second Ku Klux Klan in the 1920s, and the Make America Great Again (MAGA) movement spearheaded by Donald Trump in the late-2010s and 2020s.

The stunning lesson from the Klan and modern-day manifestations is that ignorance, anxieties, and fears about people of different colors, religions, races, languages, genders, and sexual orientations can be whipped up and exploited for political and financial gain. Imperial Wizard Hiram Evans acknowledged that in 1926 when he wrote that early kleagles of his own order were paid via commission to "sell hate at $10 a package." The hate and invisible government ideas, he added, "were what gave the Klan its great growth."[34]

In each of these reactionary movements, charismatic extremists relied on scapegoating and attacks on "the other" to build political power. The targets change but the tactics are similar. Modern-day nativist pundits and online influencers, like televangelists of prior decades, have learned that stirring up prejudice and outrage brings many eyeballs to their speeches and writings. More followers means more revenue from online ads and greater political influence.

As this book was being written in 2024, MAGA political campaigns were demonizing trans people and Haitian immigrants. While the book was being edited in 2025, the second Trump administration was orchestrating mass deportations of darker-skinned immigrants while welcoming wealthy white farmers from South Africa.

In such divided times, it's worth remembering the inspiring efforts of Oregonians who challenged the Klan when it was risky to do so. People like Portland civil rights leader Beatrice Morrow Cannady, Medford war veteran Edward Kelly, or Salem newsman George Putnam. Such bravery and heroism will be essential if Oregon is to overcome bigotry now and when it recurs in the future.

"Are the forces of religious, racial, and other forms of prejudice ever really dead and buried—in Oregon or anywhere?"[35] asked University of Portland history professor James T. Covert in 1984, in his foreword for the publication of Reverend Lawrence Saalfeld's 1950 master's thesis on the Oregon Klan. More than four decades later, and a century after the second Klan disappeared from Oregon, the answer is still no.

Acknowledgments

I'm grateful to those whose diligent research and writing about the Oregon Klan offered a rich mine of material to build upon and synthesize:

Jeff LaLande, an expert about the Klan in Southern Oregon, shared his immense knowledge, then read the manuscript and provided incisive comments.

David Horowitz freely shared his unparalleled background on the Oregon Klan. His book on the La Grande klavern minutes is a national treasure.

C. Easton Rothwell, a brilliant Reed College student during the Klan's heyday, who interviewed Klansmen and pieced together the first detailed account of the 1920s Klan in Oregon.

Eckard V. Toy Jr., a historian who focused on the 1920s Klan, starting with his University of Oregon thesis and later writings about the Klan in Eugene and Tillamook.

Reverend Lawrence J. Saalfeld, who wrote a statewide account of the Oregon Klan, especially its attacks on Catholics, for his 1950 master's thesis.

Capital Journal publisher/editor George Putnam, who penned numerous thoughtful editorials, courageously fended off a Klan boycott, and wisely assigned reporter Harry Crain to doggedly cover the Klan's activities.

Kimberly Mangun, who wrote a definitive biography of Beatrice Morrow Cannady.

Others who provided valuable assistance include:

Darrell Millner, Oregon's eminent Black history specialist, who shared his insights and encouraged me to expand my *Portland Tribune* newspaper series into this book.

Raymond Rendleman, a friend and colleague who read the manuscript and provided keen edits.

Michael Robinson, a Scottish Rite historian for Oregon, provided unpublished profiles, a photo of P. S. Malcom, and links to century-old Masonic minutes.

Robert Rynerson shared memories, a photograph, and family genealogy of his grandfather, Clarence M. Rynerson.

Bob Bussel, professor emeritus at the University of Oregon History Department and Labor Education and Research Center, offered historical perspectives on immigration to Oregon.

Professors Dale Soden and Alexander Reid Ross reviewed my manuscript for OSU Press, providing valuable feedback and suggestions.

Cartographer Sara N. Lohse generously produced valuable maps of klaverns around the state.

Many people helped me locate historical documents, photographs, and other valuable resources:

Oregon Historical Society Library staff, including reference services manager Scott Daniels and reference librarians James Scott, Nikki Koehlert, and Renato Rodriguez.

Joseph Schiwek Jr., archives and records manager at the Archdiocese of Portland in Oregon.

In addition, staff at the University of Oregon Library's special collections unit; Sarah Cantor, director of Archives and Heritage Center at the Sisters of the Holy Names of Jesus and Mary in Lake Oswego; Sister Alison (Green), archivist for the Sisters of Mary in Oregon; staff at Multnomah County Library's interlibrary loan program; volunteer Ben Truwe and others at the Southern Oregon Historical Society in Medford; Taylor Roberts, research librarian at Josephine County Historical Society; Taylor Ball, Gilliam/Wheeler County Circuit Court operations associate; Marybeth Jaeger, Wheeler Circuit Court clerk; librarian Emily Johns at the State Library of Oregon; Jeff Matsumoto, president of the Portland Japanese American Citizens League; and a descendant of Frederick Gifford's family by marriage, who asked to remain anonymous.

Friends and historians Sandy Polishuk, Harry Stein, and Jan Dilg provided general advice, and friend/photographer Brian Foulkes produced a high-resolution photo. Mark Beach offered valuable advice about publishing photographs. Bryan Stevenson of the Equal Justice Initiative inspired me to probe into my state's history of bigotry and seek to provide some form of reconciliation with its brutal past. Taylor Stewart of the Oregon Remembrance Project encouraged me to delve into Oregon Klan history.

I'd like to thank OSU Press acquisitions editor Kim Hogeland, who supported this project from the first time I contacted her, and other staff at the press.

My son Gabriel Law shared his basement, providing space for my makeshift office. My offspring Mona Eskayo offered enduring support.

Lastly and crucially, I received daily nourishment for my body and soul from the love of my life, Dawn Robbins. She willingly put up with the disappearing act of her "retired" spouse, providing constant encouragement, inspiration, and thoughtful edits of my manuscript.

APPENDIX A

Oregon Klan Chapters and Communities Penetrated by the Invisible Empire

The following list is based on documented mentions of Klan chapters or organizing across the state.

Communities listed in bold had Klan klaverns and perhaps auxiliaries for women and/or immigrants.

Communities listed in italics were the site of Klan rallies, speeches, marches, or other organizing. They may have had pockets of members, but the author found no clear documentation of full chapters. (Also see map on pages viii–ix.)

Portland Area/Northwestern Oregon

Beaverton: Klan chapter and Ladies of the Invisible Empire (LOTIE) chapter.[1]

Cascade Locks: Klan chapter.[2]

Forest Grove: Chapter chartered as Klan No. 32; Western Oregon Klonvocation staged there; Klan parade.[3]

Gladstone: Klan chapter; 110 initiated in public ceremony.[4]

Gresham: Rumors of chapter being organized in November 1922; lecture at Union High School; mass meeting at Orient Grange Hall.[5]

Hillsboro: Klan chapter; large crowd paraded around county courthouse; Western Oregon klonvocation staged there; more than one hundred paraded before November 1923 klavern meeting.[6]

Hood River: Klan chapter; 250 to be inducted in February 1923; initiation held April 1924.[7]

Oak Grove: Reverend James R. Johnson lectured there in July 1923.[8]

Oregon City: Klan arrived in September 1921; exalted cyclops was Carl Green.[9]

Portland: Klan, LOTIE, and Royal Riders of the Red Robe chapters.

Rainier: Klan chapter.[10]

Sherwood: Klan and WKKK chapters. Reverend Virgil "Bearcat" Allison lectured at Sherwood City Park.[11]

St. Helens: Klan chapter initiation held April 1924.[12]

Vernonia: Klan chapter; fifty Klansmen give money to local church.[13]
West Linn: Initiation scheduled July 1922 at Willamette Hall.[14]

Middle and Lower Willamette Valley

Albany: Klan and LOTIE chapters; exalted cyclops was J. R. Penland.[15]
Aumsville: Thirty-five Klansmen staged parade.[16]
Aurora: Klan chapter formed with eighty men.[17]
Brownsville: Reverend Allison delivered lecture in Klan regalia.[18]
Corvallis: Klan chapter; Kleagle C. W. Jones organizing there in August 1921; charter awarded May 15, 1923, in front of thousands, in joint ceremony with three other klaverns.[19]
Cottage Grove: Klan chapter; event attracts fifteen hundred people; klavern continued to meet until mid-1930s.[20]
Dallas: Klan and WKKK chapters; thousands attend open-air meeting in August 1923; chartered as Klan No. 40 in April 1924.[21]
Donald: Klan lecture at Masonic Temple.[22]
Drain: Large crowd attended February 1924 meeting.[23]
Eugene: Chartered as Klan No. 3 and LOTIE chapter.[24]
Gates: Large picnic held September 1924.[25]
Gervais: Mayor denies Klan use of City Hall.[26]
Halsey: Reverend Allison lecture in January 1923.[27]
Harrisburg: Klan chapter.[28]
Hubbard: Klan lecture held March 1923.[29]
Independence: Klan chapter with one hundred fifty to two hundred fifty members. [30]
Jefferson: Klan chapter.[31]
Junction City: Klan chapter.[32]
Lebanon: Klan charter awarded May 15, 1923, in front of thousands, in joint ceremony with three other klaverns.[33]
McMinnville: Klan and LOTIE chapters.[34]
Mill City: Klan and WKKK chapters; charter awarded May 15, 1923, in front of thousands, in joint ceremony with three other klaverns.[35]
Monmouth/Polk County: Klan chapter.[36]
Philomath: Reverend Allison spoke there in February 1923.[37]
Newberg: Klan and WKKK chapters.[38]
Salem: Chartered as Klan No. 29.[39]
Scio: Klan chapter.[40]
Silverton: Klan chapter; Reverend Allison lectured there.[41]
Springfield: Klan chapter.[42]

Stayton: Thirty-five Klansmen, including some from Stayton, paraded in Aumsville.[43]

Turner: Reverend Allison lectured at high school auditorium in June 1923; thirty-five Klansmen, including some from Turner, paraded in Aumsville.[44]

Veneta: Klan lecture in July 1924.[45]

Willamina: Klan stirred up anti-Catholic sentiments.[46]

Woodburn: Klan lecture in February 1923.[47]

Oregon Coast

Astoria: Chartered as Klan No. 2; also LOTIE and Royal Riders of Red Robe chapters.[48]

Bandon: Charter issued October 8, 1924; Catholic pastor responds to Klan propaganda against parishioners.[49]

Coquille: Klan chapter; Reverend W. L. Straub of Eugene lectured at fairgrounds in September 1923.[50]

Florence: Klan lecture in July 1924; local Klansmen joined Mapleton Klan.[51]

Mapleton: Klan chapter.[52]

Marshfield (Coos Bay): Klan chapter; organizers arrived in January 1922.[53]

Myrtle Point: Klan chapter.[54]

North Bend: Klan chapter.[55]

Seaside: Klan organized July 1923 fundraiser for Astoria fire relief; Klan donated to local church.[56]

Reedsport: Had group of Klansmen; Reverend Allison lectured in November 1923.[57]

Tillamook: Klan and LOTIE chapters.[58]

Toledo: Klan chapter.[59]

Waldport: Klan chapter.[60]

Wheeler: Klan chapter, later merged into Tillamook klavern.[61]

Southern Oregon

Ashland: Klan and LOTIE chapters.[62]

Glendale: Klan suspected of vandalism at Catholic Church.[63]

Glide: Klan lecture in June 1922.[64]

Gold Hill: Klan chapter.[65]

Grants Pass: Klan and LOTIE chapters.[66]

Klamath Falls: Chapter organized by Luther Powell.[67]

Medford: Klan chapter led by exalted cyclops Newton W. Borden.[68]

Myrtle Creek: Klan lecturer Charles Robert Mathis spoke at local theater.[69]

Oakland: Klan lecture scheduled June 15, 1922.[70]

Riddle: Klan chapter.[71]

Roseburg: Klan began organizing in August 1921; chartered as Umpqua Klan No. 5 before two thousand Klansmen; LOTIE/WKKK chapter.[72]

Eastern Oregon

Baker: Chartered as Klan No. 13; Royal Riders of the Red Robe chapter.[73]
Bend: Klan chapter.[74]
Condon: Klan chapter.[75]
The Dalles: Klan chapter established August 1921; chartered as Klan No. 19, led by exalted cyclops Charles Darnielle; LOTIE/WKKK chapter.[76]
Dufur: Local Klansmen attended ceremonial there.[77]
Elgin: Klan chapter; members include police chief.[78]
Enterprise: Klan and LOTIE chapters; also referred to as Wallowa County Klan; one hundred initiated.[79]
Hardman: Thirty men attended organizing meeting, but sheriff doubted a chapter would form.[80]
Heppner/Morrow County: Chartered as Klan No. 33, plus LOTIE chapter.[81]
Hermiston: Klan chapter.[82]
Huntington: Klan chapter.[83]
Ione: Klan chapter.[84]
La Grande: Chartered as Klan No. 14, led by exalted cyclops J. O. Reynolds; WKKK chapter.[85]
Lostine: Klan chapter.[86]
Milton: Described as a Klan voter stronghold.[87]
North Powder: Klan chapter; initiation ceremony held June 1924.[88]
Nyssa: Packed Klan introductory meeting held at Methodist Church.[89]
Ontario: Klan chapter.[90]
Pendleton: Chartered as Klan No. 4, led by exalted cyclops C. H. Conroy; Royal Riders of the Red Robe chapter.[91]
Powell Butte: Klan lecture attracted good crowd in August 1924.[92]
Union: Klan activity.[93]

APPENDIX B

What Happened to Leading Figures

George Baker: Survived 1930 and 1932 recall campaigns stemming from bribery and corruption allegations; left office in 1933. Died in 1941 at age seventy-two; body laid in state in City Council chambers.

Beatrice Morrow Cannady: Failed Oregon bar exam five times but continued practicing law, first Black woman to do so in Oregon. Lost 1932 race for Oregon House seat. Moved to Los Angeles area in 1938; died there in 1974 at age eighty-five. Happy Valley, Oregon, elementary school later named for her.

Edward Clarke: Pled guilty in 1924 to taking woman out of state for immoral purposes; fined $5,000. Organized Klan rival, Mystic Kingdom, enlisting several thousand white Protestants in Midwest. Later became a book publisher, releasing 1939 novel by Clansman author Thomas Dixon Jr.

Lem Dever: After reconciling with Fred Gifford, the duo collaborated to create Klan-like Old Hickory Club of Oregon in 1935–1936, then mounted failed bid to re-establish Oregon Klan in 1937. Died in 1946 in Portland at age seventy-two.

Hiram Evans: Became Atlanta contractor in mid-1930s, resigning as imperial wizard in 1939. State later charged him with price fixing and fined him $15,000. Died in 1966 at age eighty-four.

Fred Gifford: Destroyed Oregon Klan records.[1] Took job with Portland detective agency in April 1924. Became banking industry lobbyist in 1925. Sought to organize Klan rival, Independence Hall, in 1926. After reconciling with Dever, the pair organized Klan-like Old Hickory Club in 1935–1936, then a failed bid to relaunch Oregon Klan in 1937. Died in Portland in 1945 at age sixty-six. Daughter Lauretta married Leon Max Rothschild, a name of German Jewish origin. Their daughter Mary Jo Rothschild was buried at Catholic cemetery in Tillamook. A descendant by marriage said they were "in denial" when they heard about his Klan career. "I think I even teared up, I was that upset."[2]

Charles Hall: Ran for governor again in 1930 but lost in the GOP primary. Remained state senator through 1931 legislative session, then moved to

Portland. The Hall Building, Coos Bay's second-tallest downtown structure, was named after him.

P. S. Malcom: Passed away in 1929 at age eighty-two. Revered by Oregon Scottish Rite lodge, which displays his personal effects and portraits at downtown Portland museum.

Father Edwin O'Hara: Elevated to Montana bishop in 1930; led initiatives in Catholic rural practice, revision of Catholic catechism, and translation of the Bible. Named archbishop in 1954; died in 1956 at age seventy-five.

Governor Ben Olcott: Returned to banking career in Southern California and then Portland. Died in 1952 at age seventy-nine.

Governor Walter Pierce: Solicited support from former Klansmen for unsuccessful 1926 re-election bid. Lost initial race for Congress in 1928 but won in 1932. Became New Dealer and served in Congress ten years. Retired to Salem and died in 1954 at age ninety-one.

Luther Powell: Took civil service exam to become Portland policemen in 1924, listing Hiram Evans, George Baker, and the police chief as references.[3] Organized Klan in Alaska and the Kanadian Knights of the Ku Klux Klan in British Columbia. After a Klan parade through downtown Vancouver, B. C., in October 1925, Canada barred him from re-entering the country.[4] Went home to Louisiana, led Khaki Shirts of America, then organized for fascist Silver Shirts in 1930s. Died in 1951 in Shreveport, Louisiana, at age seventy-three.

C. Easton Rothwell: Earned master's degree from University of Oregon and doctorate from Stanford University, then worked in administration and faculty for UO, Stanford, and Reed College. Worked for US State Department; in that capacity, he helped write the United Nations Charter. Directed Hoover Institution at Stanford and was Mills College president. Died in 1987 at age eighty-four.

Reverend Reuben Sawyer: Resumed work as pastor in 1923. As Great Depression hit, became paid huckster for Theronoid, an electromagnetic device that he pitched in print and on radio as a miracle health cure.[5] Died poor at age ninety-five in 1962, in Washington.

William Simmons: Moved to Atlanta in 1926 after Knights of the Flaming Sword fizzled. Wrote book about his Klan experiences, *America's Menace, the Enemy Within*. Returned to Alabama, where he died in 1945 at age sixty-five.

D. C. Stephenson: Parole request denied in 1927 by Indiana's Klansman governor, Ed Jackson, then he testified against Jackson in the latter's 1928 bribery trial. Served thirty-one years in prison for Oberholtzer murder and subsequent parole violation. Died in 1966 at age seventy-four.

Elizabeth Tyler: Forced out of Klan by Evans in 1923. Moved to Southern California, dying in 1924 at age forty-three.

Notes

INTRODUCTION

1 Kimberly Mangun, *A Force for Change: Beatrice Morrow Cannady and the Struggle for Civil Rights in Oregon, 1912–1936* (Oregon State University Press, 2010), 123–124.

2 "Film is Protested," *Sunday Oregonian*, July 4, 1915, 3.

3 "Cheers Greet Film," *Morning Oregonian*, August 30, 1915, 7.

4 Thomas Dixon Jr., *The Clansman* (The Country Life Press, 1905).

5 David M. Chalmers, *Hooded Americanism: The History of the Ku Klux Klan* (Duke University Press, 1987), 430.

6 "Cross Burning," Free Speech Center at Middle Tennessee State University, https://firstamendment.mtsu.edu/article/cross-burning/, accessed July 11, 1925; "The History of Crann Tara," https://cranntara.org.uk/crannta.htm, accessed July 11, 1925.

7 Norman Stewart, *Abbeville Institute Press* blog, "The Legacy of D. W. Griffith," https://www.abbevilleinstitute.org/the-legacy-of-d-w-griffith/, accessed July 11, 1925.

8 Klux Klan Robes, the Anti-Defamation League, https://www.adl.org/resources/hate-symbol/ku-klux-klan-robes, accessed July 11, 1925.

9 See video clip at https://www.youtube.com/watch?v=GBzDH-Vwzy4, accessed July 11, 1925.

10 *PhotoPlay* magazine (October 1916).

11 "Mayor Baker Acts to Suppress Film," *Oregonian*, March 26, 1918.

12 "Play to Continue; Local Efforts to Bar 'Birth of Nation' Fruitless," *Morning Oregonian*, March 28, 1918, 11.

13 Mangun, 130.

14 Mangun, 131.

CHAPTER ONE

1 John Moffat Mecklin, *The Ku Klux Klan: A Study of the American Mind* (Harcourt, Brace and Co., 1924), 3.

2 John C. Lester and D. L. Wilson, *Ku Klux Klan: Its Growth and Disbandment* (Wheeler, Osborn and Duckworth Manufacturing Co., 1884), 53–59.

3 Lester and Wilson, 64–65.

4 Lester and Wilson, 22.

5 Lester and Wilson, 22.

6 Wyn Craig Wade, *The Fiery Cross: The Ku. Klux Klan in America* (Oxford University Press, 1987), 32, 453.

7 Lester and Wilson, 18.

8 Lester and Wilson, 23.

9 Lester and Wilson, 27.

10 David M. Chalmers, *Hooded Americanism: The History of the Ku Klux Klan* (Duke University Press, 1987), 10.

11 "Nathan Bedford Forrest," History.com, https://www.history.com/articles/nathan-bedford-forrest, accessed July 11, 2025.
12 Wade, 48–49.
13 Wade, 73.
14 Wade, 50.
15 Chalmers, 19.
16 Wade, 93.
17 Wade, 107.
18 Interview with author (May 23, 2022).
19 Leonard Dinnerstein, "Leo Frank Case," *New Georgia Encyclopedia*, https://www.georgiaencyclopedia.org/articles/history-archaeology/leo-frank-case, August 11, 2020.
20 Wade, 144.
21 Kenneth Jackson, *The Ku Klux Klan in the City, 1915–1930* (Oxford University Press, 1967), 4.
22 Chalmers, 30.
23 Declaration, Oregon Ku Klux Klan Pamphlets, 1921–1928, Oregon Historical Society Library, Coll 899.
24 Kenneth Jackson, 5–6.
25 Chalmers, 28.
26 Charles Jackson, "William J. Simmons: A Career in Ku Kluxism," *The Georgia Historical Quarterly* 50, No. 4 (December 1966), 351.
27 Chalmers, 29.
28 Kenneth Jackson, 6.
29 Charles Jackson, 352.
30 Charles Jackson, 352.
31 Charles Jackson, 352.
32 Kenneth Jackson, 6.
33 Chalmers, 30.
34 Ward Greene, "Notes for a History of the Klan," *American Mercury,* 5, No. 18 (June 1925), 240.
35 Kenneth Jackson, 258.
36 Charles Jackson, 353, 356.
37 Charles Jackson, 353.
38 Kenneth Jackson, 5; and Miguel Hernandez, "Fighting Fraternities: The Ku Klux Klan and Freemasonry in 1920s America," PhD thesis for University of Exeter, 2014, 21.
39 Mecklin, 68.
40 *Kloran*, Oregon Politics Collection, Box 21, folder 17, Oregon Historical Society Library.
41 Chalmers, 7.
42 Greene, 241.
43 Charles Jackson, 357.
44 Charles Jackson, 357; and Kenneth Jackson, 7.
45 Kathleen Blee, *Women of the Klan: Racism and Gender in the 1920s* (University of California Press, 1991), 20.
46 Hernandez, 167.
47 Charles Jackson, 358.
48 Kenneth Jackson, 30.
49 Blee, 20.
50 Kenneth Jackson, 32.
51 Charles C. Alexander, "Kleagles and Cash: The Ku Klux Klan as a Business Organization, 1915–1930," *The Business History Review* 39, No. 3 (Autumn 1965), 351.
52 Kenneth Jackson, 358.
53 Macon *Telegraph*, June 5, 1922, cited by Charles Jackson, 359.
54 Interview with author (May 21, 2022).
55 Chalmers, 32.
56 Timothy Egan, *A Fever in the Heartland: The Ku Klux Klan's Plot to Take over America, and the Woman who Stopped Them,* Viking, 2023, 19.
57 "Red Summer: The Race Riots of 1919," The National World War 1 Museum and Memorial, https://www.theworldwar.org/learn/about-wwi/red-summer, accessed July 22, 2025.
58 Blee, 21.
59 Chalmers, 35.
60 Mecklin, 8.
61 William Shepherd, "The Fiery Double-Cross," *Collier's*, Vol. 82, July 1928.
62 John Alexander Hamilton, "Manipulating the Masses: Woodrow Wilson and the Birth of American Propaganda," Wilson Center, https://www.wilsoncenter.org/book/manipulating-masses-

woodrow-wilson-and-birth-american-propaganda, August 2, 2021.

63 E. Kimbark MacColl, *The Growth of a City: Power and Politics in Portland, Oregon, 1915 to 1950* (The Georgian Press, 1979), 143–144.

64 "War at Home," New York State Museum, https://exhibitions.nysm.nysed.gov/WWI/phone/war-at-home.html, accessed July 22, 2025.

65 Nancy MacLean, *Behind the Mask of Chivalry: The Making of the Second Ku Klux Klan* (Oxford University Press, 1994), 23.

66 "The Deadly Virus: The Influenza Epidemic of 1918," National Archives, https://www.archives.gov/exhibits/influenza-epidemic/ accessed July 22, 2025.

67 Egan, 347.

68 Wade, 167–169.

69 Interview with author (May 21, 2022).

70 MacLean, 133.

71 Father Wilfred P. Schoenberg, unpublished book manuscript, *Ku Klux Klan in Pacific Northwest: 1921–1927*, archives of the Archdiocese of Portland, 24.

72 MacLean, 98; and Eckard Toy, "The Ku Klux Klan in Oregon, its Character and Program," master's thesis for University of Oregon, 1959, 10.

73 Kenneth Jackson, 12–13, 259, footnote 9.

74 Mecklin, 100–101.

75 "Presbyterian Church in Ireland," *Brittanica*, https://www.britannica.com/topic/Presbyterian-Church-in-Ireland, November 1, 2023.

CHAPTER 2

1 C. Easton Rothwell, "The Ku Klux Klan in the State of Oregon," bachelor's thesis, Reed College (1924), 111, 112.

2 *Confessions of an Imperial Klansman: Hot Tar and Feathers* (self-published, 1924), 10.

3 See Oregon's History, from Oregon Department of Administrative Services 2021 Action Plan, https://www.oregon.gov/lcd/Housing/Documents/2021_DAS_DEI_Action_Plan-History_Only.pdf

4 "Oregon First in Men," *Oregon Voter*, July 12, 1919, 3.

5 E. Kimbark MacColl, *The Growth of a City: Power and Politics in Portland, Oregon, 1915 to 1950* (Georgian Press, 1979), 138.

6 Rothwell, p.111.

7 Some chroniclers placed Powell's arrival in January, while historian Eckard Toy Jr. concluded it was in May, based on a first-person account by one of the initial recruits. See G. Thomas Edwards and Carlos A. Schwantes, editors, *Experiences in a Promised Land: Essays in Pacific Northwest History* (University of Washington Press, 1986), 269; and "Additional to Oregon," *The Kourier Magazine*, July 1931, 32.

8 David Horowitz, editor, *Inside the Klavern: The Secret History of a Ku Klux Klan of the 1920s* (Southern Illinois University Press, 1999), 4.

9 "Gifford and Powell Now at Outs," *Capital Journal*, November 23, 1923, 1; "The Story of the Klan on the Tennessee," *Watcher on the Tower*, July 28, 1923, 5.

10 Horowitz, 4; and Harry Crain, "Prejudice First Plea in Portland," *Capital Journal*, October 20, 1922, 1; and David M. Chalmers, *Hooded Americanism: The History of the Ku Klux Klan* (Duke University Press, 1987), 34.

11 Eckard Toy chapter in Shawn Lay, editor, *Invisible Empire in the West* (University of Illinois Press, 1992), 156.

12 Interview with author (May 29, 2022).
13 "Medford Sees Klan at Worst," *Capital Journal*, Harry Crain, October 28, 1922, 3.
14 *Kourier*, 32.
15 October 28 *Capital Journal.*
16 Harvey Elmer Tobie, "Oregon Labor Disputes, 1919–1923 I: The Living Wage," *Oregon Historical Quarterly*, March 1947, 15; "Bulletin of U.S. Bureau of Labor Statistics," September 1921.
17 October 28 *Capital Journal*; Rothwell, 117.
18 Kenneth Jackson, *The Ku Klux Klan in the City, 1915–1930* (Oxford University Press, 1967), 197.
19 Jeffrey Max LaLande, *The Jackson County Rebellion: A Populist Uprising in Depression-Era Oregon*, (Oregon State University Press, 2023), 28.
20 Jackson, 196; some chroniclers spelled his name Calloway, but it's Callaway on his death certificate and gravestone.
21 "Ku Klux Klan Puts Portland Upon its List," *Portland Telegram*, June 17, 1921, 1.
22 June 17 *Telegram*, 2.
23 U.S. Census for 1920, Oregon Population, Composition and Characteristics, Bureau of the Census, U.S. Commerce Department, Table 10, 11, https://www2.census.gov/library/publications/decennial/1920/bulletins/demographics/population-or-composition-and-characteristics.pdf
24 See Elizabeth McLagan, *A Peculiar Paradise: A History of Blacks in Oregon, 1788–1940* (OSU Press, 2022).
25 Emeritus Portland State University Black history instructor Darrell Millner, in interview with author (May 23, 2022).
26 U.S. Census for 1920, Oregon Population, Composition and Characteristics, Table 7, 5.
27 Ellen Eisenberg, *Embracing a Western Identity: Jewish Oregonians 1849–1950* (Oregon State University Press, 2015), 77.
28 Eisenberg, 16.
29 Eisenberg, 126.
30 Portland elected Jewish mayors Bernard Goldsmith in 1869, Philip Wasserman in 1871, and Joseph Simon in 1909. See Eisenberg, 126; Mayors of Portland, city auditor's office, at https://web.archive.org/web/20210121123129/http://www.portlandoregon.gov/auditor/article/4968
31 1920 U.S. Census, Oregon Population, Composition and Characteristics, Table 12, 13.
32 Catholics made up 9 percent of Multnomah County when the second Klan was formed, 14 percent of Los Angeles County, 24 percent of Manhattan, 39 percent of Brooklyn, and 44 percent of the Boston area, according to the U.S. Religion Census for 1916, https://www.usreligioncensus.org
33 "Organized Effort Wins for Coalition," *Catholic Sentinel*, June 23, 1921, 1.
34 "In the Shadow of the Slump: The Depression of 1920–1921," *Berkeley Economic Review*, https://econreview.studentorg.berkeley.edu/in-the-shadow-of-the-slump-the-depression-of-1920-1921/, March 18, 1921.
35 1920 U.S. Census, Oregon Population, Composition and Characteristics, Tables 10 and 11, 11–12.
36 MacColl, 158.
37 See "More than Hatchetmen: Chinese Exclusion and Tong Wars in Portland Oregon," Brenda M. Horrocks, master's thesis for Utah State University, 2019.
38 Lay, 154.
39 Rothwell, 117.
40 Jackson, 196–197.
41 Toy, 39–40.
42 Jackson, 196.

43 "Newspaper story denied," *Morning Oregonian*, June 18, 1921, 6.
44 "Ku Klux Signs up 1,000 Members Here," *Portland Telegram*, July 7, 1921, 1.
45 Harry Crain, "Prejudice First Plea in Portland," *Capital Journal*, October 20, 1922, 1, 7; and Rothwell, 120–121.
46 "Klan Reported Formed," *Oregonian*, July 4, 1921, 3.
47 "Salem Klan is Proposed," *Oregonian*, July 22, 1921, 6.
48 "Ku Klux Invades Hood River," *Oregonian*, July 29, 1921, 11.
49 *N.W. Ayer & Sons American Newspaper Annual & Directory, 1921, Hathi Trust, https://babel.hathitrust.org/cgi/pt?id=coo.31924087717553&seq=34, 820*
50 "Ku Klux Terrorizes the Nation," *Oregon Labor Press*, July 22, 1921, 1.
51 July 22 *Labor Press*, 4.
52 Peter Rinearson and Arthur Rynearson, unpublished Rynerson family genealogy.
53 Interview with author (November 14, 2024).
54 "Ku Klux threatens Portland man," *Labor Press*, July 29, 1921, 1.
55 "Ku Klux Subsiding," *Labor Press*, July 29, 1921, 1.
56 "Klan After Labor Press Editor," *Labor Press*, August 5, 1921, 1.
57 "The Threat of the Klan and our Answer," *Labor Press*, August 5, 1921, 1.
58 "Rynerson Gets Gun Following Receipt of Klan's Threat," *Oregon Daily Journal*, August 5, 1921, 1.
59 Rothwell, 135.
60 Interview with author (November 14, 2024).
61 Rothwell, 135.
62 "Klu Klux Klan Said to be Organizing Here and Vicinity," *Eugene Guard*, July 16, 1921, 1.
63 Rothwell, 117.
64 "Ku Klux Klan Trying to Form Local Branch," *Capital Journal*, July 21, 1921, 1.
65 "Oregon is Invaded by Ku Klux Klan," *Morning Oregonian*, July 31, 1921, 14.
66 "White Race is 'Saved;' KKK Gives Theorem," *Oregon Daily Journal*, August 2, 1921, 14.
67 "Klan Chief Stages Official Reception," *Oregonian*, August 2, 15.
68 "Local Klan Plans Action," *Portland Telegram*, August 1, 1921, 1.
69 August 2 *Daily Journal.*
70 August 2 *Oregonian.*
71 MacColl, 164, 678.
72 "Local Klan Plans Action," *Portland Telegram*, August 2, 1921, 1; "Klan's Farce is Given Aid by Public Men," *Oregon Labor Press*, August 5, 1921, 2; August 2 *Daily Journal.*
73 "Klan Claims all Election Credit," *Capital Journal*, November 18, 1922, 1; membership card in Frederick L. Gifford Papers,1920–1945, Oregon Historical Society Research Library, Mss 2218.
74 August 1 *Telegram*, 2.
75 August 1 *Telegram*, 2; and Kelly J. Baker, *Gospel According to the Klan: The KKK's Appeal to Protestant America, 1915–1930* (University Press of Kansas, 2011), 53.
76 *Labor Press*, August 5, 1921.
77 "Ku Klux Klan Head Explains to Grand Jury," *Portland Telegram*, August 4, 1921, 1; and "Nightshirt Knight Faces Grand Jury," *Morning Oregonian*, August 5, 1921, 14.
78 "Old King Kleagle Abandons Oregon," *Morning Oregonian*, August 28, 1921, 16; and "King Kleagle Abdicates His Oregon Throne," Oregon Labor Press, September 2, 1921, 1; "Calloway new King of Oregon Ku Klux; Powell Doffs Robes," *Oregon Daily Journal*, August 28, 1921, 8.
79 "Albany Get the KKK," Salem *Capital Journal*, August 8, 1921, 2; "Mysterious Klan Organizing Quietly," *Albany Evening Herald*, August 10, 1921, 1; and "Klan to

Organize Here," *Corvallis Gazette-Times*, August 15, 1921.
80 "KKK Now in Astoria," *Capital Journal*, August 11, 1921, 6.
81 "Roseburg gets KKK," Salem *Capital Journal*, August 27, 1921, 6.
82 "Governor is Asked to Join the Ku Klux," *Capital Journal*, August 20, 1921, 1.
83 "Klan Rides Pendleton," *Capital Journal*, October 17, 1922, 1.
84 *Oregon City Enterprise*, September 30, 1921, 3.
85 Toy, 86.
86 Eckard Toy Jr., "The Ku Klux Klan in Tillamook, Oregon," *Pacific Northwest Quarterly* 53, No. 2, April 1962, 62.
87 Nancy MacLean, *Behind the Mask of Chivalry: The Making of the Second Ku Klux Klan* (Oxford University Press, 1994), 125.
88 "Governor asked to curb Klan," *Oregon Daily Journal*, August 9, 1921, 5; Ben Wilson Olcott Papers, Scrapbooks, Volume 8, University of Oregon Libraries Special Collections.
89 NAACP of Portland, Oregon records, 1914–1955, microfilm 195, reel 1, Oregon Historical Society Library.
90 NAACP of Portland records.
91 Olcott Papers.
92 "Klan is Assailed in House Hearing," *New York Times*, October 12, 1921, 5.
93 October 12 *New York Times*.
94 John Moffatt Mecklin, *The Ku Klux Klan: A Study of the American Mind*, Harcourt, Brace and Co., 1924, 27–28.
95 Jackson, 12.
96 Charles C. Alexander, "Kleagles and Cash: The Ku Klux Klan as a Business Organization, 1915–1930," *The Business History Review* 39, No. 3 (Autumn 1965), 354.
97 Jackson, 12.
98 Jackson, 197.
99 "Mayor Swings Ax on Police; Expenses Cut," *Oregon Daily Journal*, December 22, 1922, 1.
100 "Will Recruit 100 Vigilantes," *Portland Telegram*, December 23, 1921, 1, second section.
101 Lem Dever, *Confessions of an Imperial Klansman: Hot Tar and Feathers* (self-published, 1924), 22.
102 See series of letters in Reuben H. Sawyer Papers, 1896–1962, Oregon Historical Society Library, Coll 488.
103 Sawyer Papers.
104 "Auditorium will be Opened Today," *Morning Oregonian*, July 4, 1917, 16.
105 Correspondence in Sawyer Papers.
106 "The Truth about the Invisible Empire of the Knights of the Ku Klux Klan," Sawyer's lecture edited and printed in booklet form, in Sawyer Papers.
107 Truth about the Invisible Empire.
108 Sawyer Papers.
109 Sawyer Papers.
110 Sawyer Papers.
111 Sawyer Papers.

CHAPTER 3

1 Ben Titus essay, KKK Records 1922–1971, Oregon Historical Society Library, Mss 22 Manuscripts.
2 Reverend Lawrence J. Saalfeld, "Forces of Prejudice in Oregon 1920–1925," master's thesis for Catholic University of America, 1950, published by Archiodesan Historical Commission in 1984, 23.
3 Kimberly Mangun, A *Force for Change: Beatrice Morrow Cannady and the Struggle for Civil Rights in Oregon: 1912–1936* (Oregon State University Press, 2010), 9.
4 Northwestern College of Law commencement program, in Beatrice Morrow Cannady Scrapbook, Oregon Historical Society Library, Microfilm 160.

5 Mangun, 11.
6 Mangun, 29.
7 Mangun, 29; Cannady scrapbook.
8 Mangun, 29; Cannady scrapbook.
9 Linda Gordon, *The Second Coming of the KKK: The Ku Klux Klan of the 1920s and the American Political Tradition* (Liveright Publishing Corp., a division of W. W. Norton & Co., 2017), 89.
10 C. Easton Rothwell, "The Ku Klux Klan in the State of Oregon," senior thesis, Reed College, 1924, 1.
11 Interview with author (May 21, 2022).
12 Eckard V. Toy Jr. "The Ku Klux Klan in Oregon, its Character and Program," master's thesis for University of Oregon, 1959, 58.
13 "1,100 are Initiated into Ku Klux Klan," *Morning Oregonian*, February 28, 1922, 5.
14 "1,200 Become Klansmen," *Morning Oregonian*, April 18, 1922, 4.
15 G. Thomas Edwards and Carlos A. Schwantes, editors, *Experiences in a Promised Land: Essays in Pacific Northwest History* (University of Washington Press, 1986), 272.
16 "Northwest Hysterias…the Klan Rides Again," *Sunday Oregonian*, April 4, 1937, 58; Saalfeld, 20.
17 "Klansmen at Churches," *Oregonian*, May 8, 1922, 5; "Klan Passes Out Bids to Lecture at Church Doors," *Oregon Daily Journal*, May 8, 1922, 9.
18 "Cicero Hogan Would Halt Klan Doings," *Oregon Daily Journal*, May 10, 1922, 13.
19 "Ku Klux Lecturer Talks While 'Riot Squad' Keeps Watch," *Oregon Daily Journal*, May 11, 1921, 11.
20 Rothwell, 121.
21 June 12, 1922, letter in Reuben H. Sawyer Papers, 1896–1962, Oregonian Historical Society Library, Coll 488.
22 "Portland's Kissing Mayor," Frank Sterrett, *Sunday Oregonian*, May 15, 1966, 154.
23 "Two Public Men on the School Question," *Catholic Sentinel*, May 26, 1921.
24 Interview with author (May 21, 2022).
25 E. Kimbark MacColl, *The Growth of a City: Power and Politics in Portland, Oregon, 1915 to 1950* (Georgian Press, 1979), 140.
26 MacColl, 140.
27 MacColl, 156.
28 MacColl, 158.
29 Saalfeld, 47.
30 MacColl, 161–162.
31 "Is There any History in your Attic?" *Oregonian*, December 4, 1959.
32 Gordon, 67.
33 Nancy MacLean, *Behind the Mask of Chivalry: The Making of the Second Ku Klux Klan* (Oxford University Press, 1994), 10.
34 Sawyer Papers.
35 David Horowitz, editor, *Inside the Klavern: The Secret History of a Ku Klux Klan of the 1920s* (Southern Illinois University Press, 1999), 45.
36 Kenneth Jackson, *The Ku Klux Klan in the City, 1915–1930* (Oxford University Press, 1967), 199.
37 "KKK at Church Doors," *Oregon Daily Journal*, May 11, 1922, 8.
38 Saalfeld, 23.
39 MacLean, 91.
40 Kelly J. Baker, *Gospel According to the Klan: The KKK's Appeal to Protestant America, 1915–1930,* (University Press of Kansas, 2011), 17.
41 Shawn Lay, editor, *Invisible Empire in the West* (University of Illinois Press, 1992), 201-202.
42 Baker, 59.
43 Baker, 14.
44 Baker, 38.
45 Baker, 36.
46 "God and Old Nick Compete Actively at the State Pen," *Western American*, July 13, 1923, 1.

47 "Mail-Order Divorce is Hideous Evil that Must be Abolished by Executive Action or by Recall," *Western American*, November 30, 1922, 1; Annie McLain, "Unmasking the Oregon Klansman: The Ku Klux Klan in Astoria 1921–1925," Pacific University Oregon, senior history thesis, 2003, 11.

48 "Don't Attend," *Western American*, July 6, 1923, 2.

49 Lem Dever, *Confessions of an Imperial Klansman: Hot Tar and Feathers* (self-published, 1924), 9.

50 "Exclusive Story of Thrilling Battle in which 'Tom Atkins' Upholds Pride of Great Race," *Western American*, December 28, 1922, 2; and Dever, "Inside the Klan: Invisible Empire Revealed," (Western America Publishing Co., Portland), 1923, 6.

51 John Alexander Hamilton, "Manipulating the Masses: Woodrow Wilson and the Birth of American Propaganda," Wilson Center, https://exhibitions.nysm.nysed.gov/WWI/phone/war-at-home.htm, accessed February 4, 2025.

52 Dever, 9.

53 January 6, 1922, letter from Dever, in Sawyer Papers.

54 Toy, 50.

55 Dever, 16.

56 See, for example, the issue of November 30, 1922.

57 Dever, 11.

58 *Western American*, December 28, 1922, 4; see also "American's Overshadowing Problem Looms in Ever-Increasing Menace," *Western American*, January 25, 1923; and "Fair Warning to Sassy Niggers," *Western American*, May 10, 1923, 4.

59 Dever, 19.

60 "Trade only with your Friends, Watch this Space Each Week," *Western American*, September 28, 1923, 4.

61 See "M. & F. Unfair Say Portland Unionists," *Western American*, January 25, 1923, 8.

62 "Sheriff Harley J. Slusher of Clatsop County, Oregon, 100 percent square, terror to evil-doers" *Western American*, October 19, 1923, 3.

63 "Beloved Grand Dragon of the Invisible Empire, Realm of Oregon, Knights of the KKK," *Western American*, January 18, 1923, 1.

64 Charles C. Alexander, "Kleagles and Cash: The Ku Klux Klan as a Business Organization, 1915–1930," *The Business History Review* 39, No. 3 (Autumn 1965), 352–353.

65 Alexander, 354–355.

66 Wyn Craig Wade, *The Fiery Cross: The Ku Klux Klan in America* (Oxford University Press, 1987), 186.

67 Charles Jackson, "William J. Simmons: A Career in Ku Kluxism," *The Georgia Historical Quarterly* 50, No. 4 (December 1966), 360.

68 Kenneth Jackson, 13; Charles Jackson, 360; Wade, 187.

69 David M. Chalmers, *Hooded Americanism: The History of the Ku Klux Klan* (Duke University Press, 1987), 101.

70 William Shepherd, "The Fiery Double-Cross," *Collier's* 82 (July 1928), 47.

71 Shepherd, 47.

72 Chalmers, 101–104; Wade, 187–189.

73 Rothwell, 125.

74 Harry Crain, "Klan Backs Recount and School Bill," *Capital Journal*, October 24, 1922, 4.

75 Dever, 34.

76 Kenneth Jackson, 198.

77 Membership card in Frederick L. Gifford Papers, 1920–1945, Oregon Historical Society Research Library, Mss 2218.

78 Rothwell, 123.

79 Klansman's Manual, 1924, 56, https://archive.lib.msu.edu/DMC/AmRad/klansmansmanual.pdf, accessed March 1, 2025.
80 Rothwell, 123.
81 Titus, 2.
82 Titus, 4.
83 Titus, 18.
84 Titus, 14.
85 "Ku Klux Klan and Jews, *Oregon Voter*, April 15, 1922, 2.
86 "The Klan is Busy," *Oregon Voter*, January 21, 1922, 3.
87 Eisenberg, 38–40.
88 "Henry Ford and Anti-Semitism: A Complex Story," The Henry Ford, https://www.thehenryford.org/collections-and-research/digital-resources/popular-topics/henry-ford-and-anti-semitism-a-complex-story, accessed July 12, 2025.
89 Hiram Wesley Evans, "The Klan's Fight for Americanism," *The North American Review* 223, No. 830 (May 1926), 60.
90 April 15 *Oregon Voter*, 2.
91 August 19, 1922, letter to William Madison, Sawyer Papers.
92 Author interview with Bob Bussel, professor emeritus at the Labor Education and Research Center and History Department at the University of Oregon (December 9, 2024).
93 Eisenberg, 43–44.
94 Interview with author (May 23, 2022).
95 "Gifford, Head of K.K.K.," *Oregon Voter*, March 25, 1922, 357.
96 *Western American*, January 18, 1923, 8.
97 "Be Ready to Act Against Picture House Outrages," *Western American*, June 7, 1923, 1.
98 Horowitz, 54.
99 "The 100 Percenters," University of Oregon Special Collections, HS2330.K6 Z63 1922
100 Rothwell 136.
101 Kathleen Blee, *Women of the Klan: Racism and Gender in the 1920s* (University of California Press), 1991, 22.
102 Gordon, 125.
103 Articles of Incorporation, KKK Records 1922–1971, Oregon Historical Society.
104 Dever, 30.
105 *Capital Journal*, July 7, 1922, 1.
106 October 1922 LOTIE balance sheet, Sawyer Papers.
107 "The Red Book," 14, Sawyer Papers.
108 Sawyer Papers.
109 "Women Joining 'Empire,'" *Oregonian*, July 10, 1922, 4.
110 Blee, 21–22.
111 Wendy P. Rielly Thorson, "Oregon Klanswomen of the 1920s: A Study of Tribalism, Gender, and Women's Power," master's thesis for Oregon State University, 1997, 20.
112 Blee, 35; see also MacLean and Gordon.
113 August 8, 1922, letter in Sawyer Papers.
114 January 8, 1923, letter from Henry Bents, Sawyer Papers.
115 August 8, 1922, letter to Elizabeth Tyler, Sawyer Papers.
116 October 17, 1922, letter from Simmons, Sawyer Papers.
117 "Dr. R. H. Sawyer Declares He is Not Connected to Klan," *Oregon Daily Journal*, November 25, 1922, 2.
118 December 27, 1922, letter from Gifford to Sawyer, Sawyer Papers.
119 January 4, 1923, letter to E. Y. Clarke, Sawyer Papers.
120 February 2, 1923, letter to R. H. Davis, Sawyer Papers.
121 February 15, 1923, sale agreement, in Sawyer Papers.
122 April 2 letter to Harry Sawyer, Sawyer Papers.
123 May 4, 1923, confidential letter from Johnson, KKK Records 1922–1971.

CHAPTER 4

1 Eckard V. Toy Jr. "The Ku Klux Klan in Oregon, its Character and Program," master's thesis for University of Oregon, 1959, 56.

2 Jeffrey Max LaLande, *The Jackson County Rebellion: A Populist Uprising in Depression-Era Oregon* (Oregon State University Press, 2023), 32; the name originated with a national article about the incidents in *Outlook* magazine.

3 "State to Prosecute Local Outrages," *Medford Mail Tribune*, July 6, 1922, 1, 8; Ku Klux in Medford," *Oregon Voter*, August 12, 1922, 9.

4 "Negro Narrates Hanging to Tree," *Oregonian*, August 1, 1922; "Victim of Hanging is Not Found, *Medford Mail Tribune*," July 28, 1922, 1; "Night Riders Will Plead August 19," *Medford Mail Tribune*, August 4, 1922, 1.

5 "Local Citizen Victim of Ku Klux Klan," *Medford Mail Tribune*, March 18, 1922, 1.

6 August 12 *Oregon Voter*.

7 "Grand Jury Invitation is Issued," *Medford Mail Tribune*, July 27, 1922, 1.

8 July 28 *Medford Mail Tribune*.

9 Jeff LaLande, "Beneath the Hooded Robe: Newspapermen, Local Politics and the Ku Klux Klan in Jackson County, Oregon, 1921–23," *Pacific Northwest Quarterly*, Vol. 83, No. 2, April 1992, 45.

10 C. Easton Rothwell, "The Ku Klux Klan in the State of Oregon," senior thesis, Reed College, 1924, 120.

11 Rothwell, 120.

12 W. R. Stewart, "Medford Klan Jury Control Injures Court," *Seattle Post-Intelligencer*, March 31, 1923, 11.

13 "Gates Objects to Masks in Secret Order," *Medford Mail Tribune*, May 15, 1922, 1.

14 "State to Prosecute Local Outrages," *Medford Mail Tribune*, July 6, 1922, 1.

15 C. E. Terrill letter to Ben Olcott, May 14, 1922, Ben Wilson Olcott Papers, Scrapbooks, Volume 8, University of Oregon Libraries Special Collections; Ax081.

16 LaLande, Beneath the Hooded Robe, 48.

17 "The Truth about the Terrill Recall," *Medford Mail Tribune*, July 27, 1922, 7.

18 "Terrill Wins, Klan Recall Effort Fails," *Capital Journal*, July 31, 1922, 1.

19 "Salem Klan not Founded on Prejudice," *Capital Journal*, November 5, 1923, 1.

20 "Ku Klux Klan Trying to Form Local Branch," *Capital Journal*, July 21, 1921, 1.

21 "Ku Klux Klan Sends Letter," *Oregon Statesman*, August 13, 1921, 3.

22 Deaconess, founded by Mennonites, later became part of Salem Hospital.

23 "Klan Letter at Hospital," *Albany Evening Herald*, October 25, 1921, 6.

24 "Ku Klux Klan is Sending Men Here for Investigation," *Oregon Statesman*, October 25, 1921, 1.

25 "White-Robed Klan has Strong Lodge in Salem," *Oregon Statesman*, November 12, 1921, 1, 2.

26 "Success Weakened Salem Klan," *Capital Journal*, November 6, 1923, 1.

27 "Steiner is Gone," *Statesman*, April 11, 1923, 1; "Gifford's Tactics Split Klan," *Capital Journal*, November 7, 1923, 1.

28 See Scandals Engulf Gifford, Chapter 9; "Klan Lists Thrown Open to Solicitors," *Capital Journal*, November 8, 1923, 1.

29 November 8 *Capital Journal*.

30 "Klansmen Done with Imperialism," *Capital Journal*, November 9, 1923, 1.

31 David M. Chalmers, *Hooded Americanism: The History of the Ku Klux Klan* (Duke University Press, 1987), 2.
32 "Documenting Reconstruction Violence," in Reconstruction in America, Equal Justice Initiative, eji.org/report/reconstruction-in-america/, accessed July 12, 2025.
33 Chalmers, 297.
34 John Moffat Mecklin, *The Ku Klux Klan: A Study of the American Mind* (Harcourt, Brace and Co., 1924), 9.
35 Nancy MacLean, *Behind the Mask of Chivalry: The Making of the Second Ku Klux Klan* (Oxford University Press, 1994), 149–158.
36 Chalmers, 49–55.
37 Timothy Egan, *A Fever in the Heartland: The Ku Klux Klan's Plot to Take over America, and the Woman who Stopped Them* (Viking, 2023), 16–17.
38 Hiram Wesley Evans, "The Klan's Fight for Americanism," *The North American Review* 223, No. 830 (May 1926), 36–37.
39 Reuben Sawyer, "The Truth About the Invisible Empire Knights of the Ku Klux Klan," (self-published in 1921), Oregon Politics Collection, Box 21, Oregon Historical Society, Mss 1513.
40 "Klan Ejects Negro From Roseburg," *The News-Review*, April 3, 1922, 1.
41 Interview with author (May 23, 2022).
42 "Oregon Stages Near Lynching Party," *The Advocate*, June 8, 1923, 1.
43 NAACP Portland branch files, 1914–1933, Oregon Historical Society Library, microfilm reel 1
44 David Horowitz, editor, *Inside the Klavern: The Secret History of a Ku Klux Klan of the 1920s* (Southern Illinois University Press, 1999), 143.
45 "Attack on Negress Puzzles Officers," *Oregonian*, October 22, 1921, 16.
46 "Ku Klux Warning to Marshfield Mayor," *Capital Journal*, August 8, 1922, 3.
47 "Official Threat is Sent Through Mails," *Oregon Labor Press*, August 5, 1921, 1.
48 Gavin Cronkrite, "The Empire and the Editor: The Ku Klux Klan in Heppner, Oregon," capstone thesis for Clark Honors College, University of Oregon, 2015, 31.
49 "Judge Calkins Advises Klan to Clean House," *Capital Journal*, June 15, 1922, 7.
50 McLagan, 121.
51 "Ku Klux Klan is Sending Men Here for Investigation," *Oregon Statesman*, October 25, 1921, 1.
52 "Threats Cause Two Colored Men to Flee City," *Evening Herald*, October 23, 1923, 1.
53 McLagan, 138.
54 "Tillamook Woman is Branded," *Eugene Register*, January 14, 1923, 1.
55 Eckard V. Toy Jr., "The Ku Klux Klan in Tillamook, Oregon," *Pacific Northwest Quarterly* 53, No. 2 (April 1962), 63.
56 "Tillamook Branders Held Not Klansmen," *Eugene Guard*, January 15, 1923, 6.
57 *Western American*, January 18, 1923, 1.
58 January 26, 1923, meeting minutes, KKK of La Grande Oregon Chapter Records, 1922–1923, Oregon Historical Society Library, Mss 2604.
59 Toy, Ku Klux Klan in Tillamook, 62; and William Toll, "Progress and Piety: The Ku Klux Klan and Social Change in Tillamook, Oregon," *Pacific Northwest Quarterly* 53, No.2 (April 1962), 81.
60 Toll, 78.
61 Toy, Ku Klux Klan in Tillamook, 60.
62 Toll, 79.
63 Toll, 79.
64 Toll, 76.
65 "Fraternal Meeting Draws Big Crowd," *Tillamook Headlight*, June 6, 1924, 1.

66 Toll, 78.
67 Ku Klux Klan Tillamook, Oregon Chapter No. 8 Records, 1922–1929, University of Oregon Libraries Special Collections, Bx 046.
68 Toll, 80.
69 June 1, 1922, letter to Klan leader Reuben Sawyer, Reuben H. Sawyer Papers, 1896–1962, Oregon Historical Society Library, Manuscripts, Coll 488.
70 "Ku Klux Klan Charter Meet Brings Crowd," *Oregon Statesman* Salem, July 16, 1922, 1.
71 Horowitz, 37; "Celebrated the Charter Arrival," *La Grande Observer*, March 19, 1923, 8.
72 Richard Botteri, "My View: Klan in Oregon sowed hatred toward many groups," *Portland Tribune*, July 22, 2020.
73 Annie McLain, "Unmasking the Oregon Klansman: The Ku Klux Klan in Astoria 1921–1925," Pacific University Oregon, distinguished senior history thesis; and Harry Crain, "Clatsop Disrupted by Ku Kluxers," *Capital Journal*, October 13, 1922, 1, 9–10.
74 "City's Official are Accused," *Astoria Evening Budget*, February 1, 1922, 1, as cited in McLain, 12.
75 Toy, Ku Klux Klan in Oregon, 62.
76 October 13 *Capital Journal.*
77 Harry Crain, "Kluxers Lose Grip in Clatsop," *Capital Journal*, October 16, 1922, 1.
78 McClain, 13.
79 "Squabble at Purity Meet," *Morning Astorian*, February 1, 1922, 1, 4.
80 February 1 *Morning Astorian.*
81 McLain, 17–18.
82 October 16 *Capital Journal.*
83 McLain, 14–15; October 16 *Capital Journal.*
84 McLain, 21.
85 "Fight Again Tears Town," *Oregonian*, March 18, 1923, 1–2.
86 W. R. Stewart, "Klan Grand Dragon Seeks Power; Rule of Oregon Declared Aim; Ku Klux Tears State into Factions," *Seattle Post-Intelligencer*, April 2, 1923, 6.
87 McLain, 23.
88 "E. P. Hawkins Resigns Position as Chief," *Western American*, February 22, 1923, 1.
89 Roger Rasmussen Collection of Baker Klan No. 13 Records, Oregon Historical Society Library, Coll 862.
90 Harry Crain, "Ku Klux Active at La Grande," *Capital Journal*, October 19, 1922, 2.
91 Personal notes by Lansing grandson Roger Rasmussen, Rasmussen Collection.
92 "Baker Sees Klan Cross," *Morning Oregonian*, October 8, 2.
93 *Western American*, February 1, 1923; Horowitz, 17.
94 Minutes of KKK Klonclave in Eastern Oregon, 1923, September 12, Oregon Historical Society Library, Coll 886.
95 Formal charges letter, Rasmussen Collection.
96 Rasmussen notes, Rasmussen Collection.
97 Margaret Meyers, SNJM, "The Ku Klux Klan in Le Grande, Oregon 1918–1924," American Catholic History Classroom, Catholic University of America, https://cuomeka.wrlc.org/exhibits/show/osc/item/292, accessed July 12, 2025.
98 Horowitz.
99 Horowitz, 12.
100 "Several Thousand People Witness Class of About Seventy Five Take Oath of Allegiance," *La Grande Observer*, July 26, 1923, 1.
101 U.S. Census for 1920, Oregon Population, Composition and Characteristics, Bureau of the Census, U.S. Commerce Department, Table 11, 12, https://www2.census.gov/library/publications/decennial/1920/bulletins/demographics/population-or-composition-and-characteristics.pdf, accessed July 8, 2025.

102 John Moffat Mecklin, *The Ku Klux Klan: A Study of the American Mind* (Harcourt, Brace and Co., 1924), 217.
103 Horowitz, 64–65.
104 Horowitz, 15, 25.
105 Horowitz, 84.
106 Horowitz, 110, 103–104.
107 Horowitz, 37.
108 La Grande Oregon Chapter Records, December 5, 1922.
109 Horowitz, 134.
110 Horowitz, 90.
111 Horowitz, 143.
112 "Ku Klux Klan Said to be Organizing Here and Vicinity," *Eugene Guard*, July 16, 1921, 1; Harry Crain, "Eugene Kluxers Exposed," *Capital Journal*, October 26, 1922, 1.
113 Shawn Lay, editor, *Invisible Empire in the West* (University of Illinois Press, 1992), 165.
114 "Ku Klux Klan is Defended," *Morning Register*, January 12, 1922, 6; "Ku Klux Klan has been Organized in City, says Sawyer," *Eugene Guard*, January 12, 1922, 5.
115 J. G. Shaw, *Edwin Vincent O'Hara: American Prelate* (Farrar, Straus and Cudahy, 1957), 104; Timothy Michael Dolan, *Some Seed Fell on Good Ground: The Life of Edwin W. O'Hara* (The Catholic University of America Press, 1992), 51, 54.
116 March 30, 1921, letter to Reverend W. G. Elliot Jr., Henry Davidson Sheldon Papers, Box 16, University of Oregon Libraries Special Collections, Coll 155.
117 Dolan, 52–53.
118 "U. of O. Newman Club Campus Home," *Catholic Sentinel*, April 7, 1921, 3.
119 May 15, 1922, letter to Dr. Joseph Shafer, Sheldon Papers, Box 16.
120 Dolan, 53.
121 Toy, Ku Klux Klan in Oregon, 170.
122 Toy, Ku Klux Klan in Oregon, 174.
123 *Eugene Register-Guard*, January 10, 1993, 1F.
124 "Eugene Kluxers Exposed," *Capital Journal*, October 26, 1922, 1, 6.
125 See election results in *Oregon Voter*, December 16, 1922, 7.
126 "New City Councilmen Will Take Seats Soon," *Morning Register*, December 22, 1922, 3.
127 Toy, Ku Klux Klan in Oregon, 168.
128 "Klan Influence Denied," *Morning Register*, March 30, 1923, 3.
129 *Oregon Voter* brief, May 26, 1923.
130 "Klan's Pictures Draw Big Crowd," *Albany Democrat*, April 27, 1922, 6.
131 "KKK," *Eugene Guard*, May 19, 1923, 10.
132 *Ashland Weekly Tidings*, May 24, 1922.
133 *Oregon Voter*, August 12, 1922, 11.
134 LaLande, *Jackson County Rebellion*, 35.
135 Toy, Ku Klux Klan in Oregon, 86.
136 "Klan Ceremony Held on Butte," *Bend Bulletin*, September 8, 1923, 1.
137 "Bend Klan is Defunct," *Oregonian*, April 12, 1925, 8.
138 "Open Air Meeting Stirs Dallas, Ore." *Western American*, August 31, 1923, 1.
139 "Gathering of Klan at Dallas," *Oregon Statesman*, April 16, 1924.
140 "Parade Held by Klan," *Oregonian*, June 16, 1923.
141 February 8, 1923, letter from D. Lillian Bancroft, Sawyer Papers.
142 "Hood River Klan to Initiate Big Class," *Western American*, February 1, 1923, 7.
143 "Klancraft Defined by Portland Chief," *Western American*, March 1, 1923, 1.
144 "Aurora Has New Klan," *Oregon Daily Journal*, November 19, 1922, 8.
145 "Ku Klux Klan Charter Meet Brings Crowd," *Oregon Statesman*, July 15, 1922, 1.
146 "Klansmen Hold Their Ceremonial in Open Air," *Eugene Register*, July 18, 1922, 8.

147 "Open Air Klan Lecture," *Vernonia Eagle*, September 7, 1923, 1.
148 "Purifying the Klan," *Oregon Voter*, December 8, 1923, 16.
149 "Mapleton has Klan," *Eugene Guard*, July 8, 1924.

CHAPTER 5

1 *Capital Journal*, March 5, 1923.
2 "Ku Klux is Busy," *Oregon Voter*, January 21, 1922, 3; "Ku Klux and F.O.P.S," *Oregon Voter*, March 4, 1922, 4; E. Kimbark MacColl, *The Growth of a City: Power and Politics in Portland, Oregon, 1915 to 1950* (Georgian Press, 1979), 386.
3 Ben Titus memoir, KKK Records 1922–1971, Oregon Historical Society Library, Manuscripts, Mss 22, 17–18; Harry Crain, "Ousting of Powell Old Trick," December 3, 1923, *Capital Journal*, 1, 10.
4 January 21 *Oregon Voter*, 14; "Gifford, head of K.K.K.," *Oregon Voter*, March 25, 1922, 5.
5 "Gifford, head of K.K.K.," *Oregon Voter*, March 25, 1922, 5.
6 Malcom Clark Jr., "The Bigot Disclosed: 90 Years of Nativism," *Oregon Historical Quarterly*, June 1974, 145–146; "Dope on the F.O.P.S.," *Oregon Voter*, August 25, 1923, 13.
7 "The Ku Klux will Pass," *Catholic Sentin*el, March 2, 1922, 4; Robert D. Johnston, *The Radical Middle Class: Populist Democracy and the Question of Capitalism in Progressive Era Portland, Oregon* (Princeton University Press, 2003), 224.
8 Eckard V. Toy Jr. "The Ku Klux Klan in Oregon, its Character and Program," master's thesis for University of Oregon, 1959, 58.
9 "Our New Bosses," *Capital Journal*, February 9, 1922, 6.
10 Clark, 148.
11 C. Easton Rothwell, "The Ku Klux Klan in the State of Oregon," senior thesis, Reed College, 1924, 129.
12 Titus, 14.
13 March 4 *Oregon Voter.*
14 "Hall is Reported Indorsed in Race for Governorship," *Oregon Daily Journal*, February 12, 1922, 2; "Who are Secret Bosses?" *Oregon Voter*, February 18, 1922, 4.
15 Rothwell, 130.
16 "The Ku Klux Klandidate," *Capital Journal*, February 23, 1922, 4.
17 Clark, 144–145.
18 Rothwell, 129.
19 Janet W. Bryant, "The Ku Klux Klan and the Oregon Compulsory School Bill of 1922," Reed College thesis, 1970, 30.
20 "W. C. Elford, Secretary," *Oregon Voter*, June 17, 1922.
21 "Secret Factions Fight," *Oregon Voter*, May 12, 1923, 37.
22 Clark, 148.
23 Bryant, 30.
24 Clark, 148.
25 "Fraternal Orders Used as Mask to Hide Real Backers," *Capital Journal*, May 17, 1922, 1.
26 "An Invasion of Civic Liberty, *Catholic Sentinel*, March 16, 1922, 4.
27 "Gifford, head of K.K.K.," *Oregon Voter*, March 22, 1922, 5.
28 George Turnbull, *An Oregon Crusader* (Binfords & Mort, 1955), 8.
29 *Medford Mail Tribune*, May 3, 1922, 2.
30 "Governor Assails Klan's Activities," *Oregonian*, May 14, 1922, 1.
31 Gov. Olcott's Proclamation, May 13, 1922, Ben Wilson Olcott Papers, Scrapbooks,Volume 8, University of Oregon Libraries Special Collections, Ax 081.
32 Turnbull, 80.
33 "Klan Head Denies Charges of Olcott," *Oregonian*, May 14, 1922, 1.

34 "Five Candidates Answer on Klan," *Morning Oregonian*, May 16, 1922, 1, 4.
35 "The Primary Election," Oregon Voter, May 27, 1922, 4.
36 Turnbull, 88.
37 Reverend Lawrence J. Saalfeld, "Forces of Prejudice in Oregon 1920–1925," master's thesis for Catholic University of America, 1950 (Archdiocesan Historical Commission,1984), 33.
38 *Catholic Sentinel*, May 25, 1922, 4.
39 Toy, 96.
40 July 15, 1922, statement, Olcott Papers.
41 Turnbull, 127.
42 "School Measure to go on Ballot," *Catholic Sentinel*, June 22, 1922, 1.
43 Arthur Bone, editor and co-author, *Oregon Cattleman/Governor/Congressman: Memoirs and Times of Walter M. Pierce* (Oregon Historical Society, 1981), 131.
44 Bone, 12. Citizens of Milton and Freewater voted to merge in 1950, creating the city of Milton-Freewater.
45 Bone, 190.
46 Bone, 119.
47 Bone, 163.
48 Harry Crain, "Use Threat of Hall to Force Pierce," *Capital Journal*, August 12, 1922, 1.
49 Titus, 22.
50 Toy, 91; Harry Crain, "Third Party to be Formed," *Capital Journal*, August 18, 1922, 1.
51 Bone, 163.
52 "Smoked Out," *Capital Journal*, September 13, 1922, 4.
53 Turnbull, 138.
54 "K. K. Nominee Retires in Favor of Pierce," *Catholic Sentinel*, September 22, 1922, 1.
55 "Pierce Sold Out on School Bill to Get Votes," *Capital Journal*, October 24, 1922, 2.
56 *Portland Telegram*, October 26, 1922, 1, as cited in Bone, 164.
57 "Pierce Leads Yellow List," *Capital Journal*, October 25, 1922, 1.
58 Toy, 114.
59 Bone, 168.
60 Saalfeld, 36.
61 "I Was a Klansman," *Portland Telegram*, November 6, 1922, 1; "Ku Klux Cyclops Sends his Own Son to Private School," *Capital Journal*, October 19, 1922, 1.
62 Father John R. Laidlaw, *The Catholic Church in Oregon and the Work of its Archbishops* (Exposition Press Inc., 1977), 29.
63 "Ticket Fake is Charge," *Oregonian*, November 3, 1922, 8.
64 Kenneth Jackson, *The Ku Klux Klan in the City, 1915–1930* (Oxford University Press, 1967), 207.
65 Jeff LaLande, "Beneath the Hooded Robe: Newspapermen, Local Politics and the Ku Klux Klan in Jackson County, Oregon, 1921–23," *Pacific Northwest Quarterly* 83, No. 2 (April 1992), 49.
66 Andrew Nils Bryans, "The Response to Left-Wing Radicalism in Portland, Oregon from 1917 to 1941," master's thesis for Portland State University, 2002, 48.
67 David Horowitz, "The Klansman as Outsider: Ethnocultural Solidarity and Antielitism in the Oregon Ku Klux Klan of the 1920s," *The Pacific Northwest Quarterly*, January 1989, 18.
68 Rothwell, 133.
69 "The Election," *Oregon Voter*, November 11, 1922, 4–5.
70 Horowitz, Klansman as Outsider, 7.
71 May 24, 1927, Pierce letter to Fred Mack, Olcott Papers.
72 Bone, 180.
73 MacColl, 170; Johnston, 225, Bryans, 61.
74 MacColl, 170; Johnston, 227.
75 Bone, 68.
76 Ku Klux Klan La Grande Oregon chapter records, 1922–1923, Oregon Historical Society Library, Manuscripts, Mss 2604.
77 David Horowitz, editor, *Inside the Klavern: The Secret History of a Ku Klux Klan in the 1920s* (Southern

Illinois University Press, 1999, 29–30.

78 "Governor Olcott Speaks of Klan," *Catholic Sentinel*, December 14, 1922, 1.

79 "I Was a Klansman," *Portland Telegram*, November 2, 3, 4, and 6, 1922, 1.

80 November 18, 1922, letter from Sawyer and Davis to Simmons, Reuben H. Sawyer Papers, 1896–1962, Oregon Historical Society Library, Coll 488.

81 "Strikebreaker," *Oregon Labor Press*, July 19, 1919, 1; and "Gifford, Head of K.K.K.," *Oregon Voter*, March 25, 1922, 5, 6.

82 Rothwell, 124.

83 MacColl 165.

84 Rothwell, 124.

85 Clark, 160.

86 Johnston, 24.

87 Lem Dever, *Confessions of an Imperial Klansman: Hot Tar and Feathers*, self-published, 1924, 43.

88 Dever, 38.

89 Kevin Miller, "Invisible Empire: Eugene Once Embraced the KKK but History Books Rarely Mention it," *Eugene Register Guard*, January 10, 1993.

90 Interview with author (May 29, 2022).

91 "Taint of the Ting-a-Ling," *Capital Journal*, May 17, 1922, 4.

92 Bone, 141, 205.

93 Bone, 125.

94 Bone, 197.

95 "Klan Factions are in Conflict," *Catholic Sentinel*, November 29, 1923, 1.

96 Jackson, 212.

CHAPTER 6

1 *Capital Journal*, "The Yellow Ticket," *Capital Journal*, October 26, 1922, 6.

2 *Capital Journal*, January 23, 1923.

3 "Street Orator Answered," *Morning Oregonian*, November 30, 1912, 1; J. G. Shaw, *Edwin Vincent O'Hara: American Prelate* (Farrar, Straus and Cudahy, 1957), 38.

4 Timothy Michael Dolan, *Some Seed Fell on Good Ground: The Life of Edwin W. O'Hara* (The Catholic University of America Press, 1992), 11.

5 Dolan, 23.

6 Dolan, 34.

7 Dolan, 32.

8 Dolan, 44.

9 Dolan, 43.

10 Malcom Clark Jr., "The Bigot Disclosed: 90 Years of Nativism," *Oregon Historical Quarterly* (June 1974), 111.

11 "Massachusetts Bay Colony Bans Catholic Priests," MassMoments, a project of Mass Humanities, https://www.massmoments.org/moment-details/massachusetts-bay-colony-bans-catholic-priests.html, accessed July 13.

12 Catherine Marie Saks, "Real Americanism: Resistance to the Oregon Compulsory School Bill, 1920–1925," master's thesis for Portland State University, 2010, 15; and Dan Stewart, "When Americans Celebrated Bonfire Night," *Time* magazine, November 5, 2015; nowadays, revelers just burn effigies of Fawkes.

13 John Moffat Mecklin, *The Ku Klux Klan: A Study of the American Mind* (Harcourt, Brace and Co., 1924), 171; and Clark, 111.

14 Saks, 34; Kelly J. Baker, *Gospel According to the Klan: The KKK's Appeal to Protestant America, 1915–1930*, University Press of Kansas, 2011, 78.

15 Mecklin, 100.

16 C. Easton Rothwell, "The Ku Klux Klan in the State of Oregon," senior thesis, Reed College, 1924, 21.

17 Timothy Egan, *A Fever in the Heartland: The Ku Klux Klan's Plot*

to Take over America, and the Woman who Stopped Them (Viking, 2023), 79.

18 Clark, 131.

19 "Catholicism in the United States, 1830–1900," https://uploads.weconnect.com/mce/f90a34bcd66e597a5d391005bf1e14a7c70f1d2c/ChurchHistory/PART%2017%20AMERICAN%20CHURCH%20HISTORY%20PART%20TWO%20DEC%202013%20tbp.pdf, accessed July 13, 2025; Julie Byrne, "Roman Catholics and Immigration in Nineteenth-Century America," National Humanities Center, https://nationalhumanitiescenter.org/tserve/nineteen/nkeyinfo/nromcath.htm, accessed July 13, 2025.

20 Papers Read at the Meeting of Grand Dragons, Knights of the Ku Klux Klan, at their First Annual Meeting Held at Ashville, North Carolina (Arno Press, 1977), 125.

21 Mecklin, 157.

22 Mecklin, 170.

23 Rothwell, 99.

24 Clark, 113–117.

25 Clark, 119.

26 Rothwell, 93.

27 *Oregon Statesman*, May 19, 1855, cited in Rothwell, 94–95.

28 Clark, 132.

29 Clark, 134.

30 *Portland Telegram*, January 25, 1894, cited in Clark, 135.

31 Clark, 135–136.

32 Clark, 137.

33 Clark, 112.

34 Promotional flyer for Edith O'Gorman lecture, Catholic Church in Oregon file, Oregon Historical Society Library, Manuscripts, Mss 1580.

35 "Nun Escapes from the Convent at Mount Angel," *Silverton Journal*, August 1, 1913, 1

36 August 1 *Silverton Journal.*

37 Clark, 142–144.

38 Father Wilfred P. Schoenberg, *Ku Klux Klan in Pacific Northwest: 1921–1927,* unpublished manuscript, archives of the Archdiocese of Portland in Oregon, chapter 1, 32.

39 "Nun 'Escapes" from Mount Angel, Stars in Lawsuits," *Catholic Sentinel*, October 6, 1995, 7.

40 John E. Hosmer, "The Escaped Nun from Mt. Angel Convent: The Last Stand of Desperate Despotism" (Silverton, 1913), archives of the Archdiocese of Portland in Oregon.

41 October 6 *Catholic Sentinel.*

42 October 6 *Catholic Sentinel.*

43 Hosmer affidavit, archives of Archdiocese of Portland in Oregon.

44 Schoenberg, chapter 5, 49.

45 March 13, 1923, meeting minutes, Ku Klux Klan La Grande Oregon chapter records, 1922–1923, Oregon Historical Society Library, Manuscripts, Coll 899.

46 "Two Women Fight at Ex-Nun's Meeting," *Morning Oregonian*, October 16, 1922, 5.

47 J. R. Murphy, "The Truth about Ex-Nun 'Lucretia,'" Lutheran Schools Committee Records, Oregon Historical Society Library, vault, Mss 646.

48 "M. Brennan Injured by Mob at Gresham," *Catholic Sentinel*, October 12, 1922, 1.

49 Elizabeth Schoffen, *The Demands of Rome* (self-published, 1917), archives of Archdiocese of Portland in Oregon, 21.

50 Schoffen, 35.

51 Schoffen, 16.

52 Schoffen, 127.

53 Schoffen, 133.

54 Schoffen, 174, 178.

55 Knights of Columbus website, https://www.kofc.org/en/who-we-are/our-history/founding-and-early-acts.html, accessed July 14, 2025.

56 David Horowitz, editor, *Inside the Klavern: The Secret History of a Ku*

Klux Klan of the 1920s (Southern Illinois University Press, 1999), 88.

57 Henry Peck Fry, *The Modern Ku Klux Klan* (Small, Maynard & Co.), 1922, 25.

58 Schoenberg, chapter 1, 35.

59 Fry, 115.

60 Schoenberg, chapter 1, 34.

61 Lem Dever, *Confessions of an Imperial Klansman: Hot Tar and Feathers* (self-published, 1924), 8.

62 Joyce McBride, "Edward Emmett Kelly," Edward E. Kelly Family Papers, Oregon Historical Society Library, Mss 1434.

63 "Judge Kelly Now Major in Signal Corps, U.S. Army," *Medford Mail Tribune*, September 7, 1917.

64 September 7 *Mail Tribune*.

65 Edward E. Kelly Family Papers.

66 "Col. Kelly Gives Views on Ku Klux Klan," *Medford Mail Tribune*, May 8, 1922.

67 "City Council bars K.K. masks," *Medford Mail Tribune*, May 17, 1922.

68 McBride.

69 Robert Kelly oral history, in Edward E. Kelly Family Papers, Oregon Historical Society Library, Mss 1434.

70 "A.E. Reames to Speak at Final Meeting Tonight," *Medford Mail Tribune*, November 6, 1922, 6.

71 C. Easton Rothwell, "The Ku Klux Klan in the State of Oregon," senior thesis, Reed College, 1924, 105.

72 Mecklin, 50.

73 Rothwell, 107.

74 *Catholic Sentinel*, July 26, 1923, cited in Reverend Lawrence J. Saalfeld, "Forces of Prejudice in Oregon 1920–1925," master's thesis for Catholic University of America, 1950 (Archdiocesan Historical Commission, 1984), 111.

75 Janet W. Bryant, "The Oregon Compulsory School Bill of 1922," Reed College thesis, 1970, 107.

76 Paula Abrams, *Cross Purposes: Pierce v. Society of Sisters and the Struggle for Compulsory Public Education* (University of Michigan, 2009), 24.

77 *Oregon Blue Book*, Oregon Secretary of State, https://sos.oregon.gov/blue-book/Documents/elections/initiative.pdf, accessed July 13, 2025.

78 Schoenberg, chapter 8, 45.

79 *The New Age* 28, No. 7 (July 1920), 322.

80 Schoenberg, chapter 2, 7; and chapter 8, 45.

81 David M. Chalmers, *Hooded Americanism: The History of the Ku Klux Klan* (Duke University Press, 1987), 34.

82 "Prejudice First Plea in Portland," *Capital Journal*, October 20, 1922, 1.

83 Eckard V. Toy Jr. "The Ku Klux Klan in Oregon, its Character and Program," master's thesis for University of Oregon, 1959, 14.

84 "Klan Claims all Election Credit," *Capital Journal*, November 18, 1922, 1.

85 Membership card in Frederick L. Gifford Papers, 1920–1945, Oregon Historical Society Research Library, Mss 2218.

86 Undated obituary in Roger Rasmussen Collection of Baker Klan No. 13 Records, Oregon Historical Society Library, Manuscripts, Coll 862.

87 Michael Robinson, Scottish Rite historian for Oregon, said the founding and fourth UO presidents were Masons. Interview with author (September 6, 2024).

88 Transactions of the Supreme Council of Scottish Rite Southern Jurisdiction, held May 17–20 in Colorado Springs, Colorado, 1920, 7, document provided to author.

89 Proceedings of M. W. Grand Lodge Ancient Free and Accepted Masons of Oregon, 70th annual communication, 95; document provided to author.

90 Schoenberg, chapter 3, 8.

91 Proceedings of Grand Lodge, 95.
92 Proceedings of Grand Lodge, 158.
93 Schoenberg, chapter 3, 9.
94 *The New Age* 28, No. 8 (August 1920), 380.
95 "Two Public Men on the School Question," *Catholic Sentinel*, May 26, 1921.
96 Oregon Voters Pamphlet, November 7, 1922, statement submitted by initiative supporters; *The New Age* XXX (1922), 502.
97 Sister Christine Mary, "Oregon School Bill: The Case of the Sisters of the Holy Names vs. the State of Oregon," 1958, Sisters of the Holy Names of Jesus and Mary archives, 6.
98 "Anti-Catholic Bills Defeated," *Catholic Sentinel*, February 2, 1921, 1.
99 Provincial House Chronicles, February 23, 1921, cited in Sister Christine Mary, 1.
100 "Organized Effort Wins for Coalition," *Catholic Sentinel*, June 23, 1921.
101 Michael Robinson, "Portland Valley Scottish Rite Temple," and Michael Robinson, "Philip Schuyler Malcom 1847–1929," documents provided to author.
102 Robinson, Philip Schuyler Malcom.
103 "Anti-denominational schools," *Oregon Voter*, July 15, 1922, 9.
104 "Education and the State," *Morning Oregonian*, October 30, 1922, 8.
105 "Masons of Oregon are the Real Kind and Here's Proof," *Western American*, June 28, 1923, 1.
106 Miguel Hernandez, "Fighting Fraternities: the Ku Klux Klan and Freemasonry in 1920s America," University of Exter, 2014, 211.
107 Hernandez, 90.
108 "An Invasion of Civic Liberty," *Catholic Sentinel*, March 16, 1922, 4.
109 "School Bill not Sponsored by Masonic Lodge," *Capital Journal*, October 16, 1922, 1; "Grand Lodge Did Not Endorse Bill," *Catholic Sentinel*, October 19, 1922, 1.
110 Schoenberg, chapter 4, 45.
111 Abrams, 37.
112 Ben Wilson Olcott Papers, Scrapbooks, Volume 8, University of Oregon Libraries Special Collections, Ax 081.
113 Schoenberg, chapter 4, 37–38.
114 Reasons flyer from A.&A.S.R. School Committee, Lutheran Schools Committee Records.
115 *Eugene Register*, November 4, 1922.
116 "Debate on School Bill," *Oregon Voter*, October 7, 1922, 14.
117 "The Cost to Oregon," *Capital Journal*, October 21, 1922, 4.
118 *Oregon Voter*, August 26, 1922.
119 Argument Against Ballot Measures 314 and 315, "Oregon Voters Pamphlet," Secretary of State, November 7, 1922, 27.
120 "Gifford, Head of K.K.K.," *Oregon Voter*, March 25, 1922, 5.
121 Hiram Wesley Evans, "The Menace of Modern Immigration," October 24, 1923, speech, 58, KKK Records 1922–1971, Oregon Historical Society, Mss 22 manuscripts.
122 Kenneth Jackson, *The Ku Klux Klan in the City, 1915–1930* (Oxford University Press, 1967), 205.
123 "Credit Masons for Great Victory," *Western American*, November 30, 1922, 7.
124 "School Fund is Denied," *Eugene Register*, October 31, 1922, 8.
125 St. Mary's Academy Chronicles, April 6, 1925, as cited in Sister Christine Mary, 16.
126 Campaign literature from Protestant and Non-Sectarian Schools Committee, Lutheran Schools Committee files.
127 Sister Christine Mary, 9.
128 Scottish Rite ad, Lutheran Schools Committee files.
129 "School Bill Not Sponsored by Masonic Lodge," *Capital Press*, October 16, 1922, 1.

130 "Former Grand Master Declares School Bill is Affront to Masons," *Capital Journal*, October 28, 1922, 1.

131 Edwin V. O'Hara, "The School Question in Oregon," *Catholic World*, January 1923, 482.

132 *Silverton Appeal*, October 13, 1922.

133 Lutheran Schools Committee files, Box 1.

134 Minutes to November 14, 1922, meeting, cited in Horowitz, 27.

135 Letter in Olcott Papers.

136 Sister Christine Mary, 9–10.

137 Sister Christine Mary, 10.

138 Dudley G. Wooten, "Remember Oregon," 1923, archives of the Archdiocese of Portland in Oregon 12–13; Saalfeld, 83.

139 "School Bill is Presented at Catholic Church," *Corvallis Gazette-Times*, October 11, 1922.

140 Archbishop Alexander Christie, "The School Question in Oregon," pastoral letter, Oregon School Bill box, archives of the Archdiocese of Portland in Oregon.

141 "The Primary Elections," *The Catholic Sentinel*, May 11, 1922, 4.

142 "General Election November 7," *Catholic Sentinel*, November 2, 1922, 4.

143 Wooten, 10, 15.

144 Wooten, 14–15.

145 Wooten, 15.

146 Abrams, 25, 31.

147 Campaign flyer in Lutheran Schools Committee Records.

148 October 12, 1922, letter from Reverend Messerli to Reverend Titus Lang at Lutheran Synod in Omaha, Lutheran Schools Committee Records.

149 Wooten, 7.

150 Oregon Voters Pamphlet, November 7, 1922, 30.

151 Appendix A, KKK Records, 1922–1971, Oregon Historical Society Library, Manuscripts, Mss 22.

152 *Portland Telegram*, November 2, 1922.

153 *The Scribe*, November 3, 1922, 3, cited by Eisenberg, 131.

154 November 3, Scribe, cited in Eisenberg, 132.

155 Sister Christine Mary, 1–2.

156 Christine Mary, preface.

157 Margaret Meyers, SNJM, "The Ku Klux Klan in La Grande, Oregon," personal reflections, Sisters of the Holy Names of Jesus and Mary archives, 1997.

158 "Klansmen and K.C. Fight," *Eugene Guard*, June 17, 1922, 14.

159 "Two Women Fight at Ex-Nun's Meeting," *Morning Oregonian*, October 16, 1922, 5.

160 F. Leo Smith oral history, September 23 to October 28, 1993, Oregon Historical Society Library, SR 1195.

161 Robert D. Johnston, *The Radical Middle Class: Populist Democracy and the Question of Capitalism in Progressive Era Portland, Oregon* (Princeton University Press, 2003), 112.

162 *Oregon Voter*, December 16, 1922, 7.

163 "The Election," *Oregon Voter*, November 11, 1922, 27.

164 Eisenberg, 132–133.

165 Johnston, 232–233.

166 See county-wide votes in *Oregon Voter*, December 16, 1922, 7.

167 Interview with author (May 29, 2022).

168 "Credit Masons for Great Victory in Adoption of Oregon School Law and Pay No Heed to Four-Flushers," *Western American*, November 30, 1922, 1.

169 U.S. Religion Census, https://www.usreligioncensus.org, accessed July 6, 2025, Catholics accounted for less than 9 percent of Washington's population in 1916 and 1926.

170 "Preparations Being Made to Test School Law," *Catholic Sentinel*, January 19, 1923, 1.

171 Baker, 77.

172 "Attempts in Other States to Abolish Private Schools," *Catholic Sentinel*, April 17, 1924, 7.
173 O'Hara, 489.
174 Saalfeld, 90.
175 "Suit Filed Against School Law in United States District Court," *Catholic Sentinel*, August 23, 1923, 1.
176 Abrams, 127.
177 Sarah Cantor, "Pierce v. Society of Sisters: The fight to preserve Catholic Education in Oregon," 2010, 1, document provided to author.
178 Abrams, 129–130.
179 "Validity of School Law Argued in Federal Court," *Catholic Sentinel*, January 17, 1924, 1.
180 Arthur Bone, editor and co-author, *Oregon Cattleman/Governor/ Congressman: Memoirs and Times of Walter M. Pierce*, Oregon Historical Society, 1981, 441.

CHAPTER 7

1 C. Easton Rothwell, "The Ku Klux Klan in the State of Oregon," senior thesis, Reed College, 1924, 84.
2 "History of American Journalism: The 1920s," University of Kansas University School of Journalism & Mass Communications, https://history-journalism.ku.edu/1920/1920.shtml; accessed July 14, 2025.
3 *N.W. Ayer & Sons American Newspaper Annual & Directory, 1921*, Hathi Trust, https://babel.hathitrust.org/cgi/pt?id=coo.31924087717553&seq=34, 811–830, accessed July 11, 2025.
4 "Laud Editor Piper for News Fairness," *Western American*, June 23, 1923, 1.
5 Reverend Lawrence J. Saalfeld, "Forces of Prejudice in Oregon 1920–1925," master's thesis for Catholic University of America, 1950 (Archdiocesan Historical Commission, 1984), 51.
6 George Turnbull, *An Oregon Crusader* (Binfords & Mort, 1955), 118.
7 Turnbull, 119.
8 "The Inquest," *Corvallis Gazette-Times*, November 10, 1922, 2.
9 Francis Paul Valenti, "The Portland Press, the Ku Klux Klan and the Oregon Compulsory Education Bill: Editorial Treatment of Klan Themes in the Portland Press in 1922," master's thesis for University of Washington, 1993.
10 Valenti, 127.
11 Valenti, 131.
12 "Tis the Telegram's Moving Day; Paper is Printed just the same at Home Date Set for Monday," *Portland Telegram*, October 14, 1922, 1.
13 *Western American*, September 29, 1923, 3.
14 Valenti, 131.
15 "Ku Klux Klan Puts Portland on its List," *Portland Telegram*, June 17, 1921, 1.
16 "Rose City Folk in Ku Klux Klan, *Morning Register*, July 8, 1921, 1.
17 "Klu Klux Klan Said to be Organizing Here and Vicinity," *Eugene Guard*, July 16, 1921.
18 "Ku Klux Klan Trying to Form Branch," July 21, 1921, 1.
19 "Ku Klux Terrorizes the Nation," *Oregon Labor Press*, July 22, 1921, 1.
20 "Oregon is Invaded by Ku Klux Klan," *Morning Oregonian*, July 31, 1921, 14.
21 "Klan Chief Stages Official Reception," *Oregonian*, August 2, 1922, 15.
22 Valenti, 167.
23 "Ku Klux Picture Exhibited," *Morning Oregonian*, December 23, 1921, 4.
24 "Throng Sees Klan Film," *Morning Oregonian*, December 24, 1921, 13.

25 Saalfeld, 50.
26 Turnbull, 83.
27 Rothwell, 135–136; Eckard V. Toy Jr. "The Ku Klux Klan in Oregon, its Character and Program," master's thesis for University of Oregon, 1959, 124.
28 Valenti, 178
29 "A Questionnaire on the KKK," *Morning Oregonian*, May 15, 1922, 8.
30 "Decadent," *Capital Journal*, May 22, 1922, 4.
31 "Ku Kluxing the State," *Capital Journal*, October 2, 1922, 4.
32 "Education and the State, part 5," *Morning Oregonian*, November 3, 1922, 10.
33 "Education and the State, part 1," *Morning Oregonian*, October 30, 1922, 8.
34 "Education and the State, part 3," *Morning Oregonian*, November 1, 1922, 12.
35 "Education and the State, part 1," *Morning Oregonian*, October 30, 1922, 8.
36 "Recommendations on bills," *Sunday Oregonian*, November 5, 1922, 8.
37 Valenti, 111.
38 "Oregonian Editor Doubts Statement of Press Control," *Western American*, March 29, 1923, 6.
39 "White Race is 'Saved;' K.K.K. Gives Theorem," *Oregon Daily Journal*, August 2, 1921, 14.
40 "Arguments Near End in 'Rider' Trial," *Oregon Daily Journal*, March 10, 1923, 1–2.
41 "The Main Issue," *Oregon Daily Journal*, August 13, 1922, 14.
42 "Let Cool Heads Take Command," *Oregon Daily Journal*, May 17, 1922, 10.
43 Valenti, 167.
44 "The School Bill," *Oregon Daily Journal*, October 26, 1922, 8.
45 "Mr. Olcott's Eastern Speech," *Oregon Daily Journal*, December 18, 1922, 24.
46 "Portland Press 'Pussyfooting' on Ku Kluxism, says Salem Editor," *Catholic Sentinel*, August 24, 1922, 4.
47 "For Editor Irvine's Attention," *Western American*," October 19, 1923, 4.
48 *Labor Press*, November 10, 1922, 1.
49 "Ku Klux Orator Called to Time by Pendleton Tribune Editor," *Catholic Sentinel*, March 16, 1922, 1.
50 Toy, 85.
51 "Mayor Outlines Policy," *Oregonian*, January 7, 1923, 7.
52 "A Casualty of Religious War," *Medford Mail Tribune*, June 1, 1923, 4.
53 Turnbull, 68.
54 Turnbull, 72.
55 Turnbull, 67.
56 Turnbull, 73.
57 Floyd McKay, "George Putnam (1872–1961)," *Oregon Encyclopedia*, a project of the Oregon Historical Society, https://www.oregonencyclopedia.org/articles/putnam_george_1872_1961_/, accessed July 14, 2025.
58 Turnbull, 72.
59 Jeff LaLande, "Robert Ruhl (1880–1967)," *Oregon Encyclopedia*, a project of the Oregon Historical Society, https://www.oregonencyclopedia.org/articles/ruhl_robert_1880_1967_/, accessed July 14, 2025.
60 *Medford Mail-Tribune*, April 12, 1922, 4.
61 Interview with author (May 29, 2022).
62 Jeffrey Max LaLande, *The Jackson County Rebellion: A Populist Uprising in Depression-Era Oregon*, Oregon State University Press, 2023, 31.
63 Saalfeld, 53.
64 "Take it to Yourselves," *Corvallis Gazette-Times*, October 28, 1922.

65 Annie McLain, "Unmasking the Oregon Klansman: The Ku Klux Klan in Astoria 1921–1925," Pacific University Oregon, distinguished senior history thesis; 14–15; Harry Crain, "Kluxers Lose Grip in Clatsop," *Capital Journal*, October 16, 1922, 1.

66 Gavin Cronkrite, "The Empire and the Editor: The Ku Klux Klan in Heppner, Oregon," capstone thesis for Clark Honors College, University of Oregon, 2015, 33.

67 Shawn Lay, editor, *Invisible Empire in the West* (University of Illinois Press, 1992), 208.

CHAPTER 8

1 "The Menace," *Capital Journal*, March 12, 1923, 4.

2 Kenneth Jackson, *The Ku Klux Klan in the City, 1915–1930* (Oxford University Press, 1967), 230.

3 Kubli Family Collection, 1911–1944, Oregon Historical Society Library, Manuscripts Coll 431.

4 Michael Helquist, "Criminal Syndicalism Law of Oregon, *Oregon Encyclopedia*, a project of the Oregon Historical Society, https://www.oregonencyclopedia.org/articles/criminal-syndicalism-law-of-oregon/, accessed July 14, 2025.

5 "Boycott Measure Meets Opposition," *Morning Oregonian*, January 17, 1917, 7.

6 Helquist.

7 Harry Crain, "Klan Coersion for Kubli," *Capital Journal*, September 30, 1922, 1.

8 David Horowitz, "The Klansman as Outsider: Ethnocultural Solidarity and Antielitism in the Oregon Ku Klux Klan of the 1920s," *The Pacific Northwest Quarterly*, January 1989, 19.

9 Reverend Lawrence J. Saalfeld, "Forces of Prejudice in Oregon 1920–1925," master's thesis for Catholic University of America, 1950 (Archdiocesan Historical Commission, 1984), 37.

10 Arthur Bone, editor and co-author, *Oregon Cattleman/Governor/Congressman: Memoirs and Times of Walter M. Pierce*, Oregon Historical Society, 1981, 188.

11 Interview with author (December 9, 2024).

12 Robert Bussel, editor, "Understanding the Immigrant Experience in Oregon: Research, Analysis, and Recommendations from University of Oregon Scholars," University of Oregon, 2008, 22.

13 Bussel, 22.

14 Malcom Clark Jr., "The Bigot Disclosed: 90 Years of Nativism," *Oregon Historical Quarterly*, June 1974, 123.

15 Clark, 131.

16 Mike Ferguson, "Historical Hate," *Medford Mail Tribune*, December 6, 1991.

17 Eckard V. Toy Jr. "The Ku Klux Klan in Oregon, its Character and Program," master's thesis for University of Oregon, 1959, 26.

18 Horowitz, Klansman as Outsider, 17.

19 Shawn Lay, editor, *Invisible Empire in the West* (University of Illinois Press, 1992), 160.

20 "Ousting the Japanese," *Oregon Voter*, January 27, 1923, 37.

21 Toy, 111.

22 Toy, 111; Greg Robinson, "Kenji Namba v. McCourt," *Densho Encyclopedia* https://encyclopedia.densho.org/Kenji%20Namba%20v.%20McCourt, accessed July 14, 2025.

23 "Change in Public Sentiment Reflected in Legislature," *Catholic Sentinel*, February 1, 1923, 1.

24 Sarah Cantor, "Pierce v. Society of Sisters: The fight to preserve Catholic Education in Oregon,"

2010, 8, unpublished paper given to author.

25 Toy, 112.

26 Toy, 112.

27 Toy, 113.

28 David Horowitz, editor, *Inside the Klavern: The Secret History of a Ku Klux Klan of the 1920s* (Southern Illinois University Press, 1999), 56.

29 Toy, 111.

30 Bone, 192.

31 "Ku Klux Lobby Fails at Salem," *Catholic Sentinel*, February 22, 1923, 1.

32 "Church Property Tax is Defeated," *Catholic Sentinel*, February 8, 1923, 1; Saalfield, 39.

33 "Ku Klux Lobby Fails at Salem," *Catholic Sentinel*, February 22, 1923, 1.

34 "Governor and Mayor Speak at Klan Fete," *Portland Telegram*, March 5, 1923, 1.

35 "Governor and Mayor Attend Ku Klux Banquet in Oregon," *New York Times*, March 4, 1923.

36 "Mayor Giesy Also Present at Klan Fete," *Capitol Journal*, March 6, 1923, p.1

37 March 5 *Telegram*, 1.

38 "The Klan Dinner," *Catholic Sentinel*, March 15, 1923, 4.

39 Bone, 194.

40 Horowitz, *Inside the Klavern*, 55.

41 March 5 *Telegram*, 3.

42 "Klansmen Honor Oregon Leader," Eugene *Guard*, March 5, 1923 2.

43 "Klertifying the Klan," *Capital Journal*, March 5, 1923, 4.

44 "Two faithless public men," *Portland Telegram*, March 8, 1923.

45 William Shepherd, "The Fiery Double-Cross," *Collier's*, 82 (July 1928), 47; Timothy Egan, *A Fever in the Heartland: The Ku Klux Klan's Plot to Take over America, and the Woman who Stopped Them* (Viking, 2023), 16.

46 David Horowitz lecture, "The Ethical Dilemmas of Tracking Down the Klan: the Oregon Ku Klux Klan of the 1920s," April 24, 1985, for the Oregon Committee for the Humanities, cassette tape at Oregon Historical Society, SR 9035.

47 Shepherd, 49.

48 David M. Chalmers, *Hooded Americanism: The History of the Ku Klux Klan*, Duke University Press, 1987, p. 201; Shepherd, 48.

49 Klan Now Out of Politics, Says Gifford," *Portland Telegram*, May 28, 1923, 2; Klan Potentate's Realm Expanded Over Big Area," *Eugene Guard*, May 29, 1923, 5; Lem Dever, *Confessions of an Imperial Klansman: Hot Tar and Feathers* (self-published, 1924), 23.

50 Hiram Wesley Evans, "The Menace of Modern Immigration," October 24, 1923, speech, KKK Records 1922–1971, Oregon Historical Society, Mss 22 manuscripts, 36.

51 Miguel Hernandez, "Fighting Fraternities: the Ku Klux Klan and Freemasonry in 1920s America," University of Exeter, 2014, 29, 168–169.

52 Shepherd, 48.

53 Horowitz, *Inside the Klavern*, 50–51.

54 Hernandez, 192.

55 Kathleen Blee, *Women of the Klan: Racism and Gender in the 1920s*, University of California Press, 1991, 109.

56 Dever, 7–8.

57 "Fox, Atlanta Klan Slayer, Gets Life Term; Victim's Widow Wanted Severer Penalty," *New York Times*, December 22, 1923, 1.

58 Chalmers, 73.

59 "State to Prosecute Local Outrages," *Medford Mail Tribune*, July 6, 1922, 1.

60 "Six Ku Klux Klan Members Indicted," *Medford Mail Tribune*, August 3, 1922, 1.

61 Horowitz, Klansman as Outsider, 8.

62 "Seek Jury to Try Kluxers," *Medford Mail Tribune*, February 28, 1923, 1.

63 Joyce McBride, "The Ku Klux Klan vs. Edward Emmett Kelly," 23,

Edward E. Kelly Family Papers, Oregon Historical Society Library, Mss 1434-2.

64 "Night Riders Face Trial at Jacksonville," *Capital Journal*, February 27, 1923, 1.

65 "State Rests in Klan Case," *Capital Journal*, March 7, 1923, 1.

66 "The Menace," *Capital Journal*, March 12, 1923, 4.

67 "State Holds Conviction Impossible," *Medford Mail Tribune*, March 15, 1923, 1.

68 "Klan to Launch School Measure in Washington," *Medford Mail Tribune*, November 16, 1922, 1.

69 "Oregon Strongest State in Northwest," *Western American*, January 8, 1923, 2.

70 Jackson, 238.

71 Jackson, 236.

72 "Local Happenings," *Lebanon Express*, August 29, 1923, 5.

73 W. R. Stewart, "Klan Dominates State Politics; Astoria Suffers," *Seattle Post-Intelligencer*, March 23, 1923, 1.

74 Saalfeld, 24; Dever, 12.

75 "Ku Klux and Catholic," *Portland Telegram*, May 5, 1923.

76 "2000 are Initiated into Ku Klux Klan," *Morning Oregonian*, June 12, 1923, 4.

77 "Klan Accounts Still Confusing," *Portland Telegram*, June 13, 1923, 1.

78 "Klan Initiation in Cemetery Opposed by Legion Auxiliary," *Oregon Daily Journal*, June 27, 1923, 2.

79 C. Easton Rothwell, "The Ku Klux Klan in the State of Oregon," senior thesis, Reed College, 1924, 130.

80 "Klan Initiation in Cemetery Opposed by Legion Auxiliary," *Oregon Daily Journal*, June 27, 1923, 2.

81 "Parade Held by Klan," *Oregonian*, June 16, 1923.

82 "Grants Pass Breaks Even," *Eugene Guard*, June 19, 1923, 4.

83 "Election at Albany Hot," *Morning Oregonian*, June 20, 1923, 7.

84 Lay, 197.

85 "Incumbents Re-elected; Bonds Beaten," *Oregon Daily Journal*, June 17, 1923, 1.

86 "Rice and Rugg are Victorious," *La Grande Observer*, June 20, 1923, 1; June 20 *Oregonian*.

87 June 20 *Oregonian*.

88 "Royal Riders Initiate," *Oregonian*, July 29, 1923, 8; "Spectacular 4-R Meet Saturday," *Western American*, July 27, 1.

89 Chalmers, 217.

90 July 29 *Oregonian*.

91 Ben Titus memoir, KKK Records 1922–1971, Oregon Historical Society Library, Manuscripts, Mss 22, 11.

92 Titus, 11; *The World*, June 19, 1922, 2.

93 Titus, 12.

94 Ben Bruce, "The Rise and Fall of the Ku Klux Klan in Oregon During the 1920s," *Voces Novae*, Volume 11, Article 2, 2019; Bruce was a student editor of *Voces Novae*.

95 Titus, 12.

96 Toy, 129; Christine K. Erickson, *Big Skies, White Hoods: The 1920s Klan and a History of Hate in Montana*, University of Oklahoma Press, 2025, 30.

97 "Royal Rider Name is Being Changed," *Western American*, September 7, 1923, 1.

98 "Gifford Appeals for American Boys in Foundation of Junior Klan Order," *Western American*, September 28, 1923, 3.

99 Dever, 19.

100 "50K Klansmen in Portland Goal of Powell Drive," *Western American*, October 19, 1923, 1.

101 Blee, 157–158.

102 "Shooting up of Klan's Meeting Place at Condon Sequel to Ousting Pastor," *Portland Telegram*, October 9, 1923, 1.

103 "Outlaws Shoot up Klan Hall," *Western American*, August 3, 1923, 1.
104 "Roman Mob Scene at Condon Amazes Peaceful Citizens," *Western American*, July 27, 1923, 1.
105 August 3 *Western American*.
106 "Governor Probes Row," *Sunday Oregonian*, August 5, 1923, 19.
107 August 5 *Oregonian*.
108 "Condon Preacher is Held for Kidnapping," *Heppner Herald*, September 25, 1923, 1.
109 Gilliam County court records for case numbers 2902 and 2903, State of Oregon vs G.A. Chaney et al., Oregon State Archives.
110 Gilliam County court records.
111 Gilliam County court records.
112 "Governor Pierce to be Recalled," *The Advocate*, June 12, 1923, 4.
113 Horowitz, *Inside the Klavern*, 108.
114 Bone, 202.
115 Titus, 21.
116 "The Klan in the Saddle," *Capital Journal*, September 23, 1922, 4.
117 Toy, 113.
118 Horowitz lecture.
119 Dever, 41.
120 November 11, 1922, letter from Hawkins, Reuben H. Sawyer Papers, 1896–1962, Oregonian Historical Society Library, Manuscripts, Coll 488.
121 "Change in Public Sentiment Reflected in Legislature," *Catholic Sentinel*, February 1, 1923, 1.
122 "Democrats Not Pleased with Pierce," *Capital Journal*, March 17, 1923, 1.
123 Bone, 196–197.
124 Bone, 197.
125 Bone, 195.
126 *Western American*, June 14, 1923, 2, 6, 8.
127 "Recall of Pierce is Called Off," *Roseburg News-Review*, United Press, June 21, 1.
128 "Do You Want to Recall Pierce?" *Western American*, June 25, 1923, 4.
129 "Warden Talks and Prisoners Run Away," *Western American*, July 27, 1923, 4.
130 "We Salute the Governor," *Western American*, August 3, 1923, 4.
131 Bone, 203.
132 Bone, 206, 443–444.
133 Bone, 207.

CHAPTER 9

1 Reverend Lawrence J. Saalfeld, "Forces of Prejudice in Oregon 1920–1925," master's thesis for Catholic University of America, 1950 (Archdiocesan Historical Commission, 1984).
2 Lem Dever, *Confessions of an Imperial Klansman: Hot Tar and Feathers* (self-published, 1924).
3 C. Easton Rothwell, "The Ku Klux Klan in the State of Oregon," senior thesis, Reed College, 1924, 127.
4 Ben Titus memoir, 15, KKK Records 1922–1971, Oregon Historical Society Library, Manuscripts, Mss 22.
5 Harry Crain, "Thirty-four Charges Suppressed by Gifford and Imperial Officers," *Capital Journal*, November 29, 1923, 1, 2.
6 Rothwell, 127. His account said there were twenty-one charges against Gifford.
7 Harry Crain, "Gifford Not Legal Klan Officer," *Capital Journal*, November 30, 1923, 1.
8 Harry Crain, "Klan Backs Recount and School Bill," *Capital Journal*, October 24, 1922, 4; Eckard V. Toy Jr. "The Ku Klux Klan in Oregon, its Character and Program," master's thesis for University of Oregon, 1959, 40.
9 "Gifford's Tactics," *Capital Journal*, November 7, 1923, 8.
10 Rothwell, 140.

11 Saalfeld, 48; Dever, 29.
12 Dever, 29.
13 "Ku Klux Project Has Fallen Down," *The World*, December 14, 1922, 6.
14 "Geo. B. Thomas, Portland School Board member, quit the Klan," *Catholic Sentinel*, December 7, 1922, 1.
15 David Horowitz, editor, *Inside the Klavern: The Secret History of a Ku Klux Klan of the 1920s* (Southern Illinois University Press, 1999), 42.
16 "Some Highlights from Salem," *Cottage Grove Sentinel*, January 10, 1923, 1.
17 Horowitz, 60.
18 January 26, 1923, minutes, Ku Klux Klan La Grande Oregon chapter records, 1922–1923, Oregon Historical Society Library, Manuscripts, Mss 2604.
19 "Join the Klan Now, and Be Economical; Raise is Due Soon," *Western American*, May 17, 1923, 1.
20 Dever, 30.
21 "Gifford Welcomed by Portland Klan; Brings Good News," *Western American*, June 18, 1923, 1.
22 "Klansmen Justified as Doubters," *Capital Journal*, November 10, 1923, 14.
23 Lem Dever, "Limelight Turned on the Klan," *The Spectator*, January 10, 1925, 7.
24 Saalfeld, 48.
25 "Klan Gives $50,000 to Children's Home," *Morning Oregonian*, June 26, 1923, 16.
26 January 10 *Spectator*, 13.
27 November 10 *Capital Journal*, 1.
28 Kathleen Blee, *Women of the Klan: Racism and Gender in the 1920s* (University of California Press, 1991), 27.
29 Dever, 31.
30 "Invisible Empire Meeting Results in Pyrotechnics," *Oregon Daily Journal*, May 13, 1923, 12.
31 Dever, 32–33.
32 Dever, 33.
33 "Women Mobilizing Throughout State for Real Service," *Western American*, September 7, 1923, 1.
34 "Klansmen Justified as Doubters," *Capital Journal*, November 10, 1923, 1; Saalfeld, 56; "Ku Klux at Roseburg," *The Eugene Daily Guard*, April 26, 1922, 6.
35 "Grand Kluxer Ball at Seaside July 6," *Western American*, June 28, 1923, 1.
36 Horowitz, 117.
37 Horowitz, 121.
38 "Off to Korvallis Host of Klansmen in Great Konclave," *Western American*, October 19, 1923, 1.
39 Klansmen to State Çeremonies of Order Tonight," *Corvallis Gazette-Times*, October 18, 1923, 1.
40 "500 Klansmen Put on Adoption Ceremonial," *Corvallis Gazette-Times*, October 19, 1923, 1.
41 Horowitz, 127, 136.
42 "Klankraft Defined by Portland Chief," *Western American*, March 1, 1923, 1.
43 "Samuel Gompers," America's Unions, AFL-CIO, https://aflcio.org/about/history/labor-history-people/samuel-gompers, accessed July 14, 2025.
44 "Welcome to Labor Given by Klansmen of the Northwest," *Western American*, October 28, 1923, 1.
45 "Labor Brands Ku Klux Klan 'Treasonable' " *Portland Telegram*, October 9, 1923, 2; "Labor Federation Unseats W. Dunne," *Eugene Morning Register*, October 9, 1923, 1.
46 "Roseburg Bars Klan's Parade," *Coos Bay Times*, November 14, 1923, 1.
47 "Eggs Halt Klan Parade," *Morning Oregonian*, November 28, 1923, 1.
48 "Says Gifford Used Klan to Help Utilities," *Portland Telegram*, November 26, 1923, 1; and "Elford Confirms Talk of Split," *Capital Journal*, November 27, 1923, 1, 10.
49 "Dope on the FOPS," *Oregon Voter*, August 25, 1923, 13–15.

50 "State of Oregon ex rel U.G. Walker vs. W.C. Elford," Multnomah County Circuit Court case number 95083, judgement issued November 15, 1923.

51 "'Yellow Ticket' in Court Limelight," *Eugene Guard*, November 27, 1923, 10.

52 W. R. Stewart, "Klan Dominating State's Politics; Astoria Suffers," *Seattle Post-Intelligencer*, March 25, 1923; Trevor Griffey, "Luther I. Powell: Northwest KKK Organizer," in *The Ku Klux Klan in Washington State*, University of Washington Civil Rights & Labor History Project, https://depts.washington.edu/civilr/kkk_seattle.htm, accessed July 10.

53 "Oregon Strongest State in Northwest," *Western American*, January 8, 1923, 2.

54 Griffey, chapter 3 and chapter 4.

55 Griffey, chapter 6.

56 Kenneth Jackson, *The Ku Klux Klan in the City, 1915–1930* (Oxford University Press, 1967), 237.

57 Griffey, chapter 1.

58 "Major Luther I. Powell, King Kleagle, Opens the Big Drive," *The Watcher on the Tower*, October 27, 1923, 1.

59 "50,000 Klansmen in Portland Goal of Klan Drive," *Western American*, October 19, 1923, 1.

60 "Klan Kall," No. 1, Oregon Politics, Box 21, Oregon Historical Society Library, Mss. 1513.

61 October 27 *Watcher on the Tower.*

62 "Ku Klux Klan Parades City and Initiates," *Oregon Statesman*, November 11, 1923, 1; "Klan Parade Here Seen by Huge Crowd," *Capital Journal*, November 12, 1923, 1.

63 November 12 *Capital Journal*, 4.

64 "Band to go to Salem," November 10, 1923, *Eugene Register*, 8.

65 November 12 *Capital Journal*, 4.

66 November 11 *Oregon Statesman.*

67 November 11 *Oregon Statesman.*

68 November 12 *Capital Journal*, 4.

69 *Capital Journal*, November 5–10, all starting on front page.

70 November 12 *Capital Journal*, 1.

71 "Klan Kleagle Inaugurates Campaign to Discredit Gifford as Grand Dragon," *Portland Telegram*, November 27, 1923, 1.

72 "Gifford and Powell now at Outs," *Capital Journal*, November 23, 1923, 1.

73 Harry Crain, "Ousting of Powell Old Trick," *Capital Journal*, December 3, 1923, 1.

74 Harry Crain, "A.P.A. Revived by Kluxers," *Capital Journal*, December 18, 1923, 1.

75 "Degree will be Given," *Morning Oregonian*, February 1, 1924, 19.

76 "Luther I. Powell Banished by Klan," *Morning Oregonian*, February 16, 1924, 17.

77 "Klansmen Oppose Gifford," *Morning Oregonian*, December 18, 1923, 17.

78 "Infamous Forgery," *Western American*, June 7, 1923, 1.

79 Blee, 109.

80 David M. Chalmers, *Hooded Americanism: The History of the Ku Klux Klan* (Duke University Press, 1987), 107.

81 "Clarke Says Klan War is Pending that will Shake Nation, Writes Coolidge," *Eugene Guard*, December 27, 1923, 1.

82 "Simmons Quits Klan for Cash Payment," *Eugene Guard*, February 23, 1924, 10.

83 Christine K. Erickson, *Big Skies, White Hoods: The 1920s Klan and a History of Hate in Montana* (University of Oklahoma Press, 2025), 112–113.

84 December 12, 1922, letter from Lem Dever, Reuben H. Sawyer Papers, 1896–1962, Oregonian Historical Society Library, Manuscripts, Coll 488.

85 "Lem A. Dever Resigns Post," *La Grande Observer*, December 12, 1923, 1.

86 Dever, 10, 1.

87 Dever, 12.
88 Dever, 13, 11.
89 Dever, 21.
90 Dever, 22.
91 Dever, 20.
92 Dever, 18.
93 "Lem Dever, Former Klan Editor, Gets 15-day Jail Term," *Oregon Daily Journal*, November 6, 1924, 7.
94 "Preached Hate on Credit," *Catholic Sentinel*, April 16, 1925; "Klan Paper Sued for $18,942 Printing Bill," *Capital Journal*, April 11, 1925, 7.
95 Horowitz, 121.
96 *Western American*, September 7, 1923, 4.
97 Dever, 36–37.
98 Toy, 118.
99 "McArthur in Race; Klan is Condemned," *Morning Oregonian*, October 19, 1923, 4.
100 "Klan Leaders Split over Baker—Kubli," *Eugene Guard*, January 22, 1924, 7.
101 "Stand for M'Nary is Taken by Klan," *Morning Oregonian*, May 14, 10.
102 Harry Crain, "Powell Not to Lack Ammunition," *Capital Journal*, November 28, 1923, 1–2.
103 "Klan Enjoined from Issuing Yellow Ticket," *Capital Journal*, May 9, 1924, 1.
104 "Klansmen Defy Order and Send Yellow Ticket," *Capital Journal*, May 14, 1924, 2.
105 Saalfeld, 43.
106 "Klan Loses in Oregon Contest," *Catholic Sentinel*, May 22, 1924, 1.
107 May 22 *Catholic Sentinel.*
108 May 22 *Catholic Sentinel.*
109 "Many Candidates of Klan Lose in Recent Election," *Oregon Sunday Journal*, May 25, 1924, 7.
110 "Return to Reason," reprinted by the *Coos Bay Times*, May 21, 1924, 4.
111 "Klan to Parade Saturday, Eugene to Have Conclave," *Eugene Guard*, June 24, 1924, 2.
112 "Klan Initiates Men Before Large Crowd," *Morning Register*, June 29, 1924, 4.
113 Lay, 176–177; and "Invisible Empire," *Eugene Register-Guard*, January 10, 1993, 1F.
114 "Klan Couple in Full Regalia are Wed at Services," *Eugene Guard*, June 30, 1924, 1.
115 Shawn Lay, editor, *Invisible Empire in the West* (University of Illinois Press, 1992), 176.
116 Chalmers, 162.
117 Timothy Egan, *A Fever in the Heartland: The Ku Klux Klan's Plot to Take over America, and the Woman who Stopped Them* (Viking, 2023), 49; Chalmers, 101, 104.
118 Egan, xv; Chalmers, 165; Wade, 233.
119 "Stephenson Heads Defiant Klansmen," *Indianapolis Star*, May 13, 1924, 1.
120 Egan, 176.
121 Jackson, 15
122 Chalmers, 171–172.
123 For more on Stephenson and Obertholtzer, see Egan; Wyn Craig Wade, *The Fiery Cross: The Ku Klux Klan in America* (Oxford University Press, 1987), 215–247; and Linda Gordon, *The Second Coming of the KKK: The Ku Klux Klan of the 1920s and the American Political Tradition* (Liveright Publishing Corp., a division of W.W. Norton & Co., 2017.
124 "The Menace of Modern Immigration," Hiram Evans speech on October 24, 1923, KKK Records 1922–1971.
125 "America of the Melting Pot Comes to an End," *New York Times*, April 27, 1924, section XX, 3.
126 Interview with author (May 21, 2022).
127 "Mention of Klan Starts Near Riot," *Catholic Sentinel*, June 26, 1924, 1.
128 Chalmers, 208.
129 "Anti-Klan Plank is Turned Down, *Catholic Sentinel*, July 3, 1924, 1.

130 "Powell Not to Lack Ammunition," *Capital Journal*, November 28, 1923, 1–2.
131 Borthwick Papers, University of Oregon Knight Library Special Collections, cited by Father Wilfred P. Schoenberg, *Ku Klux Klan in Pacific Northwest: 1921–1927*, unpublished manuscript, archives of the Archdiocese of Portland in Oregon chapter 8, 31.
132 Jackson, 212.
133 "Stand for M'Nary is Taken by Klan," *Morning Oregonian*, May 14, 1924, 10; Dever, 14.
134 Lay, 176.
135 "On Quitting the Klan," *Oregon Daily Journal*, August 28, 1924, 8.
136 Schoenberg, chapter 10, 2–3.
137 Jackson, 213.
138 Jackson, 239, 237.
139 Rothwell, 122.
140 Toy, 272.
141 Schoenberg, chapter 7, 47.
142 Rothwell, 139.
143 Lem Dever, "Limelight Turned on the Klan," *The Spectator*, February 15, 1925, 7.
144 "Claim Old Klan Records Burned," *The World*, March 5, 1925, 1.
145 "Grand Dragon of Klan Quits Place; Atlantan in City," *Oregon Daily Journal*, July 17, 1925, 17.
146 "The KKK Holds Get-Together," *Gold Hill News*, January 21, 1926, 1.
147 Ku Klux Klan Tillamook, Oregon Chapter No. 8 Records, 1922–1929, Box 1, Folder 12, University of Oregon Libraries Special Collections, Bx 046.
148 Lay, 178.
149 Chalmers, 281, 64.
150 Chalmers, 45–48.
151 Lloyd Jorgenson, "The Oregon School Law of 1922: Passage and Sequel," *The Catholic Historical Review* 54, No. 3 (October 1968), 457.
152 "Attempts in Other States to Abolish Private Schools, *Catholic Sentinel*, April 17, 1924, 7.
153 Egan, 247.
154 Chalmers, 286.
155 Terrence McArdle, "The Day 30,000 White Supremacists in KKK Robes Marched in the Nation's Capital," *Washington Post* online, August 17, 2017.
156 "Klan Ranks Thinner in Capital Parade," *New York Times*, September 13, 1926.
157 August 17 *Washington Post* online.
158 Egan, 326.
159 Gordon, 194.
160 Chalmers, 48.
161 "The Klan's Invisible Empire is Fading," *New York Times*, February 21, 1926.
162 September 13 *New York Times*
163 Chalmers, 73.
164 Chalmers, 173–174.
165 Chalmers, 291.
166 Blee, 175.
167 Jackson, 43–44.

CHAPTER 10

1 Interview with author (May 23, 1922).
2 W. R. Stewart, "Medford Club Life Suffers in Klan's Invisible Warfare," *Seattle Post-Intelligencer*, March 30, 1923, 1.
3 W. R. Stewart, "Portland Disrupted by Incursion of Invisible Empire," *Seattle Post-Intelligencer*, March 28, 1923, 1.
4 Governor Ben Wilson Olcott Papers, Scrapbooks, Volume 8. University of Oregon Special Collections.
5 Reverend Lawrence J. Saalfeld, "Forces of Prejudice in Oregon 1920–1925," master's thesis for Catholic University of America, 1950 (Archdiocesan Historical Commission, 1984), 30.

6 See, for instance, Timothy Egan's 2023 book on the Indiana Klan, *A Fever in the Heartland: The Ku Klux Klan's Plot to Take Over America, and the Woman Who Stopped Them*, Viking, 2023.

7 David M. Chalmers, *Hooded Americanism: The History of the Ku Klux Klan* (Duke University Press, 1987), 39, 280.

8 Chalmers, 4.

9 Miguel Hernandez, "Fighting Fraternities: the Ku Klux Klan and Freemasonry in 1920s America" (University of Exter, 2014), 312.

10 Interview with author (May 21, 2022).

11 Eckard V. Toy Jr. "The Ku Klux Klan in Oregon, its Character and Program," master's thesis for University of Oregon, 1959, 12.

12 Arthur Bone, editor and co-author, *Oregon Cattleman/Governor/ Congressman: Memoirs and Times of Walter M. Pierce* (Oregon Historical Society, 1981), 311.

13 Letter to Fred Mack, in Olcott Papers.

14 "Color Line Drawn; Pupils Leave Rink," *Morning Oregonian*, January 28, 1927.

15 "Klan Revival Due in Oregon, Gifford Says," *Oregon Daily Journal*, October 19, 1937, 1; "Hooded Klan Meets," News-*Telegram*, November 25, 1937, 1.

16 Kathleen Blee, *Women of the Klan: Racism and Gender in the 1920s* (University of California Press, 1991), 175; also see Chalmers, chapters 42–45.

17 Chalmers, 323.

18 Wyn Craig Wade, *The Fiery Cross: The Ku Klux Klan in America* (Oxford University Press, 1987), 275.

19 Craig Collisson, "Japanese American Wartime Incarceration in Oregon," Oregon Encyclopedia; and "Not Exactly Paradise: Japanese American Internment Camps," Oregon Secretary of State, https://sos.oregon.gov/archives/exhibits/ww2/Pages/threats-paradise.aspx, accessed July 14, 2025.

20 Greg Robinson, "Kenji Namba v. McCourt," *Densho Encyclopedia*, https://encyclopedia.densho.org/Kenji%20Namba%20v.%20McCourt, accessed July 15, 2025.

21 Wade, 361–362; Chalmers, 398; Blee, 176.

22 Wade, 364.

23 Blee, 176.

24 Wade, viii.

25 Randy Blazak, "Oregon Citizens Alliance," Oregon Encyclopedia, a project of the Oregon Historical Society, https://www.oregonencyclopedia.org/articles/oregon_citizens_alliance/, accessed July 23, 2025.

26 David Alan Johnson, Quintard Taylor, and Marsha Weisiger, "Report on the History of Matthew P. Deady and Frederick S. Dunn," University of Oregon, 2016.

27 See https://oregonremembrance.org, accessed July 14, 2025.

28 "Connections," Volume 31, Issue 4, April 2021.

29 Steve Law, "ODOT to rename stretch of I-5 that honored former KKK member," *Portland Tribune*, September 7, 2022, 1.

30 Rob Davis, "The Oregonian's racist legacy," *Oregonian*, October 24, 2022, 1.

31 Therese Bottomly, "I Unreservedly Apologize," *Oregonian*, October 24, 2022.

32 David Horowitz, editor, *Inside the Klavern: The Secret History of a Ku Klux Klan of the 1920s* (Southern Illinois University Press, 1999), 49.

33 Sister Christine Mary, "Oregon School Bill: The Case of the Sisters of the Holy Names vs. the State of Oregon," 1958, Sisters of the Holy Names of Jesus and Mary archives.

34 Hiram Wesley Evans, "The Klan's Fight for Americanism," *The North American Review 223*, no. 830 (May 1926), 36–37.

35 Saalfeld, vii.

APPENDIX A

1 *Western American,* March 1, 1923.
2 *Hood River Glacier,* March 23, 1923. 2.
3 KKK Records, 1922–1971, Oregon Historical Society Mss 22 Manuscripts; *Western American,* September 14, 1923; *Oregonian,* November 28, 1923, 1.
4 *Oregon Daily Journal,* July 31, 1922.
5 *Aurora Observer,* November 23, 1922; *Gresham Outlook,* April 8, 1924, 3; *Gresham Outlook,* April 20, 1924, 1.
6 *Oregon Daily Journal,* September 15, 1923; *Western American,* October 19, 1923; *Hillsboro Argus,* November 22, 1923, 2.
7 *Western American,* February 1, 1923; *Hood River Glacier,* April 17, 1924, 6.
8 *Western American,* July 6, 1923, 1; Reverend Lawrence J. Saalfeld, "Forces of Prejudice in Oregon 1920–1925," master's thesis, Catholic University of America, 1950 (Archdiocesan Historical Commission, 1984), 23.
9 *Oregon City Enterprise,* September 30, 1921, 3; KKK Records, 1922–1971.
10 *Western American,* May 17, 1923.
11 *Beaverton Review,* August 8, 1924; *Western American,* October 19, 1923, 1.
12 *Oregon Daily Journal,* April 13, 1924.
13 *Vernonia Eagle,* September 7, 1923, 1; *Eugene Guard,* January 22, 1924, 3.
14 *Oregon Daily Journal,* October 6, 1922, 21.
15 *Albany Democrat-Herald,* March 1, 1923; KKK Records, 1922–1971.
16 *Capital Journal,* March 17, 1924, 1.
17 *Aurora Observer,* November 23, 1922.
18 *Capital Journal,* February 2, 1923.
19 *Corvallis Gazette-Times,* August 15, 1921; *Western American,* May 17, 1923.
20 *Eugene Register,* September 19, 1923; Shawn Lay, editor. *Invisible Empire in the West: Towards a New Historical Appraisal of the Ku Klux Klan of the 1920s.* University of Illinois Press, 1992, 178.
21 *Oregon Statesman,* April 16, 1924.
22 *Western American,* March 1, 1923.
23 *Roseburg News-Review,* February 22, 1924.
24 KKK Records, 1922–1971; *Western American,* March 1, 1923.
25 *Albany Democrat,* September 11, 1924.
26 *Western American,* March 1, 1923.
27 *Albany Democrat,* February 8, 1923.
28 *Eugene Guard,* March 3, 1923.
29 *Western American,* March 1, 1923.
30 *Monmouth Herald,* July 13, 1923, 5.
31 *Eugene Guard,* February 3, 1923, and May 19, 1923.
32 *Eugene Guard,* February 3, 1923.
33 *Western American,* May 17, 1923.
34 *Western American,* March 29, 1923.
35 *Eugene Guard,* May 19, 1923; *Capital Journal,* August 11, 1924; *Western American,* May 17, 1923.
36 *Oregonian,* July 7, 1923, 3.
37 *Albany Democrat,* February 28, 1923.
38 *Oregon Daily Journal,* December 4, 1924, 3.
39 KKK Records, 1922–1971.
40 *Western American,* August 3, 1923; *Albany Democrat-Herald,* February 18, 1923; *Eugene Guard,* October 9, 1924.
41 *Capital Journal,* November 9, 1923, 12.
42 *Eugene Register,* July 18, 1922.
43 *Capital Journal,* March 17, 1924, 1.
44 *Turner Tribune,* June 21, 1923; *Capital Journal,* March 17, 1924, 1.
45 *Eugene Guard,* July 20, 1924.
46 Saalfeld, 13.
47 *Western American,* March 1, 1923.
48 *Western American,* March 1, 1923, and December 7, 1922.

49 Broadside Collection, University of Oregon Special Collections; Saalfeld, 11.
50 *Western American*, July 6, 1923; *Coquille Valley Sentinel*, September 14, 1923, 2.
51 *Eugene Guard*, July 20, 1924; *Eugene Register*, August 23, 1924.
52 *Eugene Guard*, July 8, 1924.
53 Saalfeld, 10; *The World*, January 24, 1922, 2.
54 Harry Crain, "Thirty-four Charges," *Capital Journal*, November 29, 1923, 2.
55 Saalfeld, 10–11.
56 *Western American*, June 28, 1923; *Oregon Daily Journal*, May 12, 1922.
57 *Western American*, August 10, 1923; *Albany Democrat-Herald*, November 22, 1923.
58 *Western American*, February 22, 1923.
59 *Eugene Guard*, May 19, 1923.
60 *Eugene Guard*, May 19, 1923.
61 Toy, 80; Saalfeld, 13.
62 *Western American*, March 1, 1923.
63 Saalfeld, 11.
64 *Roseburg News-Review*, June 14, 1922.
65 *Gold Hill News*, January 21, 1926.
66 *Western American*, March 1, 1923.
67 Trevor Griffey, "History of the KKK in Washington State." *The Ku Klux Klan in Washington State*, University of Washington Civil Rights & Labor History Project. https://depts.washington.edu/civilr/kkk_seattle.htm.
68 KKK Records, 1922–1971.
69 Saalfeld, 11.
70 *Roseburg News-Review*, June 14, 1922, 3.
71 *Western American*, January 18, 1923; Saalfeld, 11.
72 *Roseburg News-Review*, August 25, 1921; *Oregon Statesman*, July 16, 1922; *Western American*, March 1, 1923; *Roseburg New-Review*, April 15, 1924.
73 *Western American*, January 18, 1923; February 1, 1923; February 18, 1923; La Grande minutes, March 27, 1923.
74 *Western American*, March 8 and September 14, 1923; Toy, 86; *Boardman Mirror*, April 17, 1925, 2.
75 See Shootout in Condon, Chapter 8.
76 Rothwell, 117–118; KKK Records, 1922–1971; *Western American*, February 1, April 19, and June 28, 1923.
77 *Oregon Daily Journal*, August 5, 1924.
78 *Western American*, January 18, 1923; David Horowitz, editor. *Inside the Klavern: The Secret History of a Ku Klux Klan of the 1920s*, Southern Illinois University Press, 1999, 65.
79 *Western American*, January 18, 1923; *La Grande Observer*, February 9, 1924; *Oregon Daily Journal*, May 12, 1924, 16.
80 *Heppner Herald*, December 4, 1923, 1.
81 *Ione Independent*, February 1, 1924, p.1; *Heppner Gazette-Times*, December 6, 1923, 1; Gavin Cronkrite, "The Empire and the Editor: The Ku Klux Klan in Heppner, Oregon," Capstone thesis, Clark Honors College, University of Oregon, 2015.
82 *Hermiston Herald*, April 26, 1923, 1.
83 Minutes of a Ku Klux Klan Kloncave in Eastern Oregon. Oregon Historical Society Library. Manuscripts, Coll. 886..
84 *Ione Independent*, February 1, 1924, 1.
85 *Western American*, February 1, 1923; *La Grande Observer*, August 8, 1924; KKK Records, 1922–1971; *Western American*, January 18, 1923; Horowitz, 108.
86 *Western American*, January 18, 1923; Horowitz, 108.
87 *Coos Bay World*, September 14, 1923.
88 *La Grande Observer*, July 1, 1924.

89 *Gate City Journal*, March 16, 1923, 3.
90 *Gate City Journal*, June 27, 1924, 6.
91 Toy, 85; KKK Records, 1922–1971.
92 *Bend Bulletin*, August 27, 1924.
93 Horowitz, xi.

APPENDIX B

1 Letter from "B" to Ed Larney, December 10, 1947, KKK Pamphlets, Col. 899, Oregon Historical Society Library.
2 Interview with author (November 14, 2024).
3 "Ex-Kleagle Asks for Police Job," *Capital Journal*, May 28, 1924, 10.
4 Trevor Griffey, "Luther I. Powell: Northwest KKK Organizer," in *The Ku Klux Klan in Washington State*, University of Washington Civil Rights & Labor History Project, https://depts.washington.edu/civilr/kkk_seattle.htm, accessed July 10, 2025.
5 Reuben H. Sawyer Papers, 1896–1962. Oregon Historical Society Library. Manuscripts, Coll 488.

Bibliography

BOOKS

Abrams, Paula. *Cross Purposes: Pierce v. Society of Sisters and the Struggle for Compulsory Public Education*. University of Michigan Press, 2009.

Baker, Kelly J. *Gospel According to the Klan: The KKK's Appeal to Protestant America, 1915–1930.* University Press of Kansas, 2011.

Blee, Kathleen. *Women of the Klan: Racism and Gender in the 1920s.* University of California Press, 1991.

Bone, Arthur, editor and co-author with Pierce, Walter. *Oregon Cattleman/Governor/ Congressman: Memoirs and Times of Walter M. Pierce.* Oregon Historical Society, 1981.

Chalmers, David M. *Hooded Americanism: The History of the Ku Klux Klan*. Duke University Press, 1987.

Dever, Lem. *Confessions of an Imperial Klansman: Hot Tar and Feather.* Self-published, 1924.

Dixon, Thomas Jr. *The Clansman.* The Country Life Press, 1905. https://www.gutenberg.org/files/26240/26240-h/26240-h.htm

Dolan, Timothy Michael. *Some Seed Fell on Good Ground: The Life of Edwin W. O'Hara.* The Catholic University of America Press, 1992.

Edwards, G. Thomas and Schwantes, Carlos A., editors. *Experiences in a Promised Land: Essays in Pacific Northwest History*. University of Washington Press, 1986.

Egan, Timothy. *A Fever in the Heartland: The Ku Klux Klan's Plot to Take over America, and the Woman who Stopped Them*. Viking, 2023.

Eisenberg, Ellen. *Embracing a Western Identity: Jewish Oregonians 1849–1950.* Oregon State University Press, 2015.

Erickson, Christine K. *Big Skies, White Hoods: The 1920s Klan and a History of Hate in Montana*. University of Oklahoma Press, 2025.

Fry, Henry Peck. *The Modern Ku Klux Klan*. Small, Maynard &. Co., Boston, 1922; https://www.gutenberg.org/files/34478/34478-h/34478-h.htm

Gordon, Linda. *The Second Coming of the KKK: The Ku Klux Klan of the 1920s and the American Political Tradition*. Liveright Publishing Corp., 2017.

Horowitz, David, editor and author. *Inside the Klavern: The Secret History of a Ku Klux Klan of the 1920s*. Southern Illinois University Press, 1999.

Jackson, Kenneth. *The Ku Klux Klan in the City, 1915–1930.* Oxford University Press, 1967.

Johnston, Robert D. *The Radical Middle Class: Populist Democracy and the Question of Capitalism in Progressive Era Portland, Oregon.* Princeton University Press, 2003.

Laidlaw, Father John R. *The Catholic Church in Oregon and the Work of its Archbishops.* Exposition Press Inc., 1977.

LaLande, Jeffrey Max. *The Jackson County Rebellion: A Populist Uprising in Depression-Era Oregon.* Oregon State University Press, 2023.

Lay, Shawn, editor. *Invisible Empire in the West: Towards a New Historical Appraisal of the Ku Klux Klan of the 1920s*. University of Illinois Press, 1992.

Lester, John C. and Wilson, D. L. *Ku Klux Klan: Its Origin, Growth and Disbandment.* Wheeler, Osborn and Duckworth Manufacturing Co., 1884. Released in 1905 with an introduction and editing by Walter L. Fleming. https://www.gutenberg.org/cache/epub/31819/pg31819-images.html

MacColl, E. Kimbark. *The Growth of a City: Power and Politics in Portland, Oregon, 1915 to 1950.* Georgian Press, 1979.

MacLean, Nancy. *Behind the Mask of Chivalry: The Making of the Second Ku Klux Klan.* Oxford University Press, 1994.

Mangun, Kimberly. A *Force for Change: Beatrice Morrow Cannady and the Struggle for Civil Rights in Oregon: 1912–1936*. Oregon State University Press, 2010.

McLagan, Elizabeth. *A Peculiar Paradise: A History of Blacks in Oregon, 1788–1940.* Oregon State University Press, 2022.

Mecklin, John Moffat. *The Ku Klux Klan: A Study of the American Mind.* Harcourt, Brace and Co., 1924. https://www.google.com/books/edition/_/GkQiAQAAIAAJ?hl=en&gbpv=1&pg=PA3&dq=Oregon+Ku+Klux+Klan+

N. W. Ayer & Sons. *N. W. Ayer & Sons American Newspaper Annual & Directory. 1921.* Hathi Trust, https://babel.hathitrust.org/cgi/pt?id=coo.31924087717553&seq=43

Schoffen, Elizabeth. *The Demands of Rome*. Self-published, 1917.

Shaw, J. G. *Edwin Vincent O'Hara: American Prelate.* Farrar, Straus and Cudahy, 1957.

Turnbull, George. *An Oregon Crusader*. Binfords & Mort, 1955.

Wade, Wyn Craig. *The Fiery Cross: The Ku Klux Klan in America*. Oxford University Press, 1987.

JOURNAL ARTICLES

Alexander, Charles C. "Kleagles and Cash: The Ku Klux Klan as a Business Organization, 1915–1930." *The Business History Review* 39, No. 3 (Autumn 1965): 348–367. JSTOR.

Clark, Malcom Jr. "The Bigot Disclosed: 90 Years of Nativism." *Oregon Historical Quarterly 75*, no. 2 (June 1974): 109–190. JSTOR.

Evans, Hiram Wesley. "The Klan's Fight for Americanism." *The North American Review 223*, no. 830 (May 1926): 33–63. JSTOR.

Holsinger, M. Paul. "The Oregon School Bill Controversy, 1922–1925," *Pacific Historical Review 37*, no. 3 (August 1968): 327–341. JSTOR.

Horowitz, David. "The Klansman as Outsider: Ethnocultural Solidarity and Antielitism in the Oregon Ku Klux Klan of the 1920s." *The Pacific Northwest Quarterly 80*, no. 1 (January 1989): 12–20. JSTOR.

Horowitz, David. "Social Morality and Personal Revitalization: Oregon's Ku Klux Klan in the 1920s." *Oregon Historical Quarterly 90*, no. 4 (Winter 1989): 365–384. JSTOR.

Jackson, Charles. "William J. Simmons: A Career in Ku Kluxism." *The Georgia Historical Quarterly 50*, no. 4 (December 1966): 351–365. JSTOR.

Kedrosky, Davis. "In the Shadow of the Slump: The Depression of 1920–1921," *Berkeley Economic Review*. University of California Berkeley. March 18, 2021. https://econreview.studentorg.berkeley.edu/in-the-shadow-of-the-slump-the-depression-of-1920-1921/

Jensen, Kimberly. "Gendering White Supremacy." *Oregon Historical Quarterly 125*, no. 1 (Spring 2024): 6–33.

Jorgenson, Lloyd. "The Oregon School Law of 1922: Passage and Sequel." *The Catholic Historical Review* 54, no. 3 (Oct. 1968): 455–466. JSTOR.

LaLande, Jeff. "Beneath the Hooded Robe: Newspapermen, Local Politics and the Ku Klux Klan in Jackson County, Oregon, 1921–23." *Pacific Northwest Quarterly 83*, no. 2 (April 1992): 42–52. JSTOR.

Tobie, Harvey Elmer. "Oregon Labor Disputes, 1919–1923 I: The Living Wage." *Oregon Historical Quarterly 48*, no.1 (March 1947): 7–24. JSTOR.

Toll, William. "Progress and Piety: The Ku Klux Klan and Social Change in Tillamook, Oregon." *Pacific Northwest Quarterly 69*, no. 2 (April 1978): 75–85; JSTOR.

Toy, Eckard V. Jr. "The Ku Klux Klan in Tillamook, Oregon," *Pacific Northwest Quarterly 53*, no. 2 (April 1962): 60–64. JSTOR.

ACADEMIC THESES

Bryans, Andrew Nils. "The Response to Left-Wing Radicalism in Portland, Oregon from 1917 to 1941." Master's thesis, Portland State University, 2002.

Bryant, Janet W. "The Ku Klux Klan and the Oregon Compulsory School Bill of 1922." Senior thesis, Reed College, 1970.

Cronkrite, Gavin. "The Empire and the Editor: The Ku Klux Klan in Heppner, Oregon." Capstone thesis, Clark Honors College, University of Oregon, 2015.

Hernandez, Miguel. "Fighting Fraternities: the Ku Klux Klan and Freemasonry in 1920s America." PhD dissertation, University of Exeter, 2014.

Horrocks, Brenda M. "More than Hatchetmen: Chinese Exclusion and Tong Wars in Portland Oregon." Master's thesis, Utah State University, 2019.

McLain, Annie. "Unmasking the Oregon Klansman: The Ku Klux Klan in Astoria 1921–1925." Senior thesis, Pacific University Oregon, 2003.

Quast, Alex. "The Two Faces of Anti-Semitism: Reuben Sawyer the Klansman and Reuben Sawyer the British Israelite." Capstone thesis, Pacific University, 2019.

Rothwell, C. Easton. "The Ku Klux Klan in the State of Oregon." Senior thesis, Reed College, 1924.

Saalfeld, Rev. Lawrence J. "Forces of Prejudice in Oregon 1920–1925." Master's thesis, Catholic University of America, 1950. Published by Archdiocesan Historical Commission in 1984.

Saks, Catherine Marie. "Real Americanism: Resistance to the Oregon Compulsory School Bill, 1920–1925." Master's thesis, Portland State University, 2010.

Thorson, Wendy P. Rielly. "Oregon Klanswomen of the 1920s: A Study of Tribalism, Gender, and Women's Power." Master's thesis, Oregon State University, 1997.

Toy, Eckard V. Jr. "The Ku Klux Klan in Oregon, its Character and Program." Master's thesis, University of Oregon, 1959.

Valenti, Francis Paul. "The Portland Press, the Ku Klux Kan and the Oregon Compulsory Education Bill: Editorial Treatment of Klan Themes in the Portland Press in 1922." Master's thesis, University of Washington, 1993.

OTHER ARTICLES, PAPERS, AND REPORTS

Bruce, Ben. "The Rise and Fall of the Ku Klux Klan in Oregon During the 1920s." Chapman University, *Voces Novae 11*, Article 2, 2019.

Bussel, Robert, editor. "Understanding the Immigrant Experience in Oregon: Research, Analysis, and Recommendations from University of Oregon Scholars." University of Oregon, 2008.

Greene, Ward. "Notes for a History of the Klan," *American Mercury 5*, no. 18 (June 1925): 240–243.

Hosmer, John E. "The Escaped Nun from Mt. Angel Convent: The Last Stand of Desperate Despotism." Silverton, 1913. Archives of the Archdiocese of Portland in Oregon.

Johnson, David Alan, Quintard Taylor, and Marsha Weisiger. "Report on the History of Matthew P. Deady and Frederick S. Dunn." University of Oregon, 2016.
O'Hara, Edwin V. "The School Question in Oregon." *Catholic World*, January 1923.
Shepherd, William. "The Fiery Double-Cross." *Collier's 82*, July 1928: 8–9, 47–49.
Stewart, Dan. "When Americans Celebrated Bonfire Night." *Time* magazine. Nov. 5, 2015. https://time.com/4094948/guy-fawkes-day-america/

NEWSPAPERS AND MAGAZINES

The Advocate (Portland)
Albany Democrat
Ashland Weekly Tidings
Aurora Observer
Beaverton Review
Bend Bulletin
Boardman Mirror
Capital Journal (Salem)
Catholic Sentinel (Portland)
Coos Bay Times
Coquille Valley Sentinel
Corvallis Gazette-Times
Cottage Grove Sentinel
Eugene Guard
Eugene Register
Eugene Register-Guard
Evening Herald (Klamath Falls)
Gate City Journal
Gold Hill News
Gresham Outlook
Heppner Gazette-Times
Heppner Herald
Hermiston Herald
Hillsboro Argus
Hood River Glacier
Ione Independent
La Grande Observer
Lebanon Express
Medford Mail Tribune
Monmouth Herald
New York Times
Newberg Graphic
News-Review (Roseburg)
News-Telegram (Portland)
Oregon City Enterprise
Oregon Daily Journal (Portland)
Oregon Labor Press (Portland)
Oregon Statesman (Salem)
Oregon Voter
Pendleton Tribune
Portland Telegram
Portland Tribune
Roseburg News-Review
Vernonia Eagle
Seattle Post-Intelligencer
Silverton Appeal
Silverton Journal
The New Age
The Oregonian (Portland)
Morning Oregonian (Portland)
Sunday Oregonian (Portland)
The Spectator (Portland)
The Washington Post
The Watcher on the Tower (Seattle)
The Western American (Astoria, Portland)
The World (Marshfield/Coos Bay)

HISTORICAL DOCUMENTS

Archbishop Alexander Christie. The School Question in Oregon pastoral letter. 1922. Oregon School Bill box. Archives of the Archdiocese of Portland in Oregon.
Archbishop Christie letter to Rev. Edward Hanna, Jan. 27, 1923. American Catholic History Classroom. Catholic University of America, https://cuomeka.wrlc.org/files/original/fadcd462d79e9c853f05d14305132086.pdf
Beatrice Morrow Cannady Scrapbook. Oregon Historical Society Library. Coll. 702, Manuscripts.
Lem Dever. "Inside the Klan: Invisible Empire Revealed." Western America Publishing Co. 1923. Oregon Historical Society Research Library.
Frederick L. Gifford papers, 1920–1945. Oregon Historical Society Research Library. Mss 2218.
Gilliam County court records. Case numbers 2902 and 2903, State of Oregon vs G.A. Chaney et al. Oregon State Archives.

Gov. Olcott's Proclamation of May 13, 1922. Ben Wilson Olcott Papers, Scrapbooks, Volume 8. University of Oregon Libraries Special Collections. Ax 081.

Hosmer Affidavit. Archives of the Archdiocese of Portland in Oregon.

Edward E. Kelly Family Papers. Oregon Historical Society Library. Mss 1434.

KKK Records 1922–1971, Oregon Historical Society Library. Mss 22 Manuscripts.

Klan Kall, No. 1. Oregon Politics, Box 21. Oregon Historical Society Library. Mss. 1513.

Kloran, Knights of the Ku Klux Klan, Oregon Historical Society Library. Vault, 363.9 K95k 1916.

Kubli Family Collection, 1911–1944. Oregon Historical Society Library. Manuscripts, Coll 431.

Ku Klux Klan La Grande Oregon chapter records, 1922–1923, Oregon Historical Society Library. Manuscripts, Mss 2604.

Ku Klux Klan Pamphlets, 1921–1928. Oregon Historical Society Library. Manuscripts, Coll 899.

Ku Klux Klan Tillamook, Oregon Chapter No. 8 Records, 1922–1929. University of Oregon Libraries Special Collections. Bx 046.

Ku Klux Klan vertical file. Pacific Northwest Politics and Government. Oregon Historical Society Library.

Lutheran Schools Committee Records. Oregon Historical Society Library. Vault, Mss 646.

Minutes of a Ku Klux Klan Klonclave in Eastern Oregon. Manuscripts, Collection 886. Oregon Historical Society Library.

J. R. Murphy. The Truth about Ex-Nun "Lucretia." Lutheran Schools Committee Records. Oregon Historical Society Library. Mss 646.

NAACP Portland branch files, 1914–1933. Microfilm reel 1. Oregon Historical Society Library.

Ben Wilson Olcott Papers, 1911–1933. Scrapbooks, Volume 8. University of Oregon Libraries Special Collections. Ax 081

Oregon Blue Book, Initiative, Referendum and Recall. https://sos.oregon.gov/blue-book/Documents/elections/initiative.pdf

Oregon Politics Collection. Box 21, folder 16. Oregon Historical Society Library. Mss. 1513.

Papers Read at the Meeting of Grand Dragons, Knights of the Ku Klux Klan at their First Annual Meeting Held at Asheville, North Carolina, Arno Press, 1977.

Proceedings of M. W. Grand Lodge Ancient Free and Accepted Masons of Oregon, 70th annual communication. Portland, 1920.

Proceedings of the Supreme Council of Scottish Rite Southern Jurisdiction. May 17–20, 1920. Colorado Springs, Colo.

Promotional flyer for Edith O'Gorman lecture. Catholic Church in Oregon files. Oregon Historical Society Library. Manuscripts, Mss 1580.

Roger Rasmussen Collection of Baker Klan No. 13 Records. Oregon Historical Society Library. Manuscripts, Coll 862.

Reasons Why. A.&A.S.R. School Committee. Lutheran Schools Committee Records. Oregon Historical Society Library. Mss 646

The Red Book. Reuben H. Sawyer Papers. Oregon Historical Society Library. Manuscripts, Coll 488.

Reuben H. Sawyer Papers, 1896–1962. Oregonian Historical Society Library. Manuscripts, Coll 488.

Reuben Sawyer. "The Truth About the Invisible Empire Knights of the Ku Klux Klan," Self-published, 1921. Pamphlets: KKK 1921–1935, Oregon Politics Collection, Box 21, Oregon Historical Society, Mss 1513.

Henry Davidson Sheldon Papers. Boxes 16 and 17. University of Oregon Libraries Special Collections. Coll 155.

State of Oregon ex rel U. G. Walker vs. W. C. Elford. Multnomah County Circuit Court case number 95083. Judgement issued Nov. 15, 1923.

The 100 Percenters. University of Oregon Libraries Special Collections. HS2330.K6 Z63 1922.

Ben Titus memoir. KKK Records 1922–1971. Oregon Historical Society Library. Manuscripts, Mss 22.

Union Scale of Wages and Hours of Labor, May 15, 1920. Bulletin of U.S. Bureau of Labor Statistics. September 1921.

U.S. Census for 1920: Oregon Population, Composition and Characteristics. Bureau of the Census. U.S. Commerce Department, https://www2.census.gov/library/publications/decennial/1920/bulletins/demographics/population-or-composition-and-characteristics.pdf

U.S. Religion Census for 1890, 1906, 1916, 1926, and 1936. https://www.usreligioncensus.org/report1.php?year=1906&btype=g&allstates=yes&states%5B%5D=41. U.S. government.

Dudley G. Wooten. "Remember Oregon." 1923. Archives of the Archdiocese of Portland in Oregon.

UNPUBLISHED MANUSCRIPTS AND ARTICLES

Cantor, Sarah. "Pierce v. Society of Sisters: The fight to preserve Catholic Education in Oregon." 2010. Sisters of the Holy Names of Jesus and Mary archives.

Sister Christine Mary. "Oregon School Bill: The Case of the Sisters of the Holy Names vs. the State of Oregon." 1958. Sisters of the Holy Names of Jesus and Mary archives.

McBride, Joyce. "Edward Emmett Kelly." Edward E. Kelly Family Papers. Oregon Historical Society Library. Mss 1434-2.

McBride, Joyce. "The Ku Klux Klan vs. Edward Emmett Kelly." Edward E. Kelly Family Papers. Oregon Historical Society Library. Mss 1434-2.

Meyers, Margaret, SNJM. "The Ku Klux Klan in La Grande, Oregon." Personal reflections. 1997. Sisters of the Holy Names of Jesus and Mary archives.

Rinearson, Peter and Arthur Rynearson. Rynerson family genealogy.

Robinson, Michael. "Portland Valley Scottish Rite Temple."

Robinson, Michael. "Philip Schuyler Malcom 1847–1929."

Robinson, Michael. "Philip Schuyler Malcom."

Schoenberg, Father Wilfred P. *Ku Klux Klan in Pacific Northwest: 1921–1927.* Archives of the Archdiocese of Portland in Oregon.

FILMS AND VIDEO

The Birth of a Nation (1915)

The Birth of a Nation video clip, https://www.youtube.com/watch?v=GBzDH-Vwzy4

ONLINE RESOURCES

Blazak, Randy. "Oregon Citizens Alliance." Oregon Encyclopedia, a project of the Oregon Historical Society. https://www.oregonencyclopedia.org/articles/oregon_citizens_alliance/

Byrne, Julie. Roman Catholics and Immigration in Nineteenth-Century America. War at Home. National Humanities Center. https://nationalhumanitiescenter.org/tserve/nineteen/nkeyinfo/nromcath.htm

"Catholicism in the United States, 1830–1900." https://uploads.weconnect.com/mce/f90a34bcd66e597a5d391005bf1e14a7c70f1d2c/ChurchHistory/PART%2017%20

AMERICAN%20CHURCH%20HISTORY%20PART%20TWO%20DEC%20 2013%20tbp.pdf

Collisson, Craig. "Japanese American Wartime Incarceration in Oregon." Oregon Encyclopedia, a project of the Oregon Historical Society. https://www.oregonencyclopedia.org/articles/japanese_internment/

Connections 31, Issue 4, April 2021. State Library of Oregon. https://www.oregon.gov/library/Documents/Volume%2031,%20Issue%204,%20April%202021.pdf

"Cross Burning." Free Speech Center at Middle Tennessee State University. https://firstamendment.mtsu.edu/article/cross-burning/

"The Deadly Virus: The Influenza Epidemic of 1918." National Archives. https://www.archives.gov/exhibits/influenza-epidemic/

"Documenting Reconstruction Violence." Reconstruction in America. Equal Justice Initiative. eji.org/report/reconstruction-in-america/

"Henry Ford and Anti-Semitism: A Complex Story." The Henry Ford. https://www.thehenryford.org/collections-and-research/digital-resources/popular-topics/henry-ford-and-anti-semitism-a-complex-story

"Nathan Bedford Forrest." History.com. https://www.history.com/topics/american-civil-war/nathan-bedford-forrest

"Leo Frank Case." New Georgia Encyclopedia. https://www.georgiaencyclopedia.org/articles/history-archaeology/leo-frank-case/

"Samuel Gompers." America's Unions. AFL-CIO. https://aflcio.org/about/history/labor-history-people/samuel-gompers

Griffey, Trevor. "History of the KKK in Washington State." *The Ku Klux Klan in Washington State*. University of Washington Civil Rights & Labor History Project. https://depts.washington.edu/civilr/kkk_seattle.htm

Hamilton, John Alexander. "Manipulating the Masses: Woodrow Wilson and the Birth of American Propaganda." Wilson Center. https://exhibitions.nysm.nysed.gov/WWI/phone/war-at-home.htm

Helquist, Michael. "Criminal Syndicalism Law of Oregon." *Oregon Encyclopedia*, a project of the Oregon Historical Society. https://www.oregonencyclopedia.org/articles/criminal-syndicalism-law-of-oregon/

"The History of Crann Tara." Crann Tara: Preserving the Culture, History, Heritage & Future of Scotland. https://cranntara.org.uk/crannta.htm

"Initiative, Referendum and Recall." *Oregon Blue Book*, Oregon Secretary of State. https://sos.oregon.gov/blue-book/Documents/elections/initiative.pdf

Klansman's Manual. Knights of the Ku Klux Klan. 1924. https://archive.lib.msu.edu/DMC/AmRad/klansmansmanual.pdf

Knights of Columbus. https://www.kofc.org/en/who-we-are/our-history/founding-and-early-acts.html

Ku Klux Klan Robes. Anti-Defamation League. https://www.adl.org/resources/hate-symbol/ku-klux-klan-robes

LaLande, Jeff. "Robert Ruhl (1880–1967)." *Oregon Encyclopedia*, a project of the Oregon Historical
Society. https://www.oregonencyclopedia.org/articles/ruhl_robert_1880_1967_/

"Massachusetts Bay Colony Bans Catholic Priests." MassMoments, a project of Mass Humanities. https://www.massmoments.org/moment-details/massachusetts-bay-colony-bans-catholic-priests.html

Mayors of Portland. City Auditor's Office. https://web.archive.org/web/20210121123129/http://www.portlandoregon.gov/auditor/article/4968

McKay, Floyd. "George Putnam (1872–1961)." *Oregon Encyclopedia*, a project of the Oregon Historical Society. https://www.oregonencyclopedia.org/articles/putnam_george_1872_1961_/

Meyers, Margaret, SJNM. "The Ku Klux Klan in LeGrande, Oregon 1918–1924." American Catholic History Classroom. Catholic University of America. https://cuomeka.wrlc.org/exhibits/show/osc/item/292

Oregon Remembrance Project. https://oregonremembrance.org/sunrise-project/

Oregon's History. Oregon Department of Administrative Services 2021 Action Plan. https://www.oregon.gov/lcd/Housing/Documents/2021_DAS_DEI_Action_Plan-History_Only.pdf

Oregon Voters Pamphlet. November 7, 1922. https://digitalcollections.library.oregon.gov/nodes/view/24438?keywords=Voter+Guide+1922+Measures&type=all&highlights=WyJWb3RlciIsIkd1aWRlIiwiMTkyMiIsIk1lYXN1cmVzIl0%3D&lsk=7ce699fff6df79a34bd4801837740048

"Not Exactly Paradise: Japanese American Internment Camps." Oregon Secretary of State. https://sos.oregon.gov/archives/exhibits/ww2/Pages/threats-paradise.aspx

"Presbyterian Church in Ireland." *Brittanica*. https://www.britannica.com/topic/Presbyterian-Church-in-Ireland

"Red Summer: The Race Riots of 1919." The National World War 1 Museum and Memorial. https://www.theworldwar.org/learn/about-wwi/red-summer

Robinson, Greg. "Kenji Namba v. McCourt." *Densho Encyclopedia*. https://encyclopedia.densho.org/Kenji%20Namba%20v.%20McCourt

"War at Home." New York State Museum. https://exhibitions.nysm.nysed.gov/WWI/phone/war-at-home.html

INTERVIEWS

Bob Bussel, emeritus history professor and Labor Education and Research Center director, University of Oregon.

David Horowitz, emeritus history professor, Portland State University.

Jeff LaLande, author and architectural and historical consultant who taught at Southern Oregon University.

Darrell Millner, emeritus Black studies professor, Portland State University.

Michael Robinson, historian, Scottish Rite in Oregon.

ORAL HISTORIES

Otto Frohnmayer oral history. Edward E. Kelly Family Papers. Oregon Historical Society Library.

Robert Kelly oral history. Edward E. Kelly Family Papers. Oregon Historical Society Library.

F. Leo Smith oral history. September 23 to October 28, 1993. Oregon Historical Society Library. SR 1195.

LECTURES

Hiram Wesley Evans. "The Menace of Modern Immigration." October 24, 1923, speech. KKK Records 1922–1971. Oregon Historical Society, Mss 22 manuscripts.

David Horowitz. "The Ethical Dilemmas of Tracking Down the Klan: the Oregon Ku Klux Klan of the 1920s." Oregon Committee for the Humanities. April 24, 1985. Cassette tape at Oregon Historical Society, SR 9035.

Index